DEVELOPMENT IN EARLY CHILDHOOD

DEVELOPMENT IN EARLY CHILDHOOD

THE PRESCHOOL YEARS

D. Bruce Gardner
IOWA STATE UNIVERSITY

HARPER & ROW, Publishers
New York, Evanston, and London

DEVELOPMENT IN EARLY CHILDHOOD: The Preschool Years.

 For information address Harper & Row, Publishers, Incorporated, 49 East 33rd Street, New York 16, N.Y.

LIBRARY OF CONGRESS CATALOG CARD NUMBER: 64-12791

CONTENTS

Tables

PREFACE

THERE ARE TWO PRIMARY OBJECTIVES in writing this book. The first is to provide a general introduction to the professional field of child development. It is a new and young field and, like its subject matter, it is characterized by rapid growth. The student who seeks an understanding of this rapidly growing professional field must know a little of its history, a little of its methods in seeking answers for its questions, and a little of the major problems which still lie ahead in our efforts to understand the child. Some parts of the book are intended to help meet these needs.

The second objective is to provide a fairly concise picture of the young child as he goes about his most important task: *growing*. The emphasis is on the child under 6. But there is a more fundamental emphasis which has less to do with age, *per se: the big job of growing is a job of achieving selfhood.* This is more than merely the theme of this book; it is the theme of a child. Every child's striving, seeking, playing, working, smiling, crying, hitting, running, and wondering are variations on that theme.

The organization and philosophy of the book arise out of a firm conviction that the modern student of child development cannot be content with a knowledge of age levels and stages of human growth. Even a detailed and exhaustive study of stages in the life of the child is meaningless without insight into the manner of a child's movement from one stage to another. There are dynamic reasons underlying the varying modes and styles of growth which children select in their struggling to achieve selfhood. The challenge to the student of child development is clear: If he would understand the child, he must understand some reasons why each child moves from one stage to the next in his own unique manner. The emphasis on the dynamic forces underlying growth and change, stressed throughout the book, is based on this challenge.

Scientific progress in understanding the child is moving at a rapid pace. Research findings in a wide range of disciplines bear directly on our knowledge of child growth. My indebtedness to the many research workers and authors who have made their results and insights available will be readily apparent. At the same time, out of respect to the student's need to concentrate on ideas and major themes about the child, an effort has been made to avoid the distractions inherent in listing the vast amount of research which could be cited for each topic.

I should like to express sincere appreciation to the authors and publishers who granted permission to use quoted material, figures, and tables. To the many teachers, clinical workers and colleagues who have influenced my thinking, I should express not only deep thanks but also the assurance that any inadequacies of this book are not their responsibility. To Ila Christensen Gardner I extend heartfelt thanks for her patient and careful preparation of the manuscript. To her, and to the children who have been my most persistent and inspiring teachers, Don, Christine, and Anita, this book is dedicated.

D. Bruce Gardner

Ames, Iowa
December, 1963

Part I HOW WE STUDY CHILDREN

Part I, consisting of the first two chapters, is a unit devoted to the professional and technical discipline of child development. There is some consideration of how the current approach to the study of the child has evolved—gradually—as an accompaniment to the general development of scientific thought and also as a part of our total cultural evolution.

Part I also stresses some differences between casual observation of children and scientific observation. One's competence as an observer, as well as one's enthusiasm for understanding the nature of childhood, can be enhanced greatly by some preliminary attention to ways of observing, and to the reasons that justify careful observation and recording of child behavior.

CHAPTER ONE

What is child development? ∽ Where has this active young professional field come from? ∽ What are the relationships between child development and other disciplines and sciences? ∽ What is the work of the modern child-development specialist?

THE FIELD OF CHILD DEVELOPMENT

SOCIETY'S CONCERN—and lack of concern—for its children over the centuries makes a fascinating study in contrasts and contradictions. Man's interest in his own offspring, and his relationships with them, have undergone dramatic and revolutionary changes over the years—perhaps as revolutionary as those we have witnessed in the world of science and technology.

SOME NOTES FROM HISTORY

Certainly the well-being of children as individuals has not always been central in the thinking of adults. In some periods of history, for example, societies have accepted infanticide as a normal practice. In ancient Sparta any deformed child was killed, as the state itself forbade the raising of such children. In Athens it was up to the parents to decide whether they would accept and raise a child or destroy it at birth; in ancient times in the Orient, the practice of infanticide was particularly common with female babies. In addition, too, the practice of abandonment and exposure of infants to the elements was not at all uncommon in the Greek colonies. In fact, as Payne (10) has noted, the theme of the abandoned infant who was found and reared by someone, and who later became an outstanding figure in the society, was a popular one in the dramatic writings of the time.

Aries (3) writes that, in the Middle Ages, European civilization was marked by an unusual carelessness of its children. Aries' account of the relationship between adult and child in medieval Europe provides a startling insight into the assumptions which that society must have made about the nature of the child. He notes, for example, that no attempts were made to shield children from sex, since no one assumed that children were innocent in the first place. That artists portrayed the child as a miniature adult is held by Aries to reflect the attitude which generally permeated the medieval world. The child was apparently pretty much thrown into the adult world by the age of 6 or 7, at which time he was supposed to get along without his mother or mother-substitute.

The concept of individual differences among children—so central in our modern philosophy of child training and education—was, for all practical purposes, nonexistent during the Middle Ages. Yet, if we go back to philosophical writings from ancient Greek civilization, we can find evidences of an awareness of individual differences. Socrates (about 470–399 B.C.) had ideas for the organization of society based on differences among children, with some being fit for training along one line, and others being suited to quite different educational experiences. Plato (427–347 B.C.) also recognized basic differences among children with respect to aptitudes and talent. In his writings he encouraged the idea of discovering these individual talents at a child's early age and providing special training to develop them to the fullest.

Down through the ages, however, our ways of dealing with children have been influenced not only by philosophical considerations, but also by economic demands, military and political affairs, religious precepts, birth and death rates, and by famine and disease. Perhaps none of these factors has had as vital a role to play in prescribing our ways of relating to children, however, as have the varying conceptions of the fundamental nature of the child, held by different peoples at different times in history.

Speculative, nonscientific approaches to the study of the child have been the rule throughout the bulk of recorded history, whenever man has concerned himself with the nature of children. Anything approaching a scientific outlook on the child is a very recent innovation, historically speaking. John Locke (1632–1704), an English philosopher, stressed in his writing the importance of experience and training in the child's life. When he wrote that the child's mind was, at birth, like a blank tablet upon which his experiences would write his personality, he had, unfortunately, no scientific evidence either to support or to refute his viewpoint. Rousseau (1712–1778), almost a century later, still had little more to guide him than his own intellect and reasoning processes. He concluded that the newborn child is essentially unspoiled and natural, and that civilization has powerful, distorting effects on his personality. These in turn prevent him from achieving his potential of goodness and nobility.

EARLY SCIENTIFIC APPROACHES TO THE STUDY OF THE CHILD

Probably the first significant efforts to get away from the speculative, philosophical approach and to turn more toward a child study based on direct observation were initiated by the early child biographers of the nineteenth century. Darwin (1809–1882) and Preyer (1841–1897) kept careful notes on the development and behavior of individual children over a period of months and years. These early biographies did not, in themselves, provide much important information about children. They did, however, inaugurate a method of longitudinal study which has since proven to be a very useful research tool. These early studies also raised important questions about the nature of children—later to be answered by the results of scientific investigations (4).

It was in the late nineteenth and early twentieth centuries that the first truly scientific investigations of children were carried out. Two of the most important persons who stimulated the growth of a science of child development were G. Stanley Hall (1844–1924) in America, and Alfred Binet (1857–1911) in France (2). Each of these men was in his own way concerned with the central question of the *causes* of human behavior. Their achievements marked a turning-point in our relationships with children, for their writings, and the writings of those who followed in their footsteps, have called to the attention of mankind the need to understand the reasons underlying the behavior of children. Hall's contributions included the development of questionnaires to gain information about child behavior. In 1883 he published *The Content of Children's Minds* (cf. Dennis, 6), a study of concepts held by children upon their entrance in school. Binet's professional contributions were many, including the development of a method of testing the intelligence of children. His first intelligence scale, published in collaboration with Simon in 1905, underwent a series of revisions which led to the development of the Stanford-Binet Scales in

America. From Binet's work has been derived much of our present knowledge of child intelligence, the nature of its growth, and the means of measuring it (2).

From the work of such pioneer scientists has come the tradition, especially in America, that statements and generalizations about child behavior and development must be based on observable evidence. This has led to reliance on standardized, controlled situations in which a child may be observed in order to detect his special reactions to these situations. From these beginnings, moreover, a revolutionary new way of thinking of the child emerged, and has become a part of society itself as well as a part of scientific thought. The dramatic change was from thinking of the child as a miniature adult, whose behavior was primarily a matter of his moral fiber and will, to thinking of him as having certain psychological resources at his disposal. These resources were limited both by his unique inheritance and his maturational level. It should be clear that adult relationships with children undergo a radical change when society ceases to hold the child morally responsible for his psychological condition and begins to think of the child as an individual with peculiar and unique properties to be understood. Later, this trend of thought was to undergo considerable modification, and another feature was to be added: *the child has basic psychological needs, the satisfaction of which leads to enhanced development, and the frustration of which leads to faulty development.* The impact of this notion has been as great, if not greater, than the awareness of individual differences stimulated by the work of Binet and his followers.

But we must remember how recently, in terms of the history of Western civilization, these dramatic and revolutionary changes in thought have occurred. This should suggest to the thoughtful student that the current approaches to the study of the child, to which we now turn our attention, represent emerging and evolving ideas which are subject to continued revision and improvement.

CURRENT APPROACHES TO THE STUDY OF THE CHILD

In this section we shall examine the basic ways in which scholars and scientists have viewed the child during the twentieth century. For convenience, four major streams of thought will be described: (1) the behavioristic approach; (2) the normative-descriptive approach; (3) the field-theory approach; and (4) the psychoanalytic approach. For each of these major approaches, the work of one or two men whose contributions were central in the development of a modern conception of the child will be described briefly. It should be clearly understood that these, and other approaches that could be mentioned, were not historically independent of each other, nor do they operate in isolation from each other today. Historically, these developments were overlapping and concurrent rather than sequential. They should be considered as illustrations of the varying types of emphasis that have been placed on the central question of the nature and causes of a child's development and behavior.

The Behavioristic Approach One major development in the field of child study in the present century can be traced largely to a Russian physiologist, Ivan Pavlov (1849–1936), and an American psychologist, John B. Watson (1878–1958). Pavlov's contribution was his demonstration that animals can learn—that is, acquire new habits—by forming a new association between a stimulus and response. His experimental subjects were laboratory animals, especially dogs. His dogs "learned" to salivate at the sound of a bell, illustrating the principle of conditioned learning. Watson (*11*) was extremely interested in such kinds of learning. He saw in them the basis for much, if not all, human learning. He did not concern himself much with the basic nature of the child, apart from the influence of learning experiences. In fact, for Watson the only question of major significance was how the child's observable behavior could be modified by the presentation of special experiences. While he did recognize the importance of biological processes as a basis for human behavior, he felt that the higher level of organization was the psychological. The essential feature in the development of this higher level of human functioning was the conditioning, through experience, of new habits upon old ones. His major philosophy of child-rearing is expressed by the term "habit training."

The development of emotions serves as a good illustration of this point of view. Watson held that the complex and varied emotional behavior of growing children and adults could be accounted for by experiences that had associated a gradually increasing variety of stimuli with the primitive emotional responses (fear, rage, and love) that were part of the biological endowment of the child at birth. The newborn infant could express only these three basic emotional reactions. As he came to experience these primitive emotions in association with particular circumstances, they gradually elaborated into the complicated pattern of emotional behavior that characterizes adult life—sadness, gaiety, joy, anger, jealousy, and all the rest. Indeed, the child's total personality was essentially the outcome of his special conditioning experiences.

Watson was a spokesman for objectivity, both in the laboratories of child psychology and in the practical, everyday care of children by their parents. He was outspoken in his criticism of the sentimental, as this passage from one of his books makes clear:

> There is a sensible way of treating children. Treat them as though they were young adults. Dress them, bathe them with care and circumspection. Let your behavior always be objective and kindly firm. Never hug and kiss them, never let them sit in your lap. If you must, kiss them once on the forehead when they say good night. Shake hands with them in the morning. Give them a pat on the head if they have made an extraordinarily good job of a difficult task. Try it out. In a week's time you will find how easy it is to be perfectly objective with your child and at the same time kindly. You will be utterly ashamed of the mawkish, sentimental way you have been handling it (*11*, pp. 81–82).

Today's parents smile at such words of advice, for they are aware of the importance of close affectional ties between parents and children. At the same time, we should not underrate the significance of John B. Watson's contributions to our modern concepts of the child. He has made us aware of the need to study children objectively and, in so doing, we have learned much we could not have learned in any other way. Among other things, he has made us acutely conscious of the vital role of learning processes in the over-all personality development of the child.

The Normative-Descriptive Approach A second source of our present-day knowledge of children has been those scientists who have painstakingly observed large numbers of children, individually as well as in groups, and who have carefully catalogued the behavior typical of each age level. Arnold Gesell (1880–1961) and his colleagues and students have provided a wealth of information on development from conception to adolescence, concentrating on motor behavior, personal-social behavior, language behavior, and adaptive or intelligent behavior. In each of these areas, Gesell and his coworkers (6, 7) described the kinds of behavior typical for each age, and which might reasonably be expected of normal children. These behavior descriptions for each age level, or "age norms," provide useful reference points by which growth and behavior of a child can be described and understood more clearly.

Table 1.1, taken from the work of Gesell, illustrates this kind of information. In this table, the brief statements under each major area of growth describe the typical responses, in clinical examinations, of children at the age of 24 months. The table also illustrates the patterning of behavior at ages immediately preceding and following the key age of 24 months, enabling the examiner to establish more clearly the developmental level of the child he is examining. Comparable information has been prepared by Gesell for other ages, beginning with early infancy. Thus it is possible, if we wish to understand the growth of an individual child more clearly, to compare his development with such a set of norms. It may help us, for example, if we know that a particular child is developing more rapidly than the average, and that his behavior is more like the norms for a 30-month-old child when he is just 24 months of age. In a similar way, it may be important to know that a particular child is developing more slowly than other children, and that his behavior is on a level characteristic of children somewhat younger than he.

Being able to describe the rate of growth of an individual child as normal, fast, or slow is only one of the features resulting from the descriptive, normative approach. Another significant contribution of this line of study has been the emphasis on stages of readiness of the child; it has helped us to outline the stages through which a child normally progresses from infancy to maturity. Each stage has its generally characteristic patterns of mental and physical organization, of social and emotional behavior, and of play interests and activities. Each stage also has its characteristic degree of readiness to profit from new experience and from kinds of guidance and disciplinary measures used by adults. The general sequence of development through the first five years, beginning with conception, is illustrated diagrammatically in Figure 1.1. This representation of early development also illustrates the gradual expansion and organization of the four major areas of development studied by Gesell and his coworkers.

TABLE 1.1. *Developmental Schedules*

21 Months	KEY AGE: 24 Months	30 Months
	Motor	
Walks: squats in play (*. . .)	Walks: runs well, no falling	Walks: (dem.) on tiptoe
Stairs: walks down, 1 hand held (*24m)	Stairs: walks up & down alone	Jumps: with both feet
Stairs: walks up, holding rail (*24m)	Large ball: (no dem.) kicks	Stands: tries stand on 1 foot
Large ball: (dem.) kicks (*24m)	M. Cubes: tower of 6–7	M. Cubes: tower of 8
M. Cubes: tower of 5–6	Book: turns pages singly	Drawing: holds crayon by fingers
	Adaptive	
M. Cubes: tower of 5–6	M. Cubes: tower of 6–7	M. Cubes: tower of 8
M. Cubes: imitates pushing train (*24m)	M. Cubes: aligns 2 or more, train (*36m)	M. Cubes: adds chimney to train
Formbd: places 2–3 blocks	Drawing: imitates V stroke	Drawing: 2 or more strokes for cross (*36m)
Perf. box: inserts corner of sq. (*24m)	Drawing: imitates circular stroke	Drawing: imitates V and H strokes
Perf. box: retrieves ball	Formbd: places single blocks on (*30m)	Color forms: places 1
	Formbd: adapts after 4 trials (*30m)	Formbd: inserts 3 blocks on presenta.
	Perf. box: inserts sq.	Formbd: adapts repeatedly, error (*36m)
		Digits: repeats 2 (1 of 3 trials)
	Language	
Vocab: 20 words	Speech: jargon discarded	Name: gives full name
Speech: combines 2–3 words spontan. (*24m)	Speech: 3-word sentence	Picture cd: names 5
Ball: 3 directions	Speech: uses *I, me, you*	Picture cd: identifies 7
	Picture cd: names 3 or more	Test obj: gives use
	Picture cd: identifies 5 or more	
	Test obj: names 2	
	Ball: 4 directions	
	Personal-Social	
Feeding: handles cup well	Feeding: inhibits turning spoon	Commun: refers to self by pronoun rather than name
Commun: asks for food, toilet, drink	Toilet: dry at night, taken up (*36m)	Commun: repetit. in speech and other activ. (*36m)
Commun: echoes 2 or more last words (*24m)	Toilet: verbal. needs fairly consist. (*42m)	Play: pushes toy with good steering
Commun: pulls person to show (*24m)	Dressing: pulls on simple garment	Play: helps put things away
	Commun: verbalizes immed. experiences (*. . .)	Play: can carry breakable obj.
	Commun: refers to self by name (*30m)	
	Commun: compreh. & asks for "another"	
	Play: hands cup full of cubes	
	Play: domestic mimicry	
	Play: parallel play predom. (*42m)	

SOURCE: A. Gesell and C. S. Amatruda, *Developmental Diagnosis* (2nd ed.), New York: Paul B. Hoeber, Inc., 1947, p. 79.

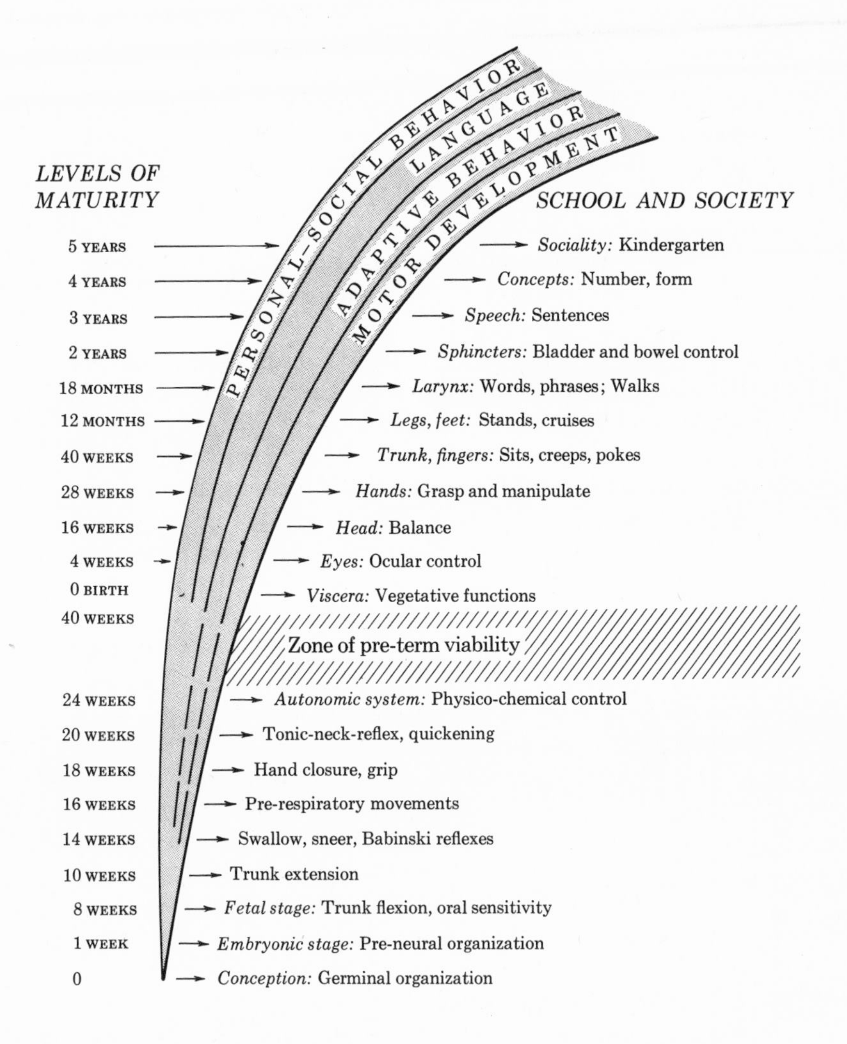

Fig. 1.1. Ages and stages—a diagrammatic representation of the trends and fields of behavior growth from the embryonic period through 5 years of age. (From A. Gesell and F. L. Ilg, *Child development: an introduction to the study of human growth,* New York: Harper, 1949, p. 63.)

Gesell and Ilg summarize the major trends and sequences of development in the early years, in the following statements:

> The first five years in the cycle of child development are the most fundamental and the most formative for the simple but sufficient reason that they come first. Their influence upon the years that follow is incalculable. The trends and sequences of this fundamental development may be summed up tersely:
>
> In the *first quarter* of the *first year*, the infant, having weathered the hazards of the neonatal period, gains control of his twelve oculomotor muscles.
>
> In the *second quarter* (16–28 weeks) he gains command of the muscles which support his head and move his arms. He reaches out for things.
>
> In the *third quarter* (28–40 weeks) he gains command of his trunk and hands. He sits. He grasps, transfers and manipulates objects.
>
> In the *fourth quarter* (40–52 weeks) he extends command to his legs and feet; to his forefingers and thumbs. He pokes and plucks.
>
> By the end of the *second year* he walks and runs; articulates words and phrases; acquires bowel and bladder control; attains a rudimentary sense of personal identity and of personal possession.
>
> At *three years* he speaks in sentences, using words as tools of thought; he shows a positive propensity to understand his environment and to comply with cultural demands. He is no longer a mere infant.
>
> At *four years* he asks innumerable questions, perceives analogies, displays an active tendency to conceptualize and generalize. He is nearly self-dependent in routines of home life.
>
> At *five* he is well matured in motor control. He hops and skips. He talks without infantile articulation. He can narrate a long tale. He prefers associative play. He feels socialized pride in clothes and accomplishments. He is a self-assured, conforming citizen in his small world (7, pp. 62–64).

The normative approach to child development has enabled us to set up reasonable levels of expectation for children. It has helped us to overcome the idea inherent in earlier philosophies that the child is a miniature adult whose job it is to do their parents' bidding while getting their growth. It has fostered the acceptance of the current philosophy that children are individuals who require, at each stage of development, experiences appropriate to their levels of readiness. It has also helped us to accept the normality of so-called "problem behavior" at certain stages in the child's career. That is, through this approach to child study, we have learned that many stages of growth are accompanied by behavior that can be difficult and trying for adults, but that is perfectly normal for that stage. It has taught us, too, that children revise their behavior as they proceed from one stage to the next and, as new stages emerge, old problems tend to disappear.

While all stages have their peculiar problems, we have discovered that some are much more likely to lead to friction with adults than others. At about age 2½, for example, most children are at a stage that can well be described as "negative." They say "No!" often and loudly in response to adult direction and suggestion. In fact, saying "No!" may be more important to them than engaging in their favorite activities, as evidenced by the fact that they will say it, at times, even when their special toy or favorite activity is suggested. This has prompted some parents to engage in a kind of "reverse psychology" by telling their child to do just the opposite of what they really want him to do. Needless to say, this is not a very sound prescription for long-range guidance. But more important, our negative 2½-year-old is illustrating an inability to live at peace either in the world of infancy from which he is emerging, or in the more mature world of the preschool child. He is at an "in-between" stage in which his life is somewhat out of balance, with strong pulls on him from his baby world and, at the same time, a grand impulse to be big, strong, and independent. The resulting conflict and instability within himself presents practical problems in his relations with others. The awareness of the normality and naturalness of these periods has enabled parents and other adults who deal with children to recognize and to accept the stages as a part of growing up. The modern mother of a 2½-year-old does not worry unnecessarily about the difficult behavior of her child, nor does she complicate matters by seeing such behavior as evidence of failure on her part.

Other contributions of the developmental approach can also be listed. Although it may appear, superficially, that this approach is designed to show how all children are alike by describing typical behavior for each age and stage, there are some ways in which it has helped us to see more clearly the importance of differences among individual children. While we have discovered that all children typically grow through the same stages of development in the same general sequence of steps, we have become more aware than ever before that each child does this in his own unique way. Using the illustration of the negativism of the 2½-year-old, we might note that each child about this time even discovers his own special ways to be negative! Furthermore, the normative approach stresses that a given child may not be equally advanced in all aspects of growth. That is, his "mental age" may be greater than his "social age," or vice versa; and his degree of emotional maturity may lag behind his physical growth. Thus, no one of these aspects of growth may be exactly at the norm for his actual chronological age. In spite of all this, he may still be a perfectly normal child in the sense that his growth and behavior are adequate, healthy, and appropriate for him.

While the normative-descriptive approach to child study has made marked contributions to our knowledge of children, it has certain limitations of which the student of child development should be aware. Norms are merely averages and, as such, tell us nothing about the rightness or wrongness, the healthiness or unhealthiness, of the behavior. If we know that the average child of 12 months has two words in his vocabulary we cannot assume that this norm is either good or bad. Nor does it give us a reasonable goal to work toward in dealing with any particular infant. If we thought this sort of information did provide us with working goals in the guidance of children, it would be reasonable to assume that we should work toward making our child negative and uncooperative by the time he is 2½, whether he wants to be or not, since that is the norm! It is important to recognize, therefore, that average behavior does not mean the same thing as "best" behavior, or "healthy" behavior.

Another kind of limitation to the normative-descriptive approach should also be kept in mind: by itself, it tells us little or nothing about the basic causes of a child's behavior. It has certainly raised many questions about the causes of growth and behavior, and it is based on the assumption that growth originates from inside the child. However, the main type of explanation provided by this approach is in terms of age level: he behaves as he does because he is 2 years old; she behaves as she does because she is 4, etc. In the final analysis, this does not really explain growth, nor was it intended as an explanation by those who have followed this approach and given us their important findings. In order to gain a better understanding of this limitation, we should consider other approaches which have as their central objective the understanding of *why* children behave as they do.

The Psychoanalytic Approach As the field of child study grew into a scientific effort to understand development and behavior of children, it was inevitable that more scholars and scientists would turn from the relatively simple problem of what children are like at given ages, to the more complex "why" questions: *Why* do they grow as they do? *Why* do they behave that way? Such questions are more difficult to answer but the answers, once available, are in many respects more helpful. For greater insights into motives, causes, and reasons for growth and behavior, many scientists have found it profitable to turn to more dynamic approaches to the study of the child.

Much of our knowledge of children derived through this dynamic approach can be traced to the work of Sigmund Freud (1856–1939). Although he was not a research scientist in the modern sense of the word, his clinical studies of adult patients, using a pioneer method of recalling childhood experiences, resulted in a number of basic insights into the role of such early experiences in the formation of personality. In addition, Freud (5) developed an extensive and elaborate theory of the nature of human personality, based on fundamental instincts and drives. These drives, he maintained, existed apart from the effects of experience; they were part of the natural equipment of the human infant at birth; they were the core of all human motivation. It was the effects of subsequent social experiences in the satisfaction or frustration of these drives, especially experiences with the parents, which led to the formation of the adult personality. Some of the experiences satisfied the basic instincts; some led to their frustration; some had the effect of distorting instinctual strivings and resulted in the formation of faulty, "neurotic" behavior.

Freud made another contribution in outlining his view of the developing child. He helped us to see that human behavior, including that of children, is often motivated at an unconscious level. This was a revolutionary idea in Freud's day. At present we take for granted the knowledge that children are unaware of many of the motives underlying their own actions. Freud saw human personality as composed of three major divisions: (1) the *id*, the reservoir of basic energy giving rise to all forms of instinctual striving; (2) the *ego*, that part of the personality concerned with, among other things, reality and the child's position in relation to the realistic elements of his world; and (3) the *superego*, concerned with moral values and the rightness or wrongness of behavior. Freud's concept of "psychosexual development" included the growing, increasingly complex set of relationships among these three basic elements of personality. Some of the contributions of psychoanalytic thought to the understanding of the child are reflected in Chapter Ten, which describes the development of personality during the preschool years.

The Field-Theory Approach A fourth major stream of thought which has had a vital role to play in our present-day conception of the child can be attributed largely to the work of the psychologist, Kurt Lewin (1890–1947). Although others before and since his time were instrumental in organizing field theory, it was Lewin (8) who was the leader in relating the theory to the growth and behavior of children. Like Watson, Lewin was concerned with the environment. However, while Watson appeared to ignore the internal growth potentials within a child and stressed only the effects of external, environmental forces, Lewin argued that a child was more than a passive receiver of stimulation from the outside. In his view, the child's personality included numerous psychological systems which interacted with his environment in an increasingly complex manner. These psychological systems had their own sources of energy for initiating behavior; however, the form of the behavior was always affected by conditions in the environment. Lewin believed that the environment included objects and persons having powers of attraction and repulsion for the child. He likened these forces of attraction and repulsion to the dynamic forces of the physical world, and attempted to explain human behavior in accordance with principles of mathematics and physics. His description of conflict situations are of special interest in the understanding of child behavior. He described three basic kinds of conflict, all of them in terms of the interaction of the individual with his environment (*11*, pp. 88–94):

1. The child is attracted, with about equal force, by two different objects. If he approaches one, it means going farther away from the other. It is comparable to the old story of the donkey which starved to death between two stacks of hay.

2. The child is caught between two forces, both of which are negative and repelling, and from which he would like to escape. However, to retreat from one of them means getting closer to another. An example

would be a threat of punishment if he does not perform some chore that is distasteful to him. A mother tells her son that unless he first does his homework he will not be allowed to watch his favorite television program. Either doing the homework or missing his program is an unpleasant prospect for him.

3. The child experiences both positive forces of attraction and negative, repelling forces in interaction with a single object. A striking example which most of us have observed is that of the very young child who encounters a strange animal—a rabbit, a puppy, or a cat—being held by another person. The child shows his wish to touch and stroke the animal and, at the same time, displays an anxious concern that it cause him no harm. So he stands perhaps a little distance away, not close enough really to touch it, and reaches his arms out as if to pet the animal.

The basic conflicts Lewin described may be seen to have implications for a host of major and minor adjustment problems for children and adults of all ages. The third type of conflict, for example, has sometimes been described as ambivalence. It is illustrated whenever we have both positive and negative feelings about the same situation, or about the same individual. We have come to recognize that such ambivalence is a very real and important part of the relationships between child and parent. Lewin also outlined the kinds of adjustments the individual child can make when he experiences conflicts. His theory, in short, has given us new insights into child behavior and has simultaneously enabled us to formulate a number of practical principles of child guidance.

Although their approaches were quite different, Watson, Gesell, Freud, and Lewin all made significant contributions to the modern field of child study. All four placed great stress on the importance of the early years in the formation of personality. All four raised basic questions about the ways in which children grow and in which their behavior develops, and all four offered tentative answers to at least some of these questions. Many of their answers are still providing fruitful insights today; other aspects of their theories have served their primary purpose in the stimulation of further research by students who followed them.

A MODERN CONCEPT OF THE CHILD

Perhaps the most fundamental development of all, and a most important feature of the modern approach to child study, is that the efforts of such men as Watson, Gesell, Freud, and Lewin have laid the groundwork for a totally new concept of the nature of the child. Through their work other men have gradually organized a point of view in which *the needs of the child are central.* The modern, need-oriented approach has created a new atmosphere and a new kind of relationship between children and adults. Before the twentieth century adults did not concern themselves with children's needs, not because they were mean or vicious or unfeeling, but because they simply had not been taught to think that way. The idea of the existence of such things as "children's needs" was unheard of, because children were conceived as miniature adults whose job it was to grow up, as quickly as possible, to become useful citizens. In some societies at certain periods of history, for example, the infant and child was not given a name, nor even regarded as a person, until reaching an age of productive usefulness. Today, it is common knowledge among parents and child-development specialists alike that children grow and behave in relation to their fundamental needs, some of which are inborn and some of which are acquired, or at least modified, by experience. It is the degree of satisfaction of these needs that a child achieves, and the manner in which he learns to achieve that satisfaction, which determine the degree of his own self-fulfillment or personality development, and which, at the same time, determine the degree to which he becomes a useful and productive citizen.

We need not go into great detail in listing the specific needs of children at this point. In one sense, the total book may be thought of as a description of those needs and their significance in the life and growth of the child. However, it may be helpful at this point to illustrate the need concept and to explain more fully the role of needs in the motivation of behavior. The following description is based on the work of A. H. Maslow (9), who has organized the fundamental needs of human beings into a kind of classification system, as follows:

1. Physiological needs, such as hunger, thirst, activity, and rest.
2. Safety needs, security, and release from anxiety aroused by threats of various kinds.
3. Love needs, including love, affection, acceptance, and a feeling of belonging in one's relationships with parents, friends, and other social groups.
4. Esteem needs, including both self-esteem from mastery and confidence in one's worth, adequacy, and capacities, and esteem from social approval.

5. Need for self-actualization through creative self-expression in personal and social achievements; need to feel free to act, to satisfy one's curiosity, and to understand one's world.

According to Maslow, it is only when the needs at any one level are satisfied that the individual is able to function at the next higher level. For example, the satisfaction of physiological needs is a prerequisite to the individual's successful operation at the next higher level of safety needs. It is the satisfaction of these safety needs, in turn, which enable him to progress to the level of love needs, and so on. Most important, it will be seen that self-fulfillment, especially through personal and social achievement, cannot occur in the absence of satisfaction of the more primitive needs at the lower levels. One implication of this is that the need approach to children is not a matter of "coddling" the child, or catering to his whims at the expense of his family and the rest of society. Instead, it may be seen as a distinct advantage to society to provide for the satisfaction of the child's needs, enabling and encouraging him to progress to a level of self-fulfillment which allows him to be the socially responsible and productive individual of which he is capable.

CHILD DEVELOPMENT IN RELATION TO OTHER PROFESSIONAL FIELDS

Child development as a professional field, and as a specialized area of study, is relatively new on the scene. While people have always been interested in their children—and throughout history there have been outstanding writers who have commented on the child and his proper upbringing—it has only been during the present century that an organized body of reliable knowledge about the child and his development has become available. In part this is due to our dependence on other basic disciplines to provide us with a foundation of solid factual material. One of the tasks of child development is the integration of the findings from these various fields into a useful body of knowledge. Child development is thus based on such disciplines as biology, psychology, sociology, and anthropology, as is illustrated in Figure 1.2.

Child development also has the function of making its integrated body of information available to a variety of practitioners, or specialists in applied services for children, including psychiatrists, educators, social-welfare workers, and home economists. This section will attempt to de-

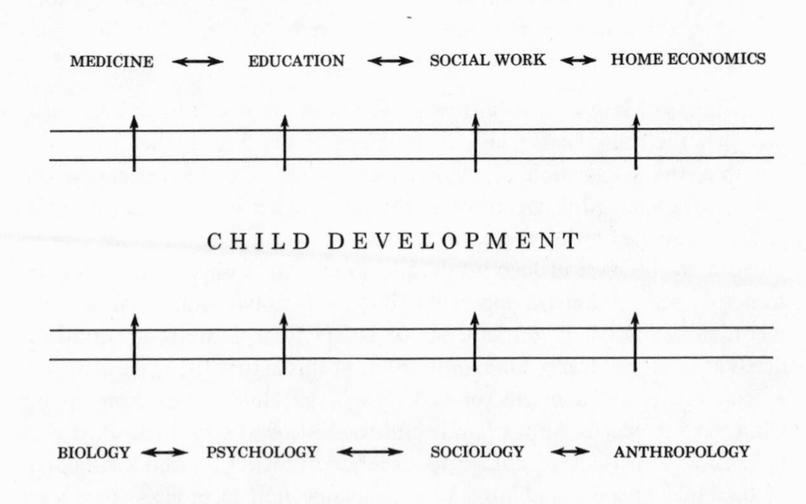

Fig. 1.2. The relationship between child development and other disciplines.

scribe each of several sources of child development in related disciplines, and each of several areas of specialized application of knowledge about the child.

Sources in the Biological Sciences Historically, child development has grown up from roots that lie, in part, in the various biological sciences. The biologist and natural scientist have shown us man's position in relation to the other species in the animal kingdom. Biologists have organized the facts of reproduction processes and, in the specialized field of genetics, have shed light on the inheritance of certain characteristics from one generation to the next. Physiologists have provided us with information on the growth and functioning of body tissues, organs, and systems. Without the wide range of factual and technical information from these and other specialized areas of biology, the field of child development as it exists today could not have come into being.

Sources in Psychology Psychology in the mid-twentieth century is an extremely broad field which is concerned with human behavior in general. It has been defined in a variety of ways, but it deals primarily with man's behavior and adjustment to his environment. One somewhat specialized area, known as developmental psychology, is concerned mainly with the chronologically progressive changes in the capacities of man to deal with his environment, and with the behavior he engages in to make adjustments to that environment. Other specialized areas in psychology deal with particular aspects of the ways in which man achieves a more or less satisfactory relationship with his world of objects and people. Some of these deal primarily with personality and its development; others are concerned largely with learning processes; some have as their major interest the processes of perceiving and knowing the world; still others deal with interpersonal relationships and the nature of adjustments made by individuals in achieving and maintaining healthy social behavior.

All of these have special significance for child development. Our interest here is in focusing our knowledge of these and related psychological problems on the central questions of the growing child: *first*, what are the laws and principles that govern the growth and behavior of all children, and *second*, how can we best account for the unique developmental and behavioral pattern of each individual child?

Sources in Sociology Sociology is a body of scientific knowledge about the behavior of human beings in relation to other human beings. It is concerned directly with understanding man's behavior in relation to the various groups in which he holds membership—especially those groups with which he is closely identified and which participate more or less directly in structuring his personality and behavior patterns. The family is one such group.

The sociologist can bring a great deal of information to bear on the question of how a child grows. Indeed, sociologists have shed much light on this question, and, over the years, have enabled us to answer significant parts of it. But in addition to describing the nature of the family and other groups which have vital roles to play in the development of the child, sociologists have helped us materially in achieving a basic understanding of the nature of society and the various institutions in society that influence our thoughts, actions, and feelings. They have helped us to see that even our perception of the physical world around us is colored and determined in large measure by the character of the social institutions which man has devised. They have helped us to see the powerful role played by such various socializing agents as the home, the church, the school, and the community in the life and personality development of the child. They have helped us to see, too, that the basic "nature" of the child is well-nigh impossible to separate from the societal environment—the milieu within which human personality is structured.

Sources in Anthropology Anthropology, broadly defined, is the study of man. It is concerned with the big questions about the nature of man and how he has come to be the way he is. While there are a number of kinds of specialists within the general field, the two major divisions of this discipline are cultural anthropology and physical anthropology.

Cultural anthropology seeks to answer the question of man's nature in relation to his inventions, including his social behavior, as this, too, is a part of what he has devised. In this connection, certain anthropologists have become vitally interested in the socialization processes of societies; that is, with the systems devised by societies for inducting children into membership and for fostering the kinds of development that allow them to participate fully in the society. In this area, the anthropologist and the child-development specialist work together in making use of knowledge about children.

Physical anthropology is concerned with man as a physical being. Man's physical status and characteristics, his origin and evolution, are the central problems. Some physical anthropologists compare the physical characteristics of man with those of the other primates (apes and monkeys); others compare the so-called "races" of man with each other. Still others specialize in physical growth and development. Through their careful measurements of the human body and its parts at different periods and stages of development, they have provided us with much useful information on the nature of the growth process.

CONTRIBUTIONS TO OTHER DISCIPLINES

As was illustrated in Figure 1.2, child development may be viewed as a specialized field which integrates the findings of other disciplines and focuses on an understanding of the growing child. It organizes these findings into a coherent body of knowledge which it makes available to a variety of fields of application. Among these fields of application are medicine, education, social work, and home economics.

~ *Medicine* Today's physician is acutely aware that the health of the growing child involves more than freedom from disease. Healthy growth is a progressive series of orderly and dynamic changes—involving higher levels of physiological and mental functioning—which reach toward the goal of maturity. The physician charged with the treatment of children, whether he is a general practitioner or a pediatric specialist, is concerned with more than keeping height and weight charts, giving inoculations, diagnosing and treating the usual childhood diseases, and prescribing vitamins. These activities have a useful and important role to play in the practice of his profession, but, beyond them, he is concerned with the total well-being of his patients. In his practice, the physician relies heavily on a thorough knowledge of human growth and development. The following statement written by John A. Anderson, a professor of pediatrics, illustrates this:

> There is perhaps no professional field in which the concept of growth and development can have fuller meaning than in the practice of medicine. A complete understanding of the patterns of growth and development and the variations in expression of these dynamic processes is necessary in order to define the existence of disease at any time from conception to birth and from birth to maturity. In addition . . . the responsibility of the physician extends further. Society demands that disease be prevented, that it be recognized in its earliest stages, and when it occurs, that the consequences of a permanent nature be prevented. Finally, if disease has produced permanent injury, the necessity of restoring functional capacity to a stage of social and psychologic acceptability is another obligation. None of these responsibilities can be met without a thorough and detailed knowledge of all phases and aspects of the process of growth and development (1, p. 227).

Psychiatry is a specialized branch of medicine concerned primarily with the treatment and prevention of mental and emotional illness. In his work with children and adults, the psychiatrist must also be familiar with normal human development in all of its aspects: physical, mental, social, and emotional. He must be able to discriminate between normal variations found among all individuals, and signs of illness, or pathological behavior, which indicate serious disturbance and call for special treatment. One interesting application of the psychiatrist's study of child development arises in his dealings with certain patients in whom growth has been retarded in one or more areas of development, or in whom there has been a reasonably adequate development followed by a regressive return to earlier, more primitive levels of behavior. The modern psychiatrist is a highly specialized, well trained, and competent individual who has a wide variety of tools and techniques at his disposal, but none of these is more vital in his practice than his understanding of human development.

Education Over the years, the professional field of education has benefited from an ever increasing knowledge of the characteristics of the growing child. The child-development point of view has permeated the schools to a marked degree. Schools attempt to design and organize their programs in keeping with the levels of readiness of the children. This trend is shown by the increasing emphasis on causes of child behavior and the seeking of mutual understanding by parents and teachers alike of the individual child in school. There has been a definite trend toward individualization of the curriculum as a result of our current recognition that the individual child brings all his special attributes—talents, attitudes, values, skills, competencies, and deficiencies—with him into the classroom. Educators have learned that the child and the subject matter cannot readily be separated from each other in the classroom. A good school program is more than a series of courses; it is based on a sound knowledge of the nature of child growth in general and on a thorough understanding of each individual child in particular.

There are different educational levels, also, at which the various principles of child development have special application. The kindergarten movement illustrates a tangible recognition of a special stage of development on the part of 5-year-olds. We are aware now that these children are not ordinarily ready for the formal experience of instruction in reading and writing. They are ready for, and in need of, a less formal kind of school experience. The kindergarten experience not only helps to prepare the child for first-grade work, it provides a unique experience in a group situation outside his home. We are now aware, also, that even before the age of 5 there are kinds of school experiences that are appropriate for most children. The nursery school, which will be discussed in greater detail in Chapter Thirteen, has developed in an effort to meet the special needs of the preschool child. While education in the formal sense of subject-matter instruction is not emphasized in the nursery school, a great deal of learning occurs in this informal setting. But it is especially a setting in which the individual child is stressed. Nursery-school teachers do not concern themselves with having every child participate in group activities. The big concern—and this stems from our knowledge of the needs of preschool children—is to provide an environment within which the child can explore freely to discover his world and the objects and materials in it, and to discover himself in the process.

There are other ages, too, for which child development has provided principles in the organization of educational experiences: the primary, intermediate, and secondary grades all make use of our expanding body of knowledge of development. It is at the adult level, however, in the education of parents, that child development has made a peculiar and unique contribution. The parent-education movement in America has been organized to familiarize parents with the nature and the needs of children, and with the principles of child guidance. Today's parents are remarkably sophisticated about children. They take for granted the principle of providing experiences and materials appropriate to the age level of the child. They recognize the importance of a child's need to express his feelings, even the negative ones, in order to learn to deal with his emotions in a positive manner. They are aware of the fact that children develop in stages, and that some of these stages involve behavior which is unattractive, difficult to cope with, and disturbing to adults, but which is, nevertheless, perfectly normal behavior.

These and many other generalizations about children which are well known to today's parents are part of the content of parental and preparental education. This educational endeavor has succeeded in making parents today the most knowledgeable, understanding, and sophisticated parents in the history of mankind. Needless to say, this has not succeeded in removing all the problems from the task of child-rearing. In one sense, it has created a new problem—we now have an increased responsibility to be aware of the current vast and growing body of knowledge about children.

Social Work Child development's emphasis on the needs of children during the first half of the twentieth century created a new atmosphere and a new philosophy for the care of all children. In particular, it led to the formulation of practices—and even of laws—which regulate the treatment of neglected, dependent, delinquent, and otherwise socially inadequate children and youth. There was a time when the emotionally disturbed or mentally retarded child was treated in the same manner—perhaps even in the same wards of the same institutions—as the psychotic or psychopathic adult. The earlier, more primitive philosophy of removing such children from society as a way of solving the problem is being replaced by the new philosophy of treatment, the goal being to help such children grow into useful and productive members of society. An essential part of this treatment philosophy, stimulated by the efforts of child-development and social-welfare workers, has been the education of professional persons (lawyers, judges, legislators, physicians, and others) as well as of the general public, to the fact that a child—especially an emotionally inadequate or disturbed child—has strong needs for the security and intimacy of a family unit. As an example of the effects of this emphasis, there has been a striking trend away from the placing of orphaned or illegitimate children in institutions, and toward placing them in private foster homes—either for continued foster care or for permanent adoption into the family. Concomitantly, there has been a strong trend toward adopting infants into private families at earlier ages, as evidence has accumulated showing the desirability of giving all children an intimate family experience from the earliest possible age.

Similarly, in the treatment of juvenile offenders and emotionally disturbed and retarded children, there has been a decided trend toward treatment based on the particular needs of the individual child. There has also been a trend toward the sound treatment of the "whole child"; that is, we have come to recognize the importance of a child's physical well-being while dealing with his psychological problems. We have come to see that the problems of the slow learning child in school are not really separate from his problem of malnutrition, and that these problems must be dealt with together as part of a total treatment program that takes all of his needs into account. Such trends have resulted directly or indirectly from the child-development point of view in our modern society.

Home Economics Home economics has had a long and illustrious career in America and has made contributions to the well-being of individuals and families in our society—the extent of which would be difficult to measure. In home economics, as in other professional fields, there have been important trends and developments in philosophy, technical knowledge, and practice. There was a time when the professional home economist was known primarily as an expert in food preparation, clothing construction, or housekeeping efficiency. In these roles, home economists did provide a wealth of technical knowledge which has benefited us all a great deal. Today's professional home economist, however, is more likely to have had special education in understanding the family as a unit of interacting personalities. While a knowledge of nutrition and food preparation, family clothing needs, art and aesthetic considerations, and principles of home management are still as important to the homemaker and the professional home economist as ever before, there is in addition an emphasis on understanding the growth cycle of the family and its individual members. This implies understanding not only the nature of the child at various stages of his development, but also the nature of the growing, changing, dynamic relationships of the child with the other members of his family at every stage of the family's life cycle.

This trend toward "interactionism" on the part of today's home economist can be attributed in part to the gradually accumulating knowledge that even such basic concerns as diet, clothing, housing, and family finance, while worthy objectives *per se*, are today conceived as means to the greater end of the development of the individual human personality. To achieve this aim, we are relying to a greater extent than ever before on our knowledge of the ways in which children grow and achieve maturity in their relationships with others. Today's home economist is learning to view herself as a specialist in human relationships, with the emphasis on the family and its development.

THE CHILD-DEVELOPMENT SPECIALIST

It should be perfectly clear at this point that the field of child development has interesting and complex relationships with other fields of specialization. These relationships make it possible and natural for the child-development specialist to be found in any of a wide variety of vocational and professional activities, in settings that differ radically one from another. Just as the engineer may be a specialist in electrical, mechanical, aeronautical, marine, or other branches of the over-all field of engineering, the child-development professional may have specialized in one or more of a variety of activities which are rapidly becoming increasingly recognized in

A child-development specialist must be competent
and understanding, and have a love for children.
(Courtesy of Mills College of Education.)

the professional world. Some specialize in early-childhood education, including the education of the preschool child. As nursery-school teachers or directors of nursery-school programs they work primarily with children between the ages of 3 and 5. (Some nursery schools admit children at the age of 2, but this is more characteristic of the day-care programs designed for children of working mothers than of the nursery school which has as its fundamental objective the social, educational, and personal development of the child.) As parents have become aware of the nursery school's contributions to the total development of children, there has arisen a strong demand for these services until at present there are both private and public nursery schools, which have different forms of financial support, and which are active in most all urban communities across the country. In some cases, these nursery schools have been made an integral part of public-school programs, thus receive state support. There is every reason to assume that our society will continue to recognize the need for such services and will improve and expand them in the immediate future.

Other child-development specialists have found a rapidly expanding field of activities in children's hospitals—especially as directors of play-therapy programs for hospitalized children. Such programs have become recognized as valuable adjuncts to the total therapy program. With the modern, enlightened awareness that the sick child is as much in need of a positive, healthy morale as he is in need of an aseptic environment, such programs have been adopted widely with considerable success. The child-development specialist in such an environment works directly with pediatrician, nurse, and in some instances with the psychiatric-treatment staff in outlining and carrying out a planned program of treatment for the individual child.

Other specialists work in a variety of social-welfare agencies responsible for the care and treatment of children—in camps and treatment centers for crippled children or in recreational programs sponsored by religious organizations and youth groups. Some work in various state extension-service programs, conducting activities for children and participating in educational programs for their parents. Some work directly in public or private schools as teachers or counselors. Some obtain graduate degrees and enter highly specialized careers as research workers and teachers at the college level, or as practitioners in specialized programs of treatment for normal or exceptional children.

Thus, there is an expanding field of work with children, affording many varied career opportunities that give personal satisfaction, and, at the same time, provide a useful service which our society is now recognizing as vitally necessary.

SUMMARY

Child development as a scientific field of endeavor had its beginnings in the late nineteenth and early twentieth centuries. It began with isolated studies of individual children, which aroused questions about the nature of children in general. These questions gave rise to longitudinal and cross-sectional studies that have provided the modern parent and the professional worker with a wealth of information about how children grow and behave at different stages of development. Four principal streams of knowledge have contributed especially to the psychological study of the child: (1) the behavioristic approach, which emphasized the observable actions of the child and the role of environment and experiences in the learning of those actions; (2) the normative-descriptive approach, which stressed that growth comes from inside the child and appears in a successive sequence of orderly stages which can be described in detail; (3) the psychoanalytic approach, which brought forth a new concept of human personality based in part on unconscious drives; and (4) the field-theory approach, which viewed the growing child in relation to the dynamic forces of his environment.

Child development has its roots in other disciplines: biology, sociology, psychology, and anthropology. A major function of the child-development field is organizing the findings of such basic disciplines and focusing them specifically on questions pertaining to the growth and behavior of children. Child development also raises some questions of its own, apart from these other disciplines, and seeks answers to them.

In turn, still other professional fields rely on the findings and organized knowledge of child development to carry out their activities with and for children: the fields of education, both for children and adults; medicine; social work, and home economics.

The child-development specialist today is a recognized professional person with specialized interests, aptitude, and training in work with children. Such a person may find a career in an increasingly varied assortment of specialized professions.

REFERENCES

1. Anderson, J. A., "Significance of growth and development to the practicing physician," in D. B. Harris (ed.), *The concept of development,* Minneapolis: Univ. of Minnesota Press, 1957, 227–233.
2. Anderson, J. E., "Child development: an historical perspective," *Child develpm.,* 1956, **27** (2): 181–196.
3. Aries, P., *Centuries of childhood,* (trans. R. Baldick), New York: Knopf, 1962.
4. Dennis, W., "Historical beginnings of child psychology," *Psychol. Bull.,* 1949, **46**: 224–235.
5. Freud, S., *New introductory lectures on psychoanalysis,* (trans. W. J. H. Sprott), New York: Norton, 1933.
6. Gesell, A., and Amatruda, C. S., *Developmental diagnosis,* 2nd ed., New York: Hoeber-Harper, 1947.
7. Gesell, A., and Ilg, Frances L., *Child development, an introduction to the study of human growth,* New York: Harper, 1949.
8. Lewin, K., A *dynamic theory of personality* (selected papers), New York: McGraw-Hill, 1935.
9. Maslow, A. H., "A theory of human motivation," *Psychol. Rev.,* 1943, **50**: 370–396.
10. Payne, G. H., *The child in human progress,* New York: Putnam, 1916.
11. Watson, J. B., *Psychological care of infant and child,* New York: Norton, 1928.

CHAPTER TWO

How can we come to understand children through observation? How can we make our observations more useful and reliable? How does the child-development scientist make use of observation procedures? What standard methods are used in reporting results of observation?

OBSERVATION OF CHILDREN

AS THERE ARE TWO LEVELS of information about children, and the student of child development makes use of both: *first,* the level of information about children in general, based on carefully controlled observations by well trained scientists, and, *second,* the level of personal insight and understanding based on one's own observations of children. One level is neither superior nor inferior to the other; they are both essential to the student. They are not independent of each other, since in the final analysis the generalizations of the scientist must become personal insights in order to be meaningful and useful to us individually. At the same time, personal insights must have validity and authenticity just as the scientist's findings do in order to be useful.

There are some close similarities—and also some fundamental differences—in scientific and informal observation procedures. It is the purpose of this chapter to outline these observation procedures as they apply to both levels of information. The first part of the chapter deals with the informal observation procedures—those we can all use to further our understanding of the children with whom we have contact. This is followed by a discussion of the techniques used by the child-development scientist in providing us with valid generalizations, and will necessarily be a bit more technical, but a careful study of this section will assist the student in understanding much of the material to be presented throughout remaining portions of the book.

INFORMAL OBSERVATION

It's an unusual adult who has not had opportunities to observe children—at home, on the playground, in school, at church, at the supermarket, in front of a television set, or perhaps even in the role of goblins at the front door on Hallowe'en. Our observations of children under such informal and "natural" conditions are probably not very scientific. Nevertheless, we cannot escape the strong tendency to form ideas, attitudes, and opinions about children on the basis of just such experiences. These ideas and opinions may or may not be accurate as far as they go; they are certain to be incomplete, however. A brief episode on a city bus, in which we observe a restless 3-year-old girl and her mother, provides an illustration. The child's restlessness leads to physical activity and loud talking on her part; the mother's embarrassed and impatient reaction is an attempt to quiet the girl. The situation worsens and the girl gives a first-class demonstration of a temper tantrum for the benefit of the other passengers. Her kicking and screaming seem to reinforce in the minds of nearby passengers the firm conviction that children should be seen and not heard. The informal observation, then, has had its impact on the observers.

Unfortunately, such observations rarely provide us with enough information; they may leave us with vague and uneasy feelings about children—just as some other kinds of observations of sweet or innocent actions leave us with a rosy, warm feeling about childhood—but they don't really tell us much. We didn't stop to observe, for example, whether the mother had made any provisions for entertaining her 3-year-old on a long bus trip; we didn't know whether this child would normally be napping at this time of day; we didn't *really* know this was the girl's mother, but just assumed it. There are many other unknown elements in the situation which make it hazardous to draw any conclusions whatever from the incident. Nevertheless, people do draw conclusions about child behavior on the basis of such meager information, on the assumption that it is, after all, mostly a matter of "common sense."

A man observes his neighbor's child, noting that the boy is slow in talking and doesn't seem to be very alert mentally. He also observes that this boy is physically strong, well coordinated, and able to throw and to catch a ball well for his age. Somehow these facts all seem to fit together in this man's mind to support and reinforce a belief which he holds: "Athletic children are likely to be slow mentally and academically." This belief, we hasten to point out, is false. It should not be overlooked that this man really held the opinion *prior* to making the observation. In fact, his very preconception was an important part of the reason he happened to observe these particular facts about the neighbor child. There is a tendency—very normal, by the way—for all of us to see those things in our world which fit and conform to the structure of the beliefs, attitudes, and opinions we already hold. One of the very serious problems, then, with informal observation is that what we unconsciously *want* to see may easily influence our perceptions of what is actually going on.

Another problem is that it is all too easy to assume that our informal analysis of a specific child's behavior is somehow applicable to children in general or, perhaps, to some broad category of children who have something in common with the one we observed. We note that an 18-month-old runs toward a stranger with his arms outstretched; we see a 2-year-old walking easily up and down stairs, alternating his feet; we hear a 4-year-old telling her father she doesn't like her tricycle any more because she knows how to ride a real bicycle and wants one of her own. All of these things might happen, and might be observed in this manner, and we might conclude in each case that the child involved is like all children and the behavior is somehow typical of children. It is not.

Or we casually note some peculiarity about a child, and almost unconsciously associate it with his behavior: if he has darker skin coloring, or fairer skin coloring, or a larger head or a smaller head, or a faster or slower manner of talking or walking, we often conclude that he is polite, unruly, aggressive, friendly, or whatever. Thus, not only may a child's behavior not be typical of other children, or of all children who have some characteristic in common—it may not even be typical of the child we are watching! What we are seeing may call itself to our attention precisely because it is unusual, even for *that* child.

For all of these and other reasons it is not safe to generalize about children on the strength of our informal observations. Yet in studying child development, we can never remove ourselves completely from these personal experiences and from their effects on our attitudes, opinions, and understanding. We cannot suddenly become completely objective and un-

There are countless opportunities for observation.
(Courtesy of Los Angeles City School Districts.)

affected by attitudes and information—and misinformation—which we have lived with for years. It is best to start with a clear recognition that our present reactions to children are very much influenced by our past experiences with them, for then we have taken the initial step in improving the quality of our observations and of making them more reliable and useful to us.

IMPROVING INFORMAL OBSERVATIONS

The usefulness of our observations will depend, in large measure, on the questions we ask ourselves before, during, and after the incident was observed. For example, we may have watched a child in the act of picking up some small object from the floor. How did he go about it? Did he bend from the waist and reach for it with one hand? Did he flex his knees and assume a squatting position to reach the floor? Did he reach with both hands? Did he make contact with the object first with the tip of one finger, or two fingers, or thumb and forefinger in opposition to each other? Or did he "palm" the object with the flat surface of what the poet called the ". . . baby's starfish of a hand"? And when he obtained the object what happened? Did he examine it with his eyes? With his mouth? While he was examining it, was the rest of his body active or still? How long did the object hold his attention? How did he react to the color, the size, the shape, the texture, and the weight of the object? There are countless questions which could be raised about an action as brief and simple as picking up and examining a small object. Some of these would appear, to most people, to be absurdly detailed and insignificant questions; but they serve a most useful purpose: they alert us to behavior which would otherwise go unnoticed. The keenest observers are those who refuse to take child behavior for granted; they are observing for a purpose, and the purpose is to answer questions. The refusal to take behavior for granted allows many questions to be raised—and answered—that might otherwise escape us completely.

The usefulness of our observations depends also on the kinds of records we make of whatever we see and hear. Keeping some kind of record serves the dual purpose of forcing us to organize our observations into meaningful statements about a child, in order to put them down on paper, and, at the same time, of providing a permanent record which can be referred to at a later time without having to rely solely on memory. In making records of observations, it is helpful to distinguish between "facts" on the one hand, and "interpretations" on the other, as suggested by Pease (5). There are some aspects of child behavior which are directly observable: we can see a child's bodily action, hear the words he says, or feel the pressure of his arms when he clings to us in a frightening situation. In the last example, however, we cannot observe the child's fear. Emotions, mental processes, attitudes, wishes, and motives are examples of things not directly accessible to the observer. We can often make reasonable inferences about their existence on the strength of the behavior we see, but this making of inferences is based on our *interpretation* of the child's behavior. If two children are quarreling, and one hits the other with his fist, we may observe the hitting action. If we record this in a meaningful way, telling exactly what happened, we have made a valid observation. If, however, we record such things as, "Jackie and Bill are aggressive and difficult children; they are always quarreling and fighting," we are writing about our personal reactions to these children.

There are many occasions when it is entirely appropriate to record our personal reactions to child behavior. Such records can help us to achieve greater insight into our own personalities by making us more alert to the kinds of behavior that we find satisfying, attractive, and desirable in children, and to those kinds that annoy, frustrate, or frighten us. As observers, however, our task is to keep a more or less objective, descriptive record of events as they occur among children. Interpretations, personal reactions, feelings about the child's behavior, etc., may then be noted separately, with full awareness on our part that these are not the same as observations.

GUIDES FOR OBSERVATION RECORDS

An adequate observation record begins with the necessary descriptive information on the setting: date, time, place, and the situation. If name and age of child are known, these should be recorded along with his sex. If the child is not well known to the observer, a brief description of his physical characteristics will be helpful. This might include eye color, hair and skin pigmentation, body build and proportions, facial characteristics, and any unusual features such as a peculiar gait or other unique mannerisms. Wearing apparel, although not ordinarily very useful in helping to identify a child later, may be important in the child's behavior, and therefore should be recorded. An example would be a nursery-school child wearing a spotless, frilly dress, who is watching the other children playing with messy materials such as clay and finger paints. She does not participate herself. The observer notes the wearing apparel, the lack of participation, and in his observation notebook writes the interpretation that these two things may be related. When he observes this child again, he is alert to note again the kind of wearing apparel and the degree of participation in messy materials. A cumulative series of records of the child's behavior may help to establish not only the nature of her attitude toward such materials, but also the reasons behind those attitudes.

The observations of child-development students are frequently based on a particular topic, or aspect of development, which the student is to single out and to devote particular attention to. This might include such topics as physical or motor characteristics of children, emotional behavior, language, problem-solving, or social behavior. An observation outline or guide is most helpful for such a procedure. Examples of detailed and comprehensive observation outlines are provided by Suchman (7). Additional insights and information on the problems of observation of children are given by Almy (1), Carbonara (2), Cohen (3), and Pease and Pattison (6).

The Diary Record In many instances the most appropriate manner of recording the observation data is in the form of a *diary record*. The diary record is a running account of the behavior of a particular child for a stated period of time. If this is a preschool child it will not be possible to keep a complete diary record for long periods without stopping to rest, even if one uses shorthand—unless the child is sound asleep! Even when a child appears relatively quiet, a keen observer keeping a diary record can find much more to write than time to write it. With practice, however, one learns to record the most significant events that relate to a child's use of the objects and materials in his environment, and the nature of his contacts with the people around him. Even so, a wise procedure is to record as accurately and completely as possible for no more than five minutes at a time, followed by brief rest periods. Such a record should be completely factual, with conscientious efforts to eliminate opinions, value judgments, and personal attitudes. An example of a well-kept diary record is provided by the following excerpt from the notebook of a student:

DATE: *Oct. 20, 1960*
CHILD: *Carol G_______, girl, 4-4*

	FACTS	INTERPRETATIONS
10:47	*Carol is playing on the big boxes and boards (outdoor play area, nursery school) with Laura and Anita. She slides, feet first in a sitting position, down a board propped against a big box. She is wearing a parka and mittens.*	*Laura and Anita seem to form a pair, with Carol being "accepted" in the play at their discretion. Carol seems to be pleased with this role, but says very little and seems to be in doubt about how much to assert herself.*
10:48	*Anita asks Carol if she is trying to get in their house (boxes) and Carol says, "Yes," and smiles. Now Carol runs over to the sandbox and says she is going to play. She fills up a pan with sand and takes it over to the boxes for their "party." She pats the sand carefully in the pan and gives it to Laura.*	*Her enthusiasm has increased now that the "party" is getting under way.*
10:52	*Laura and Anita go after more sand and Carol yells for them to hurry. Miss Avis comes out on the porch and Carol yells, "Hi, teacher! We're having a party—you can come to our party!"*	*Carol's relationship with the other children is easily disrupted by the teacher's presence.*

	Facts	Interpretations
10:54	*Carol now crawls in one of the boxes and rapidly out again, telling the teacher about their "house." Now she pushes a tricycle out of her way and runs over to the sand box again, quickly filling some more pans.*	
10:57	*She runs back to the "house," sits down in one corner and is very still and sober for a long time (about 1½ minutes). She watches the other children playing around her.*	*I wonder if Carol's behavior here means that she doesn't really care much about continuing to play with the others, or if she would really like to but isn't sure enough of herself and finds it "safer" to withdraw for a time.*
10:59	*Some of the other children are starting to go inside now, and Carol jumps up suddenly, runs to the door of the nursery school, yelling, "Let me in! Let me in!"*	

The foregoing excerpt was not selected because of any unusual incident or any special significance to the interpretive material, but because it does an excellent job of separating "facts" from "interpretations," and includes enough of the child's language and physical actions as well as the setting, objects, and other people present to enable the reader to follow the main patterning of Carol's behavior during the period of observation. It also illustrates one of the important contributions of observation—that of raising questions in the observer's mind which can lead to further attempts to understand a child. The very process of formulating a significant question is a key step in the direction of greater understanding.

Anecdotal Records In contrast to diary records, anecdotal records are not based on a unit of time, but take as their unit an event or incident in the child's interaction with his environment. In addition to the child who is the main subject of the observation, the record should include data on any other principal participants—children or adult—and the nature of the child's interactions with these persons. A given event may be long or short, routine or unusual, and pleasant or unpleasant for the persons involved. It may include many people as it progresses, or it may be carried out in isolation. The following is an example of an anecdote taken from the records of a child-development student observing in a nursery school:

DATE: *Sept. 15, 1960*
CHILD: *Linda B______, girl, age 3-9*

	FACTS	INTERPRETATIONS
10:15	*Linda has been playing by herself at a table, working a picture puzzle. Two other girls had tried to get involved in the play but she had ignored them. At this point a teacher sits down at the piano nearby and starts to sing a song, encouraging the children close to her to join in the singing. It is a song about "Miss Polly," whose dolly was sick. Linda stops playing with the puzzle and joins the other children near the piano. She acts out the story of Miss Polly with body movements but does not join in the singing with the other children and the teacher. When that song ends, they sing another; this time Linda does not participate at all, except to watch the other children.*	*Linda is a child who talks well at home but does not speak at all in the nursery school. This incident shows how she has learned to get along in the nursery school without having to use words.*

There are many variations on the basic methods of observation just described. They include varying degrees of detail and a wide range of techniques for helping the observer to note particular aspects of the child's behavior. Some techniques place primary emphasis on the individual child as he moves from one activity to another. Others shift the primary emphasis to the setting within which action occurs, and note the movements and patterns of behavior of the children as they enter into that setting, engage in action, and leave the setting. Some techniques serve to record the action of a child from one arbitrary point in time to another; others attempt to record the child's action from the beginning to the completion of some fairly clear-cut incident, regardless of the length of time involved. Some methods emphasize the child's relations with other children or adults; others stress his relationship to the objects in his physical environment. Still others are concerned largely with the peculiar characteristics of the child himself—body build, muscular action, social competence, language skill, problem-solving ability, etc.

ETHICAL CONSIDERATIONS IN THE USE OF OBSERVATION RECORDS

The child-development student learns, even after a very limited experience in observation, that some of the most personal and intimate aspects of a child's life become a part of the observation record. Four-year-old Roger, for example, may be remarkably uninhibited, fluent and expressive—even colorful—in his language. This could make Roger an interesting topic of conversation among friends. However, professional and ethical considerations forbid the discussion of individual children outside the nursery school —or wherever observations occur. More important than Roger's language might be such considerations as his statements about his parents or other relatives. Statements revealing the attitudes and habits of his parents, for example, may be accurate or imaginary but, in either case, they are not discussed among friends by the ethical student.

THE LABORATORY-NURSERY SCHOOL

The laboratory-nursery school, which will be described in greater detail in Chapter Thirteen, affords an excellent opportunity for observation. Many college and university nursery schools are designed to facilitate observation and are equipped with booths and one-way-vision screens or mirrors. These provide an excellent view—and one can remain out of the way of both the children and the teachers. Whether the observers have the use of such a booth or do their observing in the same room with the children, the nursery school is unexcelled as a place in which child behavior may be seen and understood. Facilities and programs are generally provided for children ranging in age from 2½ or 3 up to about 5 years. In some the children are grouped by age, with separate groups for 2's, 3's, and 4's. In others the ages are mixed within a group. From the observer's standpoint, there are both advantages and disadvantages to either arrangement—but in either case the opportunities for observation are plentiful.

The student observing for the first time in a nursery school will find so many things going on at once that it is difficult to assimilate all of them or to integrate them into a meaningful pattern. By getting to know individual children and by becoming somewhat familiar with the program and routines of the nursery school, the student soon becomes sensitive to the meaningfulness of the behavior of individual children. It is a most rewarding experience, and well worth the very real effort it requires.

CONTROLLED OBSERVATION

The child-development laboratory is used not only by students in training, but also by research workers who attempt to organize and further our general knowledge about children. Such research workers have, by conducting carefully controlled studies with children, learned a great deal about social behavior, mental development, physical growth, language development, and the development of motor control. Research efforts require careful attention to scientific procedures, the details of which need not be discussed here. However, it is well to point out the sources and bases of our information about children, since much of what will be discussed in the following chapters depends directly on the results of research.

Use of the Scientific Method The child-development research worker is a scientist, just as a chemist or biologist is a scientist, to the extent that he makes careful use of the scientific method. In order to make accurate generalizations about his subject the scientist must proceed in a careful and methodical manner through the following steps:

1. Defining a problem.
2. Stating a hypothesis—a possible solution for the problem.
3. Collecting data which bear directly on the problem.
4. Organizing and analyzing the data.
5. Drawing conclusions.

The data of child development are usually collected through observations of one kind or another. The observations may take a wide variety of forms—and may be aided by a large number of devices and control techniques—but the basic task in the collection of data is still one of observation. Ways to obtain useful and reliable data on child development have been described in more detail by Gardner, *et al.* (4). The data thus collected must be analyzed and reported in some manner if they are to be meaningful. We now turn our attention to this process.

DESCRIBING THE RESULTS OF OBSERVATION

Whether observations have been made in the formal setting of a psychological or physical examination of a child, or in the less formal setting of the school, home, or play group, the results of the observation must be reported clearly and in more or less standard fashion if they are to be useful. Students of child development—including teachers, parents, physicians, psychologists, social workers, and home economists, as well as college students—are continually relying on generalizations about children that have been developed through observation of one kind or another. It is important for the student to have a clear understanding of the form in which these generalizations are made.

It is important, for example, that a student know *how many* children were observed as a basis for some generalization. A study of the social behavior of nursery-school children which does not tell the student how many children were studied would be rather meaningless; for this reason, when research findings are reported, it is customary to include a report of the "N," or number of children observed in the study. It is equally important to give a description of the children that includes at least such information as their ages and sex, and any peculiar conditions in their lives which might affect the study. For example, if some generalization were made about children's social behavior, based on the observation of a group of children reared in an orphanage, it would have to be clearly stated that this generalization would be applicable only to children having a similar orphanage background and not to children in general. Similarly, generalizations about children reared in large cities may not apply to children growing up in small communities or in rural areas, and generalizations about 3-year-old girls may be quite inappropriate when applied to boys, even to boys of the same age. Because of this need for caution in interpreting the results of studies with children, it is essential that the student become aware of any special characteristics of the children that might have an effect on the behavior which has been observed.

REPORTING THE RESULTS

Studies of children are often reported in the form of test scores or in a series of number measurements of some kind. In some cases, however, the most meaningful figure will be one which gives an average for the whole group studied.

Measures of Central Tendency The average figure is often that which is most useful in describing the tendency of the total group. If we wish to describe the height of 4-year-old boys, for example, we could do so by stating that they are, on the average, 40.9 inches tall (Watson and Lowrey, 8). An average of this kind is called the *mean* and may be abbreviated as "M." Since we shall have occasion throughout the book to refer to mean scores, it may help if we remember that a mean score is simply an average obtained by adding all the scores in the group together and dividing the sum by the "N" or number of cases.

Another measure of central tendency, one which gives us somewhat different information about our group, is the *median*. Like the mean, the median provides a way of describing the total group with a single score; however, it differs from the mean in that it tells us that point in the total set of scores which divides the group exactly in half. That is, if we measured the height of 20 4-year-old boys and then ranked them in order from tallest to shortest, the median would be that score which fell exactly in the middle of our set of scores, dividing the tallest ten from the shortest ten.

Measures of Variability In addition to these figures that tell us average tendencies in a group, it is helpful to know how much variation there is in the group. We may want to know how big a *range* there is between the highest and lowest score in a group, for example. We may want to know what percent of the total group score above a given point. Or we may wish to know how much, on the average, each score in the group differed from the mean for the total group.

The most widely used measure of variation is known as the *standard deviation*. As an index of the amount of variability in scoring, it provides valuable information which is useful in many ways, but is especially useful in the comparison of two or more groups. If we wish to know whether there are important sex differences in language behavior, for example, we would want to know not only the mean score for boys and girls with respect to some measure of language development, but also the standard deviation scores for the two sexes. This would inform us as to whether or not the two sexes are equal with respect to variability in language development.

Table 2.1 shows data taken from a research study illustrating some of the basic procedures for reporting data on children. The first column identifies the group of children, and the second column indicates the number of children in each group. The third column, headed "Mean," tells the average number of trials required by children in each of the three groups to learn to push the correct button on a box. When the correct button was pushed, a marble was delivered to the child through an opening in the box. The table tells us that Group I required relatively few trials. The fourth column, "Standard Deviation," gives information on the degree of variability of performance within each of the three groups. It tells us that

TABLE 2.1. *Tabular Presentation of Basic Statistical Data*

Group	N	Mean	Standard Deviation	Range
I	24	18.62	15.60	18–87
II	15	53.93	28.98	24–124
III	19	50.95	28.02	21–135

there was much more variation in performance on the part of children in Groups II and III than in Group I. The final column tells us the range of scores for each of the three groups, and indicates that the range was relatively small for Group I in comparison with the other two groups.

Measures of Relationship Another form in which data are frequently reported is in terms of the degree of relationship between two different sets of scores. For example, we may be interested in knowing whether there is any relationship between the height of children and their intelligence. In order to find out, we could measure both height and intelligence with the same group of children and determine whether the tallest ones were also the brightest and the shortest ones also the dullest. But obviously there would be a lot of cases in which this would not be true, so we should have to check ourselves mathematically to see whether, on the *average*, there is any tendency for brighter children to be taller and duller children to be shorter. We would do this by computing a *correlation coefficient*, which would tell us whether any such relationship between height and intelligence actually exists. What we will need to know about this figure is that it tells us how strong the relationship is between two sets of data. (We need not concern ourselves with the methods used to compute it.) The limits of the correlation coefficient are +1.00 and −1.00, both of which represent perfect relationships. In the case of + correlations, the association is positive; that is, it tells us that there is a tendency for the two sets of scores to vary in the same way as each other. This means that persons who score high in one set will tend to score high in the other as well. If the correlation figure is negative, it means that persons who score high in one tend, on the average, to score low in the other. This is an inverse relationship. Thus, the negative correlation is just as meaningful as is the positive correlation. In general, the nearer the correlation coefficient is to either +1.00 or −1.00, the greater is our assurance of a real relationship between the two sets of scores.

In the field of child development it is important to know which of certain characteristics of growing children tend to be associated with certain other characteristics. For this reason, data are often reported in terms of correlation coefficients.

SUMMARY

We all make informal observations of children and, to a greater or lesser degree, make judgments and form attitudes and opinions on the basis of those observations. We can improve the quality of those informal observations, however, by being aware of the element of personal bias and by taking steps to control that bias. The laboratory-nursery school offers many unique opportunities for observation of the preschool child that can lead to keener insight into the behavior of children of this age range. Other sources of observation include playgrounds and parks, schools, camps, churches, theaters, supermarkets, public transportation, and private homes. Material collected from such observations cannot safely be generalized to apply to all children, or even to the same children at different times; nevertheless, it can sharpen our insights and raise questions in our minds which can lead to a better understanding of all children.

The scientist, as well as the student, makes use of observation procedures. It is necessary to control carefully these observations or to standardize them in some way. It is also necessary to report the results of observation in more or less standard fashion, in order to make them meaningful and useful. Techniques for reporting data frequently include such basic statistical concepts as the *mean*, the *median*, *standard deviation*, and the *correlation coefficient*. The scientific data of child growth and development make frequent use of such statistics.

REFERENCES

1. Almy, Milly, *Ways of studying children*, New York: Bureau of Publications, Teachers College, Columbia Univ., 1959.
2. Carbonara, Nancy T., *Techniques for observing normal child behavior*, Pittsburgh: Univ. of Pittsburgh Press, 1961.
3. Cohen, Dorothy H., *Observing and recording the behavior of young children*, New York: Bureau of Publications, Teachers College, Columbia Univ., 1958.
4. Gardner, D. B.; Hawkes, G. R.; and Pease, D., "Development and use of research methods in child development," *J. Home Econ.*, 1958, 50(3): 201–206.
5. Pease, D., *Child development laboratory notebook*, Dubuque: Brown, 1958.
6. Pease, D., and Pattison, M., "Observation: A method of learning about children," *J. Home Econ.*, 1956, 48(10): 755–757.

7. Suchman, J. R., *Observation and analysis in child development: A laboratory manual*, New York: Harcourt, Brace, 1959.
8. Watson, E. H., and Lowrey, G. H., *Growth and development of children*, 4th ed., Chicago: Year Book Medical Publishers, 1962.

Part II ❧ *FOUNDATIONS OF DEVELOPMENT*

Human development is not exempted from the natural laws underlying the orderliness of the universe. Understanding the growing child calls for understanding the fundamental principles that govern his development. If all of human growth may be characterized by major themes arising out of these basic principles, then every individual child may be seen as a complex variation on these great themes.

Since the main sections of the book which follow Part II will be devoted to the child from 2 to 6, we should also turn our attention to a preliminary consideration of the infancy period. This concentration on the infant, in Chapter Four, will serve to set the stage for a more detailed examination of the preschool child which follows.

CHAPTER THREE

What kinds of changes occur in the growing person that can be included in the term "development"? ◆ What general principles apply in describing each of these kinds of changes? ◆ What are the major sources or causes of development? ◆ What is meant by "interaction" as a basis for all human development?

THE NATURE AND SOURCES OF DEVELOPMENT

THE PROCESSES OF DEVELOPMENT

THE PROCESS BY WHICH a single fertilized egg cell, or *ovum*, microscopic in size, becomes a human adult containing billions of cells with markedly specialized functions, averagely weighing around 150 pounds, is nothing short of fantastic for the human mind to contemplate. We can understand this amazing process and appreciate it more fully if we examine the kinds of changes which occur in the growing individual. These changes, taken together, constitute development.

Growth in Size One of the standard bits of information that we distribute in connection with the birth of a baby, along with date of birth, sex, and color of eyes, is weight. It is possible that the tradition of providing statistics on physical status at birth has stemmed from an association between weight and health. At least this would have been a logical association in people's minds in earlier days because of the common observation that the very tiny infant was less likely to survive. We might speculate, then, that this became a way of telling friends the baby is a healthy one. We should point out, in this connection, that while there is a relationship between weight and health at birth, it is not as simple and direct a relationship as might once have been believed. In any case, growth in size is a matter of natural concern to all parents. It is of equal interest to the scientist, who has provided us with figures on average weight and length for boys and girls from birth to maturity. The consistent, regular, and steady increase in weight and length during the early months is the most obvious evidence of development. It is practically synonymous with life itself: the infant who did not undergo these early changes in size and weight would cause immediate concern, and we would have doubts about his capacity to survive. It does not follow, however, that the most or the fastest growth is the healthiest growth. Neither is average size or weight or rate of increase to be though of as necessarily best. There are other criteria by which to judge the healthiness of development. In early childhood, however, there is a correlation between body size and physiological functioning. Along with the fact that size is a fairly obvious characteristic, this has led us to associate it with normality of development.

Changes in Body Proportions Consider a normal, healthy infant, of less than a month in age. Make a mental note of the fact that his length, approximately 21–22 inches, will be multiplied roughly by three before he reaches maturity. Now visualize that infant increasing in size and becoming a 5-foot 8-inch adult, while maintaining the same body proportions as he has right now! This presents a ludicrous picture. If we were to encounter an individual having adult size but infant body proportions, our best guess might be that visitors from another planet had finally arrived.

Figure 3.1 provides a graphic contrast in body proportions between the infant and the adult. A realistic picture of the changes in body proportions that occur between birth and maturity can be obtained by considering the amount of growth which each major segment of the body must undergo:

The head will about *double* its size.
The trunk will about *triple* its length.
The arms will increase about *fourfold* in length.
The legs will increase about *fivefold* in length.

There are differences, of course, in stature and bodily proportions. These differences are associated with sex, race, nutrition, and physical condition, as well as with unique individual genetic factors. However, the summary of changes in body proportions given above is a fair estimate for the average infant.

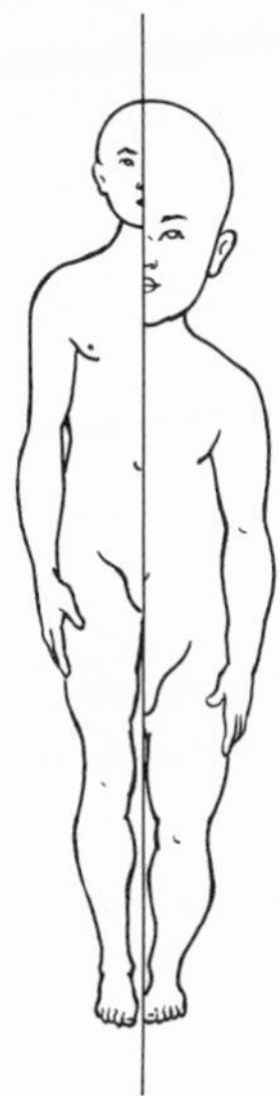

Fig. 3.1. The bodily proportions of the newborn infant and the adult. (From K. Buhler, *The mental development of the child,* London: Routledge & Kegan Paul.)

Changes in Complexity Increases in size and weight, and changes in body proportion are, of course, occurring simultaneously. At the same time, the individual is changing with respect to complexity. While it would not be accurate to describe the human organism as "simple" at any stage of development, even prior to birth, we are referring here to *relative* degrees of complexity, and from this standpoint there are marked differences from one age to another. The growing child may be envisioned as progressing from the simple to the complex in many different ways at the same time: anatomically, physiologically, psychologically, and socially. Both in *structure,* or organization of parts and systems, and in *function,* or action of the parts in relation to each other, the child becomes more complex with age. We shall devote considerable attention to the nature of these increases in complexity in later sections of the book.

It is clear that the newborn infant is not capable of reacting to his world in the complex manner of the 5-year-old child. The nature of the relationship to his world sustained by the baby is a relatively simple one, consisting of intake of food and oxygen, vague and diffuse responses to limited sensory stimulation, and elimination of body wastes, with the establishment and maintenance of adequate physiological equilibrium. By contrast, the child of 5 is capable of maintaining a fantastically complex set of relationships to his world of objects, over which he has achieved a relatively great deal of control, and to his world of people, to whom he relates with subtle cues, complex codes, and language systems.

Acquisition of New Functional Capacities This increased complexity leads to the acquisition of new capacities, which were simply not present at earlier levels of development. The infant of 6 months cannot talk; the 12-month-old can say one or two words. What is the difference? Is it merely a difference of six months of practice, or is something more involved? That there is something more involved is clearly seen in the hypothetical example of the infant who does not progress, during the second half of the first year, to the mental level of the average 1-year-old. Such an infant does not use words, nor would he even if he could have years of practice, without achieving the mental maturity necessary for active language development. Such language development is, in fact, an important indicator of mental growth in childhood. Similarly, it does not help the child to walk earlier or better if, at 8 months, we spend an hour or two every day in standing him up and coaching him in stepping, walking movements of his legs. He will walk when the functional capacity for walking reaches maturity, regardless of the kind of coaching he has had before that time.

There are many kinds of behavior which do depend on special training: learning to read and write in later childhood are good examples. But these too depend on the acquisition, through processes of maturation to be described later, of functional capacities to perform in new ways or at newer and higher levels. This achievement of new capacities has led to a concept of "readiness" in dealing with the child. The readiness concept emphasizes that the child becomes capable, through maturation, of profiting from a certain kind of experience which would have been meaningless or frustrating at an earlier period.

Disappearance of Parts and Functional Capacities In the course of development it is as natural and normal, although perhaps less apparent, for certain parts and functions to decline and even disappear as it is for parts and functions to make their appearance with new stages of growth. Perhaps this is most clearly seen in relation to aging processes, in which physical capabilities—sensory capacities such as vision, hearing, taste, and smell—may diminish or be completely lost. What is not so clear, but is equally significant to our concept of human development, is that functional capacity may diminish or disappear completely as an integral part of the *childhood* processes of over-all development. Simple examples of this form of development occur in the motor capacities of children who find it gradually more difficult to insert the toe in the mouth, or to walk on all fours with the knees straight in a bearlike fashion. But of somewhat greater significance are examples from children's intellectual and aesthetic behavior, in which progress may mean loss of the capacity to operate freely, without inhibition, in an unrestricted world of fantasy at ages 3 and 4, in order to arrive at a more realistic but clearly more restricted mode of operation at ages 5 and 6.

As Gesell (3) has pointed out, the average 4-year-old, in his uninhibited freedom of fantasy and self-expression, can portray what he wishes on paper, be it a horse, a tiger, a car, or his mother; and regardless of what it looks like to the adult it serves the child's purposes well. But the 6-year-old may be unable to do it at all; he may be unable to get started in drawing a horse, for example, because he doesn't know how to go about it. He asks someone to show him, or to do it for him in order to get it right, because by now he is concerned that his mode of expression be in keeping with reality and that his productions look to other people, as well as to himself, the way they are "supposed" to look. This loss of functional capacity is not limited to motor or psychological activities. Biologically there are some changes which illustrate this aspect of development too. The newborn infant has, as a result of his prenatal existence within his mother's body, immunity to certain diseases, provided his mother herself had established immunity through the development of the appropriate antibodies. But this immunity is only temporary, and will, in most cases, disappear during the first few months of postnatal life.

Other examples of disappearance of parts and functions can be cited: the thymus gland, located in the upper thorax, is present at birth and grows rapidly during early childhood, then grows more slowly until puberty. It then begins to decrease in size, until in the adult it is relatively small and is composed of fibrous, nonfunctioning tissue. In a similar way, the pineal gland at the base of the brain is known as a "disappearing gland" because, in the normal processes of development, it shrinks in size and appears to lose any functional capacity. The biologist can point up other, perhaps more basic processes under the heading of metabolic changes associated with development. Along with the anabolic changes that represent growth, there are the continuous catabolic changes which represent disorganization or destruction. Blood cells, for example, have a relatively short life span; new blood cells are continually being manufactured in the bone marrow to replace those which die.

Truly, life and growth are dynamic processes which can only be understood in terms of positive, building, and organizing forces operating in a favorable balance with negative, destructive, and disorganizing forces from the moment of conception until death. All of these kinds of changes, then, are important aspects of development: increase in size, changes in body proportions, increases in complexity, acquisition of new parts and functional capacities, and disappearance of old parts and capacities. It is apparent that the concept of development is a complex one which cannot be given a simple definition. From the discussion so far, however, we may summarize by presenting a general definition in terms of the kinds of changes which it includes: *development is the total complex of processes resulting from internal and external forces, leading to changes in the form, structure and functioning of the individual, and reaching toward the goal of self-realization.* In the next section of this chapter, we shall examine the internal and external forces in development and attempt to show the role they play in bringing about the changes already described.

SOURCES OF DEVELOPMENT

As defined above, development is a long-range *process* made up of many parts, rather than of a single, narrow feature of a child, or of merely one part of his personality. Some of the sources of this over-all process lie within the child himself; others are to be found outside him. The latter are the elements of his environment that participate actively in stimulating his growth. They play essential roles in the over-all drama of development. For convenience, we will describe the sources and factors in development under these two major headings: (1) factors within the child, and (2) environmental factors.

Factors Within the Child In many respects it is helpful to view the growth of a child as something which originates within the fertilized egg cell and progresses, with cell division, as an unfolding process in which the internal potentialities of the ovum gradually become realities. We shall see later that this is an incomplete picture of the total process, but for the moment it will give proper emphasis to the role of factors present within the growing organism from the moment of conception.

At the instant of fertilization of the egg cell by a sperm cell, the heredity of the new individual is permanently established. The egg cell, which contained 23 chromosomes (the bearers of hereditary traits) has become an ovum, with 46 chromosomes, with no further possibility for exchanging any one of the chromosomes in that complete set for any other. One of the chromosomes from the sperm cell determines the sex of the child. Other genetic effects determined by the unique combination of chromosomes include the color of hair and eyes, skin pigmentation, physique and bodily proportions, many basic aspects of mental and psychological capacities and, to some degree, even emotionality (9).

The period of development between conception and birth illustrates how these factors within the individual, which might be summarized as *genetic* factors, control the development process to a marked degree. At about two weeks following conception—after the fertilized ovum has undergone many consecutive cell divisions and has implanted itself in the lining of the uterus to establish a source of continued sustenance—it enters the *embryonic* period. During the embryonic stage the new individual changes from a diffuse and apparently unorganized ball of cells to a remarkably structured, patterned condition which can be identified by its several parts. The limbs, fingers and toes, head and face, sense organs, brain and spinal cord, heart and lungs, and other vital organs and systems emerge through the process of cell differentiation during the embryonic stage. At about the ninth week of the prenatal period, the end of the embryonic stage is marked and the *fetal* period is established. During the remaining portion of the prenatal period the parts and systems of the body which are essential to maintaining life apart from the mother must mature and become functional if the baby is to survive.

Aside from applying principles of nutrition, rest, exercise, and positive mental health, a mother does little or nothing to control this fascinating pattern of development which unfolds, as it were, automatically. Why do certain cells, during the embryonic period, become grouped together in form and structure and in specialized function, for example, for the reception of light waves? The child's eyes are functional, although immature in some respects, by the time he is born. How is it that by the time a child is born a slight stimulation of his cheek, chin, or lips will set off a vigorous sucking behavior of mouth and tongue? We may, of course, call this a sucking instinct or, more sensibly, a sucking reflex. However, neither expression explains anything!

The point is that there are very real forces at work during the prenatal period which insure the development of life-sustaining physiological systems, and which will be ready to function reasonably well at birth. These forces are dramatically evidenced by the regularity of development, the consistency of patterning of structure and function in the human fetus apart from any forces in the external environment. There are implications in this point that go far beyond the understanding of the nature of the newborn infant. Philosophers and scholars have, for ages, discussed and argued over the basic nature of man and the role of "nature" vs. "nurture" in his development. We no longer question which is the more important, heredity *or* environment, because we recognize the absolute importance of both of these general factors. Nevertheless, we have arrived at a point, historically, in our understanding of human development in which we find it realistic to say that there are many influences on human growth which are primarily genetic or "natural" in their operation. Other kinds of illustrations, in addition to the developmental sequence during the prenatal period, also show the powerful influences of these developmental forces operating from within the growing organism. The sequence of stages in the development of upright locomotion in the infant is one of these. These will be outlined in greater detail in a later chapter. However, the regular progression of steps, occurring in essentially the same sequence for all normal infants, gives forceful evidence that some common developmental factors, inherent in the species, are regulating this progressive achievement from one stage to the next.

Table 3.1 provides data on the average age of occurrence of each of several steps toward the goal of upright locomotion. Of course there is variation around these averages, with steps occurring earlier in some than in other infants. Concomitantly, the remarkable consistency from one child to another in proceeding through the steps in this same sequence gives dramatic evidence of the presence of controlling factors outside the experiences of the child.

Environmental Factors Even during the 280 days, more or less, of the prenatal period, there is a very active environment in operation. That environment includes physical and chemical properties as well as the

TABLE 3.1. *Age of Occurrence of Several Steps in Progress Toward Upright Locomotion*

Age (Months)	Behavior
1	Prone position, raises chin
2	Prone position, raises chest
4	Sits with support
7	Sits alone
8	Stands with help
9	Stands holding furniture
10	Creeps
11	Walks when led
14	Stands alone
15	Walks alone

SOURCE: Based on data from: *The First Two Years: A Study of Twenty-Five Babies, Vol. II* by Mary M. Shirley, Child Welfare Monograph Series, No. 7. University of Minnesota Press, Minneapolis. Copyright 1933 by the University of Minnesota.

objective and social elements that we associate with our worldly environment. For the rapidly growing and differentiating fetus the chemical and physical environments play vital roles in shaping the organization of the child, within the limits established by hereditary factors. But it is at birth that the environment broadens suddenly and dramatically to include a multitude of forces, pressures, demands, frustrations, and satisfactions that participate in the total personality development of the child. It has been said that, truly, birth is not really a beginning, but a milestone along the way. From the standpoint of personality growth, however, it is a most significant milestone in this respect: it brings to the child all the environmental possibilities for both frustration and satisfaction of needs—not merely the basic physiological needs that were automatically provided for *in utero*, but a host of others, some of which that same environment actively creates.

We shall see in later chapters the processes by which a child comes to relate himself effectively to his physical environment—the world of objects. We will also consider the over-all process of the child's learning to relate successfully to persons in his social environment. For the present, we shall merely examine briefly some evidence which points up the significance of these environmental factors in the child's over-all development.

THE PHYSICAL ENVIRONMENT. Recent studies of deprived children—that is, children who have not experienced adequate stimulation from their environments—indicate that their progress in mental development is seriously handicapped by such deprivation. To some degree, improvement in mental development takes place with an improved and enriched environment. This enriched environment includes opportunities beginning in early infancy for experience with a wide range of objects, which stimulate coordination of muscular activity with sensory processes, and which stimulate mental activity. Even the perception of the physical world is based, to a significant degree, on practice with the objects in that world. That is, a child learns to see things in three-dimensional perspective partly as a result of his muscular action in reaching farther for some things than for others and noting with his eyes the subtle cues that give him slightly different sensory impressions of the far things than of the near things.

It is the senses, then, which bring the environment to the child and enable him to derive meaning from it. It is his muscular system that enables him to deal with and modify this environment in keeping with his needs. Initially, the coordination of the sensory and muscular processes is largely a mental process. Further, continued practice in this coordination brings about mental development; hence it is not surprising that the child who is seriously deprived of stimulation in his physical world and who thus has less practice in this coordination develops more slowly in his mental life. A brief period of observing any normal 18-month-old will convince the interested student of the significance of the environment to the child. The child, if given reasonable opportunity, will poke, pinch, grasp, bite, hit, step on, pick up, and generally maul a wide assortment of objects available to him in the course of an hour or so of free play.

It should be noted in passing that for the 18-month-old, other children fit into the same category as inanimate objects. We should not be at all surprised to find this child poking, pinching, and soon, any other child who will hold still long enough to be so treated, because the motivation to explore through touch and taste his visible environment is strong in the child at 18 months. His mouth is still a primary means to exploration of his physical environment, and his natural tendency to put things in his mouth is to be understood not so much as a means of satisfying hunger pangs, but as a means of knowing his world.

Development includes the learning of many things. (Courtesy of Dalton Schools.)

The child takes important steps toward knowing his world once he begins to learn that everything has a name. As he is emerging from infancy and entering into the preschool years, he seems to get the idea that every object has a title—a word which stands for it. This is a crucial step in his developing power to deal with the physical world *symbolically*; that is, he can "manipulate" the objects of his world mentally, and in communication with others now, without necessarily having the particular objects present to his immediate senses.

To play with building blocks also illustrates an important feature of the child's need to relate himself to the physical world. Through such play the child actively engages in a process of organizing a part of his environment—of testing out his ideas about what will work and what will not. And such experiences are vital because, for one thing, there is no way of altering the basic laws of the universe: if the block tower is out of balance it will fall—every time—and consistency of effect is a powerful teacher. Painting and modeling clay, which delight the average 4-year-old, are also efforts on his part to organize his world of objects and to make sense out of them. There is a strong urge to do this—to organize our objective environments. When we see a meaningless blob of ink on a page we automatically organize it into a shape that makes sense to us—we cannot afford, psychologically, to leave it as just a meaningless blob. The child's natural urge to do this organizing—putting meaning into his objective world and making sense out of that world—is at the root of much of his most important learning.

THE CHILD'S SOCIAL ENVIRONMENT. Birth also marks the beginning of any possibility for social interaction—for the development of any kind of interpersonal relationship—between the baby and his world of people. It is evident that, at first, the most significant people in that social world are his mother and father. But the reasons for their significance have not always been clearly understood, and there are many features about parent-child interaction which require careful and cautious explanation. Historically there have been accounts, some of them very poorly documented, of children supposed to have been reared without human contact. However, there are no authenticated cases of children acquiring the essentials of normal personality development—or even normal mental ability—in the absence of at least minimum human care. In fact, over the past few years there has accumulated considerable evidence to the effect that the child needs human care not only to satisfy his biological demands, but also to develop normally his intellectual and emotional capacities. This requirement, stated in very general terms, is for active social stimulation by an adult (whether it is the child's biological mother or some other person) who is genuinely interested in the psychological well-being of that child. It is interesting to note that the basic facts of child development—gain in height and weight, development of language ability, motor co-ordination, etc.—can be both directly and indirectly affected by the presence or absence of such a person in the infant and child's life. If we can accept the reality of these important effects, it should not be difficult to accept the fact that the child's social behavior—his capacity for relating effectively to the people around him—will also be affected by these early social experiences. There are a number of research studies which show this to be the case.

Spitz (*11*), for example, studied infants who were deprived of normal mothering and were reared in institutions. He came to the conclusion that these infants were less adequate socially and were, in fact, retarded mentally as a direct result of being deprived of normal mothering. While Spitz's studies have been criticized by other research workers (*8*), there is far too much evidence of the role of mothering and the importance of the mother-figure in the life of the child to dismiss such findings as insignificant. Goldfarb (*4*), for example, found that by increasing the amount of social contact for babies residing in institutions, important gains were made in language development and in social responsiveness in the children. Some data reported by Gardner, Hawkes, and Burchinal (*2*) indicate that it does not seem to matter whether babies are reared by their own mothers or by foster or adoptive mothers. Thus there is every reason to assume that what counts is the mother's interest in the child and her desire to provide adequate care, as well as her knowledge of child-rearing—not the biological fact of parenthood. Other research has stressed the role of the father in the family setting as an important influence in the social development and behavior of the child. The child's social behavior in relation to his position in the family, and the presence or absence of older or younger siblings, has also been studied. Obviously these, too, are important factors in the social experience of any child, and, while the results do not clearly favor any *particular* status or position in the family, there is every reason to assume that fundamental aspects of the personality development of the child are based on the social relationships he sustains with other members of his family.

Generalized attitudes toward members of the opposite sex may be influenced in important ways by those members of the opposite sex in his own family. Important attitudes toward discipline and authority are undoubtedly a product of the relationships sustained within the family setting. Even the nature of what the child learns to value and to think of as being significant in his life are probably determined, to a considerable degree, by the degree of satisfaction he finds in his social relationships with people who already hold strong values and important attitudes. To the extent that the child finds it pleasant and satisfying to be around certain adults, he tends to "identify" with them and to adopt the patterns of values, as well as the patterns of behavior, that characterize the adults' way of life.

Thus, the social experiences of the child are not truly separate from his personality development at all, but are an integral part of that development. Personality would not develop, in fact, in the absence of such experiences.

THE ROLE OF LEARNING. Whether we are discussing the child's objective environment or his social world, we must go behind the obvious fact that these influence his development, and deal with the fundamental question of how this takes place. What basic processes are at work which enable the child to absorb his objective and social environments and make them a part of himself?

The vital process which concerns us here is that of *learning*. Just as we could say that the "nature" part of the child is the outgrowth of genetic factors in reproduction, so we may say that the "nurture" part of the individual is the outgrowth of the environment through the essential process of learning. Learning is the acquiring of new habits, or ways of behaving, as a result of experience with environment. There are highly complex and technical theories that account for the learning process, but we need not explore these in detail. For our purposes it is sufficient to note that children learn, by and large, in order to satisfy needs of some kind. Since we mean here that learning is the basic process in personality development which relates the environment to the child, and that learning occurs in relation to the child's needs, it will be seen that the nature of the child's needs and the manner of satisfaction or frustration of those needs in a friendly or hostile environment is a vital consideration in understanding how his personality develops in the unique ways manifested in every child.

Children are frequently described as "needing attention," for example. Whether this need for attention is a fundamental thing which must be satisfied, or simply something which the child *wants*, is not important at the moment. Assume that a given child does need attention. If this is the case, his whole being is alert for signs from his social environment which inform him that such attention is or is not forthcoming. His need, in other words, sensitizes him and focuses his sensory and mental activities on this one major question. If, while he is in this sensitized condition, he engages by chance in behavior that effectively calls attention to himself, such as "silly talk" or boisterous actions, he cannot help forming an association between the two events: *First*, his need for attention has found a kind of satisfaction, at least temporarily; and *second*, it was the silly, boisterous behavior which resulted in this satisfaction for him. It is not difficult to understand, then, his readiness to repeat such behavior when his need for attention begins to weigh heavily upon him.

In this example of learning it may appear that the child recognizes his own need and sets about to learn some way of satisfying it. On the contrary, however, it is much more likely that the child is unaware of the nature of his need, and is quite unconscious of any particular plan to satisfy it. His awareness is more likely to be at a somewhat vague level of satisfaction and dissatisfaction, happiness and unhappiness, pleasantness and unpleasantness, or tension and relaxation. It is in the movement from one condition to the other, and in the association of events that occur while he is moving, that learning takes place most effectively. In particular, events which are somehow associated with the process of moving from dissatisfaction to satisfaction are sought by the child, who wishes to reexperience the elements of this improvement in his psychological status and sense of well-being.

Learning may also occur in the movement from pleasant to unpleasant states. To put this in very practical terms, a child may learn by being punished, and it would be unrealistic to argue otherwise. Punishment as a general and continuing basis for learning, is undesirable only because it usually involves the kinds of learning that were not intended by the adult. Punishment may result in essentially negative and destructive forces in personality development, such as the association of fears—stemming from fear of punishment—with whatever positive learning processes are going on.

The Interaction of Heredity and Environment We have described two fundamental processes which, together, are the means by which all development occurs. The first of these includes the hereditary maturational processes that originate within the individual and which have the double effect of stimulating growth and initiating many of the kinds of changes which are included in development, and, at the same time, place limits on the degree or amount of such change. The second includes all those environmental forces which both stimulate and limit the developing processes. These latter operate, as the child emerges into a complex social world, through the general process of learning. Some of the environmental forces, of course, do not involve learning, at least in the sense in which we would ordinarily use the term *learning*. A child's diet, for example, is a very tangible environmental factor in development, yet, diet does not have to involve the learning process in order to have its effects on the child. Thus, while some environmental forces in the child's development may be primarily social and psychological, others may be purely physical or biological in their operations.

It is most important to understand, however, that these two processes do not operate in isolation from each other, nor can they be separated from one another. Furthermore, we can never know exactly what proportion of a given kind of growth, such as body build, is hereditary and what proportion is the result of environmental forces. We can, however, cite examples of characteristics of individuals which may be ranked very roughly in order of the degree to which they are affected by heredity or by environment. Table 3.2 provides such a comparison. This table demon-

TABLE 3.2. *Relative Significance of Heredity and Environment for Basic Human Characteristics*

Quality	Role of Heredity	Role of Environment
Eye color, complexion, body build	very high	very low
Intelligence, aptitudes, talents	high	low
Skills and abilities based on training	low	high
Attitudes, values, beliefs, prejudices	very low	very high

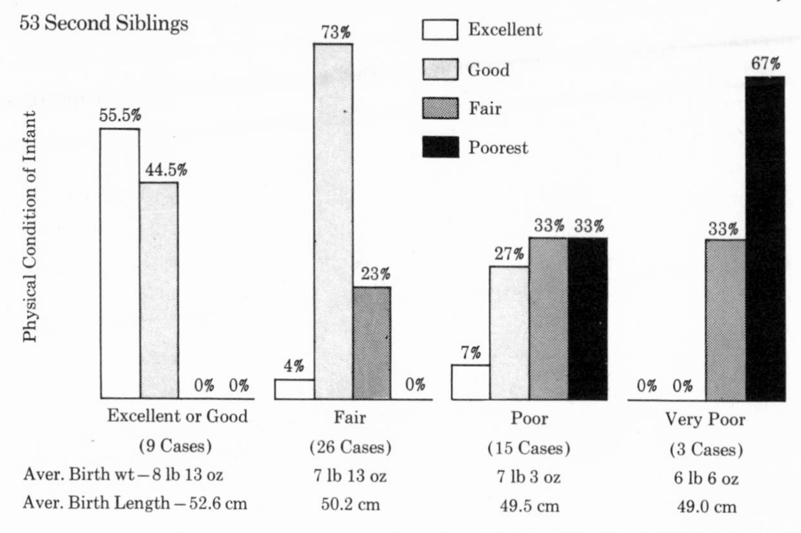

Fig. 3.2. The relation of prenatal dietary rating to the physical condition of the infant at birth. (From fig. 5, B. S. Burke, *et al.*, *J. Nutrition, 38*:462.)

strates that almost any kind of development is best accounted for in terms of the interaction between hereditary and environmental forces. Even during the prenatal period, when it is frequently assumed that only hereditary forces have had any opportunity to operate, very important environmental factors have already interacted with heredity. There is a very real biological, chemical, and physical environment for the developing fetus, and this plays a major role in allowing the genetic factors to operate; it may even place severe restrictions on these genetic factors. Certain kinds of infections in the mother's body, for example, can be transmitted to the fetus and influence its development. There is evidence too that the mother's nutritional status and diet during pregnancy makes a difference in the size, weight, and health status of the child at delivery. This relationship is depicted clearly in Figure 3.2.

Further, there is a considerable agreement among physicians that if a woman contracts *rubella* (German measles) during the first three months of pregnancy, there may be certain serious effects on the development of the fetus, including, for example, blindness. This possibility is markedly decreased if *rubella* occurs later in the period of pregnancy at, say, the sixth month following conception. Thus, we might conclude that there are times during development when the fetus is especially susceptible or vulnerable to particular environmental forces.

Similarly, there are, following birth, certain times and stages in the life of the growing child when he is especially vulnerable to specific types of environmental forces which influence his development. At other times, when greater maturity has been reached through the development of genetic factors from within himself, the same or similar forces from the environment will have little, if any, effect on his over-all progress. We may therefore conclude that hereditary and environmental forces closely interact with each other and cannot be thought of as truly separate factors in the life of the child. We no longer raise the age-old question, then, as to which is more important, "nature" or "nurture," in determining the child's personality.

SOME GENERALIZATIONS ABOUT DEVELOPMENT

Over the past few decades, as the scientific study of children has resulted in the accumulation of many significant findings, it has become possible to formulate some general principles which describe the nature of development and the manner in which it proceeds. It is not a haphazard process. Like other events and phenomena that are available to scientists for study and analysis, human development gives evidence of lawfulness and coherence. There is system to it, in other words, and that system can be described. In essence, we are stating now that the kinds of changes outlined earlier in the chapter may be summarized under a few major principles, as follows:

1. Development proceeds in an orderly fashion.
2. The rate of development is not constant.
3. Different parts, systems, and action-systems each have their own individual patterns and sequences of development.
4. Development includes processes of individuation and generalization.
5. The goal of development is self-realization.

Development as an Orderly Process From conception to maturity, development is a continuing process progressing in an orderly sequence of stages that are regular and predictable. Each stage of development is an outgrowth of the one preceding it; each stage, in turn, provides a foundation for those to follow. We shall see many examples of this stage-by-stage progression in each of the aspects of development to be described in later chapters. Another way in which the orderliness and lawful continuity of development are illustrated is in the *directions of growth,* dramatically demonstrated in the prenatal period and throughout infancy. Two major directions of development are discernible: first, development proceeds in a *cephalo-caudal* direction; that is, from the upper portions of the body toward the lower portions; and second, it proceeds in a *proximo-distal* direction; that is, from the center-line of the body outward toward the peripheral, or distant parts. Figure 3.3 represents these two directions of development.

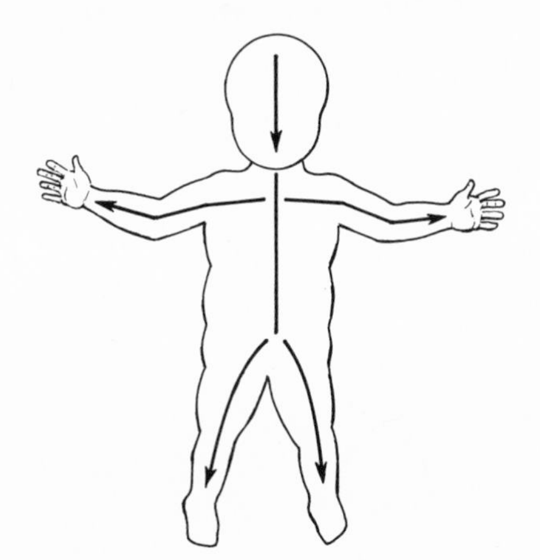

***Fig.* 3.3.** A diagrammatic representation of the directional tendency in physical and motor development. (Figure 34, page 137 from *Developmental psychology,* 3rd edition, by Florence L. Goodenough. Copyright © 1959, Appleton-Century-Crofts, Inc. Reproduced by permission of the publisher.)

The orderly, systematic nature of development from head to toe and from mid-line to periphery has important implications for understanding a child's readiness to engage in new activities. For example, we expect a child, during the latter half of his first year, to be able to sit up without support, balancing the trunk and head well, long before he stands up and walks on his feet. This is not just because to sit up is easier than to stand; it is also because the nerves and muscles which control the sitting behavior are relatively more mature, at 7 months, than the nerves and muscles which control standing and walking. Similarly, we expect a child, from infancy through the preschool years, to be relatively more adept at controlling the large muscles involved in moving whole limbs or total body action, than he is in controlling the fine muscles involved in manipulation of tiny objects with the fingers. This expectation is based on the realistic awareness that the achievement of muscular control, through maturation, proceeds from the center line of the body outward toward the periphery.

From these examples and many others which could be cited, the conclusion may be drawn that there is a basic pattern which underlies human development, and progress in the growth of the individual child must follow this pattern from one step to the next, in a sequence limited by genetic factors, toward the goal of maturity.

The Inconstancy of Developmental Rate This principle is most easily illustrated in physical growth, but has applications in other aspects of development as well. In measurements of the same child, taken at different periods in his life, it may be seen that he is growing rapidly at some times and very slowly at others. Physical growth proceeds unevenly, with the rapid spurt of infant development followed by a much slower growth during the preschool period. While the rate of visible physical growth becomes slower, however, some very important changes may be taking place in motor development, development of language, mental, social, or emotional maturity. In each of these areas, also, growth proceeds unevenly.

Rapid increases in mental development do not necessarily coincide with similar increases in other areas. There is some evidence that motor and language development may have complementary spurts of growth during the second year. During the time that a child is making dramatic progress in standing, walking, and running about there may, for a time, be a period of "motor specialization" in which language development is pushed into the background. Later, when the motor skills necessary to walking and running become well practiced, nearly automatic, and very smooth in their performance, different aspects of development—including language—become more prominent. This should not be interpreted to mean that the child who is good at motor tasks is poor at language, or that the child who is mentally advanced is compensated in his over-all development by retardation in another area, such as motor coordination or physical growth. On the contrary, we merely mean to point out that the growth spurts, common to all aspects of development, have their own timetables which do not necessarily coincide with each other.

Patterns of Individual Aspects of Development Closely related to the last one, this principle is illustrated in some of the same phenomena as have just been cited. For example, the child's "specialization" in motor development in the early part of the second year, accompanied by an apparent plateau in language growth, reveals the complex coordination of different facets of growth, each with its own timetable.

Another way to illustrate the operation of this principle is to compare different organs and systems of the body with respect to their rate of maturation, during the prenatal as well as the infant and childhood periods. Gesell (3) notes that by the early part of the fetal period, the nervous system is structurally complete; that is, it has as many nerve cells as it will ever have. By contrast, the skeletal, muscular, circulatory, and respiratory systems are relatively much further from completion. Many centers of ossification in the skeletal system do not make their appearance until the child is well along the road to physical maturity. Similar examples may be drawn from later childhood. Sexual maturity, for example, is reached only when the other basic physiological processes are well established. Yet, emotional and social maturity is not necessarily achieved at this stage.

Figure 3.4 provides a graphic illustration of the marked differences in the rate of development of different body systems. It also shows an interesting feature of development in the tendency of some parts and systems to decline in their functional capacity much more rapidly—once they have reached their highest level—than others.

Processes of Individuation and of Generalization Many of the changes with age which, together, constitute development, can be explained best by the process of *individuation.* This means that the infant or child is progressing from general behavior to specific behavior; from vague and diffuse action patterns to more precise, well defined, and clear-cut behavior. It means that the combined effects of maturation and learning bring about an increasingly greater ability to deal with the particular elements in a situation, as opposed at the earlier, more primitive levels of generalized action. For example, if a 2-year-old sits at a piano and "plays" it, his behavior is of a very general nature, and his objective is to make sounds by striking the keys. While there may be elementary rhythmic behavior involved in his action, there is unlikely to be any concern for melody or harmony. With maturity and experience he will

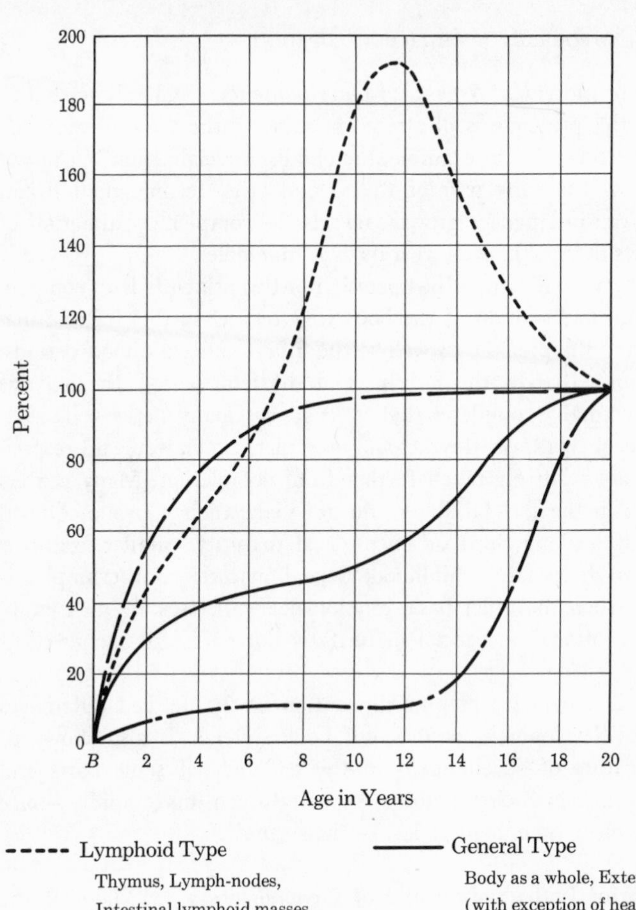

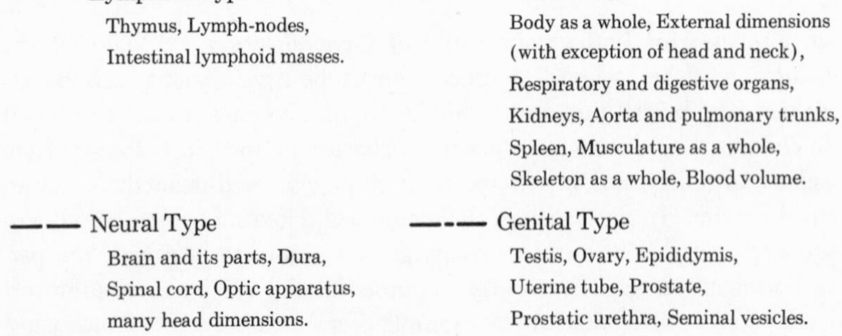

Fig. 3.4. This graph shows the major types of postnatal growth of the various parts and organs of the body. The several curves are drawn to a common scale by computing their values at successive ages in terms of their total postnatal increments (to 20 years). (From: R. E. Scammon "The measurement of the body in childhood" in *The measurement of man* by J. A. Harris, C. M. Jackson, D. G. Peterson, and R. E. Scammon. University of Minnesota Press, Minneapolis, Copyright 1930 by the University of Minnesota.)

gradually come to discern these particular elements, which make music a satisfying experience at higher age levels. Again, in learning to operate a typewriter children at first deal with the total machine, and it impresses them in a vague, generalized sort of way. The detailed operations of the various parts and units of the machine become meaningful only with maturity and experience.

Fig. 3.5. A diagrammatic representation of degrees of differentiation in child (a) and adult (b). (From K. Lewin, *A dynamic theory of personality*, New York: McGraw-Hill, 1935, p. 207.)

(*a*)

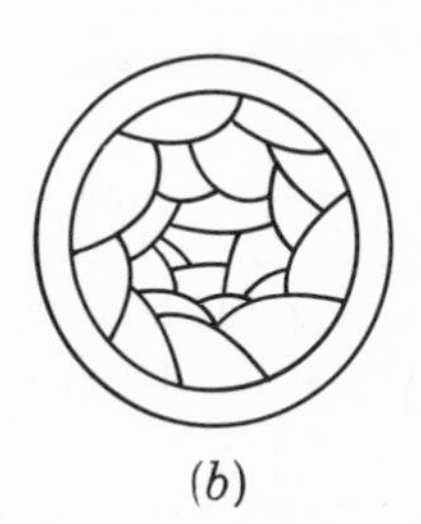

(*b*)

In social learning, too, development proceeds from the general to the specific. The child responds to the general idea of "people" before differentiating "man," "woman," and "child." It may be of some interest to note, too, that the child does not categorize people as "white," "Negro," "Indian," "Jew," "Catholic," or in any other relatively specific grouping until long after he has dealt with them as "people." These differences, too, must be learned.

The earliest emotional responses of the infant are also general, diffuse responses which might fall under the broad term, "excitement." Certainly we do not find anger, joy, jealousy, or fear in the new-born. These more or less specific emotional patterns will be developed later. And, of course, children's intellectual concepts progress from a general, nondifferentiated, diffuse state to a condition in which they are much more precise, specific, and well-defined. In general, the contrast between the younger and the older is a contrast in *degree of differentiation*, as described by Lewin (6). Figure 3.5 illustrates schematically the contrast in level of differentiation, the younger condition being characterized by (a) and the older by (b).

In mental development we also find another process occurring along with the growth from general to specific. That is, children may integrate the effects of a series of rather specific experiences into a larger unit, or generalization. Inductive thinking is like that. It is the process of developing a generalized idea, or principle, on the basis of a series of related experiences, no one of which would be sufficient to bring about the generalization. For example, a standard problem in the well-known Stanford-Binet Intelligence Test (*12*), requires a child to observe while the examiner folds a piece of paper in half, then cuts a small piece out of it from the center of the folded edge. The child is asked how many holes there would be if the paper is opened up. After the child answers, the examiner shows him, then proceeds to repeat the problem, this time doubling another piece of paper twice instead of once. Again the child is asked how many holes there will be. Again the examiner shows him how many there actually are. This process is repeated several times, each time with the paper being folded once more than in the preceding trial. At the end of the sixth trial, the child is asked if he can give a rule that will always tell how many holes there would be. His ability to generalize from the series of specific events and state that the number of holes is doubled for every additional time the paper is folded is an example of inductive thinking. It also illustrates a process of development that might be labeled *integration,* because it involves bringing together in a coherent, articulated manner the results or products of previous developments. Figure 3.6 provides a schematic representation of this general process of bringing smaller units into articulation with each other to form larger wholes, or patterns of behavior that were not discernible in the separate functioning of the smaller units.

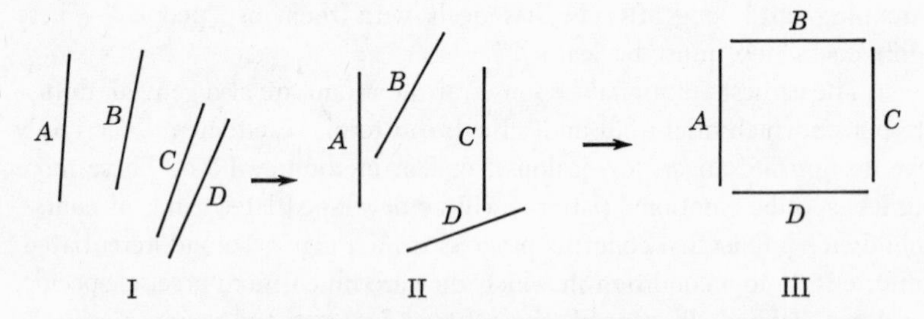

Fig. 3.6. A diagrammatic representation of the process of integration of smaller, independent units into a larger functioning unit which is greater than the sum of its parts.

This same integration, or articulation of smaller units into coherent larger units, also occurs in aspects of development other than the intellectual. In physical and motor functioning, the organization of subunits into larger, functional, whole units is not difficult to demonstrate. Skipping, which is a highly complex form of motor action for a child, does not occur until very late in the preschool period. This is understandable, since it involves a larger complex of behavior than either hopping or running, of which it is composed. But skipping is more than just running added to hopping; it is in reality a synergistic, articulated action; that is, more than the mere sum of its parts. In general, then, we may conclude that development proceeds both by a process of movement from general to specific behavior, and a process of movement from smaller, separate units to larger, integrated units.

Self-Realization as the Goal of Development The question, "What is maturity?" has been answered in a number of ways, but none of the answers has proven to be very satisfactory. The concept of physical maturity is very limited: we are all aware that a person who has achieved the maximum of his potential of height, who is sexually mature, who has achieved the secondary sex characteristics associated with adolescence, etc., may still have intellectual maturation to accomplish, and may have an even longer road ahead with respect to the achievement of social and emotional maturity. Not only is the concept of maturity somewhat vague and difficult to define, it may be quite unrealistic as a goal for development, for it is unlikely that ordinary human beings ever reach absolute maturity in the most idealistic sense of its meaning. In any case, it is clear that there is no one kind or level of attainment, applicable to all individuals, that could reasonably be called *the* goal of maturity towards which to strive. Instead, it is reasonable to conceive of an individual as having growth potentials that, given a favorable environment, will result in the achievement of a total personality which is the most desirable and effective for *that* individual. As we pointed out earlier in the description of basic needs and motives, this concept of self-realization is dependent upon the satisfaction of needs at more primitive levels.

Progressing from the more primitive to the more "mature" levels of action, however, is not just a simple, pleasant, easy, and unimpeded process of moving forward. The concept of self-realization implies the gradual achievement of higher-level habits of response to the environment, and the willingness to take the inherent risks involved in moving ahead to a higher level of action, for the sake of whatever benefits may be derived for the self and others. When a child learns to walk, he not only acquires the ability to find new satisfactions by so doing, he also acquires greater ability to run into trouble and to hurt himself. Yet the outcome is rarely to settle in favor of not walking! With older children and adults, however, one need not search long in order to find instances of preferring *not* to try a new activity rather than to risk the possibility of failure. Thus, at points along the road of development, self-realization may be compromised by the desire for safety or comfort. The self-realization concept further implies that the motivation for personal growth and development comes essentially from within the child and that the environment nurtures and satisfies this central motive, or, at times, frustrates it. As was pointed out in Chapter One, satisfaction of the self-realization motive is dependent upon the satisfaction, first, of more fundamental needs related to physiological functioning, safety, love, and esteem. Thus, the primary role of the environment is to free the child from concerns for satisfaction of needs at the more primitive levels to enable him to achieve his potential of self-development.

SUMMARY

Development may be defined as the total complex of processes arising from internal and external forces; resulting in changes in the form, structure, and functioning of the individual; and reaching toward the goal of self-realization. The internal, genetic forces and the external, environmental forces do not operate in isolation from one another, but in interaction with one another, at all levels and stages of growth.

Both the objective environment—the child's world of things—and the social environment—the child's world of people—are of vital significance in the over-all developmental process. His senses bring that environment to him, and he absorbs its effects largely through the learning process. *Learning*, defined as the acquiring of new habits or ways of behaving as a result of experiences, is based on needs and the conditions which satisfy those needs.

Development proceeds in an orderly, systematic fashion; it is not haphazard or unpredictable. It includes two major processes: (1) *individuation*, or development of specific behavior patterns from larger, more general, less organized patterns, and (2) *generalization*, or the process of bringing smaller units of behavior together into larger, articulated units. The rate of development is not constant; it proceeds, rather, in spurts and periods of slow growth. Different parts and systems have their own individual patterns and sequences of development. In general, the over-all goal or objective of individual development is self-realization, defined as the motive to achieve one's potentials.

REFERENCES

1. Burke, B. S., et. al., "Nutrition studies during pregnancy: v. relation of maternal nutrition to condition of infant at birth: study of siblings," *J. Nutrition*, 1949, **38**:453–467.
2. Gardner, D. B., Hawkes, G. R., and Burchinal, L., "Noncontinuous mothering in infancy and development in later childhood," *Child Develpm. J.*, 1961, **32**:225–234.
3. Gesell, A., and Ilg, Frances L., *Child development: an introduction to the study of human growth*, New York: Harper, 1949.
4. Goldfarb, W., "Psychological privation in infancy and subsequent adjustment," *Amer. J. Ortho.*, 1945, **15** (2): 247–255.
5. Goodenough, Florence L., *Developmental psychology*, New York: Appleton-Century, 1934.
6. Lewin, K., *A dynamic theory of personality* (selected papers), New York: McGraw-Hill, 1935.
7. Pinneau, S. R., "The infantile disorders of hospitalism and anaclitic depression," *Psychol. Bull.*, 1955, **52**:429–452.
8. Scammon, R. E., "The measurement of the body in childhood," in J. A. Harris et. al., *The measurement of man*, Minneapolis: Univ. of Minnesota Press, 1930.
9. Scheinfeld, A., *The new you and heredity*, New York: Lippincott, 1950.
10. Shirley, Mary M., *The first two years: a study of twenty-five babies*, Minneapolis: Univ. of Minnesota Press, 1931.
11. Spitz, R. A., "Hospitalism," *Psychoanal. Stud. Child*, 1945, **1**: 53–73.
12. Terman, L. M., and Merrill, Maud A., *Stanford-Binet Intelligence Scale*, Boston: Houghton Mifflin, 1960.

CHAPTER FOUR

Why is the neonatal period of critical importance to survival, health, and well-being ∽ What are the physical and psychological attributes of the neonate? ∽ What are the major accomplishments of the child during the period of infancy? ∽ In what respect is the personality of the older child based on events which occur during infancy? ∽ How does development in infancy illustrate the principles of growth which have been described in previous chapters?

DEVELOPMENT DURING INFANCY

THERE IS NO SUCH THING as an "average baby." Every newborn baby brings with him his own special characteristics and idiosyncrasies which make him unique. While he may be "average" with respect to such general characteristics as length and weight, he is certain to be unique when it comes to his own special combination of physical, physiological, and psychological characteristics. Nevertheless, there are some conditions of physical appearance and of responsiveness to environmental stimulation that are especially characteristic of the human neonate, and which apply, more or less, to all normal, full-term babies during the first weeks following birth.

THE NEONATAL PERIOD

The term *neonate* has been defined somewhat differently by various authorities. Some have included only the first week or ten days following birth in the neonatal period. Others have included the first two weeks, or the first four weeks. Some have even equated the neonatal period with the entire period of infancy. But the critical thing about the neonatal period is that during it a satisfactory level of physiological stability is established with respect to such functions as circulation, respiration, ingestion and digestion of food, elimination of wastes, and body temperature regulation. While the infant may be ready at birth to engage in these processes, the establishment of physiological stability in the processes themselves takes longer. A fair degree of stabilization is reached by the end of the fourth week following birth. For our purposes, then, we may think of this early physiological adjustment period as the period of the neonate. It essentially comprises the first four weeks.

Physical Appearance and Characteristics The neonate's birth weight, on the average, is about 7½ pounds, although there is considerable variation around this average figure, as is shown in Table 4.1. The figure varies with the sex of the child, boys weighing slightly more than girls. In America, white children weigh slightly more on the average than Negro children at birth. Whether the difference is a matter of race or of nutritional factors is not clearly understood. First-born infants tend to weigh less at birth than younger brother and sister.

TABLE 4.1. *Length and Weight Percentiles for Male and Female Infants at Birth*

	3%	10%	25%	50%	75%	90%	97%
Length (inches)							
Boys	18¼	19	19½	20	20½	21	21½
Girls	18½	18¾	19¼	19¾	20	20½	21
Weight (pounds)							
Boys	5¾	6¼	7	7½	8¼	9	10
Girls	5¾	6¼	7	7½	8	8½	9½

SOURCE: Based on data from E. H. Watson and G. H. Lowrey, *Growth and Development of Children* (4th ed.), Chicago: Year Book Medical Publishers, Inc., 1962, as adapted from original data of H. C. Stuart and H. V. Meredith, prepared for use in Children's Medical Center, Boston.

It is customary in our society for new parents to announce not only the birth of a child, but his name, sex, and birth weight. The matter of weight is of far greater significance medically than socially, however. Much of his birth weight was achieved during the last two months before delivery, and it is an important indicator of his maturity. The weight gain during the final weeks of the prenatal period is primarily an increase in fatty tissue under the skin. That tissue has some insulation properties following birth, when temperature control is not yet well established. Weight, therefore, provides an index of maturity of the degree of physiological stability and readiness of the infant for life outside his mother's body. An infant weighing less than 5½ pounds at birth is considered premature, regardless of the exact length of time since conception. An unusually large or fat baby is not necessarily in better health, however, than one of average size and weight. The neonate typically loses weight during the first few days following birth. Stitt (24) reports that a new born may lose up to 10 percent of his birth weight during the first three or four days without causing concern. This loss is mostly a matter of losing excess body fluid, however, rather than a loss of solid tissue. By the fifth day, the neonate is typically starting to regain weight, and many will have reached their birth weight about ten days following birth. Most will do so by about 14 days. Ordinarily, breast-fed infants do not gain weight quite so rapidly as those on a cow's milk formula. In the following excerpt, Stitt (24) summarizes the early changes in weight:

> Weight gain during the first three months averages approximately 1 oz. daily, then the increments gradually lessen so that although birth weight is usually doubled by 5 months, it is only tripled by one year, and quadrupling is rarely achieved before 30 months. The plump appearance and firm, resilient feel characteristic of the latter half of the first year are due largely to the subcutaneous fat which increases up to 9 months but usually diminishes soon thereafter (24, p. 102).

Table 4.1 also provides figures on birth length of normal, full-term infants. There is relatively less variation in length than in weight, as length is less affected by immediate conditions of nutrition, length of term, etc. Nevertheless, healthy infants may vary in length from 18 to 22 inches. Boys are slightly longer, as well as heavier, than girls. Changes in length are less dramatic than in weight; nevertheless, growth is rapid during the neonatal period compared with other stages of development.

There is a slight relationship between birth length and height at later ages. However, one cannot predict how tall a child will eventually be on the basis of his length at birth.

BODY PROPORTIONS. When we see a new baby, we usually think of him as having normal proportions. He does, for a baby. But the ratio of head size to body length, or body length to leg length, etc., is markedly different from that observed in older children and adults. Different parts of the body grow at different rates, during the prenatal period as well as during childhood. By the time a baby is ready to be born, the circumference of his head is approximately the same as that of his chest. In general, the upper portions of his body have grown more rapidly and are more nearly mature at birth than the lower portions. Thus the head looks very large in relation to the rest of him. The feet, by comparison, look tiny and have an "unfinished" appearance; that is, at birth his feet don't look very useful. New fathers, especially, are prone to wonder whether these absurdly immature feet at the end of markedly bowed legs will ever do a reasonable job of holding him up and getting him around! The upper part of his head and face are more developed than the chin and lower jaw. Again, his immature lower jaw and receding chin are not at all predictive of things to come. His head may be covered with a heavy growth of long, dark hair which may even extend down over the temples. The color or texture of his hair in childhood or adult life cannot yet be ascertained, however; this first crop of thick hair will largely be shed and replaçed gradually by the permanent hair growth. There is usually a wide distribution of fine hair, called *lanugo*, over the body.

At birth the neonate's skin is covered with a greasy protective coating, the *vernix caseosa*. The skin color itself is ruddy and prone to bluish tinges at the extremities. The skin is thin and tender. Since temperature control and circulation are not yet well established immediately after birth, it is not uncommon for the hands and feet to feel cool to the touch. Nails are firm and well formed in the full-term infant. The new baby's eyes are typically blue, excepting those of nonwhite children. Again, it is difficult to predict eye color on the basis of appearance at birth. The baby cannot focus his eyes well for the first few days, although the eyes are individually responsive to light and functionally ready for gross vision. Whether he is able to discriminate color at first is doubtful, however, since the cones of the retina are not yet developed.

Physiological Processes and Motor Behavior of the Neonate All of growth and, for that matter, all of life, require continual adjustment of vital body processes. At no stage of development, however, are the changes in physiological functioning more drastic or dramatic than at the time of birth. During the prenatal period the mother's body played the major role in such basic processes as respiration, ingestion and digestion of food, and excretion of body wastes. Even blood circulation, although carried on independently by the fetus, was markedly different prior to birth because the lungs were not functioning and oxygen had been provided for the baby's blood stream through the placental membranes. At birth, or at least within a short period of time following birth, significant changes in such processes must occur if the infant is to survive and to maintain his existence apart from his mother's body. He must get air into his lungs to provide oxygen and to provide for the elimination of excess carbon dioxide. He must also redirect the flow of blood to send veinous blood to the lungs for oxygenation. Breckenridge and Murphy (4) describe this change as follows:

> Before birth very little blood flows through the lungs, since there is no oxygen in them, but the blood in both sides of the heart flows through the general circulation and out through the arteries in the umbilical cord to the placenta. This is made possible by an opening between the right and left chambers of the fetal heart. In the placenta the fetal blood is aerated. When the umbilical cord is cut, this circulation must cease; the blood is forced into the lungs where oxygen can be obtained as soon as respiration is established. After pulmonary circulation is well established the opening between the sides of the heart closes (4, p. 206).

Other anatomic and physiological changes also occur when the umbilical cord is cut. The initiation of pulmonary breathing requires the beginning of expansion of the lungs. More complete lung expansion usually occurs within the first few days following birth.

Stitt (24) reports that gastrointestinal function does not proceed as rapidly, but that the healthy infant has his own supply of nutrients that will meet the needs of the first few days. The neonate is, however, capable of sucking, swallowing, and ingesting liquid food, and of other reflex action leading to evacuation of the large bowel. Functioning of the kidneys also begins shortly after birth. However, the efficiency of this function in removing waste products and in maintaining water balance in the body tissues improves gradually throughout the neonatal period.

The Neonate's Resources for Intelligent Behavior Adults are forever intrigued by the question, "what is going on in their little heads?" when inspecting a new baby. Since we can't recall our own experience at that age, and since the baby can't tell us what he's "thinking" about, we are left without much real information. William James, famous psychologist and philosopher of the early part of this century, described the infant's mental life as a "blooming, buzzing confusion" (13, p. 488). Gesell questions this, and argues that the baby probably ". . . senses the visible world at first in fugitive and fluctuating blotches against a neutral background" (10, p. 22). Gesell argues that the mental life of the baby includes sounds, the pressure of his body weight, feelings of his own movements of mouth and limbs, feelings of satisfaction associated with feeding, and of distress from hunger or cold. Even if such sensations are available to the neonate, it is highly unlikely that he can find any meaning or significance in the world outside his own skin. In any event, mental processes are based fundamentally on the activities of the central nervous system—the brain and spinal cord. It is the response of that central nervous system to stimulation from the outside world which is the basic ingredient of mental activity. The biological development of the nervous system, combined with the gradually accumulating effects of experience, result in the organization of coherent, useful mental action. Thus, to understand the neonate's potential for intelligent behavior, we must take into account the biological equipment with which he is endowed and his resources for receiving stimulation from the outside world. These latter resources are essentially his sensory capacities—his equipment for seeing, hearing, feeling, tasting, and smelling.

At birth, the brain has already accomplished a great deal of growth and maturation, and has reached approximately one-fourth the size it will be at full maturity. It has already grown much faster, relatively, than the rest of the body, and it continues to do so following birth. Watson and Lowery (27) report that about half of all the growing the brain will do between birth and maturity will be done during the first year. With respect to functioning, it appears that certain parts of the brain and spinal cord are more mature than others at birth. The outer covering of the cerebrum, or cerebral cortex, is the part which is most directly involved in the higher mental processes of learning, thinking, remembering, and reasoning. This part of the brain is what enables man to engage in the rich and complex variety of behavior of which he is capable, and which enables him to pursue complicated and indirect courses of action in order to solve his problems and to satisfy his needs. The lower portions of the brain, by contrast, are more directly involved in controlling vital physiological processes and the more or less stereotyped, automatic, and reflexive behavior that occurs in response to specific stimulation. These lower-brain centers are relatively more developed and functional at birth than are the higher-brain centers. The evidence for their functioning is found in the operation of the reflexes, some of which are well established before the child is born. One of these is the *Moro reflex*, a "startle" response to sudden change of position, jarring, or to sudden loud sounds. Typically, when stimulated in such a manner, the neonate tenses all his muscles, extends his arms widely, and then brings them toward each other as if to embrace or seize. Watson and Lowery (27) point out that a counterpart of this reaction can be seen in young monkeys when, in time of danger or emergency, they cling to their mothers, using a similar reflex action. The Moro reflex is characteristic of the neonatal period; after about six weeks it begins to disappear, and is not normally found at all in an infant beyond the first few months.

Another example of a reflex behavior pattern characteristic of the neonate which later disappears is the *tonic neck reflex*, which involves a natural coordination of the position of head, arms, and legs. The neonate, when lying on his back, may automatically assume a position with his head turned to one side—typically, to the right. The arm and leg on the side he is facing are extended, while the arm and leg of the other side are flexed. This is sometimes referred to as a "fencing position" in the infant. Researchers have observed that if the infant's head is turned by an attendant to face in the opposite direction, there may be a corresponding shift in the arm and leg positions. This reflex coordination of head and limb position persists from three to six months into infancy. The *Babinski reflex* also illustrates the fact that the neonate is equipped with certain response tendencies which will later disappear or undergo modification. The Babinski reflex is the peculiar extension and fanning out of the toes, particularly the big toe, when the sole of the foot is stimulated. The normal response of the older infant, child, and adult is for the toes to flex and tend to curl inward upon similar stimulation.

Some of the most significant reflexes—and certainly the most important from the standpoint of survival and health—are those involved in feeding. The neonate is equipped with a fairly complicated set of reflex-response mechanisms which enable him to take in food. One of these has been described by Gentry and Aldrich (8) as the "rooting reflex." This evokes a turning of the head upon stimulation of the side of the face, in the direction of the stimulus, and a simultaneous opening of the mouth. The operation of this pattern can be seen most clearly in the infant being held in its mother's arms; the turning toward the side stimulated and opening the mouth obviously increases the likelihood of making and of maintaining contact with the mother's breast. Along with this rooting reflex, sucking reflexes play an important role in the ingestion of milk during the neonatal period. Researchers have noted at various times that a very light stimulation of the infant's lips, cheeks, or chin may result in vigorous sucking movements, including coordination of tongue and lower jaw. These movements, in turn, are coordinated with swallowing reflexes. An interesting observation of the special characteristics of newborn infants is that they are able to coordinate vigorous sucking, swallowing, and breathing in a manner difficult, if not impossible, for the adult.

Many other patterns of reflex behavior in the neonate have been studied and described in the technical literature of child development. There is still disagreement among scholars on some of the finer points of these reflex behavior patterns; however, their existence provides ample evidence that the neonate is not the completely helpless creature he has sometimes been thought to be. Instead, he is endowed with a remarkably complex and adaptable set of behavior patterns which equip him for survival and adjustment in the world outside his mother's body. The relationship between such reflexive behavior and the development of intelligence, however, is another matter. Current thinking among child-development specialists is that the behavior of the neonate is pretty much subcortical. That is, it does not depend on the existence or the function of the higher brain centers that are used in thinking, remembering, and in solving problems. Where, then, is there anything in the way of "intelligence" on the part of the neonate? Some students of this problem answer it simply by saying that intelligence, as commonly defined, simply does not exist at this stage. It unfolds gradually, over time, with the maturation of the central nervous system and with experience. Nevertheless, as we have seen from the foregoing discussion, the basic reflex neural processes which underlie this unfolding of intelligence are very much in evidence anatomically and functionally at birth, and undergo rapid changes in capacity during the days immediately following birth.

The sensory capacities of the neonate have received considerable attention from child-development scholars. Investigations have been concerned primarily with the following senses: vision, tactile (touch) sense, auditory (hearing) sense, sense of taste, and olfaction (sense of smell). That the neonate does have visual sensitivity is easily demonstrated in his reflex reactions to light, including pupillary contraction as well as blinking of the eyelids. It is extremely doubtful, however, that there could be sharp visual discrimination or perception of objects at this age. The size, shape, and rapid growth of the eyeball itself at this point would make it unlikely that a sharp image could be focused on the retina of the eye. In addition, the immaturity of the muscles and the lack of motor control over them make it impossible for the neonate to focus his eyes in a coordinated manner at first. The research on neonatal reactions to different colors is not entirely conclusive. Color perception is mediated by the cones of the eye's retina, and some authorities hold that these are not functionally present during the neonatal period. There is some evidence of clear-cut response to color by the third or fourth month following birth, but this is an extremely difficult question to settle for the neonatal period.

The sense of touch exists even before birth and is quite evident in the neonate, particularly in the face. The newborn baby is especially sensitive to touch on or near the lips. Studies reveal that, while touch sensitivity is present, there is little ability at this stage to locate the source of the stimulus. The neonate, in other words, cannot tell just what part of the skin surface is being stimulated, and his response to stimulation is a very generalized, mass response involving large portions of the body, as opposed to a precise response locating the point of stimulation.

Hearing is structurally present at birth; that is, the hearing mechanism itself is complete. As Watson and Lowery remark, "The middle ear, concerned with the collecting and transmitting of sound waves to the internal ear, is practically of adult size at birth, although the drum membrane may be smaller and more oblique" (27, p. 192). This does not mean that the newborn baby can perceive clear sounds, of course. In fact, for the first few days, until the eustachian tube is well opened and any amniotic fluid or debris is cleared out of the middle ear, there may be little or no hearing of any kind. Within a few days, however, his sense of hearing becomes acute, as shown by his startle response to sounds.

Taste, also, is present at birth in a more or less diffuse, undifferentiated state. That is, the neonate does not appear to distinguish between sour, salty, and bitter substances. The sense of smell is present at birth, according to Pratt (18, p. 241). This is shown by the vigorous reactions of the neonate to such substances as ammonia and acetic acid. However, it is difficult to determine whether this is truly an olfactory response or a more general reaction to pain. In any event, the sense of smell is not yet well developed, and becomes much more acute later in infancy.

From this discussion of the sensory processes, as well as that of the nervous system, it may be concluded that the two major kinds of resources essential to the development of intelligence are present, at least in rudimentary form, when the baby is born.

Resources for Personal, Emotional, and Social Behavior The neonate's resources for personal, emotional, and social behavior—those qualities which are commonly thought of as the "personality" aspects of the child—are more difficult to establish among his characteristics and responses. However, it is clear that there are individual differences in babies from the very beginning. We are no longer likely to make the error made by some writers over the past half century in assuming that differences in adult personality are exclusively a matter of learning. Personality development is an interaction process from its beginning—interaction of internal, inherited, and biological forces on the one hand, and of external, environmental, experiential forces on the other. Because the environment was limited and restricted during the prenatal stage, the effects of genetic endowment are perhaps more clearly seen in the differences observed in neonates—and these differences are indeed significant.

Some infants, from the beginning, show marked differences in amount and depth of sleep when compared with the average. Some spend a much larger proportion of each 24-hour period in quiet wakefulness, others in crying. There are wide variations in the degree of "reactivity," that is, how quickly and sharply the infant responds to light, sound, temperature changes, and other stimuli. There are also wide variations in tempo and speed of growth, in interest in the external environment, etc. —all of which illustrate the tremendous range of individual differences present right from birth. It is never safe to make specific predictions about the relationship between these characteristics and later personality development, since many subsequent events may modify the kinds of behavior we have been describing; nevertheless, differences are there. The importance of their effects on later personality may be glimpsed when one considers that these differences not only have a direct bearing on what the child is to become, but may lead to many indirect effects, as well. One brief example of this is that of the mother who is perfectly relaxed, comfortable, and accepting toward her easy-going, placid baby, and who provides him with the kind of loving care we assume to be essential for his healthy development. She then finds herself with a second baby who is, from the time of its birth, a study in contrasts with her older child. He is wakeful and fretful day and night, upsets easily, has a different tempo of activities than the older child, and is in every respect a "difficult" baby. The very same mother finds it quite a different task to be an accepting, calm, placid, and loving parent to this child. Eventually, the fundamental difference in the temperament of the two children, present at birth, leads to a fundamentally different type of mothering from the very same woman! Thus it would be difficult to say exactly what parts of the child's personality are to be discovered in the neonate himself, and which parts are to be found in the interaction process through time of this self with the child's objective and social environment.

Outside of his needs to be fed, made comfortable, etc., the neonate is essentially asocial. Social behavior and individual personality are achieved together, during childhood, as the child interacts with others. The process of social interaction requires, for its existence, at least a rudimentary concept of oneself as a separate person, exisiting in a relationship with others. Such concepts of "self" and "others" are not available to the newborn infant; in fact, although the neonate is physically separate from the body of his mother, he is as yet psychologically undifferentiated from her, being unaware of himself as a separate person. With social behavior, then, as with intellectual behavior, it is more accurate to say that the neonate has resources and potentials for its development, rather than to imply that he engages in such behavior at this time.

Emotional behavior, however, is somewhat a different case. Admittedly, the newborn child's equipment for emotional reactions is immature and will certainly undergo much modification as he learns new ways to respond and new things to respond to. Nevertheless, he is quite capable, from the time of birth, of reacting to his environment with responses which meet all the criteria of being truly emotional behavior. At one time it was believed by certain child psychologists that the emotional responses of the newborn infant were of three specific types: fear, anger or rage, and love. Watson (28) proposed that these three basic emotions were aroused by sudden loud noises, or falling (fear), by restriction of bodily movement (rage), and by fondling or stroking (love). Later research (5) failed to bear this out, however, and instead indicates that the emotional life of the neonate is of a much more general kind. Instead of such specific emotions as anger, fear, and love, the neonate apparently responds with a somewhat vague, diffuse emotional reaction which could be termed general excitement. This is a mass response, involving the infant's entire body, and including physiological changes as well as increased body activity and crying. Emotion is aroused by internal stimulation, such as hunger, as well as by external conditions such as temperature changes and physical stimulation of various types. This general capacity to respond with emotion to a variety of stimulating circumstances stands the neonate in good stead, of course, since he has no other way of informing the world of his needs, or of correcting situations which call for attention. At first, however, a mother is not able to tell on the basis of the kind of sound he makes whether he is crying from hunger, or colic, or a wet diaper. Later, as he responds somewhat differently to each of these and many other situations, she will be able to detect differences in the kinds of emotional responses he makes, and will learn to respond appropriately.

It is very natural to think of the neonate as having a long way to go to achieve the characteristics which mark him as a responsive, purposeful human being. From our discussion thus far, however, it should be clear that some of the most vital and significant steps along this road to maturity have already been taken by the time of his birth. If we are inclined to think of the infant as helpless, we might keep in mind the truly remarkable range of functional capacities with which he is equipped at birth —capacities without which he could not possibly survive, let alone take the next wonderful steps into the world of infancy.

INFANCY

The word, *infancy*, has been defined in a number of ways and is used by different people to mean quite different things. In the legal profession, for example, "infant" may mean anyone who has not reached the age of consent, or in some cases even anyone under age 21. In its more common use, of course, the term refers to the early stages of postnatal development. Even in that sense, however, there are differences of opinion about the strict meaning of the word. Some writers define infancy as the first year of life; others suggest that the first 18 months is a more meaningful classification. The derivation of the word itself is from the Latin *infans*, formed from the combination of *in* (not) and *fari* (to speak). Thus one definition of infancy might be given as the period of development which precedes speaking. This is cumbersome, however, since we would have to refer to some 2-year-olds as infants, and admit that some 1-year-olds had already left infancy behind!

In keeping with the current usage in the field of child development, we shall be referring to the first two postnatal years when we use the term, *infancy*. This is a meaningful age span, for it includes a number of most significant accomplishments such as the achievement of upright locomotion and speech. In addition, it will provide the child-development student with a summary of the growth and development of the child up to his entrance into the preschool years. Such a summary should serve us well as a foundation for and an introduction to the period from 2 to 5 years of age, which will constitute the major emphasis throughout the remainder of the text. Our discussion of the infant, then, will be organized under the headings of the most significant achievements following the neonatal period up to the age of 2 years.

Physical Growth Achievements During Infancy The development of the infant—even his physical development—is much more, of course, than mere increase in size and weight. Yet we must not overlook the importance of such changes as these, for they have implications for other aspects of development, including the psychological. In addition, they are often a rough general indicator of the health status of the child. According to Thompson (26), there is evidence that infants from poor homes weigh less and are shorter in stature than infants from good homes. Furthermore, when infants from poor homes were supervised in the pediatric clinic, their height, weight, and body proportions soon approximated the average for a control group from ordinary homes. Hence, an understanding of the processes of physical changes and the factors involved in normal growth is essential. Furthermore, during the period of infancy, such changes occur at an extremely rapid rate—more rapid, in fact, than at any subsequent stage in the lifetime development of the individual. Figures 4.1 and 4.2, respectively, reveal the growth trends in body length and weight, for boys and girls, between birth and 12 months of age. Boys are longer than girls, on the average, at all ages during the infancy period. The differences are small but consistent throughout this entire period. However, it must not be assumed that any particular boy is, or should be, taller than any particular girl. There is considerable overlapping, with approximately 25 percent of the boys being shorter, at age 6 months, than the average for the girls. Similar overlapping is found at all ages in infancy. Weight curves also show the boys to exceed the girls consistently during infancy. It is interesting to note, however, that the average differences are greater in the middle of the infancy period, from 6 to 18 months, than during the early or late parts of the period.

The most rapid gains in length and weight occur for both sexes early in the postnatal months. The greatest gain in weight occurs during the first month, in spite of the initial loss of weight immediately following birth. The rapidity of growth during the early postnatal months is really a continuation of the accelerated growth cycle which began during the prenatal months and is gradually tapering off toward the slower, steadier growth characteristic of the preschool and school years. At no time in the child's life, even during the adolescent growth spurt, will physical development again proceed as rapidly.

Generalizations about other standard measurements of physical growth would be quite similar to those for increases in length and weight. That is, curves showing increases in head circumference, chest circumference, hip width, etc., would reveal patterns somewhat similar to those shown in Figures 4.1 and 4.2. However, it should not be assumed from this that all parts of the body are growing at the same rate. Different parts of the body grow at their own rates, thus resulting in gradual but definite changes in body proportion. The infant changes from a relatively slender newborn child to a more plump or "chunky" 1-year-old. The change is accounted for primarily by an increase in the subcutaneous fatty tissue in the early months. As Lombard (15) has pointed out, growth of bone and muscle tissue continues at a relatively steady pace beyond the first year and on into the preschool period. During this same period, subcutaneous fatty tissue is decreasing after its initial spurt during the first 9 months following birth.

Evaluation of growth during infancy. Evaluation of the physical

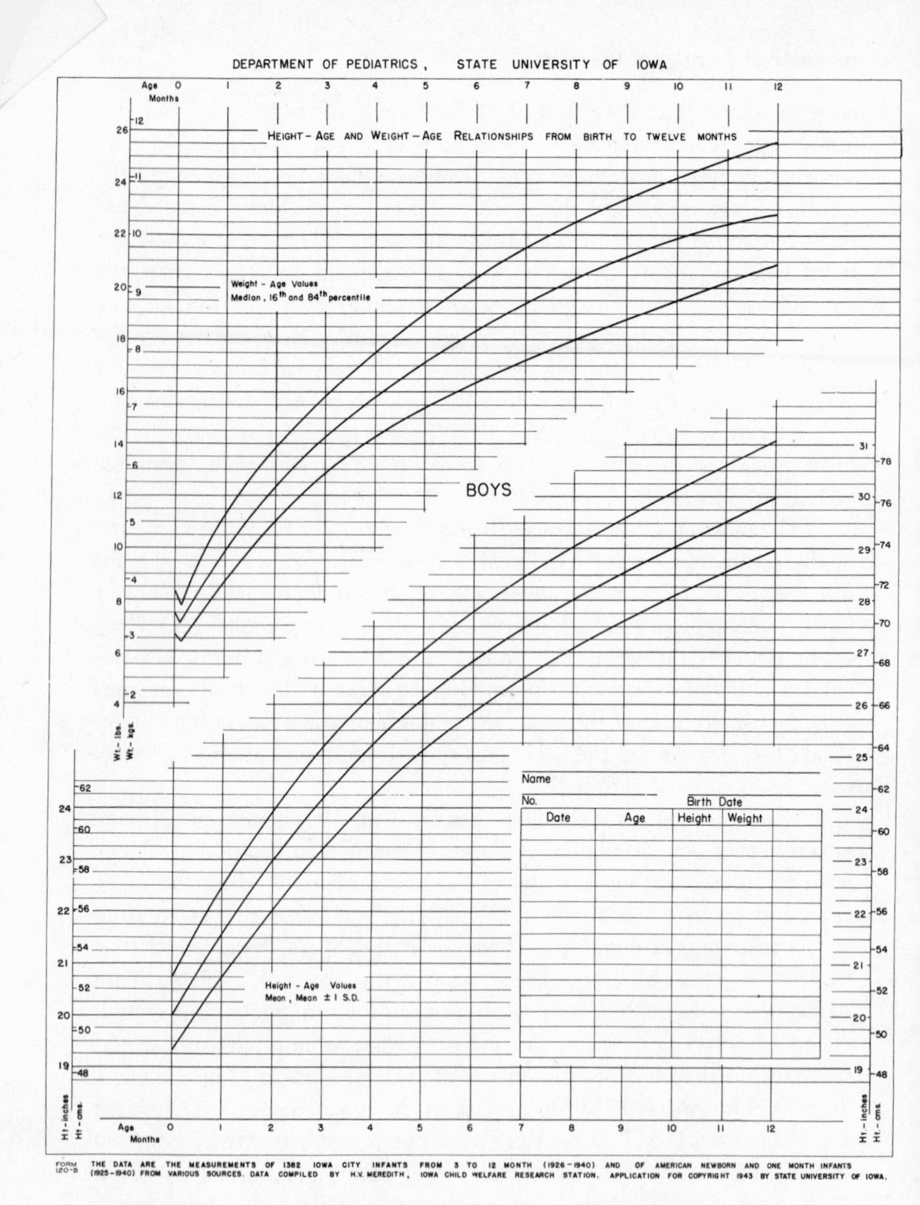

Fig. 4.1. Height-age and weight-age relationships for boys from birth to 12 months. (Data compiled by H. V. Meredith, Iowa Child Welfare Research Station. Copyright 1943 by State University of Iowa.)

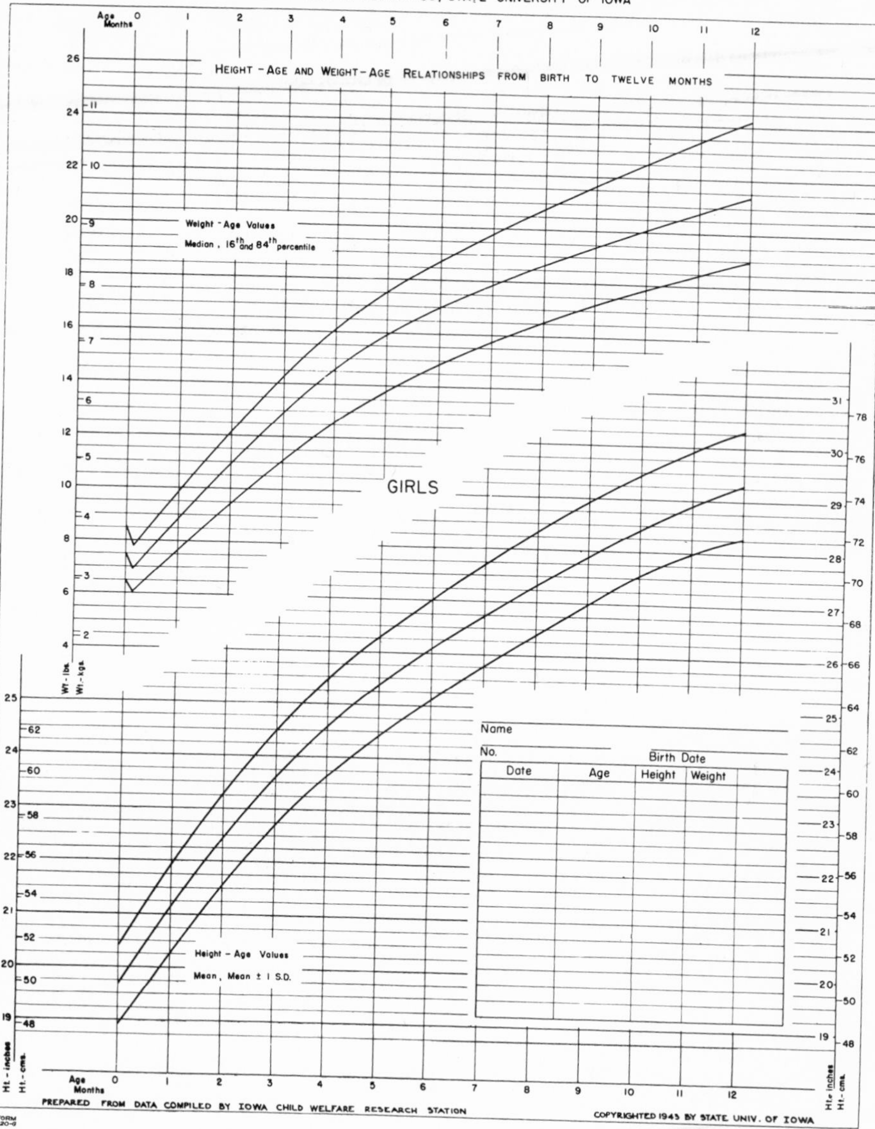

Fig. 4.2. Height-age and weight-age relationships for girls from birth to 12 months. (From data compiled by Iowa Child Welfare Research Station. Copyright 1943 by State University of Iowa.)

growth of infants is a complex matter. Many more things than length and weight need to be taken into account. Furthermore, growth of the individual infant cannot be evaluated properly by reference only to the norms, or averages for infants his age. It is essential that we be able to see the infant not only in comparison with the averages of other infants of his same age and sex, but also in relation to himself over a period of time. It is a common error to assume that average figures on length and weight, for example, represent standards of excellence. This leads to the false notion that the one baby we may be most concerned with at the moment should equal or exceed those average figures. Dr. Arnold Gesell quotes a little verse by John Kendrick Bangs which is helpful in keeping this matter straight in our thinking:

I met a little Elfman once,
Down where the lilies blow.
I asked him why he was so small,
And why he didn't grow.

He slightly frowned, and with his eye
He looked me through and through—
"I'm quite as big for me," said he,
"As you are big for you!" (10, p. 72).

In relatively recent years scientists have worked out means by which to evaluate the growth of the individual child, in comparison with himself, over a period of time. One example of such techniques is the Baby Grid, developed by Wetzel (29). This grid is based on average figures for large numbers of infants, and thus does allow for comparison of the individual baby with the average. At the same time, it provides for individual differences among infants and assumes, not that all babies should grow in the same manner or rate, but that each should normally proceed along his own "growth channel." Marked departure from the channels which cannot be accounted for by these normal developmental changes in body form may indicate the need for careful examination by the physician to determine possible causes for growth irregularity. Modern devices such as the Baby Grid also provide for recording a variety of data that, taken together, reflect adequacy of total physical growth of the infant from one medical examination to the next. It cannot be overemphasized that no single index of physical development can be interpreted meaningfully in isolation from the others. Height, weight, skin condition, subcutaneous tissue, and development of the basic body systems (circulatory system, alimentary system, skeletal system, nervous system, and respiratory system), must be considered in relation to one another by the physician in order to appraise the over-all progress of the infant. An excellent discussion of physical and physiological development in infancy, for the student who may wish to pursue this topic further, is given by Stuart and Prugh (25).

Achievement of Upright Locomotion Walking, which most of us take for granted and assume to be an easy, "automatic" behavior, is in reality a highly complex activity. It requires the coordination, not only of a number of different muscle groups, but of muscles acting in well-organized, systematic relationship with sensory processes of vision, touch, kinesthetic sense, and body-balance sense mediated in the inner ear. The sensory processes and their development will be discussed in later sections; this part of the chapter deals specifically with the changes in muscle control that lead to the development of upright locomotion. The student should keep in mind, however, that these changes are not merely a matter of muscular development.

We have already seen that the neonate shows a variety of reflex behavior patterns. When held in a standing position with his weight supported and his feet in contact with a flat surface, the baby will make rudimentary "stepping movements." These are primitive and have no immediate usefulness, except to indicate that the basic human pattern for walking is genetically determined and is present at birth. The initial neural control is reflex; that is, independent of the higher, conscious brain centers. In general, the achievement of body control of all kinds follows the basic principle of development from general to specific behavior. At first, body movements are random, vague, diffuse, and involve relatively large body segments. With increased maturation, movements become more controlled, direct, and specific, and involve the portions of the body most immediately concerned with carrying out the appropriate action. We shall have occasion to illustrate these principles in much greater detail later in the discussion of motor development of the preschool child. These principles of development can be seen rather clearly in the sequence of steps leading to walking—a sequence that has been described by Shirley (21), Bayley (2), McGraw (17), and others. While there are some minor differences in the descriptions given by these different researchers, and in the exact age at which each stage typically occurs, the investigators clearly agree on the major stages of development of upright locomotion.

Figure 4.3 summarizes the sequence of stages and the typical ages of their occurence, as described by Shirley (21). Walking is the culmination of a long, involved sequence that began, in one sense, during the prenatal period. The sequence is not truly complete when the infant takes his first steps, either. There are important changes in the walking posture, improvements of balance, learning to avoid obstacles, coordinating walking with other activities such as reaching, grasping, carrying, throwing, catching, etc. Thus, while the achievement of independent walking at a little over 1 year of age is a dramatic moment in the lives of babies and their parents, it is neither the beginning nor the end of the long and complicated sequence in the development of upright locomotion; rather, it is one important milestone along the way.

There are wide variations for individual, healthy infants, with respect to this prewalking sequence. Not only do different babies reach each stage in their own good time, but it is not uncommon for an infant to pass up a certain stage, going directly to another, more advanced one. Some infants, for example, do little or no true "creeping." Some creep, after a fashion, in ways markedly different from others. Some prefer a kind of stiff-legged "bear-walk" on all fours. Some engage in a smoothly efficient hitching along in a sitting position with one leg flexed and the other extended. Some learn to scoot backwards so well that it is easier for them to get where they want to go by turning around and backing up to it! Needless to say, then, there is no one right way to go through the creeping stage.

A second basic principle of motor development is that it occurs in a *cephalocaudal* or "head-to-foot" direction. This principle is sometimes referred to as the "law of developmental direction." In general, it means that development both of the body structure and of its functional usefulness occurs first in the upper portions of the body and later in progressively lower portions. Thus control of the head, neck, and arms appears before the infant can control foot movements. This principle is clearly illustrated in the prewalking sequence in Figure 4.3.

Achievement of Sensory-Motor Coordination The neonate's sensory contact with his environment appears to be primarily through his skin. That is, while he is not yet capable of responding in an organized, intelligent manner to the many visual and auditory stimulations in his

First steps. (Monkmeyer Press Photos.)

THE MOTOR SEQUENCE

Fig. 4.3. The motor sequence, leading to upright locomotion. (From: *The first two years: a study of twenty-five babies, vol. II* by Mary M. Shirley, Child Welfare Monograph Series, No. 7. University of Minnesota Press, Minneapolis. Copyright 1933 by the University of Minnesota.)

environment, he is very much affected by temperature changes, touch, pressure, and painful stimulations on the skin surface. Particularly in the region of the mouth, the infant's rich supply of nerve endings in the skin provide him, right from birth, with a vital sensory link with his environment. That link is essential in his earliest efforts to satisfy his hunger.

Sensory-motor development, like all other aspects of human growth, is fundamentally the outcome of both processes: *maturation*, which is the component of growth arising from internal, genetic endowment, and *learning*, which is the component of growth dependent primarily on experience. It is well-nigh impossible to separate the effects of these two basic processes when describing sensory-motor development. Nevertheless, both are well in evidence as the infant gradually acquires facility in receiving and organizing the stimulations from his environment and in coordinating his body actions in appropriate responses to the objects of that environment. Maturation of the sense organs themselves, and of the nervous system associated with them, gradually enables the infant to organize his world of sensation. The eyes, which at first he could not control, after the first few weeks become less random in their movements. Gradually they tend to fix themselves more steadily upon "interesting" objects. A significant kind of learning can occur at this point through the association of what is seen with what is touched, heard, and tasted. A prime example of this occurs in the nursing situation, which affords an excellent opportunity for the infant to associate the various sensations of warmth, touch, taste, and the visual sensations of his mother, together with his own motor response (sucking) in a total situation that leads to gratification of a basic need. The conditions for learning could hardly be better. This particular learning situation has tremendous significance for personality development, as well as merely serving to gratify the senses and to help the child learn appropriate motor responses.

One of the early evidences of sensory-motor development is the smile, which occurs by about the second or third month. Smiling itself is motor activity. Its occurrence, however, is triggered off at this age by the visual stimulus of the mother or another person, or, for that matter, even an inanimate object that is moved in the line of the infant's vision. Similarly, the sucking response can occur now without the infant's skin being stimulated; even the sound of the mother's footsteps as she approaches the crib when the baby is hungry may be enough to start the sucking activity of the baby.

The preceding discussion illustrates a kind of *coordination* of sensation with motor behavior. This coordination concept has other implications, as well, one of the most important being the use of eyes and hands together. Gesell (*10*) remarks that the infant's first attempt to grasp his environment utilizes his eyes, rather than his hands. His eyes are under his control before his hands are, and there are many lines of evidence which indicate that he understands objects with his eyes before he can understand them with his fingers, even when they might be very near his face.

Development of prehension. An important achievement during infancy is the ability of the baby to use his hands for seizing, grasping, manipulating, and releasing objects. Halverson (*11*) made use of motion picture photography to investigate the development of these abilities between the ages of 16 weeks and 52 weeks. Halverson's subjects were supported in a specially designed chair which allowed them freedom to reach for and to grasp objects presented to them on a table. A small cube was presented to each infant in a standardized manner, and the reactions were recorded by motion-picture cameras. Careful analysis of the resulting records revealed four major steps in the act of prehension: (1) the visual location of the object, (2) the approach by the hand, (3) the grasp, and (4) the disposal of the object. Each of these phases showed its special course of development during the first year, with many evidences of regularity and orderliness in its progression. Figure 4.4 charts the major developmental sequence in the achievement of prehension as described by Halverson. He summarized a portion of the findings of his investigation in this manner:

> The more characteristic reactions to the cube by the infants of different ages are as follows: at 16 weeks, infants follow the examiner's hand after she presents the cube, slide their hands about on the table, and often keep one or both hands on the table during the entire situation. At 20 weeks, infants scratch the table, and attempt to get both hands about the cube after reaching with both hands simultaneously. If they succeed in touching the cube, they either push it out of reach or simply hold it. At 24 and 28 weeks, they approach the cube in a scooping manner, sometimes using both hands, and then corral and surround the cube or push it out of reach. After grasping the

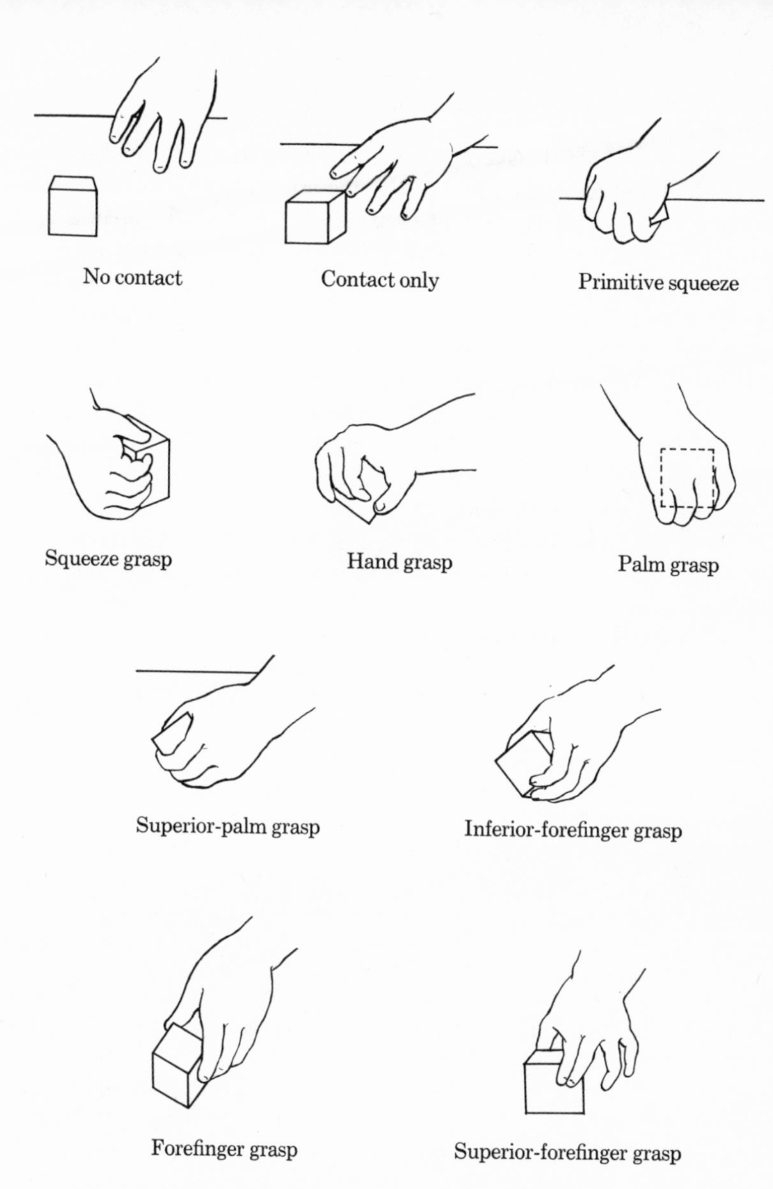

Fig. 4.4. The developmental sequence in the achievement of prehension from 16 to 52 weeks. (Adapted from H. M. Halverson, "An experimental study in prehension in infants by means of systematic cinema records," *Genetic Psychol. Monogr.*, 1931, 10:107–286.)

> cube, they hold it, take it to mouth, inspect the cube, and release it and regain it. At 32 weeks, the infants use the scooping approach to surround the cube, inspect it, take it to the mouth, release and pick up the cube again, and exchange it from one hand to the other. They often disregard the cube when there are other cubes present. At 36 weeks and at 40 weeks, the infants execute a number of bilateral approaches and shift the cube from one hand to the other. They also bring the cube to the mouth, simply hold the cube, inspect it, hold it with both hands, release and regain it, bang the table with it, exchange hands on it, execute a number of bilateral approaches, and hold it in both hands. The 52-week infants often put the cube down and pick it up again, bang the table, exchange hands on the cube, simply hold it with one hand or both hands and inspect it, but do not bring it to the mouth. The 16-weeks infants do not, as a rule, reach the cube (*11*, pp. 277–278).

Halverson's interesting and detailed study of a small sequence in the overall motor development of infants provides us with evidence of the patterning of behavior resulting from maturation processes. The study also reveals the trend of progress from the coarser, large-muscle control toward the finer, small-muscle control that has been noted by many observers of motor development. The early approach to the cube involves mainly the large shoulder and elbow action, which is relatively slow and crude. With increased maturation there is greater involvement of the hand, wrist, and fingers, with finer control of the smaller muscles leading to greatly improved performance.

Elaboration of Emotional Behavior As we have already noted, the emotional experiences and responses of the neonate are best understood as very general reactions. An early research study on this subject was done by Sherman (20). Adult subjects were asked to identify the emotional reactions of infants in response to such things as delay of feeding, sudden loss of support, restraint of head movements, and being pricked with a needle. When the subjects were informed as to conditions which precipitated the emotional reactions, they labeled the reactions without difficulty, using conventional terms. However, when the adults saw motion pictures of the infant reactions, without being informed of the stimulating conditions, they could not guess what had caused the reactions, nor could they agree with each other as to what emotion was being expressed. It is likely that our interpretation of an infant's crying as signifying anger, or fear, or any other specific emotion, is based primarily on our knowledge of whatever event is stimulating him, rather than on the reaction of the infant.

Bridges (5), another student of the early emotional development of infants, also concluded that the first emotions are vague and poorly defined, but that they become more specific, more "differentiated," with increased age. Figure 4.5 illustrates the gradual differentiation of emotional responses over the first two years. From this diagram it may be observed that distress is differentiated from the general state of excitement by about one month of age. Delight, however, is differentiated somewhat later, around 2 months of age. Delight is manifest by fleeting smiles in response to being nursed, petted, or cared for. It is more clearly defined at 3 months, and by 4 months more active signs of delight are evidenced in the form of laughter, smiling in response to another's smile, and efforts to raise the body in approach to an attentive person.

The exact age at which any specific emotional response becomes differentiated from more general emotional behavior is less important than the understanding of the sources and direction of development of the emotional life of infants. Emotional behavior is unstable throughout infancy; that is, the infant can move suddenly from one emotional state to another with little evidence of carry-over from one moment to the next. Infantile emotional behavior also tends to be of the "all-or-none" variety, in that there is, compared with older children and adults, less of a gradation from mild to extreme emotion. Instead, the infant tends to respond to any emotion-arousing condition with his whole being.

In spite of these characteristics of normal emotional behavior in infancy, a number of writers have pointed out that extreme and prolonged emotional conditions in early infancy may have serious consequences, not only for the healthy development of emotional patterns, but for the development of the total personality as well. Bowlby (3), in summarizing the research on emotionally deprived infants—those reared in institutions or somehow lacking in a normal emotional relationship with a mother-figure—concluded that the severely deprived infant shows, both at the time of deprivation and in subsequent months and years, important personality defects which take the form of inadequate personal-social behavior, shallowness of emotional reactions, and tendencies in later childhood toward

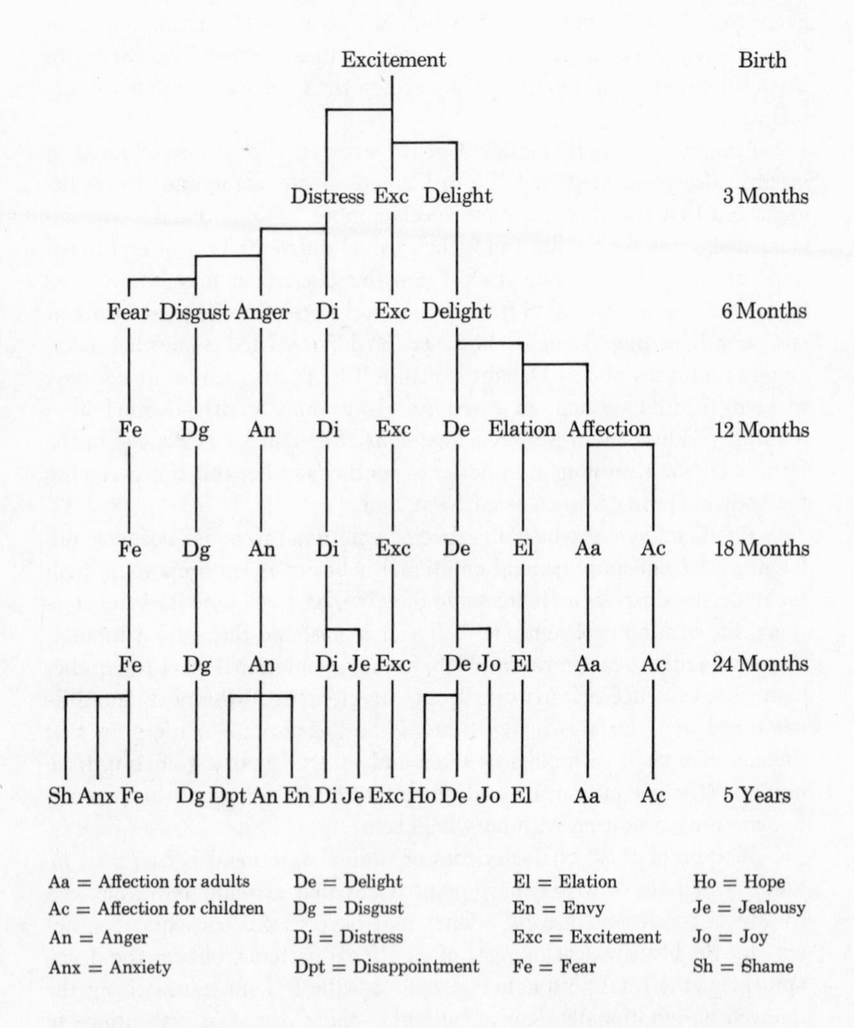

Fig. 4.5. A diagrammatic representation of the development of emotion. (From H. F. English, *Dynamics of child development*, New York: Holt, Rinehart and Winston, 1961, p. 114, as combined from two diagrams by K. M. B. Bridges, *J. genet. psychol.*, 1930, 37:524, and *Child develpm.*, 1932, 3:340.)

psychopathic disorders. Similarly, Bakwin has presented a clinical description of the deprived infant that, for all its brevity, is remarkably comprehensive:

> Infants under 6 months of age who have been in an institution for some time present a well-defined picture. The outstanding features are listlessness, emaciation and pallor, relative immobility, quietness, unresponsiveness to stimuli like a smile or a coo, indifferent appetite, failure to gain weight properly despite the ingestion of diets which, in the home, are entirely adequate, frequent stools, poor sleep, an appearance of unhappiness, proneness to febrile episodes, absence of sucking habits (1, p. 512).

These symptoms, however, are the result of extremes of emotional distortion which do not occur in the ordinary family setting. Furthermore, the healthy infant has a powerful capacity to respond in a constructive manner to the emotional experiences he has, even when these experiences are not entirely positive. While undue exposure to fearful stimulation, frustration, jealousy-provoking circumstances and the like are to be avoided, it must not be supposed that the usual emotional experiences of infancy will result in unhealthy personality development.

Achievement of Language The ability to use language in a meaningful way in the communicating of ideas, emotions, and questions to others is a remarkable achievement. True language is a uniquely human characteristic and a far more complex process than that carried on by parrots and other "talking" birds. Spoken language—oral speech—is only one form of language, and we shall later have occasion to be concerned with other aspects of communication in children. However, the period of infancy is critical in that we expect the child during this time to achieve the ability to pronounce words. Furthermore, we expect him to articulate words well enough that others than his parents know what he is saying, and we expect him to use the words appropriately, with commonly accepted meanings. We don't expect him to do all these things at once, to be sure! He will still have a long way to go in language development after he has left infancy far behind. Nevertheless, his language progress during the first two years is generally measured by these criteria: (1) *understanding the meaning of words spoken to him*, (2) *pronouncing words with clear articulation*, and (3) *using words with meaningful association, ac-*

cepted by others. We shall examine the progress of the infant, then, with respect to these three criteria.

Understanding of the words of others develops earlier, and more rapidly, than does the ability to form word sounds clearly and to use them meaningfully. Before the end of the first year the infant shows in many ways—and long before he can reproduce the same sounds himself—that he can respond appropriately to the oral speech of other persons. The process by which this early learning of the significance of words occurs is not at all a simple one. In the first place, it does not really begin with words at all, but with gestures, facial expressions, tone of voice, and perhaps many other elements of a total situation in which a word is used. The meaning of that total situation to the infant is essentially emotional: it represents comfort or discomfort, satisfaction or frustration. The infant's responses, then, are "feeling" responses. As particular situations repeat themselves in the daily cycle and routine of the infant, and as the same sounds ("words") are used consistently in given situations, the words come to stand for the rest of the elements which go to make up the total situation, and which bring forth that feeling associated with it for the infant. Lewis has expressed this process as follows:

> We have seen that the beginning of a child's responses to speech emerges in his development as a result of a number of varied factors. As always, there is a convergence between what the child does and what others do. First, he has long been responding with expressions of feeling to the sound of the human voice. Then, through babbling and rudimentary imitation, he has begun to pay attention to particular words—or, rather, particular phonetic patterns. Now he hears one of these phonetic patterns, a word or phrase, spoken by his mother in a certain intonation to which he has already been responding in ways that are expressive of the feelings that the intonation arouses in him. The word comes to him regularly in a particular situation which has emotional significance for him. As he hears the word he sees the play of expression on his mother's face, her gestures, and her movements; and all this happens in a situation in which distress or contentment, sight, sound, smell, touch, and much else are richly mingled. As the word recurs for him with varying intonations, its phonetic pattern takes over for him much of the

> expressiveness that hitherto has been held in the intonational pattern. Added to all this, the very form of the word as a typical fragment of baby-language will have a special place in the child's own speech-behaviour and his experiences (14, pp. 77–78).

In this thought-provoking and carefully worked out analysis of how children learn to understand and to speak words, Lewis has placed particular emphasis on the importance of talking to infants. While the assumption that "they can't understand our words" may largely be true at first, there is evidence of the value of being stimulated, right from the start, with words from a loving mother. It is through just this very process, in fact, that the infant begins to associate words with the vital emotional experiences of his life and thereby to develop a powerful motivation to participate, himself, in the use of language to convey significant feelings. Needless to say, his ability to differentiate words and understand meanings is no guarantee that he will always abide by them! Nothing could be more unrealistic than such expectations. Long after he "understands" the meaning of "No, no!" he may be quite inconsistent and irregular in his response to it. And of course, any mother can recount the many instances in which the infant is asked to perform some amazing feat of intelligence to impress the visitors ("pat-a-cake, darling," "Wave bye-bye, sweetheart") only to have him stare blankly at the strangers in his most uncomprehending manner. This lack of consistent performance is not at all difficult to account for in the strangeness of the surroundings and people present, and is certainly not evidence of lack of understanding on the part of the infant.

As he progresses, the infant's understanding of words is greatly facilitated and broadened by his own efforts to make word sounds. The meaning of the sound "Mama," which is found, incidentally, in infant speech in most all languages, is revised for a baby as he uses it and as significant people in his life respond to his use of it. The other criteria of language development in infancy—pronouncing words clearly enough for others to understand them, and with appropriate meaning—have been studied a great deal by researchers. In spite of this there is no perfect agreement on when the infant really says his first word. His progress toward making controlled sounds that can be understood by others is very gradual. It begins with the almost formless sounds of the neonatal period. The birth cry itself is often cited as the beginning, since it is the first time the infant's vocal apparatus is in use, and since it affords him the first opportunity to hear his own voice. However, there is no reason to place great significance on the birth cry, aside from its possible physiological and physical function in the initiation of respiration.

During the second and third months small, throaty, gurgling noises, while the infant is asleep or awake, and the beginnings of cooing and primitive babbling form the vocal exercises of most babies. By the fourth month, cooing may be observed as the response to another person's presence or attention, or to music or other sounds. Babbling may begin in earnest about this time, although there is considerable room for individual variation in the age at which it gets underway and its extent. For some infants, babbling is an extremely active and enthusiastic enterprise, and it may be observed to occur regularly at certain times of the day, in keeping with the daily routine of eating, sleeping, or wakefulness. One infant of 4 months had established a consistent routine of being "burped" after his breakfast, and then of lying contentedly on his back in the crib for a period of from 15 minutes to a half hour, during which he would babble vigorously with apparent delight. His parents observed that the babbling increased and the baby's apparent enthusiasm increased when they hovered over the crib and talked to him. The experience of these parents is not unusual. Babbling, sometimes thought of as useless and meaningless, should be recognized as a significant step, valuable and important in its own right as well as a paving of the way for the next higher stages of speech. The infant is stimulated by his own speech sounds, is encouraged to continue them, and engages in exercise of the entire vocal apparatus at the same time. Furthermore, his babbling has a natural appeal for most parents, and the response from them results in increased social stimulation which adds to the infant's well-being.

By 6 or 7 months the typical infant is vocalizing several well defined syllables, according to Gesell (9) and other investigators. Sometime during the 6- to 9-month period there may be beginnings of imitation, of efforts to duplicate the sounds he hears others make. At 11 or 12 months he may be successful in imitating such repetitious syllables as "Dada" or "Mama." A number of infant intelligence tests are based on the assumption that the year-old infant may be expected to have one or two words in his vocabulary. However, the failure of an infant to say words clearly by the age of 12 months should not be taken as evidence, by itself, of mental retardation. There are many reasons why a particular child may not be using any words at all at this age, and some of these reasons have little or nothing to do with his intelligence.

The second year is marked by considerable growth in the ability to form words clearly. This is a stage of learning to approximate the sounds of the mother tongue, and it involves not only learning how to combine sounds and to make them clearly, but also the dropping out of certain sounds that are not part of the language. As Lewis points out:

> . . . an English child does not normally hear the sound *ch* that occurs in the Scottish word *loch*. But careful observations assure us that every English child, like every other child, says *ch* during his earliest months as one of his comfort noises and in his babbling. Yet because this sound is not heard by him in the baby-language spoken to him, his use of it is not reinforced; it ceases to occur in his babbling. The time will come when he will be "unable to make it," as those who try to teach English school-children the German word *doch* know only too well. Asked to imitate *doch*, an English child of twelve will usually say *dock*, giving the nearest sound from his own repertory. With toil and trouble he may at last succeed in saying *ch*; yet at the age of six months he said it spontaneously (14, p. 92).

The second year is also the time when the infant will be observed to use a single word to express a complete thought. This is sometimes referred to as the "one-word sentence." When the 18-month-old uses the word "ball," McCarthy (16) notes, he may mean "There is the ball," or he may mean "Where is the ball?" or "I want the ball," etc. However, these first words are more the expression of emotion than the names of objects. Wishes and feelings of the infant are the primary motivating force behind this early talking; it is understandable that the words themselves are essentially expressive of feeling, as opposed to intellectual ideas. The vocabulary of the infant increases rapidly during the second year. Smith (22) observed an increase from 3 words at 12 months, to 19 words at 15 months, to 22 words at 18 months, to 118 words at 21 months, to 272 words at 24 months. Of course, these average figures were based on a small number of infants at each age, and give only a very rough index of the speed of growth in vocabulary. Incidentally, the comparatively small gain between 15 and 18 months coincides with a time of rapid motor development. It is not uncommon for the infant, at the time he is taking his first steps and learning how to balance on his own two feet, to slow down temporarily in his language development. It is as if he is using all his available energy to become accomplished at the thing that counts most at the moment, which is walking. When the walking behavior is pretty well under control, having become an "automatic" habit as it usually does by 18 months, the language development spurts ahead rapidly, as Smith's figures indicate.

Not only does the baby progress rapidly in acquiring new words, but in the last three months of the second year he begins to combine words to form larger segments of thought. By 24 months, according to Gesell (9), he uses simple phrases and sentences. This more complex kind of language behavior calls for mastery not only of word meanings, but of key relationships among words, and their appropriate use for the expression of ideas. The use of pronouns and prepositions, which are useful in the clear expression of ideas, also has its beginning about the end of the second year. Accuracy of usage, like accuracy of pronunciation, still has a long way to go, of course, following the infantile period. Nevertheless, we can conclude that the period of infancy provides for the remarkable achievement of true language, in accordance with all three major criteria: comprehension of meaning, clear pronunciation, and meaningful usage.

Beginnings of the Self The modern scientist of human growth, development, and personality is likely to place considerable emphasis on the achievement of "selfhood." Man's self-awareness is a unique quality that motivates him to great achievements and contributes immeasurably to his ability to organize and maintain a coherent society. Without self-awareness it is doubtful that there could be any sense of social responsibility. Thus, the foundation for cooperative endeavor in a free society is to be discovered in man's awareness of himself as an individual. What are the sources and early beginnings of this "self?" A truly exhaustive study of this question would take us into a number of quite different fields of inquiry: embryology and neurology, to learn of the beginnings of the central nervous system, which eventually gives the human the capacity to react to himself as a part of his world but separate from it; psychology, whose emphasis on perception, motivation, and learning would enable us to see how the individual infant's capacity for learning enables him gradually to perceive himself in relation to the objects and people in his world; sociology, whose emphasis on interpersonal relationships would help us to see how the individual infant's beginning self-awareness is influenced by the presence of significant others; and anthropology, the insights of which might allow us to understand the role of culture in determining the development of a true sense of selfhood. Quite possibly some other sciences would be involved as well. While we cannot do justice to the unique insights of all these fields, and their contributions to an understanding of self-development, we can summarize briefly the major "high points" in the development of self-awareness, as it occurs in the early months of life.

The newborn infant is not differentiated, psychologically, from his mother. That is, he does not yet conceive of himself as a person, and certainly not as a "person" separate from other "persons." The beginnings of the differentiation process that enable him to achieve this separateness are transitory, fleeting sensations reaching his brain, based on physical and physiological changes from the internal and external environments. Only gradually do these fleeting sensations become organized into meaningful patterns. They occur through a kind of repetition of sameness of stimulation and response, of frustration and satisfaction, of pain and recovery, of excitement and calm. At first, each stimulation has significance only for its own sake and is isolated from past and future stimulations. In a sense, the newborn infant lives only in the present—and frustration and satisfaction can occur only in the present. With the establishment of routine—his own biological rhythms as well as the complex of social and physical routines of his home and family environment—there is the beginning of carry-over and the emergence of "past" and "future" orientations as well as "present." It is the infant's innate capacity to respond to repeated stimulation by changing its behavior—in other words, by learning—that initiates this original carry-over from the past to the present. It is the dawning of a primitive, vague awareness best described as "This is happening again." But "this" is more than just happening in isolation; it is happening in a setting. Whatever "this" is—a sensation of pain or discomfort, a feeling of release from tension, the satisfying warm flow of milk in the mouth, a warm moist sensation in the diaper region—it occurs not independently of the other events and objects in the world at the moment, but in articulation with them. Whatever sensations are coming from the infant's total world at that moment are associated as part of one big experience.

Upon sufficient repetition of a given total experience, one element of that experience may come to represent, or stand for, the total. The infant responds to one part of it—say, to the sound of mother's approach—in the same way as he did to the total. Thus, even when it is not feeding time, the infant may react to mother's approaching footsteps by active sucking movements, because the total pattern of stimulation and response has been repeated often enough in the past for them to be associated in the infant's experience. Of more fundamental importance, however, than learning to associate any particular ideas or events, is the more general effect this repetition of routine experiences has on personality development. In the routine of daily living there is a continuing cycle of need arousal and need fulfillment. The long-range effect of this cycle, beyond its immediate implications for survival and well-being, is the development of a general outlook, or expectation, about life experiences. Erikson (6) describes that outlook as a *sense of trust,* which he contrasts sharply with the disturbed or distorted kind of outlook—basic mistrust—stemming from irregular need satisfaction in infancy. This notion of trust has far-reaching implications for the development of a mature sense of selfhood. It is the cornerstone of the healthy personality. Erikson says of trust:

> . . . *the firm establishment of enduring patterns for the balance of basic trust over basic mistrust* is the first task of the budding personality and therefore first of all a task for maternal care. But it must be said that the *amount of trust* derived from earliest infantile experience does not seem to depend on absolute *quantities of food or demonstrations of love* but rather on the *quality* of the maternal relationship. Mothers create a sense of trust in their children by that kind of administration which in its firm quality combines sensitive care of the baby's individual needs and a firm sense of personal trustworthiness within the trusted framework of their community's life style. (This forms the basis in the child for a sense of identity which will later combine a sense of being "all right," of being oneself, and of becoming what other people trust one will become.) Parents must not only have certain ways of guiding by prohibition and permission; they must also be able to represent to the child a deep, an almost somatic conviction that there is meaning to what they are doing (6, p. 195).

Another line of investigation is that followed by Harlow (12) in his research with infant monkeys. In Harlow's studies, a question of primary importance is the role of early sensory experiences, particularly in relation to the mother, in establishing affectional relationships. How does the infant come to "love" its mother? As a matter of fact, this early affectional relationship is not truly love for another person at all, since the other person is not differentiated from self in the infant's thinking at this point. Nevertheless, the early experience of a loving relationship has been shown to be a vital one for the development of the capacity to be a loving person in later life. Harlow's experiments with infant monkeys demonstrate the importance of texture and touch as a means of sensory gratification. The association of the touch experiences with the nursing situation appears to be an important feature of the early learning of love for the mother and dependence on her.

It is not always easy to sort out the features of the mother-infant relationship that are really essential to the development of healthy personality. Ribble (19), Spitz (23), Bowlby (3), and others have placed emphasis on the need of an infant for an intimate, one-to-one relationship in which a great deal of attention and "tender loving care" is consistently provided. Such an emphasis, along with its implication that any lack of such consistent, tender loving care will result in serious impairment of development, has led to considerable concern among parents, and in professional circles as well, for infants who cannot receive the most desirable kind of mothering. As one example of this concern, infants who had been placed in college home-management houses to provide an educational experience in infant care for home economics students were said to be deprived, thereby, of normal mothering. In at least one institution the infants were removed from the home-management houses on the grounds that it was harmful to their development.

Subsequent research findings by Gardner, Hawkes, and Burchinal (7) indicate that fears of this kind are largely without foundation. Not only is the human infant remarkably sturdy, physically and psychologically, but we know now that there are many different ways in which his fundamental needs can be satisfied. Warmth and consistency of mothering are, of course, important considerations. However, during the first few weeks and months of life an infant does not seem to be harmed by being cared for by a variety of mother-figures, even inexperienced ones. Similarly, the research just cited indicates that infants who live in good foster homes, or who are adopted, do not necessarily suffer from the experience. These early experiences, however, do form the basic foundation for the later development of a healthy sense of self, and for achieving a positive, creative, socially desirable personality. Thus they are of vital importance.

For our purposes at the moment, we may divide the infancy period into two major phases and note the crucial developments during each of these: (1) the early dependency period, in which need gratification is essentially provided from the "outside" upon the infant's demand, with no effort on his part other than to make the demand known; and (2) the later infancy period—particularly the second year—in which his own behavior becomes instrumental in the direct satisfaction of his needs. The distinction between these two phases in early personality development is important. It emphasizes a dramatic learning process that must occur and does, ordinarily, during this period. The learning, summarized very briefly, is to use one's own resources in the never ending struggle to satisfy needs. Complete failure in this vital learning task is not a common occurrence, fortunately. But there are degrees of success, and the infant who is overly controlled, inhibited, prevented from exploring his environment, and frustrated in his efforts to develop his own resources is, to that degree, destined to find the growth tasks ahead more difficult, frightening, and disturbing. On the other hand, the infant who is allowed and encouraged to explore his world, to meet the obstacles and to cope with them, to make use of his body in relating himself at ever higher levels to the objects, persons, and situations he finds there is fortunate indeed. He has an excellent foundation for the tasks of growth which lie ahead.

SUMMARY

The neonatal period is critical in that the baby needs to establish physiological stability with respect to basic bodily functions. There are wide individual differences in newborn babies, but the normal, full-term neonate is characterized by many resources for intellectual, emotional, and social behavior. His early behavior is largely reflexive, and the reflex functioning of his nervous system is essential to his survival and healthy growth.

The period of infancy, extending from the end of the first postnatal month to the end of the second year, is a time of major accomplishments: rapid physical growth, the achievement of upright locomotion, the accomplishment of much learning based on sensory-motor coordination, the elaboration of emotional behavior, the achievement of true language, and very significant beginnings of personality formation in the form of a sense of self.

Current techniques in the evaluation of infant development emphasize individual differences, and a respect for the child's individual growth pattern, as opposed to a simple comparison of the infant's progress with norms or averages for the population.

REFERENCES

1. Bakwin, H., "Emotional deprivation in infants," *J. Pediatr.*, 1949; **35**:512–521.
2. Bayley, Nancy, "The development of motor abilities during the first three years," *Monogr. Soc. Res. Child Develpm.*, 1935, **1**, (1): 1–26.
3. Bowlby, J., *Maternal care and mental health.* Monogr. Series, No. 2, Geneva: World Health Organization, 1951.
4. Breckenridge, M. E., and Murphy, M. N., *Rand, Sweeny, and Vincent's growth and development of the young child*, Philadelphia: Saunders, 1958.
5. Bridges, K. M. B., "Emotional development in early infancy," *Child Develpm.*, 1932, **3**:324–334.
6. Erikson, E. H., "Growth and crises of the 'healthy personality' " in C. Kluckhohn, H. A. Murray, and D. M. Schneider (eds.), *Personality in nature, society, and culture*, 2nd ed., New York: Knopf, 1953, pp. 185–225.
7. Gardner, D. B., Hawkes, G. R., and Burchinal, L., "Noncontinuous mothering in infancy and development in later childhood," *Child Develpm.*, 1961, **32**:pp. 225–234.
8. Gentry, E. F., and Aldrich, C. A., "Rooting reflex in the newborn infant: Incidence and effect on it of sleep," *Amer. J. Dis. Child.*, 1948, **75**:pp. 528–539.
9. Gesell, A., and Amatruda, C. S., *Developmental diagnosis*, 2nd ed., New York: Hoeber-Harper, 1947.
10. Gesell, A., and Ilg, F. L., *Child development*, New York: Harper, 1949. "The Little Elfman" quoted from John Kendrick Bangs, *The Foothills of Parnassus*, New York: Macmillan, 1914. Reprinted by permission of Francis H. Bangs.
11. Halverson, H. M., "An experimental study of prehension in infants by means of systematic cinema records," *Genet. Psychol. Monog.*, 1931, **10**: 107-286.
12. Harlow, H. F., "Primary affectional patterns in primates," *Amer. J. Orthopsychiat.*, 1960, **30**: 676–684.
13. James, W., *Principles of psychology* (2 vols.), New York: Holt, 1890.
14. Lewis, M. M., *How children learn to speak*, New York: Basic Books, 1959.

15. Lombard, O. M., "Breadth of bone and muscle by age and sex in childhood," *Child Develpm.*, 1950, **21**:229–239.
16. McCarthy, Dorothea, "Language development in children," in L. Carmichael, (ed.), *Manual of child psychology*, New York: Wiley, 1954, pp. 492–630.
17. McGraw, Myrtle B., *Growth: A study of Johnny and Jimmy*, New York: Appleton-Century-Crofts, 1935.
18. Pratt, K. C., "The neonate," in L. Carmichael (ed.), *Manual of child psychology*, New York: Wiley, 1954, pp. 215–291.
19. Ribble, Margaretha, *The rights of infants*, New York: Columbia Univ. Press, 1943.
20. Sherman, M., "The differentiation of emotional responses in infants: II. The ability of observers to judge the emotional characteristics of the crying of infants, and of the voice of an adult," *J. Compar. Psychol.*, 1927, 7:335–351.
21. Shirley, Mary M., *The first two years; A study of twenty-five babies*, Minneapolis: Univ. of Minnesota Press, 1931.
22. Smith, M. E., "An investigation of the development of the sentence and the extent of vocabulary in young children," *Univ. Iowa Stud. Child Welf.*, 1926, **3**:(5).
23. Spitz, R. A., "Anaclitic depression," *Psychoanal. Stud. Child*, 1946, **2**:313–342.
24. Stitt, Pauline G., "Progress during infancy," in H. C. Stuart and D. G. Prugh (eds.), *The healthy child*, Cambridge, Mass.: Harvard, 1960, pp. 92–109.
25. Stuart, H. C., and Prugh, D. G. (eds.), *The healthy child*, Cambridge, Mass.: Harvard, 1960.
26. Thompson, Helen, "Physical growth," in L. Carmichael (ed.), *Manual of child psychology*, 2nd ed., New York: Wiley, 1954, pp. 292–334.
27. Watson, E. H., and Lowrey, G. H., *Growth and development of children*, 4th ed., Chicago: Year Book Medical, 1962.
28. Watson, J. B., *Psychology from the standpoint of a behaviorist*, Philadelphia: Lippincott, 1919.
29. Wetzel, N. C., "Baby grid: An application of the grid technique to growth and development in infants," *J. Pediatr.*, 1946, **29**:439.

Part III ❧ ASPECTS OF DEVELOPMENT IN THE PRESCHOOL YEARS

The series of chapters that form Part III are an attempt to portray certain dominating themes in the behavior and development of the child from 2 to 6 years of age. These dominating themes—physical and motor development, language and communication, intelligent behavior, emotional development, and the emergence of selfhood—are inextricably interwoven in the total growth of the whole child. Their separation into chapters is justified only as a means to give proper attention and emphasis to each aspect.

Observation of individual children while studying Part III will assist the student immeasurably in maintaining a realistic sense of the relationship of each aspect of growth to the total, functioning child. Perhaps most important of all, the student should note the heavy involvement of the child's self-concept (Chapter Ten) with the aspects of growth described in Chapters Five through Nine.

CHAPTER FIVE

What are the most important changes in body size and proportion between ages 2 and 6? ∽ How has x-ray photography helped us to understand physical development? ∽ What are the major physical growth needs and health requirements of the preschool child? ∽ How does the child develop immunity to infectious disease? ∽ What are reasonable goals in the prevention of childhood accidents?

PHYSICAL GROWTH

MANY PEOPLE WHO THINK SERIOUSLY about children have tended, unfortunately, to separate the child's "mind" from his "body," and have thought of these as somewhat independent aspects of the child. The physical body and its development have been regarded, too often, as a subject for discussion quite apart from such mental attributes as thinking, feeling, perceiving, and valuing. Today's child-development specialist is aware of the complex interrelatedness of physical development with the so-called "mental" aspects of the total child; he does not try to separate these component parts artificially. The interdependence of feelings and emotions, attitudes and values, thinking and reasoning, and physical and motor development makes it unrealistic to try to maintain a separation of the child's mind from his body.

In studying this chapter, then, the student should remember that a brief concentration on physical aspects of development is intended merely to give emphasis to this aspect of total development. A separate chapter devoted to this subject should not imply that the child's physical growth is independent of the rest of his development. Indeed, the complex interaction of physical and other aspects of growth is a subject that could occupy the pages of many textbooks. It is merely for convenience that we now concentrate our attention on the physical aspects of the growing child.

SIGNIFICANCE OF PHYSICAL DEVELOPMENT

The term *growth* is often used in a limited way—to refer to increases in size and weight. *Development* is sometimes contrasted with it as a term that implies increasing complexity of functioning or of behavior. One leading authority on physical growth, Meredith, has argued that there is no useful distinction between the two terms and that they may be used interchangeably. His definition of growth is appropriate: "The entire series of anatomic and physiologic changes taking place between the beginning of prenatal life and the close of senility" (8, p. 445).

In this chapter we shall be concerned with all those changes in body size, proportions, and functioning which occur during the preschool period. It matters little whether we refer to these as "growth" or as "development," so long as we understand we are including more things than mere increases in body tissue. Nevertheless, changes in gross body size are important. They provide a rough index of nutritional status and general health, and extremes of rapid or slow growth give early warning of certain abnormalities of development. A knowledge of the normal changes in physical stature can be of practical help to adults who deal with children, for these changes reflect parallel alterations in the child's physical needs for food intake, for exercise, and for rest. If further justification for study of the physical growth of children were needed, we might even cite the argument that the child's psychological view of his world is dependent on the angle from which he views it. Thus his height may be one determiner of his "point of view," in a very real sense. A little later we shall have occasion to see that physical conditions of a variety of kinds may have important influences on intellectual, emotional, and social behavior.

CHANGES IN BODY MEASUREMENTS

During the preschool period the child is growing at a relatively slower, steadier rate than during the period of infancy. His average gain in weight, per year, is about 4 or 5 pounds (Watson and Lowry, 12). The typical 2-year-old American child weighs about 27 pounds. By age 3 he has gone up to 32 pounds. By age 4 he is about 36½, and at age 5 around 41½ pounds. There is not a large difference between boys and girls during this period, although boys are just slightly heavier, on the average, than girls at each age level from 2 through 5. It must be remembered, of course, that there are wide variations around these average figures, and that variation is not the same as abnormality. Changes in body length—or height—follow the same general rule: growth is slower and steadier during the preschool years than during infancy. The 2-year-old is about 34 inches tall; by age 3 he is nearly 38 inches; by 4 he is 40.5 inches, and by 5 he is about 43 inches (12). There is variation among normal children in height, too, just as there is with weight. However, fewer than 3 percent of children will be less than 40 inches tall at age 5, and fewer than 3 percent will be taller than 47 inches. Thus, the variation is within a fairly narrow range. For weight, by comparison, the average figure for 5-year-olds is 41 pounds. However, as many as 10 percent of normal children may weigh less than 35 or 36 pounds, and another 10 percent may weigh 48 pounds or more (12). It is evident that weight is a more variable quality than height. Figures 5.1 and 5.2 illustrate clearly the average increases in height and weight for boys and girls, respectively, from birth through age 6. These figures also show the decreasing rate of growth that occurs as the child moves from infancy into the preschool years. The range of variation around the average tends to increase, however, for both sexes.

CHANGES IN PROPORTIONS

Changes in body proportions are of as much significance as increases in size and weight. The typical change occurring during the preschool period is a "lengthening out" process as the child emerges from babyhood into true childhood. This includes a considerable loss of the baby fat associated with infancy, as well as actual lengthening of the torso and of the long bones of the arms and legs. Thus the child takes on a leaner, "harder" appearance. This is accounted for partly by the incessant activity and natural exercise of the healthy child during the preschool period. There is a heavy demand on energy for the sake of activity during this time. Changes in body proportion are the result of differing rates of growth for different parts of the body. Analysis of the total process of physical growth from conception to maturity would reveal that different parts and systems of the body approach their own level of maturity and functional capacity at quite different rates, thereby achieving maturity at different periods in the life of the growing individual.

The science of body measurements, known as *anthropometry*, is a

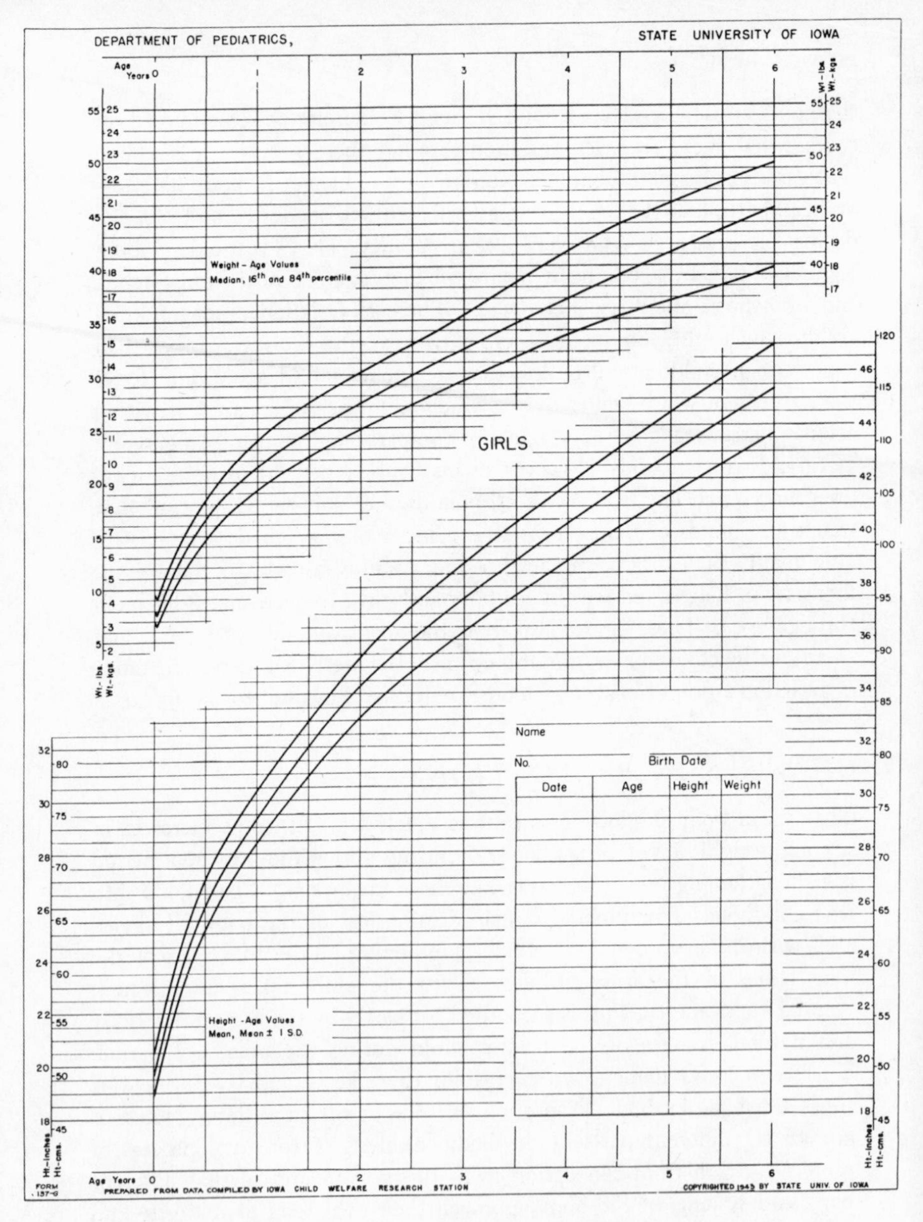

Fig. 5.1. Height-age and weight-age relationships for boys from birth through 6 years. (From data compiled by Iowa Child Welfare Research Station. Copyright 1943 by State University of Iowa.)

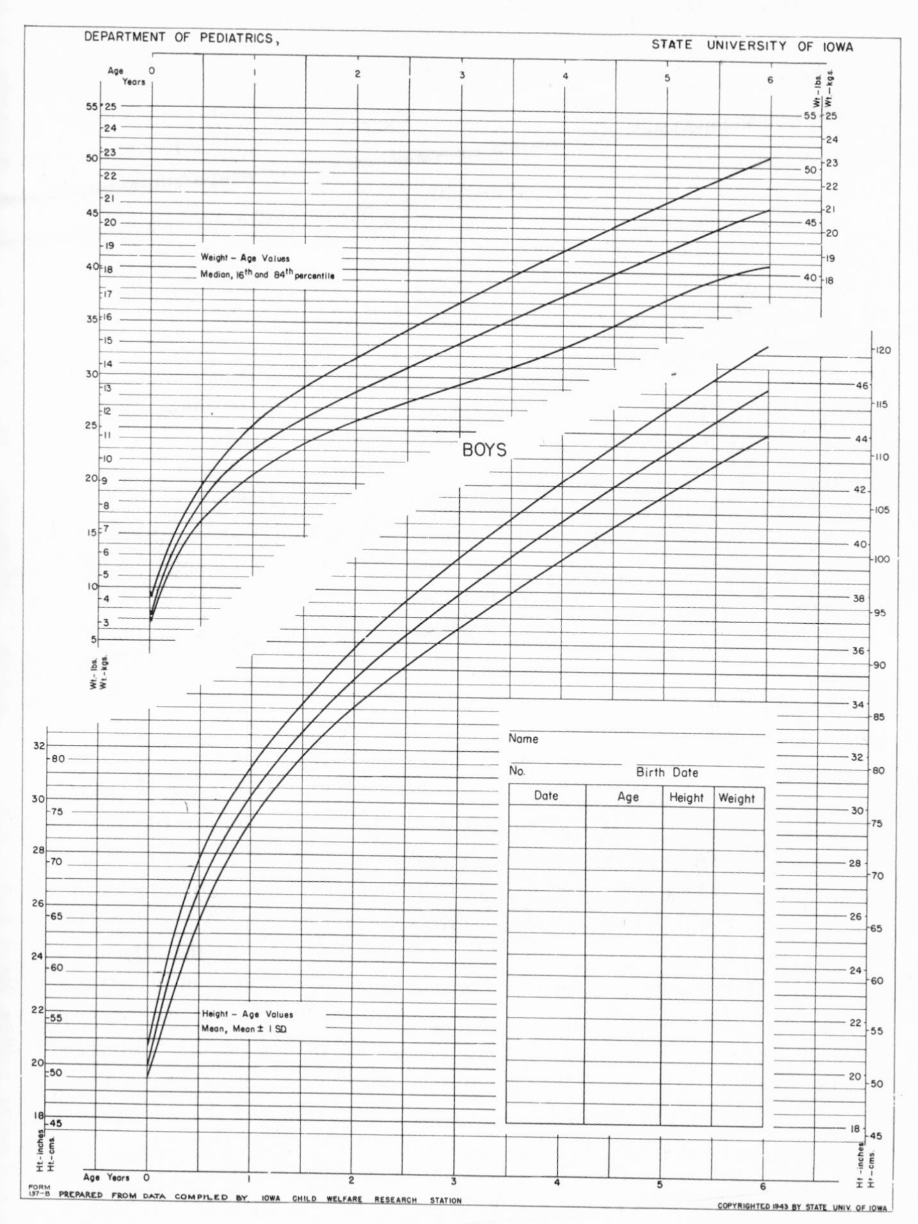

Fig. 5.2. Height-age and weight-age relationships for girls from birth through 6 years. (From data compiled by Iowa Child Welfare Research Station. Copyright 1943 by State University of Iowa.)

highly developed and complex field of study by itself. Standard measurements of height and weight, used for years to form a crude estimate of physical development, are merely two indices of growth. When combined with measurements of chest and head circumference, hip width, arm and leg length, sitting height, calf circumference, and measures of the thickness of subcutaneous tissue on the back or calf of the leg, such measures can provide a much more precise index of the physical and nutritional status of the child.

Skeletal Development Much of the change in body proportions that occurs during the growing period is attributable, naturally, to the manner in which the skeleton develops. Since different parts of the skeleton grow at different rates, and some bones are growing very rapidly while others are not, it is quite understandable that body proportions change as a consequence. We have already noted that the big change during the preschool years in body build is a "lengthening out" process. This is explained, in part, by the fact that the long bones are growing more rapidly in comparison with the rest of the body than was true during infancy.

The growth of the skeleton is an interesting phenomenon in its own right, and some of the implications of skeletal development are only now beginning to be understood. Bone development is far more complex than simple increases in the size of bones already present. During the total growth period there are changes in the number of bones in the body (both increases and decreases) and in the quality or composition of bone tissue, as well as in shape and size. Most bones have their beginnings in the form of cartilage, which is a fairly soft, plastic material—the cartilage in the tip of one's nose gives a good example of the flexibility of this material. Cartilage, which is present in the general shape of the bones that are yet to come, provides a kind of model of bone formation. Within the cartilage, ossification centers appear. These are points at which calcium and other mineral salts are deposited, resulting in the hardening of mature bone tissue. Thompson (10) reports over 800 such ossification centers in the human body. Half of them do not make their appearance until after birth, and some do not appear until adolescence.

In the long bones of arms and legs, growth takes place as follows: the cartilage increases in length and at the same time ossification (hardening, with depositing of calcium) occurs, beginning with ossification centers within the cartilage and proceeding toward the extremities. These central ossification centers form the *diaphyses*, or main portion of the long bone. Additional ossification centers appear at the ends of the cartilage, which form the *epiphyses*. Growth of the bone continues so long as the cartilage between the diaphysis and epiphysis continues to grow. When the cartilage reaches adult length, it ceases to grow and the diaphysis and epiphysis merge and unite to form a continuous and solid bone structure.

The development of bone tissue occurs in a remarkably regular, predictable manner. In recent years there has been an accumulation of much important data on bone development, most of it based on the use of X-ray photography in one form or another. These data have enabled the child-development student to understand with much greater clarity this important index of body development. The bones of the wrist and hand, especially, have been given intensive study, because they are readily accessible to X-ray, because they show a consistent regularity of patterning in their development through the growing years, and because they are a reliable index of the development of the rest of the skeleton. The most dependable and accurate assessments of the growth progress of the individual child are made by means of X-ray photography. While this is not necessary for ordinary purposes with most children, it is an extremely important source of the information we have about the course of normal physical growth. Garn states the argument for such measuring procedures very forcefully:

> At present, the only measure of maturity truly useful from childhood through adolescence is a hand-wrist X-ray. Properly taken, the gonadal exposure from such an X-ray is under 0.001 mr, equivalent to a few minutes natural background radiation, that is the amount absorbed in a few minutes of normal living! The information from such a radiograph is not equalled by any other measure we know of now (3, p. 31).

X-ray photographs of the wrist and hand bones of preschool children illustrate rather clearly the progress of skeletal development from ages 2 through 5. Figure 5.3 shows how the ossification process is occurring during this period.

One reason for the use of X-ray photography in assessing the physical development of children is that skeletal development is so closely related

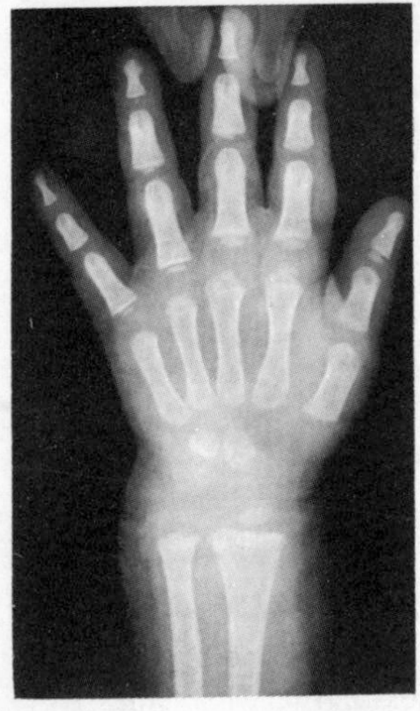

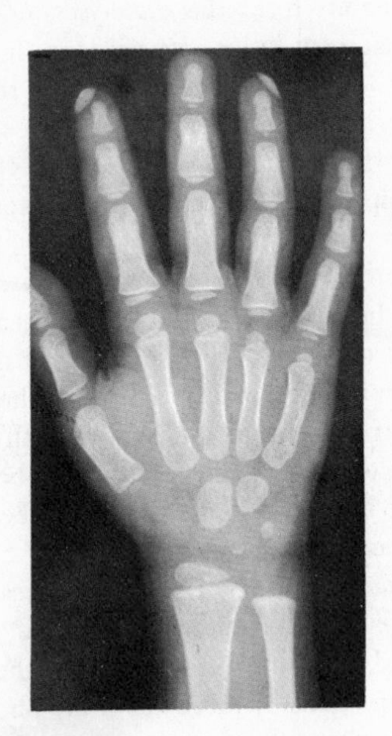

B

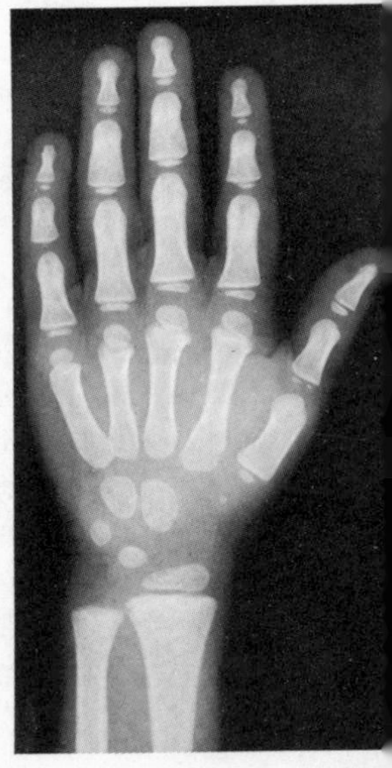

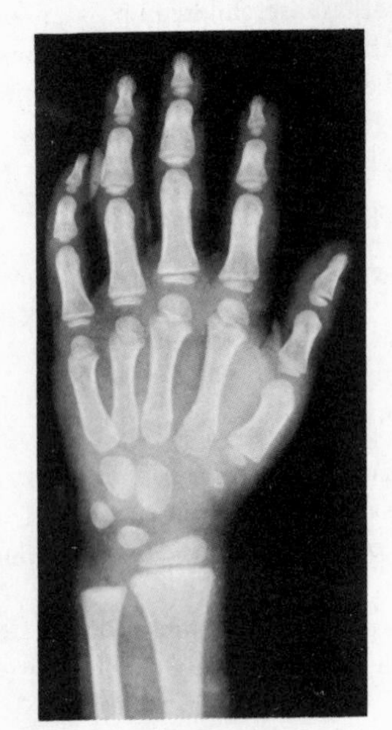

D

Fig. 5.3. Standard X-ray photographs of the wrists and hands of preschool children: A, at 2 years; B, at 3 years; C, at 4 years; and D, at 5 years. (Reprinted from *Radiographic atlas of skeletal development of the hand and wrist,* Second Edition, by William Walter Greulich and S. Idell Pyle with the permission of the publishers, Stanford University Press, © 1959 by the Board of Trustees of the Leland Stanford Junior University.)

to over-all physical growth. Conditions that affect that over-all growth leave their mark, sometimes permanently, on bone tissue. Greulich and Pyle (4), in discussing this matter, note that the development of individual bones can be impaired by illness, especially if the illness occurs at certain stages of bone development. These authorities also suggest that bone "scars" or transverse lines across the long bones, readily visible in X-ray films, may be the result of a period of serious illness and thus represent periods during which growth in the length of the long bone was interrupted. These same authors studied large groups of Japanese children who lived in Hiroshima and Nagasaki when those cities were destroyed by atomic bombs during World War II. The studies were made about two years after the children had been exposed to atomic radiation. A large percentage of the children showed bone scarring, located at about the same distance from the ends of the bones, in children of comparable ages. Such scarring was considered by the authors to be the result of the radiation and other injuries suffered at the time of the atomic bombing. The impact of dietary deficiencies and other severe illnesses on the growth of the young child can be demonstrated, then, with this very useful X-ray technique.

DEVELOPMENT OF THE TEETH

Development and eruption of the teeth also provide an index of the over-all physical development of the child. There is an orderly "timetable" and sequence in tooth eruption. The deciduous, or "baby" teeth, begin to calcify—that is, become hard—during the fifth month of prenatal life. The process of calcification is not complete, however, until about 3 years of age. The appearance of the first tooth, an event creating considerable excitement on the part of the parents, usually occurs at about 6 months of age. However, in extreme cases it may not make its appearance until as late as a year, while at the opposite extreme there are numerous cases on record of infants who display their first tooth along with their birth cry.

These first teeth are shed between the ages of 6 and 12, usually, as the permanent teeth replace them (see Table 5.1). The fact that they will be lost has led some adults to assume that care of the baby teeth is unimportant during the preschool years. For a number of reasons, however, it is vitally important that these first teeth have the best possible

TABLE 5.1. *Time of Eruption and Shedding of Deciduous Teeth*

	Eruption		Shedding	
	Lower	Upper	Lower	Upper
	Age (Months)		Age (Years)	
Central incisor	6	7½	6	7½
Lateral incisor	7	9	7	8
Cuspid	16	18	9½	11½
First molar	12	14	10	10½
Second molar	20	24	11	10½
Incisors	Range ± 2 mos.		Range ± 6 mos.	
Molars	Range ± 4 mos.			

SOURCE: J. B. Richmond, I. Schour, and M. Massler, "The Oral Cavity," in W. E. Nelson (ed.), *Textbook of Pediatrics* (6th ed.), Philadelphia: W. B. Saunders Co., 1954. Copyright 1944 by the American Dental Association. Reprinted by permission of the American Dental Association.

care. One reason is that the temporary teeth play an important role in the positioning of the permanent teeth. A second reason is simply that proper chewing of food is important in the preschool years, just as in later years, and the teeth need to be in good condition for effective mastication.

MUSCULAR DEVELOPMENT

Body movement is produced and controlled by the action of the skeletal muscles. The alternating contraction and relaxation of these muscles, in interrelated systems under the stimulation of the nervous system, provide the power, strength, and speed of body movements. Since these body movements are essential to a host of other aspects of development—motor skills, intellectual growth and problem-solving, and even social and emotional development—a basic understanding of the action and development of muscle systems is important. The voluntary muscles, those over which the child acquires more or less conscious control, are distributed rather generally over the body, mechanically attached to the skeleton by ligaments. They generally operate in pairs, with one muscle contracting while its opposing muscle relaxes, thus providing for a kind of reciprocal action which makes movement possible. The strength and size of muscles for a given age varies considerably from one child to another based, to a great extent, on inherited genetic factors. Nevertheless, nutrition, exercise, and general body health have important influences on muscular development.

Muscle fibers are present in the child's body even before birth. They are relatively undeveloped during the period of infancy, however, which helps account for the infant's lack of strength and absence of body control. During the preschool period the growth of muscle tissue is nearly proportional to the total increase in body weight. Muscle tissue makes up a significant part of body weight. Although it is a smaller proportion in early childhood than later, muscles constitute between one fourth and one third of body weight during the preschool years.

The processes of muscle growth include not only increases in gross size, but also important changes in structure. The preschool child's muscular system is composed of water (about 72 percent) and solids (about 28 percent). Zubek and Solberg (14) report that it is only much later, during puberty, that these percentages change significantly, with the proportion of solid material increasing and that of water decreasing. Because of the high water content in the child's muscles, and also because the muscles are not yet as firmly attached structurally to the skeletal system, muscle fatigue is a very significant feature of the life and routines of the preschooler. He tires easily, and adequate rest periods during the day as well as sufficient sleep at night should be important features of his daily routine.

Even in early childhood there are important differences not only in the amount and size of muscle tissue, but in strength and endurance. There are also variations from time to time in the same child, depending on his general physical well-being and nutritional status. During the preschool years there are only slight differences in muscular development which can be accounted for by the sex of the child. Hurlock (6) reports that children with broad, thick muscles are stronger, while those with smaller muscles are generally more agile and better coordinated.

PHYSICAL GROWTH NEEDS AND HEALTH REQUIREMENTS OF THE PRESCHOOL CHILD

The preschool years are of special significance in the establishment of physical health, for a number of reasons. First, growth is still progressing rapidly—although less rapidly than during infancy—and, at the same time, energy demands are high as the child's activity increases and as he explores his world through a wider range and variety of activities. Furthermore, he is not yet mature or experienced enough to be aware of the nature of his own bodily needs, nor to take responsibility for his own health routines without continuous guidance from understanding adults. For these reasons we should turn our attention briefly to a consideration of the preschool child's particular health requirements—adequate nutrition, exercise, rest and sleep, and freedom from infection. In addition, we shall consider in this section the problems of safety and of accident prevention, as these are vital factors in the health and physical well-being of the preschooler.

Nutrition Since growth is relatively slower from 2 to 6 years than during infancy, there is typically a lessened appetite and an accompanying decreased interest in food. The body is lengthened out and thinner than previously, but this thinness by itself is not evidence of malnutrition or poor health. Nevertheless, there are good reasons to be alert to the possibility of malnutrition during this period, since it is more common in the preschool period than at any other time during the growth of the child (Burke, 2). Nutritional needs are also complicated during this time by the fact that the average child is becoming more independent and likes to express his growing autonomy by refusing to cooperate in various ways with the wishes of his parents. It is understandable, then, that the parent who fails to take this special combination of conditions into account may produce stubbornness and negativism in his child in relation to the eating routine, and that this may in turn have a bearing on the child's nutritional status. The child's diet during this period should supply sufficient nutrients to perform the following functions: (1) maintenance and replacement of body tissue, (2) increase of body tissue commensurate with physical growth, and (3) provision of energy for normal activity. Burke (2) points out that a suitable diet for the preschool child can readily be obtained from the normal, well-balanced, and varied meals of the family. The construction of such a well-balanced diet does not call for drastic changes during the period from 2 to 6 years of age, but remains remarkably stable. However, it does call for intelligent planning. Table 5.2 provides an exemplary diet plan for the preschool child.

The eating habits of the child are of considerable significance: his attitudes toward food, formed during the preschool years, play a vital

TABLE 5.2. *A Diet Plan for the Preschool-Age Child*

Breakfast	Lunch	Dinner	Supper
Citrus fruit or juice	Milk or fruit	Lean meat, liver, poultry, fish, or equivalent	Egg (may be given for breakfast in place of cereal, and cereal or a prepared main dish substituted here)
Cereal, preferably whole grain, cooked		Potato, preferably cooked in skin	Vegetable
Milk, whole		Vegetables	Bread, whole grain or enriched
Bread, whole grain or enriched		Bread, whole grain or enriched	Butter or fortified margarine
Butter or fortified margarine		Butter or fortified margarine	Milk, whole
		Milk, whole	Fruit, cooked or raw
		Dessert (simple puddings, custards, etc.)	

SOURCE: Reprinted by permission of the publishers from Harold Coe Stuart and Dane Gaskill Prugh, *The Healthy Child: His Physical, Psychological, and Social Development*, Cambridge, Mass.: Harvard University Press, copyright, 1960, by The President and Fellows of Harvard College.

role in his nutritional status and development throughout his years of later childhood and adult years as well. Burke argues that the child should not be allowed to eat too many foods which interfere with normal appetites because of their excessive sugar or fat content, since the appetite may be satisfied and the caloric requirements met without necessarily satisfying the structural needs for tissue maintenance, replacement, and growth. Thus, such foods as cakes, cookies, crackers, pies, doughnuts, fried foods, gravies, soft drinks, candy, etc., should be avoided in the planned diet for preschoolers. With reference to these and similar foods, Burke comments: "The child between one and three should not have these foods, except occasionally simple desserts at regular meals. Between three and six years of age, if these foods are used to any extent, they still will replace essential foods. Parents should realize that the child does not miss what he never has had and does not need" (2, p. 173).

In the formation of sound eating habits, the child's hunger should be taken into account. That is, he should not be allowed to "nibble" between meals so that he comes to the table without hunger. The presence of hunger at meal times leads to the pleasant association of food with the relief of hunger, and thus food likes are established. Food dislikes may sometimes be traced to the opposite; being expected and forced to eat despite the absence of hunger frequently leads to an eating problem in the child, or to a specific dislike for the foods the child is forced to eat. It is also true, however, that excessive hunger can interfere with normal appetite, which suggests that the time span between meals should not be too long. Factors that interfere with appetite and that should be considered if a preschooler exhibits a marked loss of appetite include: between-meal snacks, hurry and emotional disturbance at mealtime, fatigue, excessive hunger, illness, and convalescence. Burke presents the following suggestions, which are helpful in avoiding the development of feeding problems:

> Supply the child with a pleasant, quiet place in which to eat, with furniture and utensils adapted to his size and abilities.
>
> Prepare and serve his food so that it is appetizing and attractive. Serve it in small portions to stimulate appetite and interest in self-feeding. Be sure the food is not too hot.
>
> Avoid forcing him to eat; avoid any comment on his eating; avoid "rewards" for eating.
>
> Set a well-balanced meal before him for a definite time—twenty minutes should be sufficient. At the end of this time excuse the child without comment.
>
> If he shows a particular dislike for certain foods, avoid serving these for a time. Do not discuss or demonstrate food aversions in front of him.
>
> Preferably have only one person supervise the child's feeding, one who maintains an attitude free of overconcern or oversolicitude.
>
> Do not let him nibble between meals. If he becomes hungry at such times, he may be offered a small glass of milk or some

> fruit if it will not interfere with his appetite at the subsequent meal.
>
> Prior to and during meals the atmosphere should be peaceful and tranquil (2, pp. 175–176).

Exercise Brief observation of the normal preschooler should convince even the most casual observer of the vital role played by physical activity in the child's daily routine. The basic nature of the child's growing physical body demands an almost continuous flow of activity. There is a primitive urge to make use of the muscle systems, which are gradually being brought under control. It appears to be fundamentally satisfying to the child to make use of his physical body and its possibilities for movement, manipulation, and release of stored energy. As the child moves through the preschool years there is increasing emphasis on the use of muscle action as a means to other ends—in the creation of projects, in artistic pursuits, in more highly controlled games and motor skills, and so on. But such activities find their origins in the more primitive action of the child that is initiated as an objective in its own right. That is, muscular action is good, and satisfying, and necessary for its own sake early in the preschool period long before it is used as a basis for organized projects or is applied to artistic, athletic, musical, or social action. The early preschooler loves action for its own sake—simply because it is satisfying and pleasurable. In the next chapter we shall discuss this principle more fully and give other examples of the fact that actions which begin as enjoyable and satisfying behavior in their own right become, with increased maturity and experience, the means to the achievement of other, more advanced actions, and are no longer pursued merely as goals in themselves.

The preschooler's steady diet of physical activity, which naturally tends to emphasize the large muscle action involved in gross body activities, contributes to muscular development and coordination. At the same time, however, there are many other benefits derived from the incessant activity so characteristic of this stage. The respiratory system and circulatory system are clearly involved and clearly benefited by normal muscular action; their healthy growth is stimulated by the demands increasingly placed on them as the child makes greater use of his muscles. Further, in the normal course of physical activity, the child's sensory processes are continually stimulated and much learning occurs as a result. He is continually learning to correlate the sensory images—that which he is seeing, hearing, touching, tasting, smelling, and feeling in his muscles, tendons, and body joints, etc.—with the muscle action which gradually becomes more controlled and appropriate to the sensory images received by his nervous system. We might also note that physical activity plays a vital role in the child's steadily maturing psychological and social stabilization: he experiences a "feedback" which stems from his own muscle action. The activities in which he engages inevitably result in informing him that certain behavior brings him personal, social, and physical satisfaction, and that certain other activities are likely to produce pain or discomfort, again of a personal, social, or physical variety. Thus his muscular action has a direct role to play in the establishment of knowledge about himself and his world. Certainly the significance of muscular action, in the form of the "play" of the preschool child, should not be overlooked; its role is much broader than one of merely stimulating further muscular development.

As for guidance of the exercise of the preschool child, it should not be necessary under normal conditions to impose a program of exercise on the child. As we have noted, the child's internal bodily needs provide ample motivation for him to engage in a wide variety of physical activities which normally provide his growing body with excellent exercise. The adult who will attempt to duplicate the physical activities of the normal 4-year-old for, say, a one-hour period will probably testify to the truth of this statement. Not only is there a lot of vigorous action, there is involvement of a large number of muscle systems, some of which the adult may have forgotten. It may be desirable from time to time to evaluate the child's exercise routine, giving attention to such considerations as: Are there sufficient play opportunities, in safe environments, to provide the growing child with ample exercise? Are there sufficient social contacts with other children of his age to provide the social stimulation that leads to wholesome muscular action? Are there times when the environment becomes overstimulating, leading to excessive and prolonged expenditure of energy and undue body fatigue? Symptoms of the latter condition may include irritability, lack of emotional control, difficulty in relaxing for rest or sleep, and failure to gain weight property. Control of this general condition, provided it is not symptomatic of a physical condition requiring medical attention, normally consists of controlled reduction in the amount and variety of stimulations given the child, and the provision of a consistent and pleasant rest and sleep routine.

Rest and Sleep The child's natural demands for rest and sleep provide the best guides for providing satisfaction for these needs. Since there are wide variations in the amount of rest and sleep required by individual children, it is not possible to state a precise number of hours of sleep that all children of a given age should have, or to give a precise age at which all children may be allowed to give up an afternoon nap or rest period, etc. Such rigid prescriptions, which at one time were given rather freely, do violation to our knowledge of individual differences. We do know, however, that all preschool children benefit from some planned quiet periods during the course of the day, long after they have given up a formal afternoon nap time. If these are not actually planned and arranged by parents (or teachers, in the case of nursery-school children), the child will normally show his need for such quiet periods in his behavior. It may not be so obvious, however, that the child simply sits or lies quietly, or asks the adult for a chance to rest. It may, in fact, show in the form of hyperactivity and what appears to be overstimulation, as if the child is reluctant to yield to his body's need for rest. The preschooler is still very much geared to the present—he does not succeed well in planning ahead for delayed satisfactions and therefore he does not, on his own, succeed in resting "now" for the sake of feeling better "later." He needs adult help in carrying out this kind of routine, and the constructiveness of his activities later will give ample evidence of the validity of his body's need for occasional rest.

Infectious Diseases and the Development of Immunity The incidence of illnesses of all kinds during childhood varies with the age of the child, his sex, and his individual ability to cope with infectious agents. However, childhood illnesses are such a normal part of the process of growing up that they must be considered a predictable and inevitable feature of childhood. In the Harvard Longitudinal Studies, in which detailed health and illness records were maintained for 134 children from birth to maturity, the illness records ranged from a minimum of 17 to a maximum of 104 illnesses during the first 18 years of life. These included any and all illnesses in all degrees of severity. The following description of the findings of this study, by Valadian, is revealing not only of the normality of childhood illnesses, but also of some ways in which illness records were associated with age and sex of the child:

> The majority of boys experienced from 36 to 70 illnesses while the majority of girls had 20 to 36 illnesses. The median

> number for boys was 52 whereas for girls it was 42. This greater frequency of illness among the boys than the girls is characteristic of all age periods except from 10 to 14 years, but most striking for the age periods 2 to 6 and 6 to 10 and least so during the first 2 years. It was found in this study that the median numbers of illnesses for each age period were as follows: in infancy, boys, 6.7, girls 5.8; in the preschool period, boys 16.6, girls 12.7; in the school period, boys 12.2, girls 9.4; in early adolescence, boys 6.1, girls 6.2; and in late adolescence, boys 5.6, girls 4.0. The illnesses experienced by the group tended to be mild to moderate on the average throughout total childhood. In both infancy and in the preschool period the great majority of boys and girls had about equally mild and moderate illnesses. In the school period there were considerably more girls in the mild category than in the moderate but boys were still more nearly equal in each. The highest values for both the numbers and severities of illnesses were in the preschool period with relatively high values in infancy and the school period and a definite decrease after 10 years. They reached their lowest levels in late adolescence (11, p. 28).

Elsewhere in this same study some light was shed on the general types of illnesses. It was noted that at all ages throughout the 18-year span, by far the largest proportion of cases (over 75 percent) were of a respiratory nature. However, the proportion of respiratory to total illnesses did vary considerably by age level. It was lowest during the preschool period and highest during adolescence as other illnesses became more rare. A further quotation from Valadian is revealing on this point:

> Respiratory illnesses were predominantly infections but allergies constitute a sizeable proportion. The infections were mostly mild to moderate and of the "common cold" category. For example, during the age period 2 to 6 years, 67 boys accumulated a total of 1216 illnesses of all types, of which 997 were respiratory ones. Of the latter, 418 were mild and of short duration (less than a week), 320 were moderate while 134 were severe involving both upper and lower parts of the respiratory tract, the remainder having specific area involvements or complications. Respiratory illnesses predominated to such an extent

that not a single child escaped them during their 18 years (11, p. 29).

A major consideration in evaluating the development of the normal child is his history of mild and acute infections, as well as his pattern of development of the ability to resist such infections. In one sense, this is like learning, since exposure to certain infectious agents results in improved defenses against these agents. But the ability to "learn" to resist such agents is a quality which varies from one child to another, just as do other aspects of general development.

Healthy growth, of course, is not necessarily achieved by taking precautions against exposure to such infectious agents, any more than it is safe to assume that healthy growth is guaranteed by actively exposing children needlessly to any and all infections that may be available. In the normal household and in the normal associations of a child with other children and adults there is ample opportunity for exposure to a variety of infectious agents which can stimulate the development of immunity to a large number of diseases. The same general principle is used in the planned medical programs of immunization, beginning with infancy and continuing throughout childhood and the adult years—the principle of exposure to mild and controlled dosages of the infectious agent, which stimulates the body's defense mechanisms, usually in the form of antibodies in the blood stream, thereby enabling it to ward off subsequent attacks of the same or similar types of agents. A planned program of artificial immunization, beginning in infancy, is an essential part of the healthy physical development of children today. While it will not prevent the child from having such illnesses as chicken pox, measles, mumps, and a variety of upper respiratory infections, the dramatic control of such diseases as diphtheria, whooping cough, smallpox, and poliomyelitis in childhood is a tribute to our public health campaigns and to an enlightened public which has responded favorably to modern immunization programs. Even in the cases of certain diseases for which complete immunization cannot be provided artificially, it is possible with current medical knowledge and practice to reduce the severity of the illness so as to prevent it from interfering with normal growth. Some public health authorities strongly recommend that children *should* be exposed to certain diseases in order to acquire immunity and thus prevent the diseases from occurring at a later age when the symptoms may be more serious or when the diseases may have more complications. Ipsen and Stuart make the following statement in this connection:

> There are certain complications of infectious diseases in adolescence or early adult life which can be prevented by acquiring the diseases earlier in life and these infections tend to be more severe when older people have them. Examples are the common occurrence of acute involvement of the gonads as part of mumps in adolesence and more importantly the production of congenital defects in the fetus when the mother has German measles during the early weeks of pregnancy. These preventive possibilities make it advisable to permit children in good health to have contact during the preschool and school age periods with the usual communicable diseases of childhood which cannot fully be prevented by artificial immunization (7, p. 34).

Childhood Accidents More preschool children lose their lives as a result of accidents than from any other cause. In addition to the startlingly high rate of fatal accidents among preschoolers, large numbers of children in this age range are temporarily or permanently incapacitated or crippled as a result of mishaps. If for no other reason than the impressive statistics of accidents, one should be aware of the impact of accidents on the lives of millions of children and their families. There are additional reasons, however, and a chief one is that many of these accidents could be avoided. A significant number of avoidable accidents could be prevented with sound knowledge of the nature of the growing child. Stuart cites the general figures on accidents among children:

> The prevention of accidents is a major goal of all groups concerned with the health, education, and welfare of children. Collectively they account for a large portion of deaths, temporary disabilities, and permanent defects among children. Mortality statistics for the United States for the year 1958 showed that for the age period 1 to 14 years inclusive all forms of accidental death collectively nearly equaled in number all deaths in the next four leading categories, namely "malignant neoplasms, including lymphatic and hematopoietic tissues," "influenza and pneumonia," "congenital malformations" and "major cardiovascular-renal diseases." Accidents remain the

> leading cause of death at all ages from 1 to 34 years (9, pp. 15–16).

A prime illustration of the possibility of preventing accidents is accidental poisoning, which occurs all too frequently during the preschool period. A principal factor in the large number of cases of poisoning that occur annually in America among young children is the insatiable curiosity of the children themselves. Preschoolers do not discriminate between edible and poisonous substances on the basis of taste, smell, texture, or the label on the container. Such substances, when available to the child, represent a potential hazard just as real as if one were to make a loaded revolver available to him. Unfortunately, some adults apparently assume that the child should know better or that some natural instinct will warn him of the danger of such substances. But the figures on accidental poisoning among 2-, 3-, and 4-year-old children make it tragically clear that the child does not have such knowledge or instincts. Poisonous substances should simply not be accessible to children.

Other kinds of home accidents—falls, cuts, burns, etc.—also could be reduced in number with more careful supervision and by the elimination of certain obvious hazards. A further comment by Stuart in connection with the high accident rate among preschoolers is revealing:

> It is distressing to review statistics on the causes of accidents in the home and to realize that deaths of young children commonly result from eating aspirin tablets or other medicines carelessly left about the house or in rural areas from drinking kerosene oil from drums conveniently located in the wood shed.
>
> Children differ among themselves in the types and frequencies of the accidents which they experience, not only by age but within age groups, dependent in part at least upon personality traits, physical characteristics, and major interests. The sharply higher rates among boys than girls, especially during adolescence is one indication of this. Accident rates differ also among cultures and with the basic characteristics of the communities on which the rates are based (9, p. 16).

Unfortunately, the solution to the problem of accident prevention is not a simple one. Nor is it a reasonable goal to strive for the elimination of all accidents or all possible hazards. It is evident that a child's normal

Table 5.3. *Accidents (Fatal and Nonfatal) According to Nature by Age, New Bedford, Massachusetts, 1954*

Cause of Accident	All Ages		Children < 1 Yr. of Age	Children 1-4 Yrs. of Age	Children 5-9 Yrs. of Age	Children 10-14 Yrs. of Age	Children 15-16 Yrs. of Age	Age Not Stated
	No. of Accidents	Percentage	No. of Accidents	No. of Accidents	No. of Accidents	No. of Accidents	No. of Accidents	No. of Accidents
All Causes	2097		53	708	720	442	133	41
Falls	818	39.0						
Same level	405		3	122	152	96	25	7
Different level	413		29	175	116	67	18	8
Impact	585	28.0	9	141	236	135	57	7
Cutting or piercing	225	10.7	1	42	95	63	12	12
Animal bites	143	6.8	—	38	63	36	3	3
Poison	75	3.6	2	71	—	2	—	—
Burn	71	3.4	7	36	8	14	4	2
Crushing	61	2.9	—	29	23	6	3	—
Foreign body	32	1.5	1	22	3	4	1	1
Other	87	4.1	1	32	24	19	10	1

Source: R. Haggerty, "Home Accidents in Childhood," *New England J. Med.*, 1959, 260: 1324.

progress toward independence and self-protection requires that he gradually acquire competence in meeting and handling an increasing variety of hazards which he is bound to encounter. To protect him against all such hazards throughout early childhood is not only unrealistic, but would defeat this general need to become self-reliant and independent. There is, however, a reasonable balance between the extremes of overprotection and lack of supervision. This balance somehow allows the child to experience the normal bumps and bruises of the early years without making too much of an issue of them; at the same time, it avoids the too-early introduction of hazards which the child is simply not ready to cope with. Just as we would not let the preschooler go swimming alone or without supervision, neither should we prevent him from having early and satisfying experiences in the water; this illustration may be helpful in revealing the proper balance between the two extremes.

In a review of the problem of home accidents in children, Haggerty (5) notes that in the age group of under 5, 58 percent of accidental deaths occur in or about the home. The proportion of home to nonhome accidents is similarly very high when nonfatal accidents are included. The causes of these home accidents are fairly well studied, and are an interesting reflection of the age level and the developmental characteristics of the accident victims. Unfortunately, some reported figures are misleading, since they confuse accident with other primary causes of infant and child mortality. An example of this is the fact that many reports of "mechanical suffocation" in infancy turn out, upon careful investigation, to be cases of acute, overwhelming infection. Conversely, Haggerty notes, pneumonia or shock as a complication of an accident may, in some cases, be reported as the cause of death when in reality the primary cause was the accident itself. Table 5.3, based on investigations by Haggerty, presents data which give a more precise indication of the causes of both fatal and nonfatal accidents, by age level, occurring in a one-year period in a New England community.

Haggerty noted that during the preschool age, in which accident statistics for children are usually lumped together in a single age group, there are significant variations in the types of accidents that reflect rapidly developing motor and intellectual abilities. Most poisonings occur in the early period, among children of ages 1 and 2. By age 4 there is a marked reduction in poisonings as children become more discriminating and take more responsibility for avoiding these hazards. Haggerty also reports that

> . . . Deaths from drownings, falls, and burns continue at a high level throughout [the preschool period], indicating a somewhat different pathogenesis for these accidents from that of poisoning. Falls continue as a very common but less lethal type of accident, and collision with various objects plays a major part. Mammalian bites are quite common but unlikely to be fatal (5, p. 1325).

Sex differences in accident rates among preschool children have been observed, with by far the greatest frequency of accidents occurring in males. This suggests the possibility that personality factors, differential motor skills and activities, and differential child-rearing practices for the two sexes may be contributing factors to accident patterns in children. A study by Broussard (1) suggested that differential child-rearing attitudes and practices with boys were major factors in the cause of the significantly higher accident rate among male children.

It may be concluded that accidents are the result of multiple causation, with factors in the child himself (age, sex, agility, personality), in his physical environment, in his relations with his parents, in geographical location (urban-rural; inland-seacoast, etc.), in time of day (accidents seem to increase from 3:00 to 6:00 P.M.), and other unknown variables entering into complex interaction as the cause of specific accidents. Of vital consideration, however, remains the fact that many accidents are preventable, and an understanding awareness of the developmental characteristics of the child should enable adults to be more realistic about the potential hazards of the home environment they present to a preschooler.

SUMMARY

In this chapter we have examined the general trends in physical development during the preschool period. The major change in physical appearance is a "lengthening out" process, attributable to growth of the trunk and long bones of the body and a loss of the baby fat. Gross changes in size and weight occur much more slowly between 2 and 6 than in the preceding period of infancy.

The preschool child's skeleton is still very immature, in both size and degree. Some ossification centers have not yet made their appearance. The use of x-ray photography has enabled the child-development scientist to learn much about the regularities of skeletal development. Care of the deciduous ("baby") teeth has been stressed, in part because of the role they play in the alignment of the permanent teeth. Muscular development has been seen to play a significant role in the child's expanding efforts to control his body action.

The primary physical growth needs of the child include adequate nutrition, exercise, rest, and sleep. Childhood diseases are recognized as a normal part of growth experience, and the development of immunity to them is a significant task in the child's life. The frequency of accidents, the leading cause of mortality throughout childhood, can greatly be decreased by careful attention to the characteristics of the growing child and to the materials of his environment. The most serious accidents among preschool children occur in the home.

REFERENCES

1. Broussard, E. R., "Relationship of sex to childhood accidents," *J. Fla M.A.*, 1958, **44**:1343.
2. Burke, Bertha S., "The nutrition of the preschool child," in H. C. Stuart and D. G. Prugh (eds.), *The healthy child*, Cambridge, Mass.: Harvard Univ. Press, 1960, pp. 169–176.
3. Garn, S. M., and Shamir, Z., *Methods for research in human growth*, Springfield, Ill.: Charles C. Thomas, 1958.
4. Greulich, W. W., and Pyle, S. I., *Radiographic atlas of skeletal development of the hand and wrist*, Stanford: Stanford Univ. Press, 1950.
5. Haggerty, R., "Home accidents in childhood," *New England J. Med.*, 1959, **260**:1322–1331.
6. Hurlock, E. B., *Child development*, 3rd ed., New York: McGraw-Hill, 1956.
7. Ipsen, Johannes, Jr., and Stuart, H. C., "The development of immunity," in H. C. Stuart and D. G. Prugh (eds.), *The healthy child*, Cambridge, Mass.: Harvard Univ. Press, 1960, pp. 32–40.
8. Meredith, H. V., "Toward a working concept of growth," *Amer. J. Orthod. oral Surg.*, 1945, **31**:440–548.

9. Stuart, H. C., "The principles of growth and development," in H. C. Stuart and D. G. Prugh, (eds.), *The healthy child*, Cambridge, Mass.: Harvard Univ. Press, 1960, pp. 3–21.
10. Thompson, Helen, "Physical growth," in L. Carmichael (ed.), *Manual of child psychology*, 2nd. ed., New York: Wiley, 1954, pp. 292–334.
11. Valadian, Isabelle, "General features of illness by age," in H. C. Stuart and D. G. Prugh (eds.), *The healthy child*, Cambridge, Mass.: Harvard Univ. Press, 1960, pp. 22–32.
12. Watson, E. H., and Lowrey, G. H., *Growth and development of children*, 4th ed., Chicago: Year Book Medical, 1962.
13. Wishik, Samuel M., "The importance of 'timing' in child health supervision," *Child Develpm.*, 1950, **21**:51–60.
14. Zubek, J. P., and Solberg, P. A., *Human development*, New York: McGraw-Hill, 1954.

CHAPTER SIX

Why is motor development of significance in the life of the child? ∽ What are some general trends of development that are found in the patterning of motor control? ∽ What is known about "handedness" in the child? ∽ How can we apply reasonable principles of guidance in assisting the child in his efforts toward body control?

ACHIEVING BODY CONTROL

MAN'S UNIQUE POSITION in the animal kingdom and his fantastic history of technological progress are in no small measure a reflection of his special abilities with respect to body control. Two simple but vital illustrations are (1) his uniquely precise coordination of thumb against forefinger, which allows him to engage in infinitely varied manipulatory action; and (2) his special capacity for control of a complex speech mechanism, which enables him to communicate freely his rich culture, with its expanding technology, from one person to another as it is accumulated. Both of these are examples of motor behavior. And both undergo essential developmental processes in early childhood.

By motor *behavior* we mean essentially the use of the voluntary muscles in bringing about movement and control of body action. Motor *development*, then, is the gradual process of bringing the skeletal (voluntary) muscles under volitional control. It is a long-term process leading toward gradually improved coordination of the *sensory receptors* (ears, eyes, etc.), with the *central nervous system*, and in turn with the *muscles* themselves. All three of these are essential components of motor action, and the development of all three components—*sensory*, *neural*, and *muscular*—is essential to the achievement of body control. To be human is, in part, a matter of achieving useful control of body action. It includes the accomplishment of a vast number of skills, many of which we take for granted since they are well learned at such an early age. Since motor behavior and development is so easily taken for granted, and since its importance is so easily underestimated, it will be well worth the effort to give careful consideration to the importance of motor development in the life of the growing child.

SIGNIFICANCE OF MOTOR DEVELOPMENT

Motor behavior and body control play major roles in the child's life and in his over-all development, not only because motor action is important in its own right, but because it makes possible a wide variety of activities that are not ordinarily thought of as being motor behavior. From another point of view, the failure of a child to achieve a reasonable level of body control as compared with others of his age can have great significance for the kind of personal adjustment he makes, for the kind of interests and attitudes he develops, for the feelings of achievement and competence he holds toward himself, and, in general, for the self-concept that he gradually organizes. In this section we will look at some of these implications more closely.

From the very beginning of life, motor behavior plays a part in the child's perception and awareness of his world. Motor activity brings his eyes, hands, and total body into varied and changing relationships with his world of objects and people. Through sensory coordination of his environment in this forever changing set of relationships, he gradually builds up concepts about the nature of this environment. In a sense, his own motor activity is basic to the varied experiences which allow him to engage in this process of concept building. Motor behavior is also essential for the child's development of speech. Vocal activity itself is motor behavior. The fine control of the vocal apparatus required for complex articulation of sounds is well developed during the preschool years. This requires an extremely high level of motor control, in which there is stimulation by the central nervous system of the muscles involved in the speech apparatus. There is simultaneous action of certain sets of muscles and inhibition of the action of other sets of muscles, in rapidly shifting sequences, that makes it possible to move the jaw, tongue, and lips to form the essential sounds, and to move rapidly but with clarity from one sound pattern to another. Indeed, the complexity of the motor action required for speech deserves the sincere respect of the student of child development, for the wonder is that so many children learn to talk so well in so short a time!

Motor behavior is, of course, essential to the performance of any and all activities associated with athletics. While we do not ordinarily associate athletics with the preschool child, early childhood is a most significant period in laying a foundation for the smooth performance of body action that will later be put to use in organized athletics. Already, during the preschool years, great differences in body control and smoothness of activities such as running, jumping, climbing, swinging, etc., are observable in one child and another. The role of motor behavior in aesthetic activities should also be noted. Coordination of body action is essential to dancing, which is engaged in spontaneously by most preschool children. In part, the degree of satisfaction and the motivation to develop such activities further is dependent on the degree of body control that the child acquires in these early years. Another aesthetic activity that is highly dependent upon motor proficiency is musical performance. Both singing and instrumental music require essential motor control; indeed, some instruments are exceptionally demanding of fine muscle coordination. The child's aptitude for piano playing, for example, is dependent to a great extent on sensory-motor coordination. And art, in its many forms, has a basis in motor activity also. The child's freedom or inhibition in the expression of feelings and concepts through creative media is in some respects a direct reflection of the level of mastery of body movements that he has acquired. Similarly, many of the crafts, hobbies, skills, and even the beginnings of vocational adjustment, that are being organized in the activities of the preschool child, have an important basis in motor activity and motor control. Obviously, much of the world's work requires high levels of mastery of one's body, and the significance of the early period of its development in the preschool years should not be overlooked.

But equally important to all of these considerations is the role that motor behavior and mastery of one's body plays in the development of attitudes of self-confidence and acceptance among one's peers. The well coördinated child is, other things being equal, more accepted, more sought after, more ready to assume leadership, and more likely to think well of himself during the early school years that lie ahead.

One critical aspect of personality development in early childhood has to do with the degree of autonomy, or self-directedness of behavior, which the child develops. The child who is prevented from engaging in the normal amount of exploration of his world, who is not allowed to do things for himself in the normal routines of eating, sleeping, toileting, dressing and undressing, etc., and who does not acquire the skills needed for such independence of action, can be handicapped not only in respect to the skills themselves, but in his general attitude toward himself. It is essential to achieve attitudes toward oneself that make one feel capable of mastering and controlling various elements of the environment. The failure of this aspect of development leads to an attitude of helplessness —of inability to care for one's own needs. The resulting overdependence on others is neither pleasant for the child nor for those who live with him. Neither does it allow him to make the best uses of whatever intellectual and physical resources he may have inherited.

In summary, then, we may think of body control as an aspect of the child's development which will be reflected in his total relationship with his world of people and things, and which becomes a cornerstone of his personality development.

SOME GENERAL TRENDS IN THE PATTERNING OF MOTOR BEHAVIOR

There is a systematic orderliness to the achievement of body control; general sequences of motor development may be found in all normal children, and in the same order of appearance. As in other aspects of human development, wide latitude is present within the normal range, yet, there is solid evidence of the operation of genetic laws which determine the sequence of steps in the motor behavior characterizing human childhood, and it is possible to describe the total process in terms of general principles, or trends.

Reflexive Control, Cortical Control, and Unconscious Control

Some motor activity occurs even during the prenatal period and, as we have seen in earlier chapters, there is a wide variety of motor behavior present in the newborn infant. He blinks his eyes, sneezes, hiccups, grasps with his hands, flexes his arms and legs, turns his head, and in general engages in a wide range of actions calling for the use of the skeletal muscles. The action in which the newborn infant engages is essentially reflexive in nature; that is, it is under the control of neural structures which operate in the brain stem and spinal cord but are not controlled by the higher brain centers we associate with the thinking processes. It is not necessary for the infant to be consciously aware of the bright light which, when it strikes his eyes, forces him to blink. Nor is it necessary for him to "think about" the process of grasping the adult finger to which his hand may cling, automatically. These reflex behaviors occur with no conscious thought on his part, and represent the first major stage in the development of body control. Some of the more significant reflex actions in which the infant participates are the tonic-neck reflex, the Moro reflex, the grasp reflex, and the Babinski reflex, all of which have been described in more detail in Chapter Four. For the present it is important only to note that these reflexive behavior patterns form the basis for some of the child's later achievements.

The second general stage of motor development and body control involves gradually increasing participation of the higher brain centers. Both the cerebrum, which includes a region of the brain which directs body action, and the cerebellum, which is essential in the control of body balance and coordination, become more involved as the child matures. With this increased involvement of the brain in motor behavior that is no longer automatic, it becomes necessary for the child to control behavior to a much greater extent by "thinking about" his body action. He consciously directs his hands and feet to a much greater degree than in the earlier stages.

But with continued maturation and practice in the development of particular skills comes the final and highest stage of motor control, which releases the child once again from the need to direct consciously the operation of the skeletal muscles. This is the stage of the highly developed motor habit, in which a smooth and polished action seems to occur spontaneously with no conscious effort needed. Actually, the polished performance is the result of continued practice, in which one phase of the action has consistently followed another phase so that each action serves as the "cue" or stimulus to perform the next action, the result being a smoothly flowing pattern of behavior that does not require conscious thought in order to be carried out. Walking, which involves a repetitive sequence of flexion and extension of each leg, is an illustration. As a matter of interest, we might note that the interruption of such a smoothly patterned sequence by conscious analysis of the process itself may be enough to destroy the pattern of the motor action. This could be observed in the case of the child who has developed a complex motor skill to the point of habit, who, right in the middle of the performance of the action sequence, begins to question whether or not he can move his hands or his feet in the appropriate manner. The questioning itself may seriously disrupt the performance.

This movement from the first to second and to the third stage of body control cannot be equated directly with the child's age level. Even as adults, we may be operating essentially at the first stage with respect to a given pattern of motor control. That is, our general pattern of reflexive behavior and our total pattern of motor action of a general sort may not be specific enough to allow us to engage well in some complex motor action—say, in playing the piano. While we have the essential reflexes needed to keep time and to perform the other basic functions involved, our introduction to the piano is bound to be accompanied by a great deal of conscious effort in order to perform even the simplest actions required in reading the musical notes and striking the proper keys with the appropriate fingers in approximately the proper sequence. But with consistent practice, if one is sufficiently motivated, the essential habit patterns are gradually developed to the point where one finds himself playing a sequence of notes, with harmony and accurate time, without having to give it the conscious thought that was formerly required with every hand and finger movement. A motor habit has been developed.

Since this movement from first to second to third stage is not just a matter of age, then, we should see it as the central pattern of development of motor control at any age. Many examples could be given—the fact that adults do not have to think about how to shape any particular letter of the alphabet in order to write their own names; the fact that the skilled typist does not either look at the typewriter keys or ask herself where her fingers are at any particular moment—they seem to go to the right keys by themselves; the fact that the 5-year-old who has learned to "pump" in the swing can do it gracefully and efficiently without having to tell herself consciously just how to go about it. And if that same 5-year-old has learned how to skip, she can do that also without any conscious questioning of "which foot goes next" if she has reached the third stage of motor control with respect to that activity.

It should be perfectly clear that one is not in the same stage with respect to all motor activities; the 4-year-old who is in the second stage with respect to buttoning that favorite jacket may, at the same time, be in the first stage when it comes to tying the shoelaces, and in the third stage when it comes to walking up and down stairs.

Other Trends in the Patterning of Motor Behavior

The lawfulness and orderliness of the process by which the child achieves body control is illustrated further in the operation of two additional principles: (1) there is a development from bilateral to unilateral body control and body action, and (2) there is development from maximum use of muscular action to minimum use of muscle action.

BILATERAL TO UNILATERAL CONTROL. "Bilateral" refers to both sides of the body. The neonate is essentially symmetrical, tending to use both sides of the body to about the same extent and with about the same degree of efficiency. While this generalization has an exception—the tonic-neck reflex is an early manifestation of one-sided behavior—it still may be stated that the early infancy period involves a largely two-sided, or bilateral, approach to the world.

The observations of a large number of infants by Gardner and Pease (3) have confirmed the general hypothesis that the approach an infant makes to objects presented to him while he is supported at a table is essentially a two-sided approach. That is, when cubes, spoons, pellets, and other objects used in the psychological examination of infants were presented from the opposite side of the table, and in the midline of the baby's vision, the tendency during the first half year was for the baby to approach the object in a surrounding motion, with both arms and both hands involved in the attempt to "corral" the object. Later in the second half of the first year a pronounced shift was observed, with the infants making much more use of one or the other hand while inhibiting the action of the opposite one. The implications of this shift for the development of handedness during the preschool years will be discussed at a later point in this chapter. At this point we should note that the older child has established a relatively clear-cut unilateral approach, with not only a strong preference for the use of one side of his body, but a significantly greater accuracy and level of efficiency for the preferred side in many kinds of motor activities.

MAXIMUM TOWARD MINIMUM MUSCULAR INVOLVEMENT. Early motor behavior is typically "mass" behavior, in which large segments and components of the child's body are involved even in fairly simple motor action.

The well known example of the preschool child who, at about age 5, may show interest in learning to tie shoelaces, serves to illustrate this point. In the first attempts to tie shoelaces, the child calls into action many large and small muscles that are not essential to the act of shoelace tying. With practice and increasing skill, the child will gradually eliminate the excess action of the unneeded muscle systems, and the essential action of the pertinent muscles will perform the action smoothly and without interference. As a new motor skill is being learned, however, it is natural for excess tension and muscle action to occur in parts of the body not needed for the skill.

Motor control, then, is not merely a matter of learning to use the appropriate muscles for a given act. It is also a matter of learning to inhibit the action of nonessential muscle groups. One of the reasons it is aesthetically pleasing to observe the performance of a skilled dancer, or an accomplished athlete, is that such a person has learned well how to eliminate nonessential muscle action. The result is the avoidance of clumsy or stilted movements and waste motion. We describe it as a "polished" performance.

Development of Gross Motor Control in the Preschool Years

The achievement of independent walking early in the second year is neither the beginning nor the final step in the development of upright locomotion. With increased practice, muscular and neural development, and with changes in body proportion there are important changes also in the manner of walking, and in the variations and additions to the basic walking pattern. The child's first tottering steps are taken on short legs, balancing a body that has a high center of gravity because of the proportionately large head. The body position in this first walking period is not yet completely vertical; the knees are bent and the stepping movement is high and exaggerated. The feet are placed far apart to improve balance. Often a child will walk better and with more self-assurance at first if he has something in his hand. Apparently this is because he was holding on to something such as a rail, or a piece of furniture, or an adult finger, much of the time just prior to independent walking, during which he was practicing stepping movements and gaining balance. An example of this was Don B., who for the first few days while taking independent steps consistently held his right ear lobe securely between thumb and forefinger!

Not only does the body position gradually become more vertical and at the same time more relaxed; the walking child rapidly increases the smoothness and efficiency of his stepping and balancing. Incidental skills that are related but not central to walking may be developed so rapidly as to be almost overlooked by parents. For example, the ability to go from a sitting position to a standing position without support, in the center of the floor, and move about unaided, then to sit down gracefully and easily as only the toddler can, is really quite a remarkable achievement. But in the typical parental excitement over walking itself, this skill may go almost unnoticed. It does not usually occur until some time after independent walking has been established. Table 6.1, which

TABLE 6.1. *Improvement in Control of Gross Motor Ability During Preschool Period*

Age Placement (Months)	Behavior
11.6	Walks with help
12.5	Stands alone
13.0	Walks alone
16.9	Walks backward
20.3	Walks upstairs with help
20.5	Walks downstairs with help
24.3	Walks upstairs alone; marks time
24.5	Walks downstairs alone; marks time
29.2	Stands on left foot alone (momentarily)
29.3	Stands on right foot alone (momentarily)
30.1	Walks on tiptoe
35.5	Walks upstairs, alternating forward foot
37.1	Jumps from height of 30 cm.
41.5	Jumps over rope less than 20 cm. high
48.4	Distance jump—60 to 85 cm.
49.3	Hops on right foot, less than two meters
50.0	Walks downstairs, alternating forward foot

SOURCE: Based on selected items from the California Scale of Motor Development, from N. Bayley, "The Development of Motor Abilities During the First Three Years," *Monogr. soc. Res. Child Develpm.*, 1936, 1 (1): 1-26. Reprinted by permission of the Society for Research in Child Development and N. Bayley.

is based on data provided by Bayley (1), reveals some of the important changes in motor behavior and motor control during the preschool years. Gesell and Amatruda (4) also provide normative data on motor development in the preschool years.

One of the most significant aspects of motor development during this period is the fact that behavior which is at first motivated by the child's own need to do that which his body is prepared to do, becomes, through maturation, a means to some greater end or objective. Walking and running are good illustrations. These are activities in which the child participates, at first, by concentrating all his energy, strength, and coordination on the process itself, for the sake of the process itself. The reward for the activity is the satsifaction of participating in it. But as the activity becomes a well established habit, so that balancing, stepping, starting and stopping, and all the component parts of the walking act become routine and do not call for his complete and undivided attention, the act becomes a means to the larger end of getting the child to where he wants to go—the easiest, quickest, and most efficient way.

The distinction is made more clear, perhaps, if we return to the example of the child who has just learned to walk, and who is seemingly delighted with his newly established behavior. It is almost as if he had invented walking personally, he is so pleased with himself. Nevertheless, for the first period immediately following this tremendous achievement, it is entirely possible that when he really wants to get someplace in a hurry, he will resort to creeping on all fours, which is a habit he may have established much earlier and one which he is much more certain will get him where he wants to without trouble. This is the stage, then, during which walking is satisfying in and of itself; later, with rapidly improving skill and less need to concentrate fully on the act itself, it will replace creeping as the most efficient means to the end of getting himself someplace in a hurry.

THE DEVELOPMENT OF HANDEDNESS

The question of what causes some children to be left-handed has been an interesting and, to some parents, disturbing question. To the child-development specialist, however, there is a far more basic question which needs to be answered: what causes a child to develop *handedness*, whether it be right- or left-handedness? Furthermore, what causes a child to develop dominance of one leg over the other? What causes us to develop unilaterality with respect to use of the eyes? For most of us, one eye tends to be more used than the other.

There has been much written on the subject of handedness—even from the time of the early Greek philosophers there have been conflicting theories advanced as to the cause and the proper solutions for the problem of handedness. Clearly, it can be a problem for the individual who is strongly left-handed, since society is geared, in many respects, to the right-handed majority. At the same time, there are circumstances under which the strongly right-handed person is at a disadvantage if he has never trained his left hand to do routine tasks. An example of this occurred in the life of one active preschool girl who suffered an arm injury necessitating the wearing of a cast on her right arm for a period of several weeks. This girl, 3 years old, had already established a considerable degree of right-hand dominance. However, it was interesting to observe the ease with which she reorganized such routine habits as eating, dressing, manipulating blocks and puzzle pieces, etc. Chances are that at a later age it would be a somewhat more difficult task to shift habits from one hand to the other as efficiently as she did at age 3.

In general the theories of handedness have stressed either the effect of heredity or the role of specific environmental learning as the basic cause for being either right- or left-handed. However, there is no simple explanation for hand dominance, and any theory that is put forward is probably, at best, only a partial explanation. One of the most significant theoretical aspects of the problem derives from the fact that the control of body movement by the brain is governed by the opposite side of the brain from the limb or body part involved. That is, the left hemisphere of the brain controls the motor activities of the right side of the body, and vice versa. Orton (9) has argued that hand dominance is primarily a matter of which side of the brain develops dominance over the other. This theory holds that, for most people, the left side of the brain normally develops dominance over the right side, and therefore right-handedness is a natural result. Such a theory is open to criticism on a number of grounds. In any case, it does not offer a genuine explanation for the basic cause of the condition of cerebral dominance, since it does not explain what causes the left side of the brain to develop more functional activity than the right side in the large majority of cases.

The other major theoretical argument, that handedness is primarily a matter of social learning in a world in which we expect and assume right-handedness, rests on assumptions that the infant is at first bilateral and develops handedness as he acquires experience in his social world. Other evidence has been cited to indicate that lower animals—the great apes, chimpanzees, and monkeys—are able to use both hands with about equal efficiency. This suggests that human beings, by virtue of their intelligence and culture and language, which provide each new human infant with a complex cultural environment and many rich learning experiences, force the majority of children into the pattern of right-handedness at an early age with no observable ill effects on the children—which illustrates the adaptability of the human child (*possible* ill effects will be considered subsequently). The relative ease with which most children can learn to use either hand if the need arises, as in the case of the girl with the injured right arm, would seem to uphold this general theoretical point of view. However, the arguments for both of these general theories have considerable merit and, as has been pointed out, the entire explanation of handedness has not yet been presented.

One of the interesting findings about handedness is that by far the largest majority of both boys and girls are right-handed, with the percentage being higher for girls. While a small percentage of both sexes becomes predominantly left-handed, there are few of either sex who could be called truly ambidextrous; i.e., having equal facility with either hand. The question of why more boys than girls develop left-handedness is somewhat unsettled, although certain investigators argue that it is because girls are more susceptible to training on the basis of social pressures during the period when handedness is being established. Most researchers agree that handedness remains indefinite and changeable during most of the first year. It is beginning to be well established in most children, however, by the end of the second year. Even here, however, the findings should be interpreted with caution, since it is entirely possible for a child to be right-handed in some activities and left-handed in others. Again, this has been explained partly in terms of the types of activities that are most likely to be observed and in which there is most likely to be social pressure applied to make a child right-handed.

Figure 6.1 shows the percentage of cases in which handedness is established by age level, as described by Hildreth (6). It is evident from this research that in the majority of cases it is well established before the child enters school.

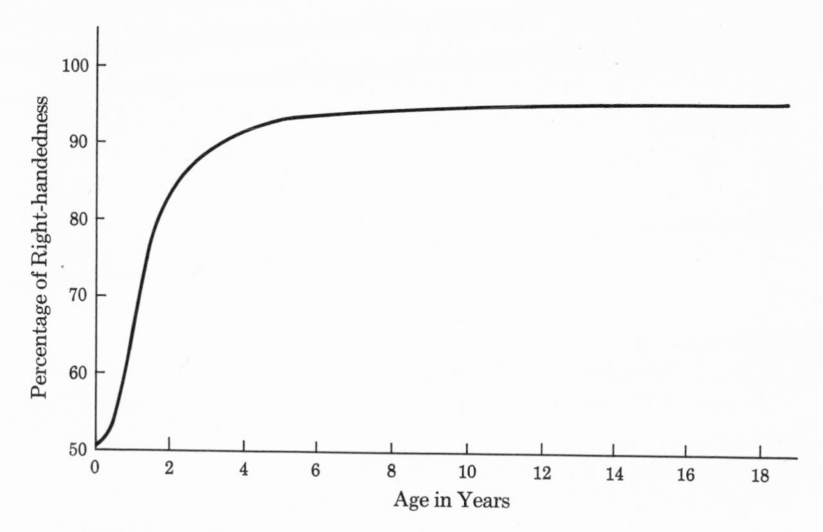

Fig. 6.1. The curve showing the increase in right-handedness that occurs with age. (From G. Hildreth, "The development and training of hand dominance: III. Developmental tendencies in handedness," *J. genet. Psychol.*, 1949, 75:221–254.)

Guidance of the Development of Handedness Because of the conflicting ideas about handedness that have been expressed by different writers, parents are often left with feelings of doubt and anxiety about the proper course of action to follow in cases where a child shows some early tendencies toward being left-handed. The advice sometimes given is that he should be trained, from the very start, to use his right hand. The consistent training from the beginning, it is argued, will avoid the problem in later years. But other writers recommend leaving the child alone and allowing him to develop handedness in his own way. This argument seems to stem mostly from the feeling that interference with handedness may also interfere with the development of speech, or may even cause severe stuttering, since speech too is a motor activity that appears to be controlled to a great extent by certain areas of the left cerebral hemisphere. The evidence that changing handedness will cause stuttering is not entirely conclusive. One reason it is difficult to evaluate such evidence is that stuttering is also correlated with excess tension. Tension, in turn, may be related to parental pressure and coercion. The same parents who enforce a change of handedness may be the ones who are coercive in other respects. Hence, if stuttering does result, we cannot be certain of the exact cause.

Nevertheless, there may be some general guides that may be useful in helping to determine whether or not it is appropriate to attempt to change the handedness of a child. Hildreth (7) presents the following criteria, not with the idea that it is either absolutely right or absolutely wrong to change the child's handedness, but as a guide to knowing under what circumstances it may be advisable:

> The child is under six years.
> The child uses both hands interchangeably.
> The handedness index is bilateral.
> A trial period shows no permanent difficulty.
> The child is agreeable to the change.
> The child is above average in intelligence.

It is Hildreth's conclusion, after careful investigation of the problem, that not all children who show signs of left-handedness should be forced to change. In fact, it might be concluded in general that if much force is required to bring about the change, it is hardly justified and may result in more problems than it will solve. For the student who may wish to explore the interesting problems of handedness still further, the discussions by Eyre and Schmeekle (2), Hildreth (5), and Thompson (10) are recommended.

GUIDANCE OF MOTOR DEVELOPMENT

The significance to the child of the achievement of a reasonable competence in control of his own body action makes it justifiable to provide a sound program of guidance to facilitate that development. In general, such a program consists of three major elements: (1) the equipment available to a child with which he can exercise his growing capacity for body control, (2) the experiences and instruction provided a child that allow for the development of skills, and (3) the attitudes of the adults in the child's life, which play a vital role in determining his own feelings about motor activity. All three are vital aspects of the guidance program.

Equipment for Motor Activities The motivation for motor behavior comes, as we have stressed, from inside the child as he achieves the capacity to engage in each new level of action. The manner of using his energies and the channeling of his motor impulses will depend to a marked degree on the kinds of play equipment available. The need for good equipment is illustrated most clearly in the child himself; if there are no other things available to him to climb on, jump from, swing on, hang from, etc., he will probably try to make use of the living room furniture for such natural activities. But providing good equipment is justified by far better reasons than protection of the living room furniture from this kind of treatment. An examination of the play area of a well equipped nursery will give an idea of the variety of play equipment and materials that can be useful in stimulating healthy motor development. Climbing, a natural and appealing activity, is stimulated by the jungle gym and similar climbing frames in both indoor and outdoor play. Swings and slides are useful in developing general body coordination. Boxes and barrels are particularly versatile items: they can be moved, piled, climbed on or in, etc., for developing strength and skill. Sturdy tricycles are always appropriate for 2- to 5-year-olds, since the skillful handling of a tricycle calls for the development of considerable coordination and timing. The circular motion of the legs is difficult to achieve before about 24 months but, once achieved, opens up an avenue of motor development that leads to important accomplishment.

While the emphasis during the preschool years is on the achievement of large-muscle control, and the aforementioned equipment is intended for gross body activity, the idea that a preschool child should not be allowed to engage in fine motor activities is a false and misleading one. The preschooler gets considerable satisfaction from a variety of activities that stimulate eye-hand coordination—painting and coloring, block building, manipulation of clay and other soft materials, cutting and pasting, and picture-puzzle play. Although such activities are assumed by most adults to contribute mostly to intellectual and aesthetic development, there are very real benefits to be derived in terms of the development of muscular coordination and of the coordination of the senses with the control of body activities. With the proper equipment stimulation occurs in a natural manner without emphasizing that the child move his hands or limbs in any particular manner. This is especially desirable since the child's focus of attention is on the process of the activity rather than on making specific movements—and motor control makes better progress in the absence of undue attention to body movement or to its inhibition.

It takes a lot of pra
(Courtesy of Dalton Sch

Experiences and Instruction Provided by Adults A variety of equipment is available which stimulate certain kinds of activities that foster motor development and concomitantly stimulate intellectual and aesthetic growth. Children need motor activity and need to acquire motor control for its own sake; nevertheless, much in the way of healthy motor development occurs almost as an incidental activity as an accompaniment to the other normal activities of children. In addition to providing the child with these materials, much can be accomplished by judicious planning and guiding the child's experiences. The motivation for activity comes from within the child; therefore a major consideration in guidance is providing a sufficiently stimulating but safe environment, with enough adult control of activities and equipment that potential hazards are kept at a minimum. Specific instruction in body skills during the preschool years is not ordinarily needed for the normal child. McGraw (8) studied a pair of twins, one trained and the other untrained in specific motors tasks, and found that maturational readiness is essential in order for the child to profit from special training. The exception is the child who requires a particular kind of therapy, such as physical therapy or speech therapy under the direction of the qualified specialist. In certain cases therapy may be indicated even in the preschool years. However, such body skills as dancing and swimming can be taught with considerable progress in the later preschool period. Many adults are surprised at the ability of 4-year-olds to control body movements in dancing and swimming under the direction of a competent teacher. However, it is inadvisable for most adults to give formal instruction in either of these activities unless they are competent both in the activities and in child development. It should be clearly understood that emphasis on specific body movements could prove, in the long run, to be more disruptive than helpful in the development of body control. The key to healthy guidance of motor development, then, would seem to be the provision of safe and age-appropriate equipment, the providing of adequate supervision in its use, and the maintenance of positive and constructive attitudes on the part of adults.

The Role of Adult Attitudes in the Guidance of Motor Development Much of the child's task in the over-all achievement of healthy motor development is the maintenance of healthy attitudes toward himself. More particularly, it is essential that he have a generally competent feeling about his ability to handle himself and the objects and situations which confront him. Such an attitude is based on having had satisfactory experiences, over a long period of time, which lead him to feel confident that he can handle himself adequately in whatever situations arise.

The role of parental attitudes in fostering feeling of confidence in the child is paramount. Attitudes of fear and doubt, reflected in overprotectiveness and sheltering of the child from the normal bruises and bumps of the preschool period, will engender an overly anxious, unduly cautious approach in the child. Essentially this is an approach characterized by conflict. The child's conflict, rooted in his own doubts and fears about his ability to handle himself in climbing, tumbling, jumping, or whatever activity may be involved, is expressed in the physical inhibition of a smooth flow of motor activity. The resulting "jerkiness" and roughness to the behavior reflects a "start and stop" attitude on the child's part. This very inhibition of the smooth, spontaneous line of action interferes with the effectiveness of the action, and reinforces the feeling of the child that he cannot do things well. Thus, a vicious circle of uncoordinated, inhibited action leading to attitudes of incompetence, which in turn lead to more faulty, inhibited action, can be the result. On the other hand, attitudes of acceptance of the naturalness of bumps and bruises, of the inevitability of risk if one is to achieve normal motor control, if held by parents from the time the baby first moves himself about independently will carry over in significant ways to the child. For one thing, parents holding such attitudes are not likely to make a big production out of a small bump, and the child is thus less likely to develop a distorted notion of the significance of such routine events in his life.

It is possible, however, to go to extremes in allowing the child complete motor freedom in an unsupervised setting. We are not proposing complete lack of concern for the child's welfare. It helps to remember that the child himself contains the essential motivation for engaging in motor activities. He will adapt very rapidly, given sufficient freedom and adequate equipment and stimulation, to the limits of his own ability to keep himself out of serious trouble. The contrast here again may be illustrated in a nursery-school setting. The nursery-school playground is fenced off, typically, to insure safety from traffic or from children wandering off, and to increase the probability of good adult supervision. But, within the limits of the play-yard fence, the children are not much restricted as to what equipment they can use and what they cannot. If a child wishes to climb on a jungle gym, his motivation to do so is typically consistent with his ability to handle himself in that situation. The nursery-school teacher does not, however, place him on top of the jungle gym and leave him to his own devices. The distinction between this and allowing him to do the thing which his body is ready to handle—allowing him to climb it himself when he is ready to do so—is a vital one. Normally, the child does not get himself into situations which he cannot handle, particularly when the equipment is geared to his age level and there is reasonable supervision.

SUMMARY

Motor development may be defined as the gradual achievement of control over body action involving the voluntary muscles. It is based on steadily improving coordination of sensory, neural, and muscular action. The importance of motor development is seen not only in improved muscular coordination *per se*, but in major contributions to aesthetic, intellectual, social, and personality development. The child's self-concept is dependent in no small measure on his feelings about his ability to control his own body movement and to control the objects and tools of his environment. General trends in the achievement of body control include (1) the sequence from reflexive to cortical to unconscious control, (2) the movement from bilateral to unilateral control, and (3) the trend from maximum toward minimum muscular involvement.

The preschool years are a time of incessant gross motor activity, during which there is continual practice and improvement in locomotor action with all its variations, manipulation of objects, and increased skill in coordinating body action with sensory stimulation. The prevalence of large-muscle activity among preschoolers does not mean that the child is uninterested in small objects, or that he should not be allowed to exercise finer muscle coordination.

Positive guidance of motor development includes attention to three major considerations: (1) equipment for motor activities, (2) experiences and instruction provided by adults, and (3) adult attitudes toward the child's motor action.

REFERENCES

1. Bayley, N., "The development of motor abilities during the first three years," *Soc. Res. Child Develpm. Monogr.*, 1935 (1).

2. Eyre, M. B., and Schmeeckle, M. M., "A study of handedness, eyedness, and footedness," *Child develpm.*, 1933, **4**:73–78.
3. Gardner, D. B., and Pease, D., "Performance of infants on three standardized scales," unpublished research report, Iowa State Univ. Agricultural and Home Economics Experiment Station, 1961.
4. Gesell, A., and Amatruda, C. S., *Developmental diagnosis*, 2nd ed., New York: Hoeber-Harper, 1947.
5. Hildreth, G., "The development and training of hand dominance: I. Characteristics of handedness," *J. genet. Psychol.*, 1949, **75**:177–220.
6. Hildreth, G., "The development and training of hand dominance: III. Developmental tendencies in handedness," *J. genet. Psychol.*, 1949, **75**:221–254.
7. Hildreth, G., "The development and training of hand dominance: V. Training of handedness," *J. genet. Psychol.*, 1950, **76**:101–144.
8. McGraw, M. B., *Growth: A study of Johnny and Jimmy*, New York: Appleton-Century-Crofts, 1935.
9. Orton, S. T., "Some studies in the language function," *Proc. Ass. Res. nerv. ment. Dis.*, 1934, **13**:614–633.
10. Thompson, G. G., *Child psychology*, 2nd ed., Boston: Houghton Mifflin, 1962, pp. 223–270.

CHAPTER SEVEN

What differences are there between learning to speak and learning to communicate? In what respects is language basic to the development of human personality? What are the main functions of language in the life of the child? What specific tasks must the child accomplish in order to communicate well with others?

COMMUNICATING WITH OTHERS

TRUE LANGUAGE is a distinctively human accomplishment. It is probably the most tangible and overwhelming bit of evidence of the superior place of man in the animal kingdom. At the same time, it is through language that much of his intellectual, emotional, and social development takes place; indeed it could not take place in the absence of this fundamental process of communicating with others. For these reasons it is essential that we examine carefully the processes of language development as they occur in the life of the preschooler. In addition to understanding language as a basis for the child's intellectual, emotional, and social development, however, we may discover, as students of this process have done in the past, that it can be a fascinating subject in its own right. In the first place, it is about as complex an activity as the human mind can contemplate. Language encompasses much more than just oral speech and hearing. It includes all forms of human interaction in which a person is made aware of a thought, feeling, or question experienced by another person. In its broader sense, then, language is the vehicle for all human communication, including speech, writing and printing, gesture and pantomime, code signals, musical notations, mathematical symbols, and many other devices for conveying thoughts, feelings, and questions. In this larger sense, it is the task of every child to become acquainted with a seemingly endless array of techniques of communication. In order to become a competent member of his society he must become familiar with an assortment of languages, some of them formal and rather rigidly defined, as the English language; some fluid, subtle, and poorly defined, such as the language of body posture and facial expression. In the latter, as in many other languages, the child eventually learns that a whole system of messages may be conveyed, quite apart from the specific meanings of any words spoken.

Speech, in contrast to language, constitutes a much narrower range of human experience. Speech occurs whenever distinct vocal sounds are articulated by a person and understood by a listener. This definition may help us to recognize the difficulty of pinpointing the age at which a child is truly speaking. As we noted in the earlier discussion on development during infancy, the first "words" of an infant may not be easy to recognize, except perhaps by his parents. However, if his vocal effort represents a consistent attempt on the infant's part to convey a particular thought or feeling, and if the articulation is understood by a listener so that both the infant and the listener are dealing with common ideas, then speech has taken place. If both, for example, think,"that solid, white, warm cylinder with a rubber tip at one end, from which warm fluid flows," when the infant says, "ba-ba," then his effort represents true speech. Obviously no infant who is unable to say "bottle" is going to think in the terms used here; the point is that the mental image of the infant and that of the adult are roughly comparable when the infant articulates a sound. If he uses that particular sound consistently and is consistently rewarded, it serves the purpose of communication remarkably well.

When we speak of the communication process we are speaking of the basic process of human interaction—a process fundamental to the development of human qualities of thought and action. Personality does not develop in a vacuum. It is only through interaction with others that it can come to fruition. Language, in a sense, defines the limits and possibilities of personality development for every individual. It becomes the child's primary device for translating raw experience into meaningful units that can be dealt with coherently and his technique for the solution of myriad problems. It also becomes his way of responding to frustration. It is, in fact, the organizing essence of his basic personality.

Speech development, then, is only a specific illustration of the larger problem that confronts the child—the problem of communicating with his world in an effort to make sense out of that world. Yet speech development, while a relatively smaller matter than this total problem, can certainly become a *big* problem when something goes wrong, or when, for some reason, the child does not speak when his parents think he should. Parents frequently are heard to ask, "Why doesn't he talk"? or, "I think there's something wrong; he's older than Susan next door and she's been talking for months now." Sometimes, when discussing that which we take so for granted, it helps if we change the question around; instead of asking, "Why doesn't Danny talk?" we might ask ourselves, "Why does *Susan* talk?" Why does *any* child talk? If we can get a good answer to that question, we are in a much better position to discuss the child who is not talking.

Our beginning preschooler, at 2 years of age, has already found it very satisfying to say words. He has been rewarded in many ways for his efforts to make intelligible sounds. The babbling of infancy, satisfying for its own sake as a vocal exercise that gave pleasure to the vocal apparatus as well as to his ears, has given way to short but highly meaningful assertions and questions about his world of people and things.

THE FUNCTIONS OF LANGUAGE FOR THE CHILD

As we have already stressed, language is more involved and accomplishes more than the mere transmission of ideas from one person to another. The purposes that it serves are many and varied, and they are intimately connected with basic aspects of personality itself.

For convenience, we can group the purposes served by language under the following five major headings: (1) language as a means to make wants and needs known, (2) language as a means for the expression of emotion, (3) language as a device for gaining information and skill, (4) language as a means of initiating and maintaining social interaction, and (5) language as an aid to the achievement of personal identification. Our task will be to understand these functions of language and the special ways in which the preschooler uses the developing skills of communication to fulfill them.

Language as a Means to Make Wants and Needs Known Occasionally, when an inexperienced parent voices concern about the child who is not talking at the expected age, a keen observer—usually a more experienced parent—may note that there is a relatively simple reason. The reason has nothing to do with the child's intelligence, or the condition of his vocal apparatus, or the adequacy of his hearing, any one of which may have been suspected by his parents. The child may be failing to talk, or may be failing to use anything more complicated than grunting and pointing, simply because he has *no need* to engage in more complex language behavior at this point. Such behavior as grunting and pointing on the child's part, with the parents then running through a series of guesses as to what he wants, provides a clue to this kind of situation. Why should he learn to use a variety of words when one grunt will serve all his purposes? And especially when parents seem to pay so much attention to him if he persists in using this one sure-fire technique. It seems to be a pretty good device for getting him what he wants, including attention, so why spoil a good thing? Obviously, the way parents react to this can make a lot of difference. The presence or absence of older siblings or other children can make a difference, too. Many things can. But most important of all, what leads the child beyond this stage is his own need for more complex communication. The 2-year-old who is still getting whatever he wants with crude communication techniques will, in all likelihood, soon discover that there are many situations which are not gratified by these simple devices. He needs something that will tell much more precisely what he wants to simply because he has become aware of so many more possibilities in his world of objects and people and wants to partake of these possibilities. Language, like other important human skills, is learned. In order for the learning to occur, there must be motivation on the part of the child. The child must somehow discover that he can satisfy his own needs better by talking than by not talking, and by talking well rather than poorly. In later chapters, in our discussion of intellectual and social development especially, we shall see that the world of the 2-year-old normally becomes far too complex to let him be satisfied to remain at the "grunt and point" stage.

Language as a Means for Expression of Emotion During infancy laughing, cooing, and crying are the chief means by which the child expresses pleasure and displeasure. At first, in fact, there is little need to express more than these in the way of emotional response. As the world broadens into the exciting, stimulating, and often frustrating world of the

2-year-old, however, there arises a need to express many more things than simple pleasure and displeasure. At first, much of the emotional reaction is expressed directly, physically, in such behavior as hitting, running away, biting, hugging, etc. This is wordless action. True, such behavior may be accompanied by gross vocal activity, in an 18-month-old, for example, as squeals of delight, screams of fear or frustration. But during the preschool years an important shift is occurring: the child is becoming much less direct, much less physical, much more symbolic in his expression of emotion. Instead of hitting, he learns to use "hitting" words. Later, he finds more helpful and constructive words to help him deal with social frustration.

Language as a Device for Gaining Information As a child's world of people and things broadens and becomes more inclusive, it is understandable that many questions of "what?" "where?" "when?" and "why?" will occur to him. Asking questions and getting answers is an important activity, for the child is learning much about his world and about himself and, it is to be hoped, he is continually learning to ask better questions. In addition to the direct question-answer sequence which provides so much curiosity-satisfying information to the preschooler, there is the use of language in negative assertions, in the presence of adults and other children, as a technique for clarifying knowledge and opening up new possibilities. For example, when Terry, struggling with a jig-saw-puzzle, says, "It won't work," and is about to give up disgustedly, a nearby adult makes a casual suggestion about two colors or shapes that are alike, and Terry quickly sees the possibilities. Terry's assertion that it wouldn't work led to success in this instance, and she also learned a new clue in the fitting of puzzle pieces together. These negative assertions may be seen as devices or techniques put forth for the essential purpose of being confirmed or denied. They are devices intended to help the child clarify his world. The 2-year-old may make assertions with clarification as the essential motive. When he asserts something—and incidentally, it is frequently in a negative form—he is using a verbal technique in an effort to determine the form, the organization, and the boundaries of his world. The answers he gets to his assertions provide him with vital information on the nature of his world, both the physical world of objects and the social world of people. We shall say more about such motivations on the child's part in our discussions on personality development in later chapters.

A child learns to talk—and to listen.
(Courtesy of Dalton Schools.)

Language as a Means to Social Interaction The child of 2 and beyond is strongly motivated to engage in social behavior of a variety of kinds. He has already learned that many of his most important needs are dependent for their satisfaction on the presence of other people, both children and adults. It is natural, therefore, that his expanding skill in communication should be inextricably involved with his social motives. Indeed, language is the basic adhesive that binds a society together. Even the most primitive groups of which we have any record have relied on language in some form as a means of organizing for group action and cooperation. Through language it is possible to assign roles: "You will do this and I will do that, and together we can do something which neither could accomplish separately." And that is the basis of social organization.

For the preschooler, language is at first primarily a means of getting, from someone else, something he wants. This is to be expected, since the preschooler is essentially egocentric, and other people are not recognized as having equivalent thoughts, feelings, and needs, let alone equal rights. According to Piaget (13), the child's early stages of language use are consistent with this egocentrism, and reflect his need to *get* from a world whose purpose it is to minister to his wants. Piaget's concepts have been seriously questioned on the basis of recent research studies; nevertheless, it is not difficult to demonstrate that the young preschooler uses language in a self-centered way and that his social contacts via language are of this quality. At the same time, it will be through language that the child gradually becomes more aware of the objective realities of his social situation. He learns that his need to receive love and affection and all the more tangible rewards of social living is paralleled by a responsibility to give consideration to the needs of others. Language enables him to learn this fundamental lesson, thus preparing him for more mature social interaction. He learns, too, that language becomes a pleasant means to the social objective of living with and trusting other people. He learns that the sharing of ideas, thoughts, feelings, anxieties, hopes, frustrations, excitement, and disappointment with loved and trusted persons adds flavor to the positive feelings, and makes bearable the negative ones.

Perhaps most of all, it is only through language that one can truly reach agreements with others—not agreements in the sense of liking and disliking the same things as others, but agreements about the fundamental nature of things experienced. Language is the only device by which human beings can avoid being overwhelmed by the psychological threat of isolation. Man needs others of his kind if he is to fulfill his potentials as a human being. Language is the device through which he can truly give and receive in interaction with others of his kind.

Language as an Aid to Personal Identification We have already seen that, in order to learn to use language, a child must be motivated; he must have a reason before he talks. In the final analysis the most powerful motive of all, which serves to stimulate language development as well as a host of other kinds of growth, is the motive of self-realization. The drive to define oneself as a person, separate from but related to and respected by other persons, is an intense and fundamental drive in all of us. It is with language that one reaches out, tentatively at first, to make assertions about what he is and what he might be. The answers given to him gradually modify elements of his own definition of himself. The self-definition, as we shall have occasion to note from time to time, is a vital determiner of one's behavior. The child who learns early to think of himself as one who can take care of himself and solve his problems behaves, in emergencies, quite differently from one who has learned to think of himself as helpless and incapable of meeting crises constructively. The beginnings of such differences are made very early, and the language which the child experiences, especially from those he loves and on whom he is dependent, forms a large part of that self-definition.

THE TASKS OF LANGUAGE DEVELOPMENT

The remainder of this chapter will be devoted to a discussion of the two major tasks of language development which confront the child between 2 and 6 years of age. The emphasis in this section will be on the development of oral speech, since this is the major language task for this age period; it is also the aspect of total language development that has received the most attention from researchers. It is, in fact, an area in which a great deal is known—far more than could possibly be included in one brief chapter. The two major tasks of speech development for the preschool child are (1) the task of clear expression, and (2) the task of comprehension. The tasks do not occur in this order, but are developing simultaneously and interdependently. In the section that follows, each of these tasks will be explained as it applies to the preschooler, and our knowledge of the processes through which a child goes to fulfill them will be summarized.

The Task of Clear Expression Much progress has been made in the pronunciation of words by the time the typical child reaches the age of 2. But oral speech is a word-shaping and word-combining process, among other things. It is a complex motor skill requiring literally years of practice to become perfected. The infant could not make mature speech sounds even if his mental ability and experience were such that he knew how to go about it. The reason is simply that the vocal apparatus itself is still immature; the complex speech sounds made by older children and adults require coordination of the tongue against the teeth, among other things, which would not be possible for the infant.

According to McCarthy (12), and in keeping with the experience of most observers of children, the child typically acquires a basic mastery of spoken language between the ages of 1 and 5 years. McCarthy adds that the child whose language development is seriously delayed for any reason ". . . labors under an almost insurmountable handicap in his social and academic relationships" (12, p. 494). Articulation, the clear and accurate pronunciation of speech sounds, has its beginnings during infancy, with the native equipment with which the infant is endowed. In the normal course of events the infant's more or less random babbling and cooing, consisting of most of the vowel sounds and many of the consonants, goes through a refining process in the latter part of the first year. Part of this process includes the forming of distinct syllables, meaningless to the infant himself, which are easily repeated. Interestingly enough, the easiest and perhaps most common example is the "ma" syllable, which the infant pronounces with the vowel sound similar to that in the word "cat." He has achieved sufficient maturity of the sensory and nervous systems by this point that his own production of such a sound stimulates him to repeat it. It appears to give him satisfaction to do so. Most infants go through a late babbling stage known as "echolalia," in which there is a powerful stimulus to repeat such primitive syllable sounds. Understandably, then, sounds such as "ma-ma-ma . . ." and "da-da-da . . ." both of which are relatively easy for the infant speech apparatus to form, provide a basis for the first "word."

As the infant moves into the second year, which is generally the most dramatic one from the standpoint of speech, Smith (15) reports that the child has three words in his vocabulary, on the average. There is a strong drive now to imitate the sounds he hears, especially sounds made by those who attend to his needs. This is the psychological process of *identification* in operation. In it, it is as if the child, by reproducing the sounds made by those who care for him, can guarantee the repetition of that care. It is as if he were taking upon himself the power to minister to his own needs through reproducing the sounds made by those who have done just that in the past. Imitation is the basis of the rapid expansion of vocabulary which occurs in the second year. Table 7.1 reveals the remarkable speed of vocabulary growth throughout the preschool period. At no other time in the child's life is there such a rapid flowering of language development.

But learning to express oneself through oral speech is more than a matter of learning to say individual words. Soon after the vocabulary begins to expand in the second year, another kind of expansion can be noted:

TABLE 7.1. *Average Size of Vocabularies of 273 Children From 8 Months to 6 Years*

Age Group				Vocabulary	
Years	Months	Number of Children	Average IQ	Number of Words	Gain
	8	13		0	
	10	17		1	1
1—	0	52		3	2
1—	3	19		19	16
1—	6	14		22	3
1—	9	14		118	96
2—	0	25		272	154
2—	6	14		446	174
3—	0	20	109	896	450
3—	6	26	106	1,222	326
4—	0	26	109	1,540	318
4—	6	32	109	1,870	330
5—	0	20	108	2,072	202
5—	6	27	110	2,289	217
6—	0	9	108	2,562	273

SOURCE: M. E. Smith, "An Investigation of the Development of the Sentence and Extent of Vocabulary in Young Children," *Univ. of Iowa Stud. Child Welf.*, 1926, 3 (5): 54. Reprinted by permission.

the child uses words not only as names of individual objects, persons, or ideas (bottle, dada, mama, bed, night, etc.), but suddenly he seems to be using a single word to express a complete thought. It is not simply that the child associates "bottle" with his own feeding; we must realize that he may be saying, in effect, "I want my bottle—and I want it *now!*" when he uses the one word "bottle." The combining of two words to form a more complete thought is now not far away. Gesell (5) indicates that children combine two words in ordinary speech by the age of 21 months. Other researchers place it variously at between 18 and 24 months. In any case, it is clear that late in the second year the idea of putting words together, and the ability to do so in order to express a complete thought, is very much in evidence.

The order of occurrence of the parts of speech is of some interest in this connection. The first words of most children are predominantly nouns. This seems to accompany the rapid growth in naming objects in the middle of the second year—about that time the child seems suddenly aware of the fact that everything has a name, and his job is to know it. However, it should be kept in mind that the overwhelming predominance of nouns noted in the research studies of young children's speech may, in part, be due simply to the fact that nouns predominate in the language, and research methods commonly employed base their estimates on the proportion of words spoken to the number of words in the language itself. McCarthy (12) points out, however, that when a young child uses a noun, he may not *mean* it as a noun. For example, in the one-word sentence of the 18-month-old, a noun can easily function as a combination pronoun, verb, and noun, so far as the apparent intent of the child is concerned.

About the end of his second year, the child typically begins to use pronouns. His understanding of the concepts underlying the use of pronouns, however, is still very limited, and he will continue to make many errors in their use throughout the preschool period. From 2 through 5 years of age the use of nouns does not decrease, but the relative proportion of modifying and clarifying words—adjectives, adverbs, interjections—all increase along with size of vocabulary and length of sentence.

Sentence length as a measure of language development has been given considerable attention by research investigators. It provides a reliable index to the level of language maturity of the child, and it is a relatively easy one to measure. Table 7.2 gives a summary of the growth of average sentence length for the preschool years. As is true of all the measures of language development for which average figures can be given, there is a great deal of variation here, which occurs in two major ways: (1) variation from one child to another, some having much longer sentence constructions than others at each age level, and (2) variation for a given child, from one time to another, depending on the circumstances, the need for long or short constructions, the degree of stimulation, factors of inhibition, etc.

The feature of the expressive language of children that most calls itself to the attention of adults is probably *articulation*. This is the ability to pronounce speech sounds that are clear, accurate, and comprehensible to the adult listener. Speech sounds of 2-year-olds and many 3-year-olds are difficult for most adults to understand. The competent nursery-school teacher, however, develops considerable skill in comprehension. This brings up one of the most vital points about the guidance of children's language development: a child needs people around him who will make a real effort to understand his vocal productions, in order to encourage him to keep trying. His efforts represent continuous practice in a skill that requires long years to perfect; a little encouragement along the way can make a lot of difference. The ability to pronounce speech sounds correctly is closely tied to chronological age. A study by Wellman *et al.* (17) reported a correlation of .80 between age and the ability to articulate speech sounds during the preschool years. The same study indicated that about 32 percent of the total number of sounds were made correctly at age 2. The percentages at ages 3, 4, 5, and 6, respectively, were as follows: 63%, 77%, 88%, and 89%. It appears that between the ages of 2 and 3 there is a marked increase in accuracy of articulation.

In this connection, Jersild tells an interesting story of a conversation between a mother and her two small daughters, Peggy (age 2) and Marian (age 3):

> MOTHER: *Oh, look, there's a monkey wearing a red coat!*
> PEGGY: *Oh, yook!*
> MARIAN: *Don't say yook, say wook* (9, p. 407).

This suggests that even the nature of the errors and their gradual correction follows some patterning and regularity. A major factor in the child's correction of his own articulation errors, assuming there is no defect in the speech apparatus itself, is the speech model available to him. It is not necessary to call the child's attention to his errors; in fact, it is ordinarily

TABLE 7.2. *Mean Length of Sentence in Spoken Language as Shown in Three Investigations*

Author and Type of Study	Date	Group	Age							
			N	2	2½	3	3½	4	4½	5
McCarthy: Representative group, 50 responses with adult.	1930	Boys	67	1.4	3.2	3.1	4.2	4.3	4.6	
		Girls	73	2.1	3.1	3.8	4.4	4.4	4.7	
		All	140	1.8	3.1	3.4	4.3	4.4	4.6	
Smith: Miscellaneous cases in child-child and child-adult situations.	1935	Boys	153	1.5	2.4	3.3	4.3	4.4	5.0	4.9
		Girls	152	2.0	2.6	3.8	4.2	4.7	4.9	5.0
		All	305	1.8	2.5	3.5	4.3	4.6	4.9	5.0
Young: Nursery-school children in four situations.	1941	Boys	37		3.1	3.3	4.2	4.6	4.7	4.9
		Girls	37		3.3	3.9	4.6	4.8	5.0	5.5

SOURCE: Adapted with permission from D. McCarthy, "Language Development in Children," in L. Carmichael (ed.), *Manual of Child Psychology* (2nd ed.), New York: John Wiley & Sons., Inc., 1954, pp. 492–630.

inadvisable. As Jersild comments, the child will, in his own good time, "correct his earlier mispronunciations even though no adult is hounding him" (9, p. 406). The risk of adult correction is that a sensitive child can be made to feel that it is better to avoid certain words—or, in extreme cases, to avoid talking altogether in the presence of adults—rather than to make mistakes. Obviously, this does not lead to healthy attitudes toward his own speaking ability. Thus, it may be concluded that most of the articulation errors will have disappeared, without special attention, by the end of the preschool period. This assumes the availability of a good speech model, one who talks clearly and not too fast to the child, and one who has a good all-round personal relationship with the child.

There are many children, however, who for any of a number of reasons do not completely overcome their articulation errors by age 6. This by itself is certainly not to be taken as evidence of mental retardation. A child who is still making serious errors in speech sounds at age 6 should receive, in addition to a regular medical examination, treatment from a qualified speech therapist.

INFLUENCES UPON THE DEVELOPMENT OF EXPRESSIVE ABILITY. The variation from one child to another in the ages at which they first begin to talk, in the speed at which they increase their vocabulary, in the extent to which they talk, in the length of their sentences, and in every other index of expressive language development is indeed remarkable. No one factor or condition accounts for this wide variation. It is always a combination of forces that results in the individual child's unique development of expressive ability. Some of the forces lie within the child himself: his native intelligence, the rate of maturation of his nervous system, the physical condition of his speech apparatus, etc. Other conditions lie outside him as a part of his social and objective environment. Although each of these will be discussed as separate factors, it is well to remember that their effect on the child is usually in interaction with a number of other factors—that there are no isolated causes of fast or slow speech development.

Conditions within the child. It is natural for most people to associate the child's speech development with his over-all intelligence. Research findings bear this out. However, the relationship is not a simple one of cause-and-effect, with the brighter child always talking earlier and better than the average or retarded child. One of the strongest fears of parents when a child does not talk or talk well at an age when most children are is that their child is retarded. We can be pretty certain that a child who does talk at a normal age or earlier must have at least average intellectual development. The converse, however, is not a safe generalization. We can never be certain, on the basis of retarded speech development alone, that a child is mentally slow.

TABLE 7.3. *Correlations of Several Language Indices with CA and MA, and Intercorrelations Among the Language Variables*

N = 38	MA	Speech Sounds	Word Usage	Length of Unit	Complexity	Completeness	Van-Alstyne Vocabulary	Smith-Williams Vocabulary
CA	.56	.31	.43	.54	.41	.45	.36	.16
MA		.12	.49	.78	.55	.59	.52	.47
Speech sounds		.91	.64	.60	.61	.62	.16	.01
Word usage		.60	.94	.62	.80	.57	.36	.27
Length of unit		.69	.42	.86	.65	.80	.56	.37
Completeness		.58	.66	.41	.89	.74	.41	.21
Complexity		.60	.38	.67	.61	.87	.56	.41
Van Alstyne vocabulary		.57	.13	.28	.16	.36	.84	.59
Smith-Williams vocabulary		.08	.09	.04	—.02	.22	.76	.87

NOTE: Reliabilities are shown on the diagonal. Zero order *r*'s above and to the right. Partial correlations holding CA and MA constant below and to the left.
SOURCE: Reprinted with permission from D. McCarthy, "Language Development in Children," in L. Carmichael (ed.), *Manual of Child Psychology* (2nd ed.), New York: John Wiley & Sons, Inc., 1954, p. 575 (after Williams, 1937).

Table 7.3 presents a portion of the data obtained by Williams (18) in an important study of language development in 3- and 4-year-old children. In this table, it may be seen that mental age (MA) is correlated in varying degrees with eight different measures, or indices, of expressive language development. From the size of these correlation coefficients we may safely conclude that a child's ability to express himself verbally is greatly dependent on his mental maturity. What complicates the relationship between intelligence and speech development, however, is the fact that some children who are average or who are even very bright in their mental development simply do not talk until they are well beyond the average age for talking. In such cases, the rate of speech development is usually rapid when it does get underway. The reasons for this slowness in talking among a small percentage of bright children are not entirely clear. One suggestion is that, partly because of their brightness, they become highly proficient in communicating without having to speak. They may develop a fairly elaborate gesture language which, because they are more "fluent" in this respect than other children, may serve them for a longer time and make speaking less necessary at first. During the later preschool years and in subsequent development throughout childhood, over-all language development is the best single index of intelligence available to psychologists. Most good tests of intelligence measure vocabulary, directly or otherwise, along with the other standard items of intelligence testing.

Another significant internal factor in expressive language development is the condition of the sensory processes, especially those of vision and hearing. Deafness, of course, has a direct bearing on speech development. In the normal course of events, the child hears his own speech and gradually modifies it to make it sound like the speech of others around him. Hence the deaf child is at an extreme disadvantage, and must, if he is to learn to speak, go through a somewhat different psychological process in the learning. Children who have only partial hearing are relatively less handicapped than the totally deaf child. The degree to which speech is affected depends a great deal on the age at which the hearing loss occurs as well as the degree of hearing loss. Much has been learned about specialized techniques for teaching speech to hard-of-hearing and deaf children, with encouraging results in large numbers of such cases.

Loss of vision has a less direct influence on speech development; some studies even indicate that certain aspects of speech may be accelerated in blind children. In research conducted by Maxfield (10), it was found that among a group of eight totally blind preschool children there was a great deal of talking; more, in fact, than had been observed in certain studies among normal preschool children. Further, these blind children as a group asked more questions and resorted less to nonverbal language. Other studies of the speech of blind children do not entirely support the findings of Maxfield, however, nor do they indicate any significant speech retardation among these children. It has been suggested that any effects of blindness on speech development may operate indirectly, through the experiences the blind are provided with and the attitudes of the important people in their lives. Many blind children, for example, may be given a different kind and quality of attention by their parents and may be exposed to a different quality of speech stimulation from them because of their blindness. In any event, it is safe to conclude that blindness, *per se*, whether it be congenital or the result of disease or accident during childhood, need not be a significant cause of delayed or distorted speech.

There are a variety of other pathological conditions that may have direct or indirect effects on the establishment of expressive language. Among these are cerebral palsy, aphasia, and cleft palate conditions. We need not discuss these factors in detail, however, as our primary concern is not with pathological conditions, but with understanding normal speech development and the parts played in it by a variety of processes in the child's life.

The factors of sex and sibling position have also been studied in relation to speech development. There is considerable agreement in research literature that girls talk at an earlier age than boys and that their vocabularies are consistently larger. In most studies the differences are not sufficiently large to be of statistical significance; however, the consistency with which this finding has been made, in repeated studies, by so many different students of speech development, leaves little doubt about there being a real difference in favor of girls. As with other factors, the reasons for sex having this effect are less clear than the effect itself. It could be explained in part by the fact that girls simply mature more rapidly. For example, it might be related to the fact that myelination of the nervous system occurs at a more rapid rate for girls, on the average, than for boys. In part, however, the explanation may lie in the different kinds of speech stimulation provided for girls and boys in our society by most parents. Further research is needed to explain such differences in a satisfactory manner.

Order of birth is known to be related to progress in speech development, but also the extent to which children associate with other children or with adults. These should properly be considered as environmental factors. McCarthy (11) found that children who associated chiefly with adults were accelerated in their language development. Apparently these children get more practice in the use of mature language forms. A number of research studies have shown that twins and triplets are slower in their speech development than singletons, with triplets seemingly more affected, even, than twins. This difference is not a matter of intelligence, but is also apparently related to the kind of social environment and degree of stimulation presented to the children, and thus, too, should properly be classified as an environmental factor. It is certainly an interesting factor. Day (4) studied 80 pairs of twins and found them to be markedly retarded in all aspects of language development, compared with singletons. One of Day's conclusions is especially interesting: the average length of response for 5-year-old twins was slightly below that of 3-year-old singletons. The differences were accounted for primarily in terms of the reduced need on the part of the twins to form broader social relationships beyond the relationship with the other twin. Other studies also indicate that it is primarily the home situation during the preschool period which has the retarding effect on twins. Later, when the children enter school and are stimulated by a broader range of experiences, their language development tends to catch up with that of their peers, according to Davis (3). Presumably the effect becomes greater in proportion to the number of children born at any one time. In studies of the Dionne quintuplets carried out by Blatz, Fletcher, and Mason (1), it was found that the girls were retarded by 16 to 18 months when less than 3 years of age. Their case was complicated by the fact that they grew up in a bilingual home. Nevertheless it appeared that being quintuplets did affect speech progress.

One other feature of normal speech development has to do with timing. That is, growth in active expressive language does not occur in one smooth curve. When the history of a particular child is followed carefully, spurts of rapid development and periods of little or no apparent progress may be observed. This is merely in keeping with other aspects of human growth; yet, for some reason, it seems to cause a certain amount of concern to parents if their children go through a long stage of no apparent progress. We should emphasize the word *apparent,* since the child's total language development may be progressing without there being any obvious change in his vocabulary or increase in the length of his sentences.

It helps to understand that at certain points in the child's growth he seems to focus most of his available growth energy on a particular task until he achieves a reasonable level of perfection. Reaching it, he is then free to go back and pick up other tasks and move ahead in them. It is not really a matter of "going back" at all, but merely a matter of resuming the active attention to a task that had been held in abeyance for a time, while specializing in something else. This explanation should help us to see what normally happens to many children in the later infantile period, when it becomes so important to get up on two feet and walk around under one's own power. That is no small task. It takes a lot of concentrated effort to get the nerves and muscles and body balance senses to coordinate properly and acquire sufficient bodily control to walk well.

It is understandable, then, that talking, which typically has its beginnings before a child learns to walk, should be sidetracked for a time while skill in walking is achieved. Once walking has become more or less automatic, however, and no longer requires the concentration or effort it took at first, the child can then command a broader perspective of his own world, which is suddenly bigger and more stimulating with things and people, and which calls forth his latent language capacity, demanding that he exercise it. Even the number of questions posed by the runabout child indicates how his rich multitude of daily experiences, many of them new ones each day, stimulate him to question and to discuss his world. Language, at this point, becomes a vital means to a gallant end: the satisfaction of human curiosity.

Environmental factors in speech development. We have already referred to one or two factors in the child's environment which seem to have important effects on the growth of active language. We have yet to see just how the environment operates to stimulate a child in his use of words or, in some cases, to retard his speech growth. It should be remembered that there is no such thing as "natural" language. Left completely on his own, without the stimulating effect of significant people in his life, the child would be completely without speech. It is the concept of "*significant people*" which should be stressed here. Perhaps the mother is the most significant of all. From the very beginning she is the one who has had most to do with the satisfaction of the infant's needs. It is precisely around and within that need-satisfaction setting that language learning takes place. The language the child learns is, without planning or intent on her part, her language. When we speak of a child learning the "mother-tongue" there is more involved, indeed, than learning the language of one's country!

A number of research investigations have brought out the fact that children raised apart from a loving mother-figure have been retarded in language development as a consequence. Children reared in institutions such as orphanages have been shown to talk less and at later ages than children reared in ordinary households. The studies of Goldfarb are of interest in this connection. Goldfarb (6, 7, 8) showed that not only were young children affected in their language development by living in institutions, but that the effects persisted on into adolescence. Spitz (16), Rheingold and Bayley (14), and others have demonstrated that when children suffer from inadequate mothering, their language development is likely to be an area in which the effects are most marked. Part of the explanation for this is that in many institutional settings need satisfaction—to the extent that it occurs—takes place in a relatively impersonal setting. There is not the close, one-to-one relationship, the give and take of intimate language interaction, which occurs in ordinary homes around the routines of eating, bathing, household chores, dressing and undressing, health care, etc. It is the close identification of the child with a loving parent that seems to be a central ingredient of the motive for talking. Without such motivation language development is, at best, a slow and difficult process. According to McCarthy (12), it is not just the amount of contact with the mother that is important. After reviewing the research on the subject, McCarthy concludes that even in ordinary homes the quality of the mother-child relationship has an important bearing on the acquisition of language. The kind of quality most helpful to the child is difficult to describe or to measure scientifically, but it is made up of many things: how much the mother wanted the child; the extent to which she feels she is competent to take care of him; the amount of tension and anxiety she feels while caring for him; the extent to which she talks with him or, on the other hand, is silent and preoccupied while giving mere physical care; and the extent to which she develops a truly close relationship with him, in contrast to being impersonal and psychologically distant.

Throughout the preschool years, parent-child relationships enter into language development in a variety of ways. The pattern of speech for children is established by their parents, particularly by the mother. During this same period identification with parents becomes pronounced; that is, children take upon themselves many of the psychological attributes of the parents. It is through language that the child is enabled to carry out many of his specific identification tasks. By using the words his parents use he takes unto himself some of the strength, power, and authority of his parents, which is a part of what he seeks during this time. Thus there is a powerful incentive to talk like them. This means that the parents become highly significant speech models for their children, whether they wish to be or not. Voice inflections and mannerisms; choice of words; use of speech to show aggression, hostility, fears, and other emotions; use of speech to cajole and threaten; development of verbal humor; and a host of other things are a part of the pattern established for the child by his parents. Perhaps of utmost significance is the child's learning, or failing to learn, how to use speech as a way of relieving tension and reducing anxiety. Again, it is the parents who teach this, without ever necessarily thinking about it or planning it.

One other significant element in the preschool child's language development, which we have said very little about thus far, has special significance in the parent-child relationships—the matter of asking questions. Preschoolers are notorious question-askers. When the Brandenburgs (2) kept careful records of the verbal behavior of their own child, they discovered something which many parents will regard as a conservative underestimate: during the course of *one day* their 4-year-old asked 397 meaningful questions. The mother of one 4-year-old asked the child psychologist who was directing a meeting of nursery-school parents and teachers, "What can I do? My child talks incessantly, he talks when he's supposed to be resting; he talks when he's supposed to be eating; and when he's just playing, he asks so many questions so fast I don't have time to answer one before he asks another one! It isn't that I want him to stop talking and asking questions; it's just that I'd like time to get my work done!" There is a bit of humor in this—and a bit of insight for us, too—when we understand that mother: she was by far the talkingest and questioningest mother in that parent group, and it is not straining anything to see a relationship between her own language habits and those of her 4-year-old!

Nevertheless, there is a legitimate question for all parents: how does one react constructively to the barrage of language that often comes from the preschooler as he "blooms" into a true user of language? And it is complicated by the knowledge that many of the questions he asks cannot be answered once and for all; they will be raised again and again, perhaps at more sophisticated levels of understanding, possibly at the very same level as before. But children are using their questions for more than the mere purpose of getting a specific factual answer to a particular question. The solution to the mother's problem, if there is one, is in her understanding of why the child is using language the way he does. He is using it for a variety of purposes, including to get and to hold his mother's attention. Knowing this, she can find a number of ways to provide him with that which he needs—possibly special times when she can be alone with him and provide her undivided attention. She should know, also, that his questions are not just designed to get at "the facts." He is after the kind of security that comes from reassurance that the world is orderly, safe, and to some degree predictable. His questions arise from his need to experience and re-experience her own convictions in these matters, to prove continually to himself that his own experiences check out and square with the rest of the world. He is seeking her strength, and language is a powerful means to that end.

Other environmental conditions also play important roles in shaping the language development of children. One of these is the socioeconomic status of the child's family. This is really a complex of factors rather than a single one—and the factors are inextricably interwoven with each other. It is known, for example, that there is some relationship between adult intelligence and socioeconomic status. It is also known that intelligence is to a considerable degree a matter of biological inheritance. Hence the bright child whose parents are of a relatively high socioeconomic status and who learns to express himself well verbally at an early age is only demonstrating that many forces are at work in producing that effect. His early vocabulary development, partly based on his keen mind, may also be a function of the number of books in his home, the level of education of his parents, the family practice of reading and speaking well—their greater facility in verbal expression, in other words. It is not easy to separate the effects of heredity and environment in such a big undertaking as the acquisition of speech. Nevertheless, some research has demonstrated that the environment has some very real effects on the language of the emotionally deprived. Included here would be those studies on the effects of living in institutions and having inadequate mothering during infancy and early childhood. In such studies it has been a rather consistent finding that, if the environment is threatening and depriving to the child, it is in the area of language development that the effects are most severe and damaging.

The Task of Verbal Comprehension Every child and, for that matter, every adult who has learned to speak has two basic kinds of vocabulary. One of these, the most obvious to the observer, might be called the *active* or *expressive* vocabulary. The other, which we shall now discuss briefly, has been termed the *understanding* vocabulary.[1] At all ages from infancy on we understand and respond appropriately to a larger

[1] Some writers have referred to this as a "passive" vocabulary, since it does not involve open expression; as we shall see here, the term "passive" is not an accurate description of this aspect of language development.

number of words and a greater variety of words than the ones we speak to other people. The infant is quite capable of reacting intelligently to verbal commands and prohibitions for some time before he is able to use the words himself. Throughout the early stages of single words, one-word sentences, short phrases, and on through the preschool years to the development of mature language patterns, the child continues to progress more rapidly in the understanding of words and phrases than he does in the expressive use of them. Perhaps the reason for this is in part that their use for expressive purposes demands at once a basic understanding as well as something in addition: the psychomotor skill and coordination in forming thoughts into audible, articulate speech sounds. By contrast, the understanding vocabulary demands only comprehension.

The difference, however, is less clear-cut than this might imply. Understanding of verbal speech is not merely a passive process of absorption of the sounds of someone else and knowing what is meant! It requires a very real and active participation on the part of a child to understand a word or phrase. Here lies one of the vital keys to understanding children. For the child, cooperation with the world around him, in the form of attending to things said by others and understanding those things in the way they are intended, is not just an automatic process, but a dynamic activity which must be learned, and which is subject to many influences that make it sometimes more, sometimes less efficient. This is part of the monumental task confronting a child who is in the process of becoming a communicating human being.

To understand is, in a sense, to reach an agreement with another—an agreement on the meaning of a common experience. In the final analysis these meanings are always unique and individual experiences. It is only by testing under many and varied circumstances that children gradually approximate, in their individual experiences of meaning, the meanings that words and phrases hold for the adults around them. It is a long and difficult process, fraught with many frustrations and potentialities for misunderstanding. The wonder is not so much that parents and children often misunderstand each other, but that there are so many occasions when they come so close to genuine understanding.

The measurement of children's understanding vocabularies has been accomplished through the use of various vocabulary tests. Many of these, however, demand that a child have the ability to explain with expressive language the meaning of the terms presented to him. Such is the case with many of the vocabulary tests used as part of standard intelligence tests. Vocabulary tests for young children and for others whose expressive capacity is sharply limited cannot rely on such techniques. Some efficient tests have been developed which allow a young child to respond to pictures by signifying which of a number of possibilities represents the term or expression used by the examiner. The usefulness of this procedure is illustrated in the case of Linda, a 4-year-old who had been in nursery school for almost a year. Linda did not talk at nursery school, and questions were raised about her intellectual development. However, she did talk at home, and she also communicated fairly efficiently through gesture language at school. The usual tests of intelligence, relying heavily on the child's expressive ability, were inappropriate for her. Instead, she was given a performance test, which measures the child's ability to respond appropriately to a variety of designs, visual patterns, mazes, and puzzles. In addition, she was given a vocabulary examination that merely required her to identify which of four pictures portrayed each of the terms spoken by the examiner. In both of these tests Linda scored well above average, indicating superior general mental ability and in addition a keen grasp of the meaning of words. Thus, the procedure was useful in establishing the sharp cleavage between a child's expressive language ability, which in this case was limited in the nursery-school setting, and her understanding vocabulary, which was unusually good. The reasons for the unusual discrepancy between the two kinds of language ability noted in this case go outside the area of discussion at the moment. They are tied, in rather complex ways, to the child's emotional development and to her having learned at an early age that whenever there is a "threatening" or "dangerous" situation it is safer not to talk.

Estimates of the total understanding vocabularies of normal children, while extremely difficult to establish accurately, are impressive in the number of terms and concepts understood at relatively early age levels. Verbal understanding, of course, involves something more than merely comprehending isolated words. It involves the whole matter of organizing meanings of phrases, words used in a variety of contexts and with many shades of meaning, long and complex sentences, etc. It involves understanding idiomatic expression—a form of understanding which is somewhat removed from the literal, or dictionary, definition of the words used. Again, the task of the child is seen to be a challenging one, indeed. Factors in the development of verbal understanding are, in many respects, identical with those which we have discussed in the section on active language. Perhaps the special emphasis in connection with the understanding vocabulary should be placed on the factor of native intelligence, since that serves as the initial basis for such language development. Home conditions, family patterns of speech, the family values placed on literary and verbal activities, and the nature of the parent-child relationships also enter in, however. The response of parents to the child's questioning is rather crucial—for through that response a child learns or fails to learn not only the specific answer he is seeking through his immediate question, but also whether or not the process of questioning is a safe and legitimate way to explore his world. He learns whether his questions are of any significance or not, according to whether or not the significant people in his life value them.

There is room for a great deal of wise guidance from parents and nursery-school teachers for the preschool child in his efforts to achieve verbal understanding. The preschool years are remarkable years of discovering that words can be powerful means to the end of organizing and understanding the world and gaining a measure of control over it. The chief element of a sound program of guidance of this aspect of the child's personality is, beyond any reasonable doubt, a respect for the validity of the child's need to understand and for the limitations of his experience that prevent him from having greater understanding.

SUMMARY

Speech occurs whenever distinct vocal sounds are made by a person and understood by a listener. Language is a broader category including all vehicles for human communication. The child is confronted with the task of learning many languages, including the language of facial expression, gestures, body posture, and pantomime, as well as spoken language. Language is the basic process of sharing among individuals, and lies at the core of social interaction. It is also the basis for the development of human personality as we know it.

The preschool years represent the period of the most rapid progress in language behavior, in both expressive language and understanding language. Growth of language behavior is orderly, progressing in a natural and predictable sequence but with a remarkably wide range of individual differences among normal children. Factors associated with these individual variations include intelligence, rate of maturation, sex, efficiency of sensory processes such as hearing, sibling relationships, quality of speech model available, motivations for language, and amount and kind of social stimulation provided by adults.

The two major tasks of language development between 2 and 6 are (1) the achievement of clear, understandable articulation of words and word combinations, with appropriate meanings; and (2) understanding the language of other children and adults. In both of these tasks, the role of the most significant adults in the child's life is paramount.

REFERENCES

1. Blatz, W. E., Fletcher, M. I., and Mason, M., "Early development in spoken language of the Dionne quintuplets," in W. E. Blatz et al., *Collected studies of the Dionne quintuplets*, Toronto: *Univ. Toronto Stud. Child Develpm. Ser.*, 1937 (16).
2. Brandenburg, J., and Brandenburg, G. C., "Language development during the fourth year," *Ped. Sem.*, 1919, **26**:27–40.
3. Davis, E. A., "The development of linguistic skill in twins, singletons with siblings, and only children from age five to ten years," *Inst. Child Welf. Monogr. Ser.*, Minneapolis: Univ. of Minnesota Press, 1937 (14).
4. Day, E. J., "The development of language in twins: I. A comparison of twins and single children," *Child Develpm.*, 1932, **3**:179–199.
5. Gesell, A., and Amatruda, C. S., *Developmental diagnosis*, 2nd. ed., New York: Hoeber-Harper, 1947.
6. Goldfarb, W., "The effects of early institutional care on adolescent personality," *Child Develpm.*, 1943, **4**:213–223.
7. Goldfarb, W., "Effects of psychological deprivation in infancy and subsequent stimulation," *Amer. J. Psychiat.*, 1945, **102**(1):18–33.
8. Goldfarb, W., "Emotional and intellectual consequences of psychologic deprivation in infancy: A revaluation," in P. H. Hoch and J. Zubin (eds.), *Psychopathology of childhood*, New York: Grune & Stratton, 1955, pp. 105–119.
9. Jersild, A. T., *Child psychology*, 4th ed., New York: Prentice-Hall, 1954.
10. Maxfield, K. E., "The spoken language of the blind preschool child: A study of method," *Arch. Psychol.*, 1936 (201).

11. McCarthy, D., "The language development of the preschool child," *Inst. Child Welf. Monogr. Ser.*, Minneapolis: Univer. of Minnesota Press, 1930 (4).
12. McCarthy, D., "Language development in children," in L. Carmichael (ed.), *Manual of child psychology*, 2nd. ed., New York: Wiley, 1954, pp. 492–630.
13. Piaget, Jean, *The language and thought of the child*, New York: Harcourt, Brace, 1926.
14. Rheingold, H. L., and Bayley, Nancy, "The later effects of an experimental modification of mothering," *Child Develpm.*, 1959, **30**: 363–372.
15. Smith, M. E., "An investigation of the development of the sentence and the extent of vocabulary in young children," *Univ. Iowa Stud. Child Welf.*, 1926, **3** (5).
16. Spitz, R. A., "The importance of mother-child relationship during the first year of life," *Ment. Hlth Today*, 1948, 7:7–13.
17. Wellman, B. L., *et al.*, "Speech sounds of young children," *Univ. Iowa Stud. Child Welf.*, 1931, **5**:(2).
18. Williams, H. M., "An analytical study of language achievement in preschool children. Part I of development of language and vocabulary in young children," *Univ. Iowa Stud. Child Welf.*, 1937, **13**:(2).

CHAPTER EIGHT

Why is intelligence difficult to define? What differences are there between the intelligent behavior of adults and that of children? What are the components of intelligence? Do young children reason? At what age is it possible to reason effectively with a child? How do children acquire general concepts? How do we measure intellectual development in young children? How reliable are the results of mental tests with infants and preschool children? What are the causes of individual differences in the intellectual growth of children?

THE DEVELOPMENT OF INTELLIGENCE

EVER SINCE THE APPEARANCE of the first intelligence tests early in the present century, there has been an increased interest in this more or less mysterious aspect of human personality. There has also been much misunderstanding about the nature of intelligence, its growth during childhood, the significance of individual differences from one child to another, and the techniques for estimating the level of mental ability of children. In this chapter we shall attempt to portray the meaning of intellectual ability and the nature of its growth during early childhood.

THE MEANING OF MENTAL ABILITY

In popular thinking, intelligence has frequently been defined as the ability to learn. It has been closely identified, for the school-age child, with the ability to perform well in school subjects. Certainly it is true that the more intelligent child is able to learn more efficiently than the less intelligent child, other things being equal. But learning ability and scholastic achievement, while affected by intelligence, should not be thought of as synonymous with intelligence. Alfred Binet, one of the first psychologists to experiment with intelligence tests, and probably the most important single influence in the development of the mental-age scale for testing mental ability, defined intelligence in terms of the child's ability to act in relation to goals and to revise his behavior if need be to reach a goal. Other psychologists have provided varying definitions, stressing such qualities as abstract thinking, comprehension, creativity and originality, and the ability to make use of past experience in the solution of problems. Some have tended to view intelligence as a more or less unitary quality, a general level of efficiency of mental functioning. Others, in contrast, have viewed it not as a unitary trait, but as a series of relatively independent qualities (factors), which may exist in markedly different degree within the same child.

There is no one right definition of intelligence, but these considerations give some impression of the breadth of the area to be covered. It is the gradual elaboration of the processes and characteristics included in such definitions that constitutes mental development.

Verbal and Nonverbal Intelligence One major consideration in mental development is the distinction often made between verbal intelligence and nonverbal mental ability. The first of these consists of all of those mental functions that rely heavily for their operation on the ability of a child to organize a problem into words (which may or may not be spoken) and to deal effectively with that problem through the use of words. Thus this aspect of mental behavior is closely tied to language development; indeed it would be impossible to draw a sharp line between mental behavior and language behavior, since the two are not really independent processes at all. Nonverbal intelligent behavior, on the other hand, presumably relies on the capacity for organizing problems and dealing with those problems without necessarily resorting to the use of formal language symbols.

These two aspects of mental behavior are not independent; other things being equal, the child who is advanced in one will be advanced in the other, and the child who is retarded in one will probably be retarded in the other. At the same time, it is often a useful distinction to make, especially when dealing with children who have special circumstances that for one reason or another place the child at a disadvantage in one of these aspects of mental behavior. A simple example would be the deaf child, who is obviously handicapped in his language development and whose mental growth may be slowed in some ways with respect to the achievement and use of verbal concepts. On the other hand, this child may have a well developed central nervous system, so that his native capacity for intelligent behavior, particularly of the nonverbal variety, may be markedly superior to his language intelligence.

Social Definitions of Intelligence In the final analysis, the most important definitions of intelligence are not those ordinarily given in textbooks or manuals for the testing of mental ability. The basic criterion of intelligent behavior is a social criterion: to what degree is the child capable of reacting constructively to the countless problems presented by living in his physical and social environment? In this sense the only real test of intelligence is the test of life itself, which measures the child's capacity for living effectively in a complex world. In the following section, we shall attempt to understand how psychologists estimate children's ability to adapt to their physical and social environments. The psychologist's use of tests is, in one sense, merely an attempt to make predictions about the child's resources for adapting effectively to his world.

THE MEASUREMENT OF INTELLIGENCE IN YOUNG CHILDREN

In any attempt to understand the intellectual development of a child, we must be concerned with two questions: (1) what is the child's present status with respect to performance of intellectual tasks, and (2) what is the trend of the child's growing and expanding capacity for task performance? The use of standardized scales or "tests" of intelligence provides us with the basic information we may use to answer these questions. The intelligence test is merely a device that allows the examiner to compare the performance of one child with that of many other children in response to a series of standard tasks or problems which demand a variety of mental activities and operations. The test is given under carefully controlled conditions, and the examiner follows a rather elaborate set of instructions in presenting the tasks to the child. Otherwise there would be no basis for comparing one child with all the others. The comparison is made by checking the child's performance on the tasks with the "norms" or standards provided in the manual for the test. These norms have been derived by the examination of large numbers of children, and they represent the average performance of children in the general population.

The Concept of Mental Age One of the most significant developments in the history of mental testing was Binet's concept of mental age. While there are certain limitations and disadvantages to its use, especially with older children, it paved the way for the establishment of sound testing procedures. The mental-age concept is a fairly simple, straightforward notion in its basic features: *mental age is the average performance, on standardized tests of intelligence, of children of a given chronological age*. Thus if we had a set of tasks that was known to require intellectual ability for their performance, we might theoretically present the tasks to all children of a given age, say 4 years. By scoring the performance of every 4-year-old and averaging the scores, we could determine what the "typical" 4-year-old behavior is with respect to these tasks. It is this typical behavior of the children of a given chronological age which provides a basis for the mental-age concept. Presumably if we gave the same tasks to all 5-year-old children, their average performance would be somewhat superior to our 4-year-olds. The difference in the performance of the two age groups represents the difference between mental age 4 and mental age 5. From this we develop an age scale which provides us with the performance levels for each chronological age. It follows that mental age will necessarily mean something slightly different when measured with a different set of tasks. This is important to keep in mind, since it means that a child's mental age, as measured by one test, may not be identical with his mental age on another test. There are many tests in use.

When we wish to know the level of mental ability of a given child, we present him with the same tasks of intellectual performance as were given those on whom the test was standardized. We determine from his test performance how he compares with the norms. If his performance equals that of the average 4-year-old, we say he has mental age of 4, regardless of his actual chronological age. A child who is actually 5 years old may perform at the 4-year level; we would say his mental development is significantly below average. A child of 4 whose performance is equal to the 4-year average would be described as having normal mental de-

Taking a standardized intelligence test.
(Suzanne Szasz.)

velopment. A child who is actually 3 years old, but whose performance equals that of the average 4-year-old, would be described as having accelerated mental development; he is significantly above average in rate of mental growth.

The IQ Another very useful device which makes it easier to draw valid comparisons among children is the *intelligence quotient*, commonly abbreviated as IQ. This is simply the ratio of the child's mental age to his chronological age, as given in the following formula:

$$IQ = \frac{MA}{CA} \ (\times\ 100)$$

With this formula, we obtain an index that is very useful in estimating the child's mental abilities. If a child's mental age and chronological age are identical, the quotient is always 1.00. When multiplied by 100, the resulting IQ score is 100. We commonly think of 100 as representing average IQ. In the case of the examples previously given, in which two children whose actual ages were 5 and 3, respectively, both of whom had mental age scores of 4, the IQ figures would deviate considerably from 100. In the case of the 5-year-old, the IQ would be computed as follows:

$$IQ = 4/5\ (100) = .80\ (100) = 80$$

In the case of the 3-year-old with a mental age of 4, the IQ computation would be:

$$IQ = 4/3\ (100) = 1.33\ (100) = 133$$

In theory, a child's IQ should remain relatively stable from one age to another, on the assumption that an individual child's rate of mental development is fairly consistent. That is, the bright child whose mental age is accelerated at 3 years of age will continue to progress more rapidly than the average and maintain approximately the same ratio of MA to CA. At age 6, for example, his mental development is likely to be that of the average 8-year-old, which would still provide an IQ score of about 133.

There are a number of reasons why a child's IQ score will not be exactly the same from one age to another, however. Many things can affect the actual performance of a child in an intelligence test: the nature of the examination; the competence of the examiner; the degree of rapport (agreement or harmony) between child and examiner; freedom from distractions, fatigue, or boredom, etc. Thus, any score obtained with an intelligence test is, at best, an *estimate* of mental ability, based on the child's performance under the conditions at the time of the examination. A different examiner, using a different test, in a different room, at a different time in the child's life, with a different level of rapport, would probably arrive at a somewhat different estimate of the child's intelligence.

In addition to these effects on test performance, it is also important to note that individual children may not progress in their mental development in the same manner as others. Some of the research studies by Bayley (1) indicate that children have their own unique patterns of development of intellectual capacity, and that a rapidly maturing infant, who would score high in mental age on an infant scale, does not necessarily continue to progress rapidly in the capacity to perform the kinds of tasks used in scales of mental development for preschool children or older children. Figure 8.1 gives dramatic evidence of the extreme dissimilarity in patterning of mental development from one child to another.

Such theoretical problems as these make it extremely difficult to predict with any degree of accuracy what a child's intelligence will be at some later date if the test is given at a very early age. Thus, infant tests of mental development, which provide for computing mental age scores and IQ scores even during the first few months of life, are not reliable indicators of intelligence in later childhood or adult years. Figure 8.2 provides information on the degree of relationship between tests given during the preschool years and at subsequent ages, up to 18. It is clear that the correlation decreases as the length of time between tests increases. It is also true that tests given at very early ages are less reliable than those given during the school years.

Of the many tests of intelligence that are in use with individual children, the most widely used at the preschool-age level is the Stanford-Binet Scale. Form LM of this scale (13) has age norms beginning at the 2-year level and progressing through the adult level. It is a well organized scale, based on sound theoretical principles, and well standardized. In the hands of a highly skilled examiner it can yield important information about the mental development of the individual child. The child's verbal intelligence as well as his performance and problem-solving ability in

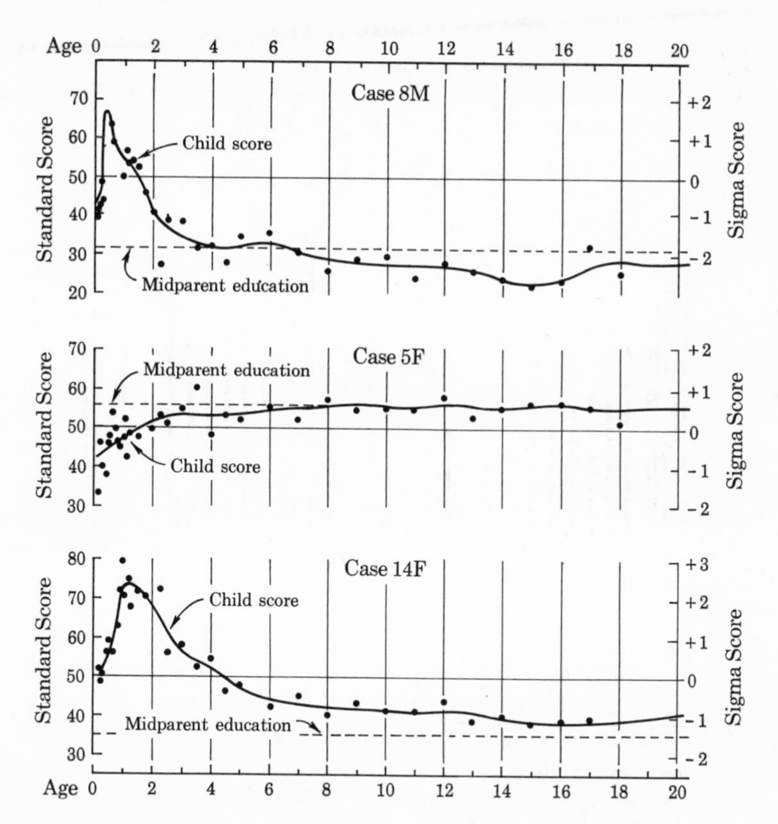

Fig. 8.1. The relative intelligence scores, by age, of three children, shown in relation to the educational levels of their respective parents. (From N. Bayley, "Individual patterns of development," Child Develpm., 1956, 27:45–74. By permission of N. Bayley and the Society for Research in Child Development.)

nonverbal tasks is tested with this scale, which includes an evaluation of such mental operations as vocabulary, form perception, identification of common objects, comprehension, the ability to understand analogies, and the ability to make aesthetic comparisons.

Tests of preschool children, while yielding important information about the level and organization of mental ability of a child at the time

Relation of 21 Month Mental Test Scores to Scores at Other Age Levels

Calif. Preschool Schedule I or II
Stanford Revisions
Wechsler-Bellevue
Coefficients of Correlation
1.00
.80
.60
.40
.20
0
2 4 6 8 10 12 14 16 18
Age in Years

Relation of 3 Year Mental Test Scores to Scores at Other Age Levels

Calif. Preschool Schedule I or II
Stanford Revisions
Wechsler-Bellevue
2 4 6 8 10 12 14 16 18
Age in Years

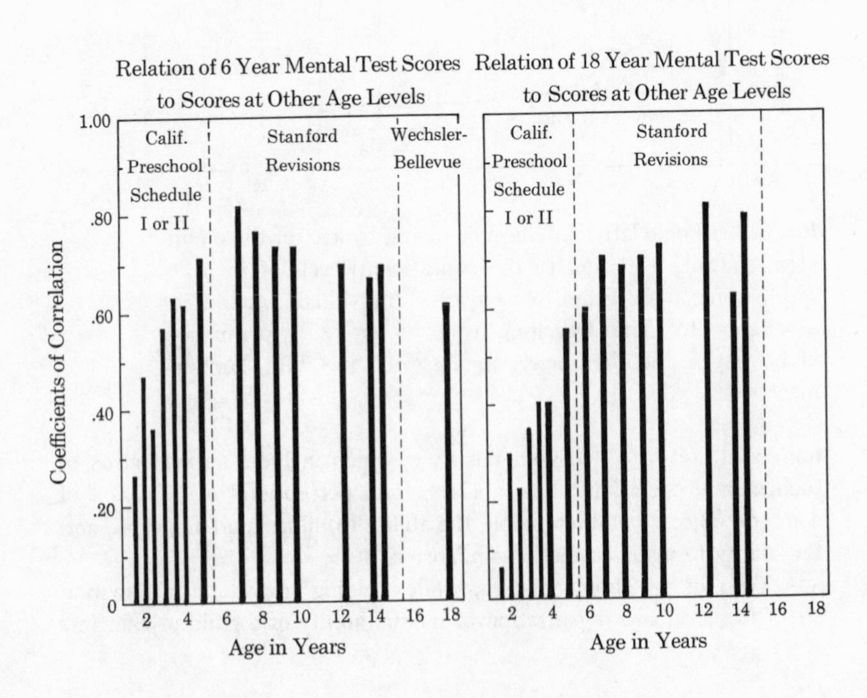

of the test, are of questionable value in predicting intelligence levels of his later life. Nevertheless, they can be extremely helpful in providing information about the intellectual resources of the child. For instance, a child who did not talk well and who was obstinate and difficult in many ways was thought of by his parents and other adults as being mentally slow. Careful testing revealed that the child's mental ability was, in fact, very superior, and indicated that the source of his problem behavior lay in the fact that people did not recognize his intellectual capacity or provide experiences in keeping with his level of ability. Similarly, there are many cases on record in which far too much was expected of children on the assumption that they had normal mental development, when in reality their mental growth was slower than average. One of the basic contributions of intelligence testing is that it makes possible more realistic expectations on the part of adults, thereby serving as a basis for more effective child guidance in a wide variety of situations. It is both frustrating and threatening to a child to be expected to perform like others his age if his mental ability is significantly less developed than that of the others. It is equally undesirable to expect nothing more of the child who is markedly advanced for his age.

In individual cases, then, there may be important reasons for obtaining as much information as possible about a child's intellectual development. The experienced examiner, in an effort to get the most reliable indication of mental development, will make use of the most appropriate scale available, since one test is not the equivalent of another. Some tests are designed specifically to measure the performance (nonverbal) intelligence. Others are more highly verbal in nature. In the case of the child with certain handicaps or other conditions that might affect his performance on tests, it may be necessary to select a test specifically designed for children who do not speak the English language. Some tests may even be given in pantomime, making it unnecessary to speak a single word to the child. When it is desirable for any reason to administer a test of intelligence to a preschool child, it should be done only by a qualified psychological examiner. Ordinarily this is a clinical psychologist

Fig. 8.2. The relation of mental test scores at 21 months, 3 years, 6 years, and 18 years to scores at other age levels. (From M. P. Honzik *et al.*, "The stability of mental test performance between two and eighteen years," *J. exp. Educ.*, 1948, 17:309–324.)

or an educational psychologist with special training in the administration and interpretation of psychological tests. It is particularly important that a preschool child not be "labeled" with his IQ. Test results are to be used judiciously, and with full recognition of the limitations surrounding the testing of any preschool child.

EQUIPMENT AND RESOURCES FOR INTELLIGENT BEHAVIOR

The child's intellectual behavior is, of course, not separate from the rest of his personality. We speak of it, for convenience, as if it were something apart from his physical being, his emotions, or his attitudes, but this is not an indication that we believe intelligence to be a thing apart. Intelligent behavior is coordinated by the central nervous system, especially the higher-brain centers which are so essential to thought, reasoning, and problem-solving. In addition, vital roles in intellectual development are played by the sensory mechanisms, especially those of seeing, hearing, and touching, and by the motor mechanisms which are concerned with control of body action. Intelligent behavior, then, is not merely a matter of the efficiency of the brain itself. Instead, it involves coordination of sensory stimulation, with memory in the form of past experiences, and with action—which may be muscular, neural, glandular, or some combination of all three. Mental development really involves development of all the systems of the body involved in intelligent behavior.

Sensory Equipment The child's first explorations of his environment are of three or four major types, all of which have a strong sensory component. First, he explores with his mouth, for it is through his mouth that the first and most significant bodily needs must be met in order to insure survival. The sensory capacities of the mouth are well developed at birth, and the sensations they provide are basic to the continuing need satisfactions of the nursing experience during infancy. Exploration with the mouth takes on additional significance later in infancy; the natural tendency of older infants to suck on things—toys, clothing, fingers, and whatever is available—can be understood partly as an effort to explore their world and to satisfy their curiosity about the nature of objects. Basically, of course, it is a pleasant sensation which is sought in such activities. But in the process of satisfying this urge, the infant learns a great deal about the texture, size, shape, and weight of objects.

Oral sensations are also involved in the process of language development. Early stages of language development, beginning in the preverbal sequence in infancy, apparently involve a good deal of sensory gratification. Some of this stems from the infant's hearing his own babbling, and it is likely that there are pleasurable sensations emanating from the vocal apparatus itself. It appears to "feel good" to the baby to engage in vocal play. This probably leads to increased effort to vocalize. The resulting increase in babbling activity is a direct antecedent of the early verbal behavior that forms an important ingredient in early mental development.

Sensations arising from touch also play an important role in stimulating mental development. As with tactual sensations in the mouth, touch sensitivity of fingers, toes, face, and body also convey to the child many fundamental impressions of the nature of his environment. These are essential to his gradual understanding of and effective dealings with his world—one way of defining the essence of intelligent behavior.

Vision and hearing play a big part in allowing the child to achieve understanding and mastery of his world. The most dramatic evidence of the importance of these sensory avenues is provided in the case histories of some individuals who have been deprived of normal vision or hearing during the early years. The long, arduous, and unusual training required to achieve the basic intellectual concepts that are taken for granted with nonhandicapped children gives clear evidence of the vital role played by these sensory processes. The story of Helen Keller makes us aware of their importance, not only in learning to speak, but in formulating ideas about the nature of the world, which can then be used to represent it and to deal with it effectively. The following excerpt from Miss Keller's autobiography is a poignant example of the role of sensation in the achievement of coherent concepts of the nature of one's world:

> The most important day I remember in all my life is the one on which my teacher, Anne Mansfield Sullivan, came to me. I am filled with wonder when I consider the immeasurable contrasts between the two lives which it connects. It was the third of March, 1887, three months before I was seven years old.
>
> On the afternoon of that eventful day, I stood on the porch, dumb, expectant. I guessed vaguely from my mother's signs and from the hurrying to and fro in the house that something unusual was about to happen, so I went to the door and waited on

the steps. The afternoon sun penetrated the mass of honeysuckle that covered the porch, and fell on my upturned face. My fingers lingered almost unconsciously on the familiar leaves and blossoms which had just come forth to greet the sweet southern spring. I did not know what the future held of marvel or surprise for me. Anger and bitterness had preyed upon me continually for weeks and a deep languor had succeeded this passionate struggle.

Have you ever been at sea in a dense fog, when it seemed as if a tangible white darkness shut you in, and the great ship, tense and anxious, groped her way toward the shore with plummet and sounding line, and you waited with beating heart for something to happen? I was like that ship before my education began, only I was without compass or sounding-line, and had no way of knowing how near the harbor was. "Light! Give me light!" was the wordless cry of my soul, and the light of love shone on me in that very hour.

I felt approaching footsteps. I stretched out my hand as I supposed to my mother. Some one took it, and I was caught up and held close in the arms of her who had come to reveal all things to me, and, more than all things else, to love me.

The morning after my teacher came she led me into her room and gave me a doll. The little blind children at the Perkins Institution had sent it and Laura Bridgman had dressed it; but I did not know this until afterward. When I had played with it a little while, Miss Sullivan slowly spelled into my hand the word "d-o-l-l." I was at once interested in this finger play and tried to imitate it. When I finally succeeded in making the letters correctly I was flushed with childish pleasure and pride. Running downstairs to my mother I held up my hand and made the letters for doll. I did not know that I was spelling a word or even that words existed; I was simply making my fingers go in monkey-like imitation. In the days that followed I learned to spell in this uncomprehending way a great many words, among them *pin, hat, cup,* and a few verbs like *sit, stand,* and *walk.* But my teacher had been with me several weeks before I understood that everything has a name.

One day, while I was playing with my new doll, Miss Sullivan put my big rag doll into my lap also, spelled "d-o-l-l" and tried to make me understand that "d-o-l-l" applied to both. Earlier in the day we had had a tussle over the words "m-u-g" and "w-a-t-e-r." Miss Sullivan had tried to impress it upon me that "m-u-g" is *mug* and that "w-a-t-e-r" is *water,* but I persisted in confounding the two. In despair she had dropped the subject for a time, only to renew it at the first opportunity. I became impatient at her repeated attempts and, seizing the new doll, I dashed it upon the floor. I was keenly delighted when I felt the fragments of the broken doll at my feet. Neither sorrow nor regret followed my passionate outburst. I had not loved the doll. In the still, dark world in which I lived there was no strong sentiment or tenderness. I felt my teacher sweep the fragments to one side of the hearth, and I had a sense of satisfaction that the cause of my discomfort was removed. She brought me my hat, and I knew I was going out into the warm sunshine. This thought, if a wordless sensation may be called a thought, made me hop and skip with pleasure.

We walked down the path to the well-house, attracted by the fragrance of the honeysuckle with which it was covered. Some one was drawing water and my teacher placed my hand under the spout. As the cool stream gushed over one hand she spelled into the other the word *water,* first slowly, then rapidly. I stood still, my whole attention fixed upon the motions of her fingers. Suddenly I felt a misty consciousness as of something forgotten—a thrill of returning thought; and somehow the mystery of language was revealed to me. I knew then that "w-a-t-e-r" meant the wonderful cool something that was flowing over my hand. That living word awakened my soul, gave it light, hope, joy, set it free! There were barriers still, it is true, but barriers that could in time be swept away.

I left the well-house eager to learn. Everything had a name, and each name gave birth to a new thought. As we returned to the house every object which I touched seemed to quiver with life. That was because I saw everything with the strange, new sight that had come to me. On entering the door I remembered the doll I had broken. I felt my way to the hearth and picked up the pieces. I tried vainly to put them together. Then my eyes filled with tears; for I realized what I had done, and for the first time I felt repentance and sorrow.

> I learned a great many new words that day. I do not remember what they all were; but I do know that *mother, father, sister, teacher* were among them—words that were to make the world blossom for me, "like Aaron's rod, with flowers." It would have been difficult to find a happier child than I was as I lay in my crib at the close of that eventful day and lived over the joys it had brought me, and for the first time longed for a new day to come (8, pp. 21–24).[1]

Motor Equipment In Chapter Six we noted that the child's achievement of body control plays an important part in his coming to deal effectively with his world. Intellectual behavior frequently expresses itself in motor action of one kind or another. In addition, it is often through the operation of motor behavior that the child engages in trial-and-error processes in the solution of problems. The "meaning," to a child, of any particular cue or stimulus in his environment is often a matter of what he *does* about that stimulus. Just as it is reasonable to assume that for the infant the bottle is "to suck," it is reasonable that for the 2-year-old the crayon is "to scribble," for the 3-year-old the tricycle is "to pedal and ride," and for the 4-year-old the big boxes are "to climb on and jump from." The child's repertory of motor responses is both a resource and a limitation for his imaginativeness, his inventiveness, and his degree of variability in coping with his world.

A brief review of a laboratory study of children's learning (3) will serve to illustrate the combined roles of sensory and motor processes in intellectual behavior. In this study children were taken individually into a testing room, where they were seated in front of a "discrimination box." On the front panel of this box was a row of four colored lights, two red ones and two blue ones. There were also two large buttons to push, one colored red and the other blue. When one of the lights came on, the child could push the button of the same color, and would be rewarded by a marble delivered through a small opening at the bottom of the box. If the child pushed the wrong button, he received no marble. Preschool children learned this task very quickly, and not only were they eager to push the appropriately colored button when the light was turned on, but they actively avoided the "wrong" button. Such remarks as, "Oh, no! I almost

[1] From *The Story of My Life* by Helen Keller. Reprinted by permission of Doubleday & Company, Inc.

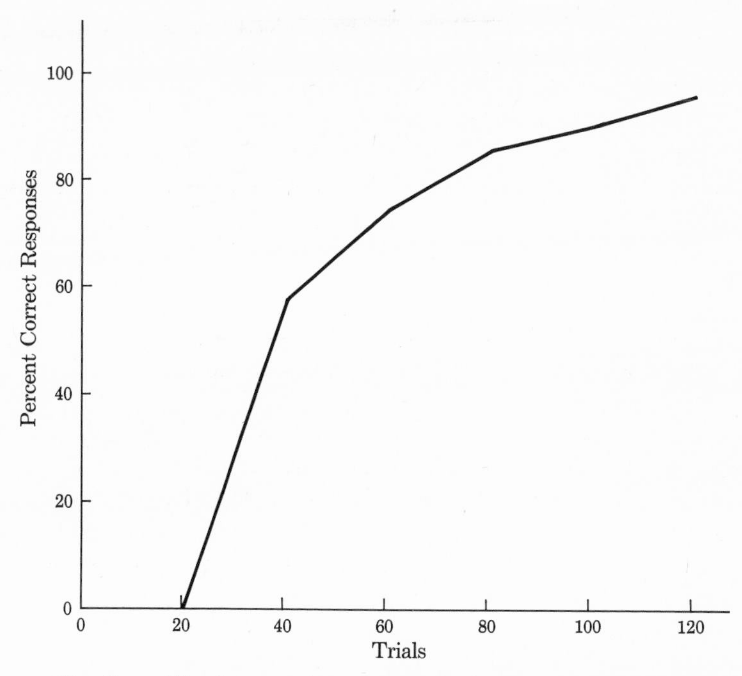

Fig. 8.3. The increase in percentage of correct responses in a learning problem, by number of trials, for 57 preschool children.

pushed the wrong one!" were not infrequent. It was clearly evident that solving the problem meant coordinating a specific sensory impression with a well defined motor act. In nonlaboratory settings it is perhaps less obvious, but intellectual behavior is frequently of this very sort. The *meaning* of a given stimulus is to be found in *what one does about it with his muscles.*

The Central Nervous System The role of the brain and the rest of the central nervous system in intellectual behavior and development is rather obvious. The manner in which the central nervous system carries out intellectual activity, however, is far from obvious. Figure 8.4 shows a highly schematic representation of intelligent behavior, in which some of the major intellectual processes are depicted. The "sensory input" box represents sensations received from the environment. The "central nervous system" box illustrates the process of correlating the residue of past ex-

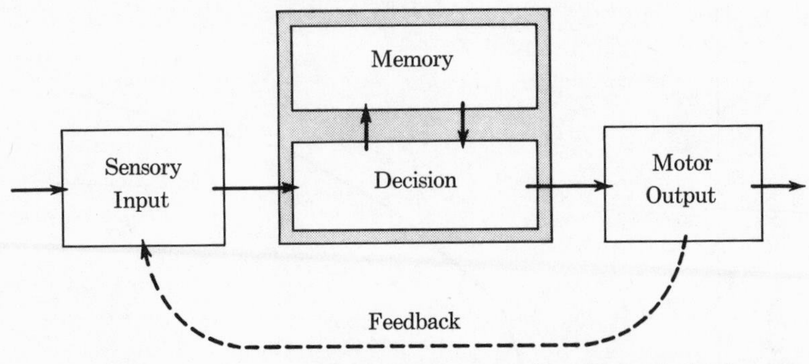

Fig. 8.4. A diagrammatic representation of intelligent behavior.

perience (memory) with the present sensations, and making an appropriate decision for action. That action may take the form of motor behavior, depicted by the "motor output" box. The "feedback" line portrays the child's ability to perceive the effects of his own motor action, which enables him to make appropriate corrections when necessary. This schematic portrayal is not intended to do justice, of course, to the complexities of the central nervous system. Its purpose is merely to illustrate one major function of that system, which is to correlate sensory impressions with motor action. The objective of this correlation is to bring about appropriate responses to the environment.

With increasing maturity of the brain it is possible to engage in increasingly complex decision-making actions. It is possible to take into account a wider range of potential courses of action. It is also apparent that with an increasingly rich store of remembered experience, the child is gradually able to bring more memory to bear on the decision of the moment. Thus the growth and elaboration of the nervous system, plus the increasingly rich memory resulting from experience, are central in the development of intelligent behavior.

FACTORS IN THE PRODUCTION OF INDIVIDUAL DIFFERENCES IN MENTAL GROWTH

The preceding discussion should serve to emphasize the "wholeness" of intelligent behavior in the child; that is, intelligent behavior is not merely the functioning of the brain or of the central nervous system apart from the rest of the child. Indeed, his total personality is inevitably involved in all intelligent behavior: his body and its various systems, his emotions, his motivational forces, and his attitudes—including his attitudes toward himself, other people, and the world of objects. It remains for us to note the important reasons that underlie differences, from one child to another, in degree and rate and quality of mental development. These differences have been observed ever since people became aware of the individuality of children. However, it has only been since the beginning of this century that we have explored scientifically the nature and extent of individual differences in mental functioning from one child to another.

All sources of variation are either hereditary or environmental, or some combination of the two. In reality, neither hereditary nor environmental forces can operate to affect intelligence in the absence of the other. Be that as it may, there are some ways in which intelligence is relatively more a function of environment, and other ways in which it is much more dependent upon heredity.

The Inheritance of Mental Abilities One way of studying the effects of heredity on intellectual development is to compare the mental growth of identical twins, since twins are essentially duplicates of each other with respect to inherited characteristics. This approach presents some problems in research, however, if the twins are raised together in the same family; under these conditions, if they turn out to have the same intelligence, we cannot be sure whether it is because they inherited the same capacities or because they were given nearly identical treatment and experienced nearly identical environmental influences. To get around this problem we must find identical twins who have been reared in quite different environments and note the degree of similarity in their intellectual capacities. Any significant differences in their mental ability should reflect the extent to which environmental forces operated in determining their intelligence. In one study of 30 pairs of identical twins reared apart, Burt (2) reported that the degree of correlation between pairs of twins was .85 with respect to intellectual status. This is a strong relationship, indicating that there were powerful genetic factors operating to bring about similar levels of mental development for the two members of each pair. The correlation reported for identical twins reared together was .92. Burt also reported that the correlation with respect to school achievement for identical twins reared together was about .90, in comparison with .72 for identical twins reared separately. The general conclusion is that academic achievement was affected much more by the environmental differences than was basic intelligence.

Other studies, notably that of Newman, Freeman, and Holzinger (9), have reported somewhat higher correlations between intelligence test scores for identical twins reared together than for twins reared apart. In cases of extreme differences in environment, these researchers observed wide variations between test scores of certain pairs of twins. Such findings suggest that unusual degrees of environmental distortion may have very significant effects on mental growth, even though the major component in intellectual development remains that of genetic endowment.

Intelligence, however, does not seem to be a single, unitary quality but, rather, a complex of functions and processes. It is not only possible to compare children with respect to the *amount* or *level* of mental development, but with respect to the *organization* of mental abilities. That is, one child may be relatively more advanced in those aspects of intelligence which call for speed of mental action, while another may be more advanced in those elements of intelligence which call for abstract reasoning ability. It is possible that the two children may show the same over-all *level* of mental growth, as reflected in their mental-age scores, and yet be quite different with respect to the way in which the various components of intelligent behavior are organized. The exact role of heredity in producing these differences among children in intellectual organization is not clear. Nevertheless, it appears that such differences are, at least in part, determined by genetic factors.

The sex of the child, which of course is an inherited condition, also appears to play a role in the development and organization of intelligence. Girls tend to develop those mental abilities which depend upon language behavior more rapidly and to a higher level than do boys, during the preschool years. However, it is likely that this difference is a reflection of the differential treatment given boys and girls in our society, rather than an inherited difference in mental ability. Goodenough (5) reports that males excel in general information, especially information of a scientific, mathematical, or mechanical variety. She also reports some studies which would indicate that the range of intelligence tends to be greater for boys than for girls. That is, if such studies were to be finally verified, it would indicate that more boys are located at the extremes of both high and low intelligence than girls.

Environmental Factors in Mental Development The question of the effects of environmental forces in mental development is an interesting and a complex one. Much attention has been given this question, often without clear-cut results. The question, for example, of whether or not attendance at a nursery school will raise the IQ level of a child has been investigated. While this would appear to be a simple enough question, it is in reality a very difficult matter to sort out the effects of such experiences on basic intellectual growth. In general, it appears safer to conclude that the child whose mental development has not been hampered by an extremely impoverished environment prior to attendance in nursery school will not show significant gains in mental growth as a result of nursery-school attendance. Mental development, of course, is not the main purpose of a nursery school anyway, as we shall see in a later chapter; many other significant gains can and should occur through nursery-school attendance. Nevertheless, it seems that we cannot realistically expect the normal child, living in a normal home environment, to achieve significant gains in mental growth as a result of nursery-school attendance.

There is the exceptional child whose experiences have been so limited, and whose home environment is so restricted and lacking in mental stimulation, that his performances on standard intelligence tests at age 3 would be very low—much lower than his original native capacity. Attendance in a *good* nursery school over a period of months may, indeed, reflect itself in significant gains in performance on intelligence tests at age 4. In such cases, it would seem that the enrichment of this child's environment might lead to better test performance, more in keeping with the native capacities of the child. In this, as in other questions about the intellectual growth of children, it is important to distinguish between *native capacity*, which is never measured directly by any intelligence test, and *performance*, which can be measured and used as a basis for estimating the child's capacities. It is the performance, not the capacities, which seems to be most markedly influenced by environmental factors.

In some growth studies of infants who were deprived of normal mothering experiences (Spitz, *11*; Goldfarb, *4*) it has been reported that mental growth, as well as other aspects of development, were adversely affected, and that, if the maternal deprivation continued over a significant period during infancy, the trend toward inferior mental development became irreversible, so that no amount of special treatment later could compensate for it. Such studies dealt with very unusual situations, and there is considerable doubt as to the validity of the generalizations which might be drawn from them in reference to the child with more normal experiences.

THE DEVELOPMENT OF REASONING AND PROBLEM-SOLVING ABILITY

Terman (13) defined intelligence largely in terms of the ability to carry on abstract thinking. While others would not agree that this is a complete definition, certainly few authorities would question that abstract reasoning ability is a central component of intelligence—and a vital one. Some efforts have been made to trace the child's gradually developing ability to engage in abstract thinking and reasoning processes. Piaget (10), for example, has written extensively on the stages children go through in achieving a mature ability to reason and think logically.

The development of the ability to think logically and engage in abstract reasoning processes is really the development of understanding of one's world and the ability to manipulate symbols which represent different aspects of that world. Early sensory experiences form the basic process by which the world becomes differentiated into such categories as "me," "thing," and "other person." The senses make it possible for the infant to discriminate, gradually, one class of experience from another class. To some degree, each class of experience has an element of need satisfaction, or "reward," attached to it; or it has an element of frustration, disappointment, or unpleasantness associated with it. This pleasantness-unpleasantness component is central to the child's differentiation process. It sharpens the definitions of events, objects, and situations in terms of their affective (need-satisfying) implications for him.

Piaget (10) described the early infantile condition as egocentric, meaning that the infant's perception of significant events is based entirely on their implications for *him*. The following passage by Stone and Church conveys the meaning of this condition rather nicely:

> In earliest infantile experience, the world is only a diffuse field with objects coming and going but without a fixed frame-

> work. To begin with, events or objects come into the baby's awareness in terms of immediate threat or gratification to him. Soon after, there may be connections between things, but the connection is always personal, through the infant. Orange juice may signify that a bath will follow, but these are related as things that happen to *him* in close succession, and not as events in a world which includes his mother's schedule, too. Similarly, the kitchen where he gets his juice and the bathroom where he takes his bath may be tied together in terms of personal relevance, but there is no notion that they have geographical relationships as well. And here is the difficult part for most adults to grasp: although, for the infant, everything is related to "my" immediate needs, wants, and experiences, there is no *me*. There simply *is* Hunger, and Wetness, and Orange-Juice-Followed-by-Warm-Immersion, all in a context of familiar person and place; but there is *no* "I am" hungry, or "I feel" wet, or "I taste" orange juice, and so forth. The baby's experience is *personal,* as we have said, because, after all, it is only his own hunger and wetness and pleasures that he has any knowledge of. But there is no me until a me (*the self*) has emerged as an entity from the total welter of experience (*12*, pp. 85–86).

The meaning of experience, then, is first primarily an emotional one for the infant. During infancy it is this more or less emotional impact of specific experiences which serves as a basis for the child's making any mental discriminations that even define the object or the situation involved.

This same process, in its various forms, is central throughout the early development of understanding of the world during the entire preschool period; that is, the child reacts to only those aspects of his world which have affective meaning to him. Those things which do not have any emotional impact on him are, in a sense, not a part of his psychological world and are not discriminated by him. This is partly a matter of what things have action possibilities for *him*. The child's discriminations are refined and made more clear-cut in terms of the uses to which he can put various objects. As a natural accompaniment of physical growth, which makes him more mobile and increases his capacity for using and for relating himself to objects, his discrimination capacities similarly increase. But throughout the preschool years it is the meaningfulness of things to himself, and the uses to which he can put things, which serves as the driving force behind his growing awareness of the nature of the world. In other words, it is less a matter of his deriving meaning from the objects around him than it is a matter of his giving meaning to those objects.

Concept Formation During the Preschool Period A concept is an abstract idea separate from its specific manifestations. For example, the concept "boy," exists independently, apart from its manifestation in any particular boy. Concepts are central in the thinking process; they form the content of much mental activity. The child's store of concepts and the adequacy of these concepts are directly related to his mental ability as well as comprising the subject matter of his mental manipulation of environment. Concepts are formed through repeated experiences with objects, people, events, and situations, but they always involve something more than the specific meaning of a particular person, object, event, or situation. It is this "something more" which must be understood if we are to appreciate the task of the child as he attempts to organize his world into meaningful and useful concepts. Consider a child's experience with "mother." It is clear that the concept "mother" can be an abstraction, a general idea which can be manipulated as a mental symbol apart from any particular mother. But in this abstract sense of the term, it is a meaningless and irrelevant idea in the life of the infant and very young child. In fact, it is only through a long series of meaningful experiences with his particular mother that a child comes to acquire any important idea of her as a separate person.

An additional and very important step must be taken by the child in order to achieve a truly abstract idea of "mother" apart from his own mother. For this to occur, he must have some kind of experience with other women who fill similar roles in relation to children. First, he must become aware of the reality of the separate existence of other children and then of the significance of the women who play roles in relation to these children that compare to the role his mother plays in relation to him. Thus it still comes back to utilizing his own personal experience as the basis for developing concepts, even though the concepts may enable him to go, mentally, beyond the narrow bounds of his specific experience. The child's ability to form useful concepts is not only a reflection of his level of mental development; it is a direct aid in his intellectual growth, with meaningful concepts serving as the basis for the development of other, additional concepts. One builds on the foundation of others.

Language is a most useful and necessary process in concept formation. It helps a great deal in sorting our experiences and giving them meaning if we can label the experiences and put them into a class with other experiences having something in common. It is understandable that the child's first words are typically nouns, because of the importance to him of naming objects and persons that are important to him. His sense of security seems to be enhanced by the ability to name those things in his environment—his bottle, his mother, his bed, etc.—which represent the predictability of experience and the orderliness of the world around him. Later, too, as concepts become more involved and much more abstract, the role played by words in formulating concepts is fundamental to the child. "Mother" conveys a host of meanings derived from his own experience with his mother. The term enables him to deal effectively with that whole wealth of specific meanings under one very useful heading.

The general process of concept-formation moves from the concrete, tangible, and specific toward the more general, less tangible, and more abstract. A delightful example of concepts in action comes from a 4-year-old boy whose mother was awaiting the arrival of a baby. This boy had never asked his mother about babies or where they came from until early one morning, as she was busily preparing pancakes for the family's breakfast. Then he chose the rush hour of the day to ask the classic question. This mother, anxious to give the boy an honest and complete answer, interrupted her meal preparation long enough to tell the child everything she could think of, from beginning to end, about human reproduction! The boy appeared duly impressed and evidently made the appropriate associations with his mother's condition, for after she returned to the breakfast chores he went about his play. A few minutes later he made a grand entrance into the kitchen, having stuffed a pillow down inside his shirt and trousers. The ensuing conversation was most revealing:

BOY: *"Hey, you know what's inside there?"*
MOTHER: *"Yes, I'll bet I do know what's there."*
BOY (grinning): *"What?"*
MOTHER: *"I'll bet you're going to have a baby, too."*
BOY: *"Naw; that's not a baby in there. Them's pancakes!"*

The 4-year-old still tends to deal in limited concepts, based on only those ideas which are meaningfully related to his own experience. The sex-education lecture he had received may well have created a need to explore his feelings about birth, but it could not succeed in providing realistic concepts so far removed from his experience. But *pancakes*—now that was a concept he could really relate to, and something which could understandably make his middle pretty big! Concept-formation is a continuing and never-ending process, and the child's task—when viewed from the angle of the rich and complex variety of concepts that he must establish in order to deal with the adult world—is truly a staggering one.

The child's use of language is a helpful index to observant adults as to the level and accuracy of children's concepts. One religious body has a statement of belief which begins something like the following: "We believe in being honest, true, chaste, benevolent . . ." The kindergarten child who was being instructed in the memorization of this statement came forth with the following interpretation: "We believe in being honest, truly, and chased by an elephant." Now the words of that statement are, of course, highly abstract words which are quite beyond the concept level of the ordinary preschool child. This child's version was another reflection of the need to apply concepts that he *did* have in order to make some sense of an otherwise meaningless experience.

Development of Reasoning Ability According to Piaget (10), the preschool child is essentially prelogical; that is, his approach to the world is not based on a logical, critical examination of the evidence for or against any given proposition; but instead, is based on the significance of the proposition as it bears directly on him. This is consistent with what we have noted already about the child's early mental development. Piaget argued that the child tends to reason only in terms of isolated cases, dealing with specifics rather than generalities. He also noted something of which most persons experienced in the ways of children have been at least vaguely aware: the young child is not able to take the position of someone else and to reason from the other person's point of view. Perhaps one of the true marks of maturity is the very capacity for seeing things from another person's viewpoint. That the young child does not have this capacity is well brought out by one or two of Piaget's classic experiments. In one, a child was asked, "How many brothers do you have?" He answered correctly, "Two, John and Peter." Then he was asked, "How many brothers does Peter have?" The child's response: "One, John." Piaget interpreted the child's error as evidence that he cannot see himself in the role of brother, since "brother" in his experience is something that he *has*, and not yet something that he *is*. Such limitations on the child's ability to see the world from the viewpoint of another may help to account for the many quarrels, conflicts, and disagreements among preschool children. Any nursery-school teacher can testify to the fact that her charges are not very sophisticated as to the effects of their behavior on other children or adults; they are simply not able to place themselves in the position of the other people and to recognize the impact their behavior has on others.

An interesting characteristic of children's reasoning is that it tends to be "magical" in its quality; that is, part of the prelogical approach to the world is the tendency to explain things in terms of magic or mysterious forces. One form which this tendency often takes is known as *animistic* thinking; which attributes animal powers, motives, and characteristics to nonliving things. If an automobile, an airplane, or any other machine moves and makes noises, it may not be differentiated from living things so far as the child is concerned. Piaget has given many examples of animistic thinking in children and has stressed that this is one of the ways in which children's thought processes differ from those of adults.

A homely example of more or less animistic thinking occurred in the writer's experience when, some years ago, his family made a major purchase —a somewhat modest station wagon. The children almost immediately named the car "Wag," and it remains Wag to this day. But the animistic thinking about the car did not end with its name. When the family could afford a luggage carrier for the top of the car, it was christened "Lug," and Wag and Lug have always been good friends, with many human qualities and warm characteristics so far as the children are concerned. On one or two occasions, when Wag developed symptoms of illness associated with the aging process, and the writer expressed his opinion about the car's foibles in the presence of the children, it was as if one of the members of the family were under attack. It was truly fascinating to observe the degree of family feeling the children developed for that piece of machinery. Like siblings, they come to its defense!

While it is undoubtedly true that, with experience and maturity, the child's prelogical explanations of events and of his world give way to more realistic interpretations, it is also true that this kind of thinking is not sharply limited to children of any particular age level. Many examples might be given of the use of prelogical and "magical" thinking by adults when confronted with situations they do not understand. There are many comparisons that can be drawn between children and adults, and, while there may be valid distinctions, there are also many common characteristics. Jersild cites the following anecdote as an illustration of the fact that children and adults may have qualities of *both* logical and prelogical thinking:

> One three-year-old girl, for example, when asked, "What makes the wind blow?" answered, "It blows itself." When asked, "What makes a car run?" she answered, "The motor." The second answer is the more acceptable from the adult point of view, yet it probably meant little more to her than the first. In any event, the two answers do not seem to represent two different kinds of thinking but, rather, the best explanation the child was able to supply at the moment (7, p. 358).

There is not a clear-cut distinction, then, with respect to the prelogical and logical stages. It does seem evident, however, that children's thinking is more likely to be based on wish, as opposed to reality in contrast to adults, and it seems likely that they tend to use more magic and animism in their thinking than do adults.

Intellectual Curiosity and Creativity It is important to distinguish between raw intelligence, on the one hand, and intellectual curiosity and creativity on the other. The first is essentially the inherited capacity of the child to engage efficiently in the variety of mental processes that have been described in this chapter. The latter terms, *intellectual curiosity* and *creativity*, imply characteristics of children that are less restricted by the limits of inherited capacities than is raw intelligence.

Current research in creative thinking is revealing that the truly creative person has some essential personality characteristics, apart from intelligence, *per se*, which allow him to make unusually good use of his native abilities in the solution of problems. This is a relatively new and unexplored area, but already we are beginning to learn that early childhood experiences make it possible for some children to think creatively and to see unique solutions for problems, while others, perhaps equally bright, learn very early to see problems and solutions only in terms of the features presented to them in the traditional manner. Obviously, we need to learn more about what makes some children exceptionally creative. It is reasonable to assume that the child who is severely restricted in his early opportunities to learn about his environment will not develop the same kind or degree of intellectual curiosity as the child who has many opportunities and much stimulation to explore his world. The child whose environment is continually challenging and stimulating and who is encouraged to find satisfactory answers to his questions, would seem to have a healthy start toward strong intellectual curiosity. It is for this reason that the manner of answering children's questions takes on special significance in fostering curiosity and creativity.

Responding to Children's Questions As pointed out in the chapter on communication, a preschool child can ask more questions during a day's activity than most adults can possibly find the time or resources to answer. But these questions, even when impossible to answer thoroughly in every case, deserve a great deal of respect, encouragement, and understanding. A child is not only learning the information provided when his question is answered with respect and consideration, he is also learning that his question was a worthwhile endeavor. The attitude that he gradually builds up after experiencing this kind of relationship with adults carries over into his other efforts to understand his world. It is an attitude that assures him of the validity and significance of his curiosity about his world, and helps him to feel that the only logical thing to do when a problem arises is to seek the answer.

SUMMARY

Intelligence has been defined in many different ways. As used here it refers to the efficient operation of a complex of functions involved in a wide range of problem-solving activities. Some aspects of intelligence are primarily verbal while others are mostly nonverbal. The ultimate criterion of intelligence is a social one: the ability of the child to adapt successfully to his world. In this concept of intelligence, however, there is room for creativity and inventiveness, as well as mere adaptation to the status quo.

The child's progress in developing intellectual processes is measured through the use of standardized tests. Some of these provide a mental age (MA) score, from which the IQ may be derived. The IQ is a useful index of the child's brightness in relation to the average, but it must be interpreted with caution, especially when referring to a preschool child.

Resources for intelligent behavior include the child's sensory and motor systems as well as his central nervous system. The major factor determining intellectual growth is genetic, although unusual or extreme distortions and deprivations in early childhood may have a significant effect on mental growth.

The process of concept-formation is both a reflection of the mental maturity of the child and an invaluable tool in his further elaboration of mental growth. In the process of concept-development, language plays a helpful role, which is one of the reasons that language development and mental growth are highly correlated. Children's reasoning tends to be highly wishful and need-oriented. While there are qualitative differences in the thinking and reasoning of children as compared with adults, there is a great deal of overlapping from one age to another with respect to the kinds of mental processes employed. Just as adults may at times be prelogical in approaching problems, children may at times demonstrate logical thought.

Providing a challenging and stimulating environment and satisfying answers to children's questions with respect for the needs which motivate the questioning is important in a program of child guidance designed to stimulate intellectual curiosity and creativity.

REFERENCES

1. Bayley, Nancy, "Individual patterns of development," *Child Develpm.*, 1956, **27**:45–74.
2. Burt, C., "The inheritance of mental ability," *Amer. Psychol.*, 1958, **13**:1–15.
3. Gardner, D. B., and Judisch, J. M., "Transfer of discrimination learning across sensory modalities in preschool children," unpublished paper presented at the 1963 Biennial Conference of the Society for Research in Child Development, Berkeley, California.
4. Goldfarb, W., "Emotional and intellectual consequences of psychologic deprivation in infancy: A revaluation," in P. H. Hoch and J. Zubin, (eds.), *Psychopathology of childhood*, New York: Grune & Stratton, 1955, pp. 105–119.
5. Goodenough, F. L., "The measurement of mental growth in childhood," in L. Carmichael (ed.), *Manual of child psychology*, 2nd. ed., New York: Wiley, 1954, pp. 459–491.
6. Honzik, M. P., Mcfarlane, J. W., and Allen, L., "The stability of

mental test performance between two and eighteen years," *J. exper. Educ.*, 1948, **17**:309–324.

7. Jersild, A. T., *Child psychology*, 5th ed., New Jersey: Prentice-Hall, 1960.
8. Keller, Helen, *The Story of My Life*, New York: Grosset & Dunlap, 1904. Reprinted by permission of Doubleday & Company, Inc.
9. Newman, H. F., Freeman, F. N., and Holzinger, K. J., *Twins: A study of heredity and environment*, Chicago: Univ. of Chicago Press, 1937.
10. Piaget, J., *The language and thought of the child*, New York: Harcourt, Brace, 1926.
11. Spitz, R. A., "The importance of mother-child relationship during the first year of life," *Ment. Hlth. Today*, 1948, 7:7–13.
12. Stone, L. J., and Church, J., *Childhood and adolescence*, New York: Random House, 1957.
13. Terman, L. M., and Merrill, Maud A., *Stanford-Binet Intelligence Scale*, Boston: Houghton Mifflin, 1960.

CHAPTER NINE

What are the fundamental components of any emotional behavior? ~ What general pattern of emotional development exists during the early years? ~ In what respects is emotional behavior a matter of both maturation and particular learning experiences? ~ Is it unhealthy for the child to experience such emotions as anger, fear, and jealousy? ~ What is meant by "emotional conflict" in the child?

EMOTIONAL DEVELOPMENT

THE STUDY OF EMOTIONS, whether those of adults or those of children, has proven itself to be a fascinating one to many people. We are always interested in knowing more about our own feelings—our changes in mood—and we have all had occasion, no doubt, to wonder how our emotional life came to be the way it is. But emotions are more than a matter of curiosity; they form such a basic part of our everyday lives that, in a very real sense, everything we do is directly dependent on their operation. The very motives that arouse our activity and sustain and direct it in our daily activities are essentially emotional in nature. Our system of values, our attitudes toward people and things, our personal goals and ambitions, our likes and dislikes, our standards of behavior and, perhaps most important of all, our mental images of our own personal selves, all are emotional in nature. Certainly emotions are not just negative or undesirable things, then, to be "gotten rid of" or ruled out of our lives. On the contrary, they are necessary in providing for each of us an essentially human characteristic, enabling us to relate to the people and things in the world around us in satisfying and constructive ways.

But it is obvious that emotions do not always work to the advantage of human beings. Almost any kind of emotion, out of control and aimless, can work to the detriment of man, just as it might, under more favorable circumstances, work to his advantage. Emotion, then, is like raw energy in that it is not, of itself, either a good or a bad thing. Directed and channeled into constructive outlets, it becomes a powerful force for the satisfaction of human needs and for the development of creativity. Undirected and uncontrolled, it becomes an equally powerful force for the destruction of human creativity.

THE MEANING OF EMOTIONAL DEVELOPMENT

When we speak of emotional behavior, we are referring to three main processes, which can be described separately though realistically they occur together: (1) the physiological changes within the body, including changes in circulation, respiration, glandular activity, and sensory processes; (2) changes in the observable behavior pattern of an individual, such as laughing, crying, fighting, frowning, being "silly," or being moody; and (3) changes in the conscious experience of emotional awareness, which represent the "feeling" component of emotion. The distinction among these three can be kept in mind by noting that the first can be measured with sensitive apparatus and electronic equipment, and the second can be observed by anyone. But the third is available only to the individual experiencing it, and can be described only indirectly to another person.

Our concern is to understand how normal emotional development proceeds in early childhood and to recognize the role played by various forces in the child's life in developing a constructive use of his emotional resources. This includes the understanding of how he comes to deal with all three of the major components of emotion described above.

In attempting to understand the role and development of emotions in the life of the young child, we can approach the subject from two quite different points of view. First, we can ask ourselves just what the typical emotional reactions are for infants and children at each age level up to about age 6. The answer to this question will be a description of the characteristic emotional behavior of each age level. The second question we might ask goes a bit deeper. It concerns itself with the nature of the relationships a child sustains with important people and things around him, and the ways in which these relationships affect the pattern of emotional behavior he acquires.

The answers to both of these questions are important to understanding the individual child and his emotional needs. They are important also for understanding what principles might be applied in helping a child gradually to achieve mature control and direction of his emotions so that they will work for him instead of being his master.

The remainder of this chapter, then, will consist of these fundamental considerations: (1) a description of the course of emotional development, outlining the major stages of emotional growth up to the end of the preschool period; (2) a discussion of the dynamic factors and forces in a child's life that play vital roles in directing and channeling his emotional behavior; and (3) suggestions for guidance of the child's emotional development.

STAGES OF EMOTIONAL DEVELOPMENT

We have already noted in Chapter Four that the infant is born with the sensory, neural, glandular, and muscular capacities for becoming aroused emotionally in a very general sense, but that he does not experience specific emotional states such as anger, hate, love, or jealousy. We also noted that as the infant matures more specific emotional states gradually become differentiated. The general direction of development, emotionally, seems to be from the general to the specific.

The development of specific emotional responses during the period between ages 2 and 5 is much less clear-cut and predictable than the earlier, infantile period. Nevertheless, there is a regularity of patterning during this time also. Katherine Bridges (*1*, *2*), to whom we are indebted for the general outline of emotional development during the infantile and preschool periods, noted that "fear" at 24 months becomes differentiated into "shame," "anxiety," and "fear" during the preschool period. "Anger" during the same period becomes "disappointment," "anger," and "envy." "Delight" becomes "hope" and "delight." Thus it would seem that the preschool years are a time of sharpening the degree of differentiation of general emotional reactions into increasingly specific ones. More than this, the preschool period also represents a time of complex emotional learning. This includes the association of feeling and emotional reactions with particular objects, events, situations, and people. Not only does the child's maturing body allow him to experience a wider range of emotional response,

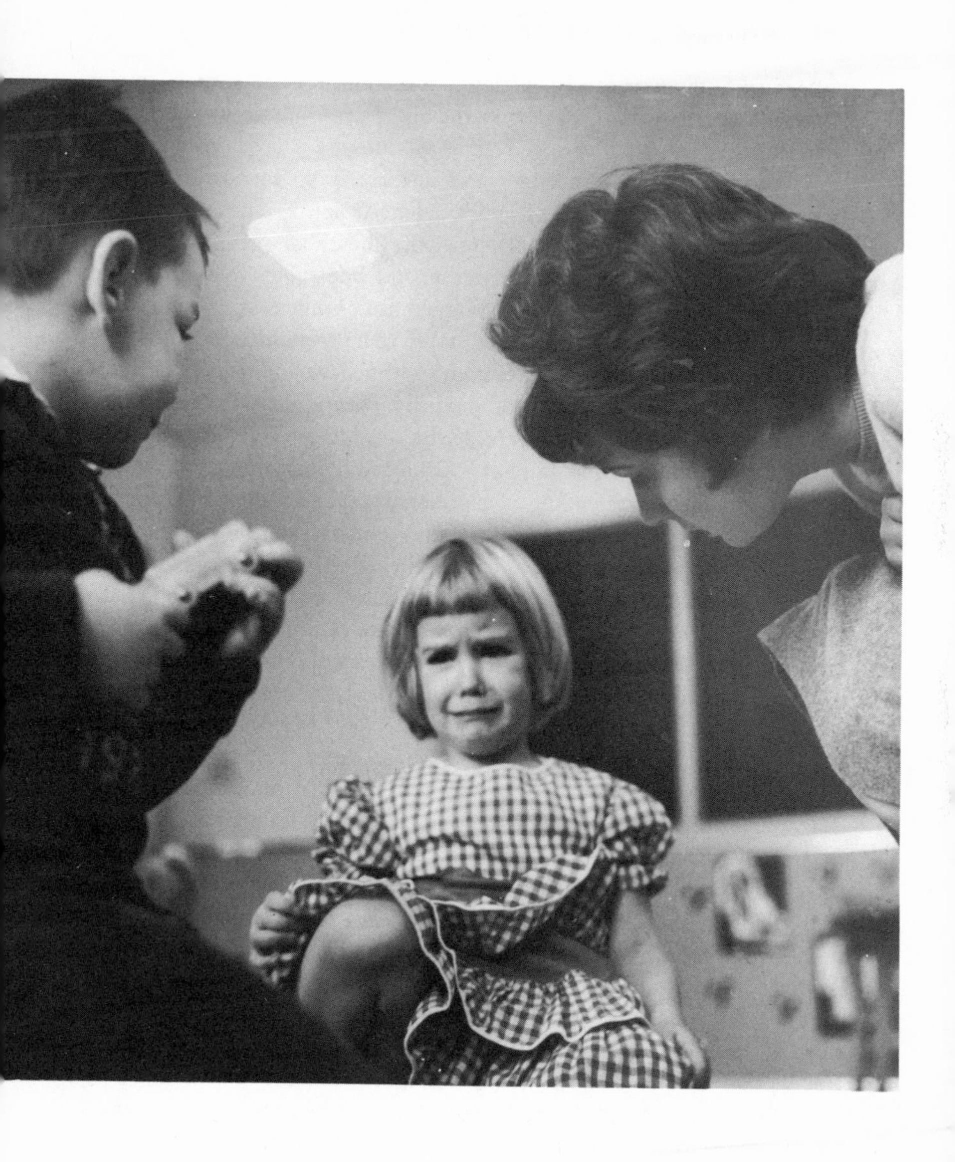

Strong feelings are real; we learn to accept them.
(R. Fred Sponholz.)

but his expanding circle of experience takes him into an ever increasing variety of situations that teach him the appropriateness of whatever reactions he uses.

There are important changes, too, in the ways in which various emotions are manifest as the child grows older. At age 2, when the child is really just emerging from infancy into the preschool period, emotional arousal is still relatively sudden, intense, and brief. This means that the observable emotional tone of the 2-year-old can change drastically in a very short time. To the casual, untrained observer he appears to be unpredictable and unstable in his pattern of emotional behavior. But with increased age, experience, and greater mental maturity, there appears to be more of a carry-over from one event in the child's life to another. Instead of the sharp separation of each emotional incident from those preceding and following it, there is more of a blending of emotional responses along the time dimension. He moves more slowly from one emotional state to another, and there is greater variation in the degree to which he expresses his feelings. This is understandable. After all, his increasing maturity as well as his broadening experiences give him a greater range of situations to respond to emotionally. They also give him the need to express finer degrees of reaction than the "all or nothing" response which worked well in infancy.

EMOTION AS A RESPONSE TO ENVIRONMENT

The human infant is born with the capacity for emotional behavior, limited, vague, and general at first, but gradually becoming more specific, direct, and definite. The capacity is merely a potential, not an active emotion. The child's muscles, glands, and nervous system are the resources necessary, to result in emotional behavior, *when they are appropriately stimulated*. Part of understanding the child consists of understanding what kinds of situations and events lead to his emotional reactions. This, in turn, provides clues to the effective guidance of a child's emotional life. In this section we shall be examining a number of kinds of emotional behavior and their causes. In each case, it should be remembered that an emotional reaction is the product of a unique relationship between an individual child having his own potential for emotional behavior, and the particular stimulus that triggers the emotion. There are countless individual variations in the manner of expressing emotions, and we can only point out some of the general features here.

Anger This is a complex emotion, which takes different forms and which results in quite different behavior at different age levels and in different children. Still, there are some things that seem to be true of all anger: first, it involves some physiological changes in the body; these include activity of the nervous system, and endocrine gland system in particular; second, there is the feeling aspect of the emotion, which is a very subjective experience but which is reported consistently by children and adults as a part of the total anger experience. These two components would seem to be general, widespread, and somewhat similar from one person to another in the case of anger. The third level of behavior, however—the observable reaction of the angry child—is highly variable from one child to another, and, for a given child, from time to time. Another common feature of the anger response seems to be its stimulus. What is it that triggers anger? The most important stimulus to anger seems to be some kind of blocking, thwarting, or frustration of a child's motives. Any motive might be involved, from his wish to get an attractive toy and to play with it, to his wish to keep his mother for himself and for her not to leave him (at home with the sitter, at the nursery school, in bed in his room by himself, etc.). In other words, anger results not from some specific kind of situation, but from any of countless situations in which some significant motive in the child's life is blocked and he is prevented from fulfilling the demand of that motive. The emotional reaction is generally less intense if a substitute motive can be satisfied when the child is blocked in some respect. The reaction is typically more intense if no other motive can be evoked at the time a significant one is blocked. The implications for guidance in these instances will be discussed later.

One of the things that determine whether or not a given event will result in anger is, simply, the child's age. In the infant, some experimenters have noted "angry" reactions when physical activity is restricted; i.e., when arms and legs are held firmly in place and movement is sharply limited. While there is no universal agreement on this point, it serves to illustrate the kinds of frustration which can motivate infantile anger. Obviously, restriction of physical activity is more of a motive during his active waking hours than at sleeping times, and the different results of various experiments can be accounted for, in part, by this.

During the preschool years, a child's anger responses will depend primarily on three things, according to Jersild (7): (1) his urges and strivings, (2) his activity tendencies, and (3) his personal limitations. All of these change rapidly between the ages of 2 and 5; therefore, it is understandable that outbursts of anger occur in response to rapidly changing conditions. A child's own limited motor coordination may prevent him from satisfying his urges or strivings, as when he would like to swing but cannot yet coordinate his body properly to "pump" and make the swing go. Again, a guidance principle may be drawn from this: equipment for the child that stimulates activity but demands a level of action beyond the ability of the child proves frustrating and essentially negative in its effects, since it produces anger and is a stumbling block in the way of need satisfaction. On the other hand, equipment which is stimulating but which lies within the realm of the child's control serves to increase his feelings of competence, allows for need satisfaction, and generally makes the anger reaction less probable. Nevertheless, a child's own activity tendencies may run, at times, well in advance of his physical and mental readiness. Stimulated either by the presence of equipment, or by the activities of older or more advanced children, a youngster may tackle activities that are inappropriate for him, leading to inevitable frustration, and frequently to colorful displays of anger. A 4-year-old, for example, likes to play in her own neighborhood with 6-, 7-, and 8-year-olds, one of whom is her sister. She wishes to do exactly the same things as the others, but when the others run fast from one yard to another, the preschooler is always last, and always gets angry. "No fair!" she screams, and her anger is a natural reaction to a kind of frustration inherent when children of such age differences play together.

A classic research study which reveals some of the changes in anger reactions that come with age was made in 1931 by Goodenough (3). Incidents involving anger were recorded in detail by parents. Among children under 1 year of age, one fourth of the incidents developed in connection with some child-care routine, such as dressing or bathing. Another fourth of the incidents were related to minor physical discomforts. Only 6 percent of the anger reactions were based on a direct restriction of bodily movement. The establishment of routine physical habits was the basis for a large proportion of the anger responses among 2-year-olds. Conflict with persons in authority, in situations not concerned with routine physical habits, was a second major cause of anger. Problems developing around social relationships at this age were also a source of anger reactions.

Blocking of the motive or need to think well of oneself may also lead to anger. All human beings old enough to have achieved even a rudimentary self-definition, or sense of personal identity, need to view themselves in at least a moderately favorable light. Admittedly there are wide ranges of variation in the ways this need operates, and there are countless distortions of the need in the unhealthy personality. Nevertheless, as a general characteristic of the development of the healthy child, nothing appears to be more central or significant, or more critical as a motivating factor in behavior, than this need to think well of oneself. At a very early age, children discover and make use of complex techniques for protecting and enhancing the gradually developing self-image. They even discover numerous ways to avoid facing some of the realities of their own behavior and misbehavior if, through self-deception, they can think more highly of themselves. If it is true, then, that a good deal of psychological as well as physical energy is devoted to maintaining and enhancing one's self-image, it may be better appreciated that a child (or, for that matter, a childish adult!) can become very angry indeed if something comes along which threatens that self-image. Such an event represents a thwarting of one of the most powerful of human motives, the need to see oneself in a favorable light. Anger reactions, in this case, arise in the immature personality which has not yet achieved self-assurance sufficient to withstand readily such threats to self-esteem. They are essentially defensive reactions, designed to protect a somewhat "tender" self-image.

With children who anger when they must give in to authority, for example, it is likely that the real cause of the upset is that they are forced to view themselves as being less powerful and less significant than someone else. Fortunately, there are many ways in which the growing child can be given ample experience with situations in which the net effect is a favorable view, on his own part, of the person he is. In her study of the anger responses of young children, Goodenough presented detailed data on 45 children ranging in age from 7 months to 7 years, 10 months. Daily records were kept by mothers of the children. Included were such data as: every manifestation of anger, rage, or marked irritation; immediate cause or provocation of the incident; type of behavior shown by the child (undirected energy, resistance, retaliation, motor or vocal behavior, or some combination of these); behavior following the outbursts (cheerful, sulky, fretful, continued sobbing, resentful); methods of control used, and by whom used; and the outcome (whether or not issue was settled, and in what manner, if it was settled). This detailed study yielded some interesting generalizations about the nature of children's anger responses, which can be summarized as follows:

1. Overt manifestations of anger reach a high frequency during the second year of life, and fall off rapidly thereafter. After the second year boys show anger more frequently and more violently than girls, but with wide individual variations for both sexes.

2. With advancing age, angry behavior becomes more openly directed toward a given end. Outbursts of undirected energy decrease in frequency, while angry retaliation increases. Indirectness increases also, as does the frequency of after-reactions such as resentfulness and sulking.

3. The duration of outbursts of anger remains fairly constant during the first eight years. Most of them do not last as long as five minutes.

4. The frequency of anger outbursts is related to the child's general health status and physical condition at the moment.

5. There is a positive relationship between the number of adults present in the household and the frequency of anger in the child.

6. Anger occurs more frequently at certain times of the day, especially just before meals (3, pp. 244–249).

Other findings of this study related to the methods of control used by parents and to the outcome or results of particular kinds of control methods. The author's own concluding words are revealing:

> A subjective judgment of the total home situation secured by a consecutive reading of all records for each child leads to the conclusion that the control of anger in children is best achieved when the child's behavior is viewed with serenity and tolerance, when the standards are adhered to with sufficient consistency to permit the child to learn through uniformity of experience, without such mechanical adherence to routine that the child's emotional or physical well-being is sacrificed to the demands of an inflexible schedule. However, when departures from the established schedule are made, they should be determined by a recognition of the needs of the child and not simply by the convenience or mood of the adult in charge. Self-control in the parents is, after all, likely to be the best guarantee of self-control in the child (3, p. 249).

The problem of "self-control in the parents" deserves cautious consideration. There are conditions and circumstances under which emphasis on parental self-control may work to the detriment of the child, as well as to the parent. Nevertheless, as a general statement on parental guidance of anger reactions, the quotation from Goodenough remains remarkably sound advice today. We need only add that Goodenough's suggestions have broader implications for emotional development than the mere control of anger responses; indeed, they apply to the whole range of emotional reactions of which the child is capable.

Variations in the manner of expression of anger among preschool children was also studied. Goodenough noted that at age 4, about half the anger reactions were directed toward the specific object of the child's frustration. This was in marked contrast to the kind of anger observed at earlier age levels, which was more explosive, less well aimed, and less effective in removing or overcoming an obstacle. Besides becoming more directed and focused, the preschool child's anger also appears to take on more "carry-over" along the time dimension. That is, with age and maturity he is more likely to be affected for a longer time by frustration, and he is a little less abrupt in his shifts in mood into and out of anger. Further, his tendency to retaliate as a means of gaining revenge seems to increase during the preschool years. Goodenough observed that threats appeared between ages 2 and 3, and became more frequent following that period.

Jersild (7) calls attention to the fact that as soon as the child begins to direct his anger toward specific objects and people, he encounters strong social pressure to control or inhibit his angry behavior. Such pressure takes a variety of forms, including not only the unwillingness of others to accept his anger, but also the child's own realization that his anger may backfire in the form of a counterattack. As a result of this pressure to keep anger under control, the child embarks on a search for ways to deal with his feelings of anger and hostility. The success or failure of this search for methods of handling one's anger have vital implications for the adult personality as well as for the growing child. Jersild comments on the variety of substitute behavior designed to provide some kind of emotional outlet that is relatively safe and acceptable to other people. Not all substitutes are equally safe, nor are they equally acceptable socially. Nevertheless, they represent ways in which individual children endeavor to deal with their feelings of anger and hostility: Verbal aggressiveness (as fighting decreases, quarreling increases), teasing, swearing, the expression of hostility through fantasy and play, displacement of hostility (if it is not safe to be angry toward a person, for example, it may be safer to get angry at one's toys), cruelty, development of prejudice, bullying, antisocial tendencies, self-inflicted pain or punishment, projection of hostility onto someone else, the development of a variety of physical (psychosomatic) symptoms, and finally, neurotic reactions such as feelings of abuse or martyrdom (7, pp. 886–891). Some studies suggest that different cultural groups lead their children to quite different ways of responding to their own anger and aggressiveness, but that the problem is evidently present in all societies.

Fear Anger and fear are closely related emotional experiences, and in many instances are difficult or impossible to differentiate properly. The emotional reaction of fear can, in extremes, be most devastating and perhaps most conducive to unhealthy personality development in the young child. Nevertheless, fear is not abnormal nor pathological, but is one of the important components of the child's total emotional capacity. It is an emotional resource which must undergo its own maturation and growth process. If it is to become a positive and constructive force in the over-all development of the child, ways must be found to direct the action of this powerful emotion so that the child does not become dominated by obsessive or abnormal fears.

The range of things, situations, and people that a child may come to fear is almost without limit. Some of the things and situations feared by children represent appropriate fear stimuli. In responding with fear to these, the child is not only showing his normal capacity for emotion, but may perhaps be saving his own life in the face of a real danger. In such situations fear can lead to fast action, greater muscular exertion, and intensely concentrated effort where such would not normally be possible. But fear can also lead to panic, a disorganized and disruptive emotion which gets in the way of effective action, which paralyzes instead of stimulates, and which breaks down even well-developed habits of efficient behavior. A severe case of stage fright in a child asked to perform before a large audience for the first time is a case in point. This tremendous raw energy in the form of fear is, like most forms of energy, a source of strength and protection and advancement, and at the same time, a potential source of disorganization and destruction.

Some authorities regard fear as a kind of initial, internalized running away from a situation with which one cannot cope in any direct way.

Any situation which can be conceived of as a potential source of danger may serve as a fear stimulus. In infancy, responses that have all the earmarks of "fear" have been noted frequently. The conditions which cause them are varied. Sudden changes of physical position, as when the infant is moved abruptly, may result in a fear reaction. Loss of support, as when he is allowed to fall through the air briefly, causes a fear reaction. Sudden loud noises stimulate a fear response in the normal infant. As Jersild (7) points out, sudden intense stimulation of most any sensory modality (visual, tactual, auditory, etc.) may lead to a fear response.

Fear of strange persons, objects, and situations may appear in the latter half of the first year of life. A number of researchers have noted that between 5 and 9 months of age many infants show fear of persons they have not been around previously. One scientist, Valentine (10), noted in 1930 that things which may not ordinarily have aroused fear may do so in the presence of an unusual, novel, or strange situation. Fears of the strange and unfamiliar are explained by Jersild on the grounds that the individual has no prepared response with which to meet the situation. Previously learned habits of behavior do not seem appropriate in these cases, and the child is suddenly called upon to make adjustments in his own "inner" life to make it fit with the outer reality of the strange situation. The result is fear.

Developmental studies of emotion indicate that children are continually being exposed to unfamiliar situations and are constantly in the process of absorbing these into their personality, incorporating them into the larger body of what has become the familiar. Healthy emotional development includes the gradual, orderly expansion of the child's sphere of living, with sufficient support from familiar outside sources (parents, siblings, friends, nursery-school teachers, etc.) to adjust constructively to new experiences and to incorporate them into the larger body of what is familiar. With experience and maturity even an unfamiliar situation becomes less threatening, and the child's adjustment to this sort of experience is aided by the assurance he has gained from past experience that new experiences need not be completely devastating.

Certain kinds of fear reactions of children have long held special interest for parents and researchers alike. Among these are fears of the dark, of pain or injury, of animals, and of imaginary creatures. These fears show definite developmental trends; that is, they are much more likely to be found at one age than at another. Fear of separation from

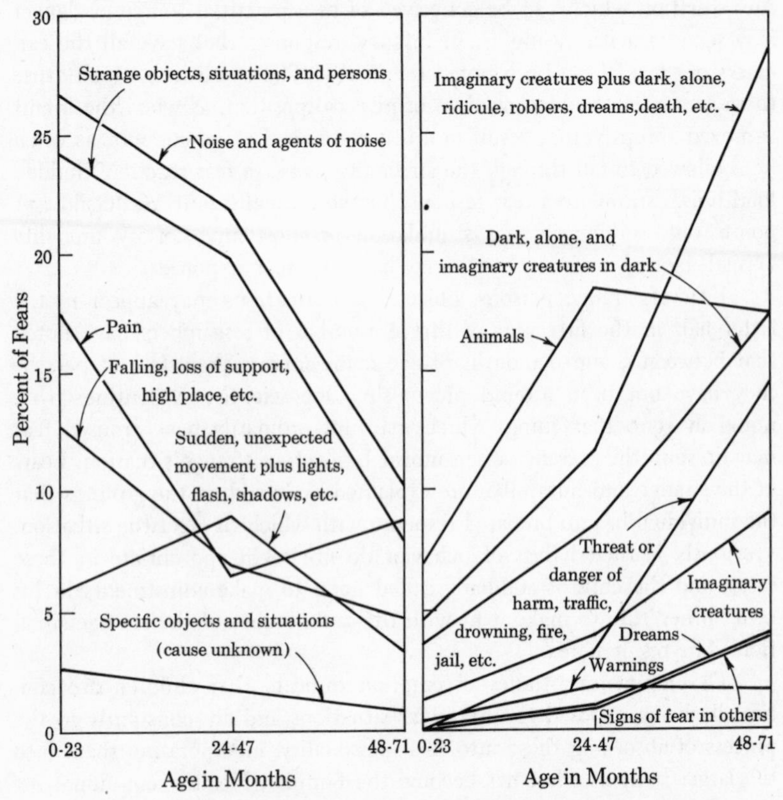

Fig. 9.1. The relative frequency of various fear situations as described by parents and teachers, including 146 records of observation of children for periods of 21 days, combined with occasional records of 117 additional children. (Reprinted with permission from A. T. Jersild, "Emotional development," in L. Carmichael (ed.), *Manual of child psychology* (2nd ed.), New York: Wiley, 1954, p. 867.)

parents, for example, did not appear in subjects of the Jersild and Holmes (8) study until after 12 months of age. During the second year, however, it was reported in 13 percent of the children. More would undoubtedly have shown fear had they been subjected to abandonment or separation from their mothers. Figure 9.1 indicates rather clearly that some types of fears increase rapidly during the preschool period. Others, however, show equally sharp decline. From these diagrams it may be concluded that fears of strangers and unfamiliar situations, of responses to sudden noise, of pain, falling, sudden movement, etc., tend to decrease in frequency during the preschool period. At the same time, however, fears of imaginary creatures, of the dark and of being alone, as well as some realistic fears of such things as traffic, drowning, fire, etc., are increasing. Some of these are very understandable when the child's increasing capacity to understand his environment is taken into account. As he becomes aware of the potential hazards of such things as automobiles and fires but is still not sufficiently mature to be able to control them, it is natural that some fear reactions may develop.

The child who is intellectually mature enough to understand the potential threats in strange situations—for example, entering nursery school for the first time—may be somewhat fearful and anxious until the situation and people in it become more familiar, and until he has developed a number of ways of responding that help to make it more "safe" to him and less threatening. The wise mother and nursery-school teacher, observing the process of adjustment by a newly enrolled child, will assist in the process by having the mother remain in the group for a time, until the child is ready to let her go. Another reaction to the newness and strangeness of the nursery school is illustrated by a child who does not wish to have his coat removed when he comes into the playroom. Again, the wise teacher is aware that the coat represents more than a way of keeping warm; it is a prime, tangible source of "familiarity" which he needs at this point and which is much more vital than the custom of removing outer garments on entering a playroom!

The child's familiarity or lack of familiarity with a situation is of fundamental importance if we are to understand the causes of fears and to provide experiences designed to help to overcome them. All of us, at any age, are more likely to be afraid of that which we do not understand—the unfamiliar. In one study of the process of overcoming fears of children (6), it was observed that familiarization and the development of ways of dealing with the feared situation were the keys to progress.

The effect of particular learning experiences on the development of children's fears has been illustrated in a number of classic studies of emotional "conditioning." One of the best known of these studies was reported years ago by Watson and Rayner (11). The technique was simple. It involved introducing a harmless furry white rat to an infant boy, "Albert," whose reaction was to reach toward the animal. Just as Albert reached, the experimenter made a loud sound, startling the child. The same procedure was repeated several times, with Albert becoming less willing to reach toward the animal each time. Finally he was withdrawing and attempting to get away from the animal, whether the sound was made or not. This concept of emotional conditioning in infancy has many implications for understanding how children's fear reactions come to be what they are. Not every specific fear of a child can be accounted for in terms of such simple conditioning, nevertheless, it is quite likely that many fears of particular things develop because of their close association with something already feared. Perhaps the young child's reaction to a puppy will illustrate this to some extent. At first, if he is introduced to a quiet, sleepy puppy in a basket, his natural curiosity leads him to touch it, discover what it feels like and what it will do. If he can build up sufficient familiarity with the quiet puppy at close range, and with noisy, active dogs at a safe distance, then gradually he can blend them together into a picture of a nonthreatening animal. If, however, his introduction to the puppy is sudden, at close range, and includes a lot of violent antics typical of puppyhood, plus considerable "yipping," it is not likely that he will respond favorably. Instead, it is highly probable that the youngster will, as Albert did, try to escape the loud sound and unpredictable movement of the animal, and avoid it in the future. Thus, one type of the beginning of a fear of dogs can be explained. This might be reinforced from time to time by otherwise harmless incidents, such as a playful dog that wants attention and who in the process of jumping up may knock the youngster off balance. Needless to say, well trained dogs that do not jump up on people are the exception rather than the rule, and it is unrealistic to assume that one's child will never have such an experience. He is fortunate, however, if he has the support of an understanding adult when such events do occur. A child's incipient fear of animals can be alleviated, at least to some degree, through reconditioning; that is, by providing positive, nonthreatening, and pleasant experiences with quiet animals, and allowing the child's natural interest and curiosity to lead him into participation once the arrangements are made. A good nursery school provides many such experiences, which prove most helpful in introducing the unfamiliar in safe, nonthreatening ways to make it familiar and to avoid needless fears.

One of the most significant implications of the work of Watson and other experimenters with the conditioning of emotions is the phenomenon of *stimulus generalization*. When a child comes to fear a particular object, person, or situation, it often happens that he generalizes from the specific elements involved to a whole class of objects, persons, or situations having something in common with the feared one. In the case of Watson's subject, for example, it was found after he had come to develop the fear of the furry animal that other furry animals also aroused the same reaction. Generalization went even further. The child showed similar reactions to a variety of objects having something in common with the furry animal: a fur coat, a piece of cotton wool, a Santa Claus mask.

A child who has experienced pain and fear in connection with a visit to the doctor's office may generalize this fear to all doctors, or perhaps to all persons wearing white coats, or perhaps to rooms having bright shiny instruments. A boy's fear of going to the barber shop can be accounted for, perhaps, if he has already experienced fear in connection with a doctor or dentist. This generalization property of children's fears makes them extremely complex and frequently leads to kinds of fears which are difficult to understand. One of Watson's major contributions to understanding the child's emotions was his insight into emotional conditioning and into the fact that fears, perhaps even unusual and intense fears, can come to be associated with harmless situations. These in turn can be generalized to include a multitude of similar situations or events having perhaps some obscure thing in common with the original feared situation.

It is never easy to determine just where the line lies between the normal fears of childhood and the abnormal, pathological fears found in the emotionally disturbed child. If a child's health is being impaired through loss of sleep resulting from fear of nightmares, it is evident we are dealing with an emotional disturbance that requires professional treatment. However, there are many normal fears of the developing child which are not so extreme, which do not interfere with the normal activities of eating, playing, sleeping, and the other routines of the child's daily life. Parental acceptance and understanding of the normality of fear is the only treatment required, since the child's own developmental progress will bring revision not only in the types of things that bring out his fear reaction but in the degree of his need to be afraid.

However, in the case of children who are exhibiting more than the ordinary number of fears, or unusually intense fear reactions to situations only somewhat fearful for other children, it is reasonable to consider parental practices as a possible cause. One important reason for this is that the preschool child identifies very strongly with the powerful people in his world; that is, he takes upon himself some of the psychological qualities and characteristics of those people. A boy, for example, identifies strongly with his father, for to him his father is powerful and wise. Similarly, a girl tends to identify with her mother and in the process takes upon herself many of the qualities and characteristics, mannerisms, ways of speech, facial expressions, gestures, body postures, etc., of her mother. This identification process is generally unconscious—the child is not aware of doing this at all—and is perfectly normal. However, it goes far beyond imitation of merely superficial mannerisms into some of the core elements of personality itself. Identification is one of the processes by which children attach emotional reactions to particular situations. An extreme example is the case of a mother who could not stand electrical storms. When a thunderstorm came up, she would throw herself on the floor and cover her head with something. Her children soon came to do likewise—but this was more than mere imitation of their mother's observable behavior. The children were afraid, and there was nothing in their mother's behavior to help them deal constructively with their fear. Instead, her behavior told them rather clearly that thunderstorms are things to be afraid of. A point should be added in this connection. None of the foregoing material should be interpreted to mean that a parent should put on a false front of "bravado" in an attempt to deceive the child. If anything, the child needs to identify with a person who does have honest emotions, including fear, but who has developed constructive ways of dealing with those emotions. If the child is fortunate enough to have such parents, then there is everything to be gained and nothing to be lost through the child's gradually increasing awareness that the strong persons in his life also have fears at times.

Anxiety Anxiety is closely related to fear. But anxiety has some special features that should be considered in a somewhat different light. In the case of anxiety, the child is not dealing with a sudden, sharp, intense feeling of impending disaster. Instead, there is a prolonged high level of tension best described as a feeling that things are not going to work out well. This has very important implications for over-all personality development. Just as fear represents a natural response to a threat of some kind—

real or imagined—anxiety represents a response to pressures and to vague, poorly defined threats that do not produce sudden, sharp fears. Examples of anxiety operating in the life of the child would include a concern over the possibility of losing the mother, or concern about losing the mother's affection, or concern about not measuring up to expectations, or concern about one's own impulses, etc.

The real relationship between anxiety and fear, or anxiety and other emotions such as anger, is extremely complex and deserves much more study. However, a point may be made about the kind of reciprocal relationship that may sometimes be observed. Anxiety may serve to inhibit and suppress other emotions; that is, the anxious child may inhibit the direct expression of such emotions as anger, fear, or hostility. In fact, his anxiety might well reflect a prolonged concern over the expression of emotions of various kinds. This might be true of the child who learns at an early age that the free expression of emotion is somehow dangerous or in conflict with some other needs, such as the need for acceptance by a loved person. In such a case, the anxiety-arousing factors in his life might well be reinforcing themselves continually as he strives to keep his more explosive emotions under control. When, on occasion, the more violent upheavals do break through the inhibitions and express themselves openly, he is likely to feel guilty and strive all the harder to prevent it from happening again. But the continuing fear that it *might happen* again is a form of anxiety itself.

From this discussion it might be assumed that the major approach to the prevention of excessive anxiety in the life of the child is acceptance by the loved persons around him. This is precisely the correct interpretation. Every normal child has emotions. It is all too easy, however, to add to the emotional burden of the child by making him feel guilty or anxious over the existence of the strong feelings which these emotions include. Healthy emotional development includes the gradually increasing awareness that one's own feelings—even the strong ones and negative ones—are natural and can be coped with.

Jealousy Jealousy as an emotional reaction in early childhood deserves special mention, inasmuch as it is both a common reaction of most children and also a powerful force in motivating the child's behavior. Jealousy can be a significant determiner of his personal adjustment and the adjustment of those around him. Its major causes are not obscure and can easily be understood by most adults. However, we must remember that the child himself probably has very little understanding of the feelings he harbors, or of the reasons for their existence.

Sibling rivalry, the basic cause of much jealousy, is usually accepted by parents as a natural and almost inevitable condition when there is more than one child in a family. Indeed, depending on the intensity, the manner of its direction, the way it is handled by parents, and other factors, sibling rivalry itself may be a positive force for healthy personal development in the life of the individual child. At the same time, if it leads primarily to deep resentments and jealous reactions, as it may well do if one child is forever subjugated to another or presented in unfavorable comparisons with another, the net effects are most likely negative. In such circumstances, the child's natural reaction is to build a system of defense of his own ways of dealing with the hurt which arises from the unfavorable position he holds in relation to his sibling. The ways of dealing with this hurt may be open and direct or, as is more likely the case when such conditions are prolonged, more secretive, hidden, and indirect. It is the indirect jealous reaction that is most difficult to understand and to deal with intelligently. Even the child is not likely to know *why* he engages in devious efforts to throw blame or suspicion upon his brother or sister, or *why* he is overly critical of the sibling, or *why* he is uncooperative or negative or hostile where that sibling is concerned. The jealous reaction takes many forms, but at the core of all of them is the fundamental feeling of having been deprived of favorable status with a loved person as a result of the existence of someone else.

Sibling rivalry is not the only condition involved here. It is quite possible for a child to be jealous of his father for his mother's affection. (For that matter, we might note that it is entirely possible for a *father* to be jealous of his child, for the same reason—but that is another story).

Since affection and the threat of loss of affection from a loved person seem to be at the heart of this matter, guidance of emotional development in this sphere requires considerable understanding of the child's affectional needs. Furthermore, it requires an emotional capacity in the adult involved to provide the kind of affection that is developmentally appropriate for the child. The demonstration of affection to a child must, of necessity, undergo revision as the child grows. Behavior that represents love to him as an infant may symbolize restriction or discipline to a 2-year-old, and similarly, the love given a 3-year-old should not take the same form as that provided a 5-year-old kindergarten child. Affection that is freely given and developmentally appropriate for an individual child (who is truly perceived as an individual by his parents) can go far to avoid the negative, destructive affects of deep-seated jealousy. Again, however, one must remember the natural, almost inevitable existence of a certain amount of jealousy in any healthy child, and avoid treating it as a sign of emotional disturbance.

Joy and Happiness In some respects there is less known about such positive emotional aspects of the child's life as joy and happiness than there is about such feelings as anger, fear, and jealousy. Nevertheless, joy and happiness do play a vital part in the child's over-all development.

As was shown in Figure 4.6, joy and elation responses do appear very early in the infancy period. At first glance such emotions seem to result from relief of tension. An example of this would be the kind of excited elation observed in a group of preschool children upon being released from a Sunday school class. Their emotional state at this point may include a good deal of shouting, laughing, running, and miscellaneous motor activity that represents the child's best ways of discharging the tension that had built up during the period of relative restriction of activities.[1] But on closer examination we may observe that joy and happiness in children occur not only in relation to discharge of excessive energy but also may accompany a building-up of tension. An example of this can easily be seen at a birthday party for 4-year-olds (which, incidentally, can be a devastating experience for all concerned if poorly handled, and is not recommended here!) At such a party it is not at all uncommon for the children to get progressively "higher" and louder and more active, all of which are evidences of increased tension, as the party progresses. Whether such emotional reactions are properly termed "joy" and "happiness" may be a somewhat debatable semantic question. Perhaps they would be better labeled "gleeful excitement." In any case, the condition under consideration is accompanied by a great deal of tension.

Spontaneous expressions of joy and happiness in the preschool child are, other things being equal, indicators of the general health and well-being of the child. They reflect an over-all satisfaction on his part with

[1] The wise Sunday school teacher, if she has a group of preschoolers, learns constructive ways to avoid an excessive buildup of this tension while the children are in the class. Physical activities interspersed with quiet activities are usually helpful.

his life circumstances and indicate that he is finding reasonably adequate ways to meet his various psychological needs. Obviously this changes from one time to another, and the child is less likely, when ill or fatigued or frustrated, to show such pleasant emotions.

According to Jersild (7, p. 902), important sources of pleasure, joy, and happiness for children include the satisfying of physical appetites, pleasures associated with food and drink, fragrant odors, the comforts of rest and relaxation. Jersild points out that for the normal child pleasant emotional states such as joy and happiness tend to occur with greater frequency than unpleasant states. This same finding happens to be true of normal adults as well.

Love and Affection Children begin to display affection for others during the first year. Some authorities hold that the beginnings of affection occur pretty much as a spontaneous action of the child, without much need for social stimulation from others. Both maturation and experiences, however, play vital roles in determining the course of the child's ability to express affection as he grows through the preschool years. Recent experiments with rhesus monkeys carried on by Harlow (4) provide important data about the development of affectionate behavior. While no one would say that the human infant is identical in emotional behavior with the infant rhesus monkey, both are primates, and the similarity of emotional behavior and factors involved in normal and pathological emotional development should not be overlooked. In any event, certain of Harlow's findings are of special interest. His research methods included rearing monkeys apart from their mothers, providing for them, in cages, two types of dummy "mother surrogates." The first of these was simply welded wire mesh shaped into a cylindrical form, with a crude wooden head at the top. The second was similar, except that the wire mesh was covered by a soft terry cloth. In one phase of the study, eight newborn monkeys were placed in individual cages, each cage being equipped with a cloth mother *and* a wire mother. Four of the infants received their milk from the wire mother, and four from the cloth figure, the milk being provided by a nursing bottle with its nipple protruding from the mother's "breast." In both experimental setups, the infant monkeys made the same progress from the physiological standpoint: both groups drank the same amount of milk and both gained weight at the same rate. But there were remarkable differences in the two "mothers" from the psychological standpoint. The infant monkeys in both groups spent a lot of time clinging and climbing on the cloth-covered mothers; they spent little time clinging to or climbing on the wire mothers. Those that received nourishment from the wire mother spent no more time with her than was necessary for feeding.

Harlow's studies strongly suggest that the source of the love relationship between the mother and infant is not so much the fact that the mother is the source of food as the fact that she is the source of bodily contact. It appears that love develops, at least in part, in the rhesus monkey, through the skin. Harlow's research also reveals much about development of other emotions, particularly fear. As the monkeys grew older, they were subjected to a number of experiences, some of them designed to frighten them. In response to fear, the monkeys ran, as might be expected, to their mothers. But they did not run to the wire apparatus; even those who had been nurtured by the wire dummies ran, when frightened, to the cloth-covered figures. The words of Harlow on this point are instructive:

> Whether the infants had nursed from the wire mother or the cloth mother, they overwhelmingly sought succor from the cloth one; this differential in behavior was enhanced with the passage of time and the accrual of experience. Early in this series of experiments the terrified infant might rush blindly to the wire mother, but even if it did so, it would soon abandon her for the cloth mother. The infant would cling to its cloth mother, rubbing its body against hers. Then, with its fear assuaged through intimate contact with the mother, it would turn to look at the previously terrifying . . . [stimulus] . . . without the slightest sign of alarm. Indeed, the infant would sometimes even leave the protection of the mother and approach the object that a few minutes before had reduced it to abject terror.
>
> The analogy with the behavior of human infants requires no elaboration. We found that the analogy extends even to less obviously stressful situations. When a child is taken to a strange place, he usually remains composed and happy so long as his mother is nearby. If the mother gets out of sight, however, the child is often seized with fear and distress (5, pp. 70, 72).

It should be evident from this that the child's emotional development from its very beginnings is dependent on the sensory experiences he has with his mother. In the development of the affectionate relationship, the sense of touch appears to take on special significance.

There are developmental changes in the love and affectional sphere of the child's life, both in his needs for such experiences and in his own manner of expressing affection for others. Jersild has summarized some of these developmental changes:

> We know from everyday observation that as time passes the child's affections expand in scope. He shows affection for his parents, immediate members of his family and, as time passes, for other persons in his environment. Eventually he becomes capable of a wide range of loyalties that contain an element of affection.
>
> Likewise, from an early age, the child begins to acquire affection for pets and things and places, his doll, his favorite toy, an old blanket, the family cat, the house and grounds wherein he lives, and so on.
>
> With the passing of time there are changes also in the quality of his affection. As he develops, he increasingly gains in ability to appreciate the feelings of others, to sympathize, to feel compassion, to respond to loved persons with thoughtfulness and tenderness, to give to others out of love (7, p. 893).

The child's ability to express emotion is closely interconnected with his developing mental capacities. One example of this, referred to briefly above in Jersild's summary of the changes in the child's love relationships, has to do with the child's expression of sympathy for others. To be truly sympathetic, a child must have the capacity to suffer *with* another person. Murphy (9), in a study of the sympathy responses of preschool children, concluded that 2- and 3-year-old children did not respond with sympathy to external evidences of suffering such as bruises, swellings, pictures of accidents or funerals, the crippled, etc. At age 3, most children did show sympathy in response to bandages, blindness, injuries, crying, accidents, attacks by another person, deprivation of toys, deprivation of the mother, or confinement to bed. The ability to develop sympathy and compassion for others would seem to depend, in part, on one's mental maturity and capacity for seeing the implications of events in the lives of others. This is correlated both with mental age and with any special experiences of the child that might lead him to be more sensitive to such events. In any case, it would appear that the early preschooler is not especially sensitive to the welfare of others; considerable progress is made in this direction during the preschool years.

CONFLICTING EMOTIONS

We are talking in this chapter, of course, about the child's feelings—the way he feels about the important objects and people in his world. Perhaps one of the most significant things that can be said about these feelings in describing the nature of the preschool child is that they are decidedly mixed and overlapping. The words we have been using here—fear, anger, love, jealousy, etc.—are words of convenience to describe the more obvious themes of feeling that appear in early childhood. But seldom, even at this age, are there unmixed feelings.

Consider, for example, a child's general relationship with his mother. In her role as mother she must not only provide nurturance and tender loving care; she must provide restrictions, limits, discipline, and all those things that represent the boundaries of permissible behavior. It is natural and inevitable that the child's feelings toward his mother, who is both nurturant and controlling, both loving and restrictive, will include some positive and some negative elements. At times the negative elements will come to the fore around some particular incident or item of behavior, and the child's demeanor, if not his actual words, will say clearly to his mother, "I hate you!" At other times—it is to be hoped a larger proportion of times—his manner and perhaps even his words will tell his mother clearly that he holds great affection for her. Most of us do not wish to be disliked, especially by our own children. But one of the tasks of parenthood includes acceptance of the reality of the negative feelings our children hold for us. Only through such realistic awareness of these feelings, only through the recognition that they are normal and inevitable can we be of real service to the child whose task is to learn how to deal with his own combination of negative and positive feelings.

There is a word which aptly describes the condition in which we feel two ways about the same person: *ambivalence*. We almost always feel ambivalent toward the people who are closest to us. If we love them, our wish to possess them exclusively may run into conflict with their wish to hold affectionate relationships for others, too. Our ensuing jealousy may take the form of anger against the loved person. Hence our feelings are mixed. Something like this is continually happening in the emotional life of the child in his intense relationships with parents, siblings, and other children. It is well to understand that the child's emotional behavior is motivated, in all likelihood, by a complex of feelings rather than a single, clear-cut emotion. Emotional conflict, seen from this standpoint, is not an abnormal condition experienced only by unbalanced children. Instead, it is an inevitable consequence of living in a world which both gives and takes, which both nurtures and controls, which both grants freedom and imposes bondage, which is both satisfying and frustrating. Obviously, in this world, there is nothing wrong with the *child* who experiences emotional conflict; indeed, we should have cause to be concerned about his normality should he fail to respond to such disparate conditions with no evidenced conflict. His task and the task of those charged with guiding his emotional development is essentially a learning task—which can be expressed as a question: How can the child learn to adapt himself to such conflicting emotional demands in such a manner as to lead to optimum self-development?

SUMMARY

The emotional life of the child includes physiological changes, observable changes in behavior, and feelings. His growth toward emotional maturity is, in large part, a matter of coming to terms with the reality of these components of emotional life. The early stages of emotional growth illustrate, in the gradual movement from general reactions toward more specific emotional behavior, the process of differentiation. There are consistent changes in the patterning of emotional responses through the preschool years, which give evidence of the role of maturational factors in development. The particular mode of response in a child exposed to an emotion-arousing situation, however, is determined to a great extent by his learning experiences.

Anger, a response to the thwarting of satisfaction in some need, undergoes considerable modification between 2 and 5. By the end of the preschool period the child is much more adept at modulating his responses to frustration. Children's fear reactions also undergo important changes during this period. Anxiety, jealousy, joy and happiness, and love and affection are other examples of major themes in the emotional life of the preschool child. All these manifestations of emotion become greatly differentiated and associated with a wide variety of circumstances, situations, people, and objects before the child reaches school age.

Conflicting emotions are normal experiences for children, and the resulting disturbance does not, by itself, indicate the existence of illness. Effective guidance of emotional growth includes, as its major prerequisite, an understanding and acceptance of the inevitability of emotional conflicts.

REFERENCES

1. Bridges, K. M. B., "A genetic theory of the emotions," *J. genet. Psychol.*, 1930, **37**:514–527.
2. Bridges, K. M. B., "Emotional development in early infancy," *Child Develpm.*, 1932, **3**:324–341.
3. Goodenough, Florence L., *Anger in young children*, Minneapolis: Univ. of Minnesota Press, 1931.
4. Harlow, H. F., "Primary affectional patterns in primates," *Amer. J. Orthopsychiat.*, 1960, **30**:676–684.
5. Harlow, H. F., "Love in infant monkeys," *Sci. Amer.*, 1959, **200** (6): 68–74.
6. Holmes, F. B., "An experimental investigation of a method of overcoming children's fears," *Child Develpm.*, 1936, **7**:6–30.
7. Jersild, A. T., "Emotional development," in L. Carmichael (ed.), *Manual of child psychology*, 2nd ed., New York: Wiley, 1954.
8. Jersild, A. T., and Holmes, F. B., "Children's fears," *Child Develpm. Monogr.*, (20), 1935.
9. Murphy, L. B., *Social behavior and child personality*, New York: Columbia Univ. Press, 1937.
10. Valentine, C. W., "The innate bases of fears," *J. genet. Psychol.*, 1930, **37**:394–420.
11. Watson, J. B., and Rayner, R., "Conditioned emotional reactions," *J. exp. Psychol.*, 1920, **3**:1–14.

CHAPTER TEN

What elements must be included under the heading of the child's personality? ∽ *What is there about personality growth that leads to inevitable conflicts? What major conflict is there inherent in the process of growing up?* ∽ *What major tasks of childhood must be accomplished in order to achieve a healthy sense of self?* ∽ *What are the main stages through which the preschool child progresses in developing a sense of self?*

ACHIEVING SELFHOOD: THE PERSONALITY OF THE PRESCHOOL CHILD

IT IS IMPOSSIBLE to write or to talk about the child without referring to his personality. His emotional life; his intellectual behavior; his muscular coordination; his relationships with family and friends; every one of the things that we have discussed up to this point is part—*an essential part*—of his personality. At the same time, we are accustomed to think of the child's personality as somehow going beyond anything that could be included under muscular, mental, social, or emotional behavior. Personality is more than the sum of these attributes. Whatever else it may be, it seems to represent the total orientation of the child toward his world, and in that orientation the child acts as a unified whole—not as a muscular system, or a mental or social or emotional system—that is greater than the sum of its parts.

When we use the term *personality* here we refer to something more than "traits" such as honesty, or aggressiveness, or tenacity, or inferiority feelings. All such traits may be important characteristics and most of them have been investigated, at one time or another, in research studies on human personality. Again, however, we shall concern ourselves with the "something more" which is manifest in the child's total orientation toward his world. While we may have occasion to note, in later chapters in Part IV of this book, that certain kinds of treatment of children are more likely to result in the development of certain kinds or degrees of these traits,[1] this chapter places primary emphasis on the child as a complex, highly organized behaving unit.

THE MEANING OF PERSONALITY

Psychologists define *personality* in many different ways. The word *persona* as used in ancient Rome referred to a theatrical mask. From this was derived the notion of one's *appearance* as the crucial element in personality. That is, the way in which one is viewed by others has been held by many to be the central point in a definition of personality. Such a definition also implies that personality is essentially the "mask" of behavior a person adopts in order to present some particular view of himself to the world.

Other key elements in historical definitions of personality include the concept of the *role* played by an individual, or, more correctly, the complex of many roles he learns to play in relation to the objects and persons in his world. A final basic component of personality is that of the *player* himself —the actor—the individual who wears the mask and who portrays the roles.

Personality, as discussed by Bronfenbrenner and Ricciuti (2), includes three major elements: (1) the ways in which a child responds, (2) his motives, and (3) the way he stimulates other people. The following quotation from their discussion illustrates each of these three characteristics:

> A personality characteristic ordinarily implies a tendency toward behavior associated with a particular person under a given set of conditions. Most commonly, this behavioral tendency refers to a disposition to act on the part of . . . the person himself.

[1] One approach to the study of child personality places primary emphasis on individual differences. This usually involves a discussion of personality characteristics, or "traits," and the possible causes of their variation from one child to another. There is significant literature on this approach to child study, some of which is referred to in other sections of this book. The present chapter, however, is concerned with a more unified approach to the personality ot the preschool child, in which "traits" do not represent major considerations.

> For example, Mary cries whenever she sees another child crying, Tom avoids the company of boys his own age . . . We also . . . consider a personality characteristic any tendency [of a child] to evoke a particular response in others under a given set of conditions. For example, John is picked on by boys his own age, Tom is "mothered" by females older than himself. All together, we have found it necessary to distinguish three types of personality characteristics, which we designate as *response tendencies, motives, and stimulus characteristics.* The first two refer to dispositions toward action on the part of [the child] himself, the last to tendencies to evoke responses in others (2, p. 771).

Although we are not concerned at the moment with particular traits of personality, the preceding quotation indicates rather well the breadth and scope of the concept of personality. It also suggests that if we are to understand personality development during the preschool years we are obliged to understand the achievement by an individual child of his own unique ways of responding, his own special system of motivation, and his own peculiar ways of affecting other people. We need only add that these three components operate in complex interaction with each other—not as separate or isolated elements.

Personality, as defined by representatives to the Midcentury White House Conference on Children and Youth, includes concepts derived from psychology, sociology, physiology, and psychiatry: "We mean by personality the thinking, feeling, acting human being, who, for the most part, conceives of himself as an individual separate from other individuals and objects. This human being does not *have* a personality; he *is* a personality" (11, p. 3). This statement brings out one of the key concepts to be understood. The popular notion of a person as "having" or "acquiring" or "losing" or "strengthening" something called personality doesn't ring true to modern psychological researchers. The self, which is the organic and psychological individual, *is* the personality.

The first part of the definition presented above stresses another point central to understanding the growth of the child. That is the self-awareness aspect of personality. Current thinking on this subject has placed primary emphasis on the self-concept—the achievement and enhancement of a sense of personal identity. This self-concept has vital bearing on the child's relationship with others and with the objects in his world. The self-concept, rapidly growing during the preschool period, includes expanding *awareness* of who one is and, at the same time, continuously fluctuating *evaluation* of one's worth.

It is the evaluation, perhaps more than anything else, which influences one's kind and quality and amount of participation in social interaction. It also influences interaction of the child with the tools of his world. This becomes readily apparent in the older child—the 7-year-old who takes so much pride in the development of tangible skills—riding a bicycle, roller skating, reading, playing the piano. This pride in accomplishment is meaningful and understandable as a direct outcome of one's own self-picture. It is, furthermore, a vital factor in the revision and expansion of the self-picture. When the child envisions himself as being "one who can ride a bicycle," then that operation is incorporated into the child's self-definition. It now includes all the status, prestige, power, and privileges that were formerly withheld from him and available to the select "others" who participated so grandly in bicycle riding. While such tangible accomplishments are less obvious in the preschooler, there is every reason to believe that a child's actions, including his skills, become part of him in a very real sense. As he gains confidence and skill in handling his own body under varying circumstances, he revises and modifies the "picture" he carries of himself.

The achievement of selfhood is not a simple, direct, easy growth process. It involves a continuous movement between assertions and questioning; between thrusting ahead and retreating; between pushing and hauling on the environment and being pushed and driven by the forces of one's world. Jersild describes the over-all process in colorful and understandable language that brings out the complexity and the paradoxical qualities of self-development:

> Each child strives to be himself, to realize his own resources, to come into his own. In other words he strives for selfhood. But while the self shows a powerful impetus to grow, it also, as part of its essential character, has a strong resistance to change.
>
> This is the paradox of the self: It is a changing, growing phenomenon, and it comes into existence by a process of learning, yet it also is strongly geared to prevent change. It is both flexible and rigid. From the time when the child begins to be-

> come aware of himself, and to take thought of who and what he is and begins to have attitudes regarding himself, he is constantly in the process of expanding his perception of who and what he is, and he is constantly involved in experiences that might help to revise or redefine his conception of who he is or might be. Yet from an early age he also is eager to preserve whatever concept of himself he then may have, and he may strongly resist anything that might threaten to change it (6, p. 32).

This point of view on self-development is parallel with the philosophy expressed by Lecky (7) in his concept of self-consistency. For Lecky there is only one major drive, or goal, or objective of all human striving. This objective is the achievement and maintenance of self-consistency. It is an internal self-condition in which the various self-operations are harmoniously allied one with another, without serious discrepancies or conflicts among them. The goal of therapy for the disturbed person, according to this point of view, is the removal of conflict and restoration of internal harmony.

Other writers have stressed similar views, although varying considerably in detail. Maslow (8, 9), for example, has written that the essential motivating force behind human action is self-realization, or self-actualization. This, in essence, is using one's potential for action of all kinds, freely, creatively, and with great personal satisfaction. Maslow's concept of the self-actualizing person, however, includes the satisfaction of more fundamental bodily and psychological needs. The individual is in a position to function at the self-actualizing level if his love and affectional needs are met. These needs, however, represent the focus of his energy if they remain unsatisfied. One is unable to operate even at the "love and affection" level if his self-esteem needs are not met. These in turn are dependent upon the satisfaction of safety needs, which arise out of physiological needs. Thus, Maslow is really describing a hierarchy of needs systems, beginning with the most fundamental physiological ones. The satisfaction of essential needs at each hierarchichal level releases the individual to focus his energies at higher levels. So long as the needs remain unsatisfied at a given level, however, one does not go beyond that stage; his motives and energies and life activities will be mobilized at that level.

The implication from such theoretical systems is that a child's needs must be satisfied if society is to receive the greatest return from its investment in him. It is quite similar to the philosophy expressed by most authorities in the field of child development. The need-satisfaction approach is not novel, nor is it seriously questioned today. Still, there are somewhat different approaches to the outlining of the growing child's fundamental needs, as well as to proposed means of meeting those needs. In the section which follows, we shall summarize two major approaches to understanding the special growth needs of the preschool child. It is implied throughout this discussion that, other things being equal, the satisfaction of these needs tends toward the development of a healthy, well-functioning self during the preschool years, and that the failure to satisfy these needs somehow restricts, hinders, or impedes the healthy development of selfhood.

PERSONALITY AS THE "WHOLE CHILD"

Before we go into a detailed discussion of the development of personality and its significant changes during the years from 2 to 5 or 6, it may be well to stress again the total nature of the concept with which we are dealing. One way to do this, perhaps, is to stress the interdependence of various aspects of personality. For example, a child's motor behavior is frequently discussed, for the sake of convenience and practical guidance, somewhat apart from the rest of his personality. There is reason to believe, however, that the smoothness of a child's motor action is, in part, a matter of the degree of confidence he holds in his ability to control his body. This confidence, in turn, appears to be dependent on the experiences he has had that have reinforced his conviction that his motor behavior is safe, productive, and valued by others. In other words, he will be able to engage in smooth, spontaneous, and well coordinated motor behavior to the extent that his past experiences have led him to feel that his motor action is "worthy." Worthiness, as here used, includes elements of safety, elements of productivity, and elements of social value. In contrast, if we consider the likely effects of continued and repeated inhibition of motor activities in a social context, associating in the child's experience such things as "motor behavior leads to danger," or "motor behavior leads to social error," or "my own muscle control doesn't get me what I want; I'd better rely on someone else's ability to control things," it appears that the inhibited child reflects a combined attitudinal-motor orientation to his world in which the point where one (motor) leaves off and the other (attitude or inhibition) begins is extremely difficult to discern.

Another example of interdependence of personality traits might be seen in the relationship between physical characteristics and emotional attitudes. The latter are obviously personality ingredients. The former are also, but are perhaps less likely to be considered when one speaks of the child's personality. It is not difficult to see, however, that a child's emotional attitudes toward food and eating behavior can readily influence his nutritional status, at least if intense attitudes persist over a considerable period of time. His nutritional status, in turn, plays a significant role in the ways in which he relates to other people and in his stimulus value in relation to others. It may, in fact, directly affect the vigor with which he approaches social and objective situations.

Many other examples of interdependence of personality variables could be cited to support this general theme. Any discussion of the personality of the child should take into consideration the organized complexity of the child, and the fact that the child's total orientation toward himself and toward his world cannot realistically be separated into independent, isolated units such as motor behavior, emotion, attitude, social, nutritional, physique, intelligence, etc. The child *is* a personality, and that personality is best described as the unique orientation of one growing individual toward himself and toward his social and objective environments.

TASKS IN THE ACHIEVEMENT OF SELFHOOD

In the achievement of personality, or selfhood as we have chosen to call it here, there are three fundamental tasks which the child must accomplish. They are not independent; indeed, the accomplishment of any one of these tasks is dependent on the achievement of a degree of success with each of the other two. They are not achieved in chronological sequence, but progress simultaneously.

The Task of Living with Tools The first of these tasks may be described as the *mastery of the world of tools*. In this, the child's need is to acquire skills that promote independence and allow him to function effectively and successfully in meeting his own needs, of whatever kind.

Tools come in all shapes, sizes, and varieties. Some of them are very tangible tools, such as play equipment, blocks, dolls, puzzles, climbing frames, swings, slides, etc., and such items as shovels, rakes, and hammers. Other kinds of tools are less tangible, such as the social customs that people use to enable them to interact successfully with others—the folkways and mores described by sociologists and anthropologists. Language is such a tool—and a most significant one. In fact, it might be argued that of all the tools a preschool child is learning to use effectively, none is more essential and basic to his personality growth than that of language.

The mastery of all tools implies more than the immediate satisfaction gained by the successful operation of some particular implement, or some other immediate action dependent on the use of any tool. It goes far beyond into the realm of one's attitudes toward self and other people, as we shall see in the discussion of the other two central tasks of personality development.

The Task of Living with Others The second central task of the growing personality is the *task of living successfully in a world of other people,* or social adjustment. This involves, for the preschool child, a rapidly expanding awareness of the individuality of other people, both children and adults, and an acceptance of the reality of the needs of others. It involves a wide variety of skills in interaction with others, including the language skills and nonverbal communications skills which allow the child to recognize the feelings, attitudes, and needs of others as well as the intellectual content of the things said or implied by others. It involves the development of a degree of sympathy and feeling for others before the end of the preschool years, and the ability to await one's turn, postponing one's own satisfaction for the greater satisfaction of being acceptable socially by being capable of sharing and taking turns. Living in a world of others implies more, however, than just yielding to others or being altruistic in relation to their needs. It implies learning to make the best use of one's own resources, and the resources of others, for the sake of cooperative activity of all kinds. It implies awareness of the values of teamwork, or cooperative behavior, and the recognition that there are certain satisfactions to be derived from successful articulation of the resources of a group.

In Part IV we shall have occasion to analyze some of the institutions and forces in our society that play vital roles in the shaping of a child's ability to adapt to a world of others. Such personal traits as aggressiveness, rivalry, competitiveness, hostility, cooperation, and leadership, all of which are important personality characteristics, will be discussed in relation to some of these social forces. At this point in our discussion, however, we are merely noting that social adjustment is one of the key tasks of the child if he is truly to achieve a reasonable degree of selfhood.

The Task of Living with Self The third central task in the achievement of selfhood is that of *learning to live with the impulses and needs that arise from within himself*. This obviously overlaps with the other two tasks we have discussed, but it deserves to be emphasized: we should not overlook the vital importance to a child of finding acceptable ways of dealing with the powerful feelings, the intense drives, the emotional attitudes, the conflicts, doubts, and questions that stem from within his own personality. Some of these arise in relation to the experiences he encounters as he grows older. Others arise out of his own organic tissue needs and include a variety of conditions and circumstances that in former years might have been labeled "instincts." Whatever their source, the bewildering array of impulses and feelings experienced by any normal child will inevitably challenge his own capacity for handling them and for channeling them into acceptable activities, or inhibiting them while substituting other means of finding need satisfaction.

Baruch (1) has stressed the importance of helping a child to live with himself, by helping him to accept the normality and rightness of these feelings, urges, and impulses. This does not necessarily include allowing him to express whatever impulses arise without restriction or inhibition, but it does include an awareness by adults in the child's environment that the impulses are there, that they are real, that they are valid, and that they will not go away merely by our insisting he is not supposed to have such feelings! Learning to live with oneself also implies the gradual awareness of one's resources, strengths, and capacities, as well as the more or less negative feelings and impulses that require a certain amount of direction and channeling.

THE COURSE OF THE ACHIEVEMENT OF SELFHOOD

Implicit in the discussion of the nature of personality up to this point is the concept of a central theme; a core idea that is the focal point of personality organization and integration. This focal point, or central idea, is perhaps better expressed in the form of a question rather than in any simple statement. The question is asked repeatedly as a child progresses through the various stages of personality organization, not in so many words, and not necessarily in words at all—nor is the child necessarily aware of the fact that this is a central question. It is the same question asked by countless numbers of individual adults who, for one reason or another, have cause to question their own personality development or personal adjustment, though they, too, may be unaware of the nature of the question, much less able to provide a reasonable answer to it. The question is well put by Carl Rogers, a psychotherapist, who gives his view of this central theme in the following quotation:

> As I follow the experience of many clients in the therapeutic relationship which we endeavor to create for them, it seems to me that each one has the same problem. Below the level of the problem situation about which the individual is complaining—behind the trouble with studies, or wife, or employer, or with his own uncontrollable or bizarre behavior, or with his frightening feelings, lies one central search. It seems to me that at bottom each person is asking, "Who am I, *really?* How can I get in touch with this real self, underlying my surface behavior? How can I become myself?" (10, p. 196).

While Rogers is speaking about the adult who is seeking help with personal adjustment problems of some kind, his statement is singularly appropriate as a description of the central question posed by the child in his search for selfhood. Rogers' remarks do not imply that there is anything morbid or pathological in the child's search for personality growth; on the contrary, they suggest that large numbers of adults, still searching for helpful answers to this fundamental question, failed somehow to derive a sufficiently satisfying and constructive answer to the question at each critical stage of development along the way, during those periods of childhood when answers were so desperately needed. It is no mere coincidence that Rogers and other psychotherapists working continually with patients in need of help with their personal adjustment problems have found it fruitful—indeed essential—to create a therapeutic environment in which the patient can reconstruct, safely, elements of personality which for one reason or another they were not able to bring to satisfactory levels of maturity at the appropriate stages of their development.

Current approaches to understanding the development of selfhood place great emphasis on the importance of the years from infancy through about age 6. They are important, in part, simply because they come first and provide a framework of experience, ideas, feelings, attitudes, and concepts within which later childhood and adolescent personality development can occur. But these years are important, too, in their own right. The preschool child is not merely a "personality potential," or "prospective" self. He is a very real person, having all the components and ingredients that go into any reasonable definition of selfhood. True, they are immature; they are "in process" of achieving all of their possibilities. Nevertheless, they are all there.

Growth, according to Jersild (6), is not just a pleasant series of steps forward. Every step ahead is accompanied by certain threats, risks, and inherent dangers. When the infant learns to walk, he achieves not only the grand possibility of getting himself around on his own two feet under his own power and the resulting capacity for better satisfying his own needs in his newly fascinating world, he also achieves a much higher level of potential for getting into trouble with his world! The same is true of any significant step forward. With each achievement of every significant task, there are new threats, as well as new advantages, with which the child must cope. This means that the important thing is not only the accomplishment of the task, but also of a positive feeling about the self that accomplished. There is a balance between the positive forces striving for growth, achievement, increase in productivity, creativity, and positive action, on the one hand, and the "negative" forces demanding safety, security, satisfaction with the status quo, and all those forces that represent threats to one's feeling about himself if he risks movement ahead. For the normal child, the net effect of these two general forces is a balance in favor of growth, of forward progress. But this progress is not accomplished without cost of pain. There is, in normal growth, an irregularity in the speed of forward progress. The whole pattern of the achievement of selfhood is marked by rapid spurts ahead and slower periods of doubt and questioning and consolidation of the resources in preparation for the next movement ahead.

One of the net effects of this balancing of forces in the child's total effort to achieve selfhood is the development of ambivalence about his own growth. It is as if, in every normal preschooler, there are really two "selves." There is the one that wants to be big, strong, independent, achieving, productive, expansive, and self-actualizing. And there is the other that wants to be small, protected, dependent, secure, nurtured by the strength of others. The first seeks responsibility, the second seeks to avoid responsibility. The first joyously enters into relationships with his world of objects and people; the second seeks to protect itself against the intrusion of threatening elements of its world of people and things, and tries to avoid encounters with the strange, the novel, the threatening.

The distinction is well illustrated in the following two incidents, which occurred in the normal routine of two different nursery-school children. The only thing exceptional about these two children was that they were perhaps better able to verbalize the conflict described above than some other children at the age of 3. The first, Christine, was being taken to nursery school by her father. She was riding in the back seat of the car, when her father suddenly realized that she had gotten down off the seat and was crouched low on the floor of the car. "Where's my girl?" he teased; "Doesn't she want to look outside and see all the pretty things?" The 3-year-old's muffled answer was not forceful in volume, but it packed a lot of power in insight: "Sometimes the pretty world is too big to look at." This girl had made an excellent adjustment to nursery school; she was never reluctant to go or to stay and let her mother or father leave her. In other words, the balance of the positive, outgoing, self-developmental forces in her life was favorable in all discernable aspects. Nevertheless, even for this girl there are times when the whole world looks too big and one needs to protect oneself from the bigness of it all by shutting some of it out. Nursery school is a wonderful experience, but there are times when it can be a bit threatening, too, and demands a form of maturity which can burden.

The other incident also involved a 3-year-old girl who had made a reasonably good adjustment and who looked forward to going to nursery school each day. She too had the capacity for expressing, verbally, an insight which some of us as adults would do well to remember. On getting in the car after a busy, strenuous morning in school, Anita and her father started toward home. The nursery-school teacher had mentioned to the girl's father some of the interesting things Anita had been doing, and how she had taken a very mature role in some of the social play with the other children. But as they progressed toward their home, Anita, who was riding in the front seat of the car with her father, leaned her head over onto his knee and sighed, "I want to go home and be Mommy's baby." Then she put her thumb in her mouth. She had been a grown-up, nursery-school girl for about as long that day as she could manage.

Both of these incidents are revealing of the dual nature of the striving for selfhood during the preschool years. It is the desire to be big and the desire to be little at the same time. It demands that reasonable adults understand both of these wishes and provide an accepting environment in which the balance of forces will eventually be in favor of the wish to grow. This is accomplished, in part, by complete acceptance of the reality of the other wish and of the immature behavior that it arouses, which may take diverse forms. The wish to be small can lead, sometimes, to unreasonable crying, to clinging, dependent behavior, to tantrums and jealous reactions, to aggressive and hostile behavior, and to unwillingness to share. It can even lead to the loss of established controls such as sphincter control, or the upsetting of established routines such as eating and sleeping. Truly, this aspect of the self-concept *is* personality in the broadest sense; it *does* involve the child's total orientation to his world, and there are times when that total orientation wants to be a small and dependent and secure one.

The writings of Erik H. Erikson (3, 4) have stimulated another approach to the understanding of self-development. Erikson, whose point of view is based on psychoanalytic theory, has attempted to outline critical stages in the development of human personality, beginning with infancy and extending through the adult years. At each of the eight major stages in personality growth, or self-development, there is a kind of "crisis" in which the balance of positive, growth-producing forces and negative, handicapping forces is for a time in question. The successful accomplishment of certain psychological objectives at any one stage is essential to smooth progress throughout that stage and provides a foundation for further personality development. Like most of the modern, productive ideas about self-development, this approach has strong implications for the role of early childhood in the achievement of adult personality. Erikson also comes closer than other writers on the subject to presenting a theoretical answer to the question posed by Rogers, as the central question of the individual whose personal development and adjustment is self-doubted: "Who am I, *really?*"

For Erikson, the answer to this question comes in a series of steps, or "crises," which arise partly in relation to the child's social environment but primarily are a result of his biological nature. The steps are viewed as essentially built into the nature of man because he *is* man, and because he must follow these steps, at least in general outline, if he is to achieve his potential of selfhood.

The Sense of Trust The steps begin with infancy, during which time the crisis is described by Erikson as *Trust vs. Basic Mistrust* (3, p. 219). During this time the balance, and therefore the crisis, is between those forces in the child's life that represent, on the one hand, confidence, a feeling of safety, and a "prediction" or assumption on the infant's part that his needs will be satisfied, and, on the other hand, all those forces that represent threat, failure of essential need satisfaction, or disturbance of the basic physical, physiological, and psychological rhythms of the child.

We can define *trust*, at least in general terms, through the words of James L. Hymes, Jr. as "that sure feeling: everything is O.K.!" (5, p. 4). It is a general assumption that the world is safe, friendly, nurturant, and need satisfying. It brings into oneself an attitude of certainty, based on the regularity of events and cycles of one's own body and of events and cycles in the outside world. People frequently use the phrase "sense of security" in reference to the infant, stressing the need for the child to feel sure of his world and his place in it. This comes fairly close to the concept of trust we are describing here. But what is security made of? In essence, security, or trust, the foundation of healthy selfhood, is made of the ability to predict the continuity and regularity of need satisfactions. It is based on regular experiences with need satisfactions of all kinds in connection with the everyday routines of babyhood—eating, sleeping, eliminating, being warm and comfortable, and being in close contact with a loving mother. The accumulation of successful, need-satisfying experiences around these everyday routines builds up in the infant an assumption, or willingness to predict, that such experiences will continue and will always be available. This, in essence, is security and a feeling of trust and confidence in the world.

The role of a loving mother—her willingness and ability to satisfy needs of her infant as they arise—is clearly important here. With increased age, maturity, and experience will come the capacity of the child to delay satisfaction of needs without threatening this sense of trust. But for the infant, whose only time orientation is his own biological rhythm of needs and need satisfactions, the policy of delaying need satisfaction in order to "train" him in the realities of family routines is inconsistent with the objective of healthy self-development. This is part of the explanation for the effectiveness and success of self-demand scheduling of infant feedings.

The achievement of a healthy sense of trust should not be viewed as an "all or nothing" thing, of course. It is never a question of having it or of not having it; it is a question of the degree, or of the quality of the balance between the forces working toward trust and those forces which work toward basic mistrust. Figure 10.1 helps to explain the nature of the relationships between trust and later critical stages in the development of selfhood. "Trust" is not a stage that is fully accomplished at any particular point in the child's development. In one sense, it persists as an issue right on through childhood and into the adult years. But the diagram in Figure 10.1 is intended to show that the sharp features of the crisis of trust vs. mistrust will have been resolved and the issues decided, with the balance relatively stabilized and the individual child's unique quality of his own balance in this issue settled as he moves out of infancy into the periods of toddlerhood and the preschool years.

First Stage (about first year)	BASIC TRUST	Earlier form of AUTONOMY	Earlier form of INITIATIVE
Second Stage (about second and third years)	Later form of BASIC TRUST	AUTONOMY	Earlier form of INITIATIVE
Third Stage (about fourth and fifth years)	Later form of BASIC TRUST	Later form of AUTONOMY	INITIATIVE

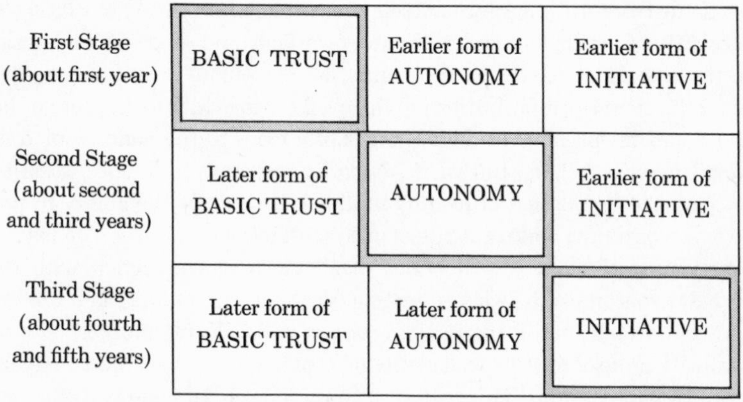

Fig. 10.1. A diagrammatic representation of the interaction among stages in healthy personality development in infancy and the preschool years. (From E. H. Erikson, "Growth and crises of the healthy personality," in M. Senn (ed.), *The healthy personality; Supplement II: Problems of infancy and childhood,* Transactions of the Fourth Conference on Infancy and Childhood, New York: Josiah Macy, Jr. Foundation, 1950, pp. 91–146.)

Returning for a moment to the question of selfhood and self-definition, we should note that the infantile version of the question "Who am I, really?" must be answered in terms of the affection and consistency of need satisfactions available to him as gifts, rather than as a function of anything he must do or be. His answer is essentially, "I am whatever the world gives to me." To the extent that his world satisfies his basic needs, he is a real person; to the extent that his world fails to be need-satisfying, he is nothing, so far as selfhood is concerned. By the time a child gets up on his own two feet and takes active steps, physically and psychologically, in the exploration of his world, he inevitably enters into a crisis described by Erikson (3, p. 222) under the heading of "*Autonomy vs. Shame and Doubt.*"

The Sense of Autonomy Hymes has also expressed the essence of this period as follows: "That strong feeling: I–I–I" (5, p. 6). As children are progressing through their second year what seems to matter most is to try themselves out, to discover the limits of their own personal resources, and to see how far those resources will take them in their expanding world of people and things. Parents, dealing with children during this crisis period, describe a wide (and wild) array of behavior and misbehavior with seemingly countless variations—but these are variations on one central theme: the need to discover how far the child can go on his own two feet and still be in control of himself and his world. What the child *seems* to be doing and saying suggests that he wants complete freedom and independence. What he *really* wants and needs, however, is not the complete freedom and independence that his behavior suggests, but instead the reasonable limits which tell him precisely and kindly and understandingly the sphere of the world over which he does have control.

The nature of this crisis and its title suggest correctly that a child must have an area in his personal world where he is in charge; where he makes decisions that count; where, if he says "No!" his word is respected. His saying "No!" is, of course, one of the hallmarks of this stage. His words are an effort to assert himself and establish himself as a real person, apart from anyone else. To be a real person at this point requires being a real decision maker—a real controller of one's own destiny to some degree. The task of adults at this stage is to provide a degree of autonomy, or self-direction, for the child without making him feel ashamed or doubtful of his ability to be a real person.

Shaming a child into "being good" in order to avoid the inevitable conflicts of this stage is risky. The risk is that we may force a child to feel that his impulses to be big, to be strong, to be independent, are somehow evil and unworthy. Perhaps this is better understood if we keep in mind one of the central tasks of growing up during this period: toilet training. One general kind of training, which rigidly emphasizes the need of a child to conform to adult expectations about time, place, facilities, clothing, cleanliness, etc., and which fails to consider the child's need to be somewhat autonomous in deciding how, when, and where, takes the matter of elimination out of the child's domain of control. This can result in some absurdly artificial situations between mother and child, illustrated by the complaint of one mother to her child's pediatrician: "My 2-year-old boy simply refuses to have a bowel movement for me!" Now perhaps it is not even necessary, at this point, to raise the question of whose bowel movement this is, anyway! At the same time, in a society that places as much emphasis on proper toilet behavior and habits of elimination as ours does, it is not too farfetched to assume that many 2-year-olds find such basic biological functions being removed from their sphere of control or, to be perhaps more realistic, find that their own efforts to retain some semblance of control are countered by adult forces leading to shame and doubts about the rightness or worthiness of their own behavior.

The entire issue of autonomy vs. shame and doubt does not revolve around the establishment of sphincter control, of course. But this is a fairly tangible example of the nature of the issues which arise during this period. Again, there is the central question, "Who am I, *really?*" And again, the answer that accrues to the child's expanding sense of selfhood comes in terms of the daily life experiences with those people and things closest to him. The answer somehow takes the form, "I am whatever my domain or sphere of control is." But the child needs more than freedom and autonomy and independence during this time. He is still very much influenced by the crisis of the earlier stage, and the need for trust, confidence, and security that was so strong in him before. Autonomy, then, must somehow include reasonable limits that tell the child where he stands. Limits to autonomy should not be viewed as opposite to or incompatible with trust. Not only are they completely compatible, but limits appear to be essential to the full and complete development of trust. One way to understand this is to view the problem of the child who is given too much freedom, on the assumption that if a little autonomy is good, then a lot of it must be that much better! Such a child finds himself confronted with a world too large, too complex, and too threatening to handle. The threat is directed toward his sense of trust and confidence in his world and in himself, as well as toward his emerging sense of autonomy. The resulting doubts are doubly significant in that they threaten his confidence in both his world and his ability to deal with it and to make good decisions about it.

ဖ *The Sense of Initiative* The next significant crisis stage outlined by Erikson (3, p. 224) is described by the phrase "*Initiative vs. Guilt*". It occupies a place of supreme significance in the self-development process during the preschool years.

As the term *initiative* implies, this stage is concerned with plans, ideas, and action. Sometimes the action is a bit wild and, in the words of Arnold Gesell, "out of bounds." But the child feels good about himself to the extent that his plans and ideas count for something. He has already established himself, if he has a reasonably adequate sense of autonomy, as a real person. Now, when he is 3 and 4 and 5, he is working hard to establish *what kind of person* that self will be. A quotation from Hymes again may help clarify the meaning of this stage:

> They are not always pretty plans and ideas. This is the age that can get into the furniture polish and smear it all over the rug. This is the age that can puncture holes in the screens, but in such a nice design. This is the age that wakes up before you do and decides that this is the day for scrambled eggs . . . and scrambles them all over the kitchen (5, p. 11).

This is also a time of questioning: "What can I do? What can I make of this self which I have discovered and established as a real person? What can I be? What can I become?" And all this means that there is a good deal of imagination and fantasy mixed up with the real world of people and things. The later preschooler has enough mental ability to discern great possibilities in his world—possibilities for doing, being, and becoming—and some of them can even be frightening to the child himself! The 4-year-old, for example, has such a fluid imagination that he can "be," within a very short space of time, a tiger, a bunny, a wild charging horse, and a big enough, strong enough man to tame the tiger, to ride the horse, or to be a tender and nurturant adult who can protect the weak bunny. In this fantastically fluid mental imagery, he is doing more than merely pretending or playing a part. He is *living out* the intense feelings encompassed within the richly complex personality of the typical late preschooler. He is making all these feelings an acceptable part of himself, and trying to discover satisfying modes of operation which incorporate them into a total, growing self.

During these years, there is a fundamental psychological process that reaches a high point of development in the child's relationships with the important adults in his life. This is the *identification* process, in which a child strives to experience the ways in which the grown people cope with the complicated world. It is an age during which a child incorporates many things into his personality that typify the strengths and weaknesses of those grown people on whom he is still dependent. It is a period when, as one slightly bewildered father expressed it, "My son is becoming so much like me, it . . . it *frightens* me!"

If children of this age do go out of bounds and off limits, at least it is a considerable refinement of the cruder, physical limit-testing behavior of the 2-year-old. Much of this change can be traced to the fact that at 4 our preschooler uses words—not always nice words, to be sure, but words—to take the place of the direct physical approach to aggression and hostility and other emotions. Once again, we recognize that personality growth and self-development encompass all the other components: emotional, social, motor, physical, and language behavior. They do not occur apart from these.

Another key to the nature of the child's strivings at this time is his creative action of all kinds. Through drawing, through dancing and other rhythmic activities, through dressing up and playing parts, through creating roles with other children and living them out in tea-parties, doll-play, etc., and through all manner of building, organizing, constructing and reconstructing, the preschooler is exploring the world of possibilities as to what he can do, what he can be. At the same time, he is integrating his emotional feelings about all of the exciting things that are opening up to him.

The failure to achieve some semblance of initiative results, in its most gross and tragic form, in an overwhelming sense of guilt. Again we should stress that in every healthy child there will be, in all probability, some signs of guilt. It is still a matter of the balance between the freedom to explore one's world as a self-actualizing person, and the crippling, inhibiting effects of extreme guilt. This is an age when conscience is developing. And because it is having its first significant development during this time, the child is particularly vulnerable to adult efforts to organize his conscience too soon and too completely. The child can be made to feel guilty about too many things, with all too little effort on the part of well meaning adults. Guidance and discipline techniques which rely primarily on shaming or, in other words, on forcing the child to think less well of himself on

Exploring the world of tools.
(Nancy Rudolph.)

account of his behavior, are particularly inappropriate. They are self-defeating in the long run. The trick during this age is to find enough ways to help the child feel truly good about all aspects of the person he is and wants to be, keeping shame and guilt to an absolute minimum. Erikson (4) suggests that much of the adult motives of overdoing, overcompensating, overachieving and never feeling satisfied with himself as a person stem from the guilty feelings arising during the period when conscience is developing.

But it need not be a time of excessive guilt feelings. This is where adult respect for an individual child's unique manifestation of initiative plays a crucial role. The adult's responsibility is to understand, appreciate, and respect the child's efforts to discover anew an answer to that same question: "*Who am I, really?*" At this period, his answer comes to him primarily in this form: "I am whatever I can dream about, whatever I can express through fantasy or action or words, whatever I can imagine myself to be."

SUMMARY

The achievement of selfhood during the preschool years includes the meeting and resolving of a number of fundamental crises and the accomplishment of basic tasks. These center on such major themes as (1) learning to live in a world of tools, (2) learning to live with other people, and (3) learning to live with oneself. The manner in which a child accomplishes these tasks constitutes his own individuality, his unique self.

The achievement of selfhood may also be viewed as a developmental process, in which one phase serves as the foundation for the next. During infancy and the preschool period, the critical phases include the development of a sense of *trust*, the achievement of personal *autonomy*, and the establishment of a sense of *initiative*. It is in and around these critical steps in self-development that the child attempts to answer the major question of self-definition: "Who am I, really?" The central striving of the child may be viewed as an effort to answer that question, and the answers that accrue to him become the core of his self-concept.

REFERENCES

1. Baruch, D., *New ways in discipline*, New York: McGraw-Hill, 1949.
2. Bronfenbrenner, U., and Ricciuti, H. N., "The appraisal of personality

characteristics in children," in P. H. Mussen (ed.), *Handbook of research methods in child development*, New York: Wiley, 1960.

3. Erikson, E. H., *Childhood and society*, New York: Norton, 1950.
4. Erikson, E. H., "Growth and crises of the healthy personality," in C. Kluckhohn and H. A. Murray (eds.), *Personality in nature, society, and culture*, 2nd ed., New York: Knopf, 1953.
5. Hymes, J. L., Jr., "A healthy personality for your child," *U. S. Dept. Hlth, Educ. and Welf.: Chld's. Bureau Publ.*, No. 337, 1952.
6. Jersild, A. T., *Child psychology*, 4th ed., New York: Prentice-Hall, 1954.
7. Lecky, P., "The personality," in C. E. Moustakas (ed.), *The Self*, New York: Harper, 1956, pp. 86-97.
8. Maslow, A. H., "Self-actualizing people: A study of psychological health," in C. E. Moustakas (ed.), *The Self*, New York: Harper, 1956, pp. 160–194.
9. Maslow, A. H., "Personality problems and personality growth," in C. E. Moustakas (ed.), *The Self*, New York: Harper, 1956, pp. 232–246.
10. Rogers, C., "What it means to become a person," in C. E. Moustakas (ed.), *The Self*, New York: Harper, 1956, pp. 195–211.
11. Witmer, Helen L., and Kotinsky, Ruth (eds.), *Personality in the Making*, New York: Harper, 1952.

Part IV THE SOCIETY OF THE PRESCHOOL CHILD

The first three segments of this book were intended to give a general introduction to the field of child development, to describe the nature and patterning of child growth, and to explore the various facets of development from infancy through the preschool years.

The primary objective of the remainder of the book is to examine the process of child socialization; that is, the process by which a child comes to use whatever resources lie at his command to relate himself effectively to the world of people and things.

In this process many institutions and elements of society participate and make contributions of varying degrees of significance. The child does not grow and develop in a vacuum, but in a society rich with stimulating as well as inhibitory influences. It is the shaping forces of the child's society to which we now turn in an effort to understand the complex relationships between the child and his efforts to achieve selfhood.

CHAPTER ELEVEN

What is meant by the term "culture?" ∽ *How does the concept of culture help us to understand the personality of the child?* ∽ *What important aspects of child-rearing differ from one culture to another?* ∽ *What examples could be given of cultural inconsistencies that effect the middle-class American child?*

THE CHILD'S CULTURAL HERITAGE

A THE STORY of the introduction of the American game of basketball to the Hopi Indians has often been told, and is worth repeating here. It is said that the Hopi children took up the sport with great enthusiasm and vigor. There was one problem, however: the Hopis would not keep score. No matter how long the two teams would play, neither side could be induced to keep track of who was winning!

In American sports, while we occasionally tell ourselves that "it isn't whether you win or lose—it's how well you play the game that counts," the fact that we insist on keeping score suggests that we get some satisfaction from knowing who is winning. As a matter of fact, some rather cynical people have suspected that we don't even think about this higher moral value—that it is not the winning or losing, but how well you play that counts—unless we find ourselves unfortunately identified with a losing team! Whether this is true or not, few would argue that competition plays a strong role in motivating sports activities in our society. For that matter, the intense role of competition for us seems to permeate so much of our social, economic, political, aesthetic, and even religious ways of life that it is difficult to conceive of a society lacking this intense competition between individuals and groups as a prime motivating force.

The example of the Hopi children and basketball, however, reminds us that competition as a motivating force is not an innate human characteristic. At least, if man is instinctively competitive, there are some societies that have been able to control it successfully. The Hopi child not only fails to be competitive in sports but is, in fact, noncompetitive in his whole relationship with people, with things, and with nature. The difference between him and his white cousins is illustrative of the role of culture in determining differences in the personal development of children.

THE MEANING OF CULTURE

The term *culture*, has been defined in many different ways by various authorities on the subject. Nevertheless, it remains easier to say what it is *not* than what it is: (1) it is *not* something which individuals *possess* or which some people or families *have* to a greater degree than others; and (2) it is *not* something that can be transmitted biologically from one generation to the next. Sometimes culture is defined as *the learned behavior of a people*. However, this is an abstract concept and does not refer directly to the specific learnings of any particular individual. Thus, while particular modes and themes pervade the art forms of a given society in the twentieth century, it would not be appropriate to say that a particular artist has more culture than someone who has no interest in art. Each of these individuals is living and behaving in a society which holds cultural values and cultural techniques, including the values and techniques relating to art forms. Each is affected, consciously or otherwise, by the existence of these values and techniques. Further, it can be demonstrated that a specific culture determines not only the variety of gadgets, modes of transportation, communication, economic matters, assorted customs, folkways and mores, not only style of dress and manner of speech, not only systems of expressing emotional involvement or lack of involvement, but also the most fundamental internal processes of the human nervous system. One's very mode of thinking, as well as the content of his thought, is affected by culture.

Anthropologists, in making detailed observations of various societies, have noted that different groups, living in different parts of the world, have quite different ways of categorizing their experiences and of viewing their world. It has been observed, for example, that certain Alaskan Indian groups have in their language many nouns that represent the thing we label "snow." Because their economy and life-activities are so thoroughly and inevitably intertwined with snow, their language in reference to snow is richer and more elaborate than ours. Thus, there is a noun which stands for each of many kinds of snow, and many nouns for conditions in which snow might be encountered. Similarly, the Arabian camel-driver has a large and rich vocabulary pertaining to the types of camels and the accessories associated with the care and use of camels. By contrast, his vocabulary concerning automobiles is probably very limited. Terms such as "automatic transmission," "power steering," "dynaflow," and "windshield washers" have elaborated in our highly mobile society, which has, over the last half-century, literally put itself on wheels.

These different ways of categorizing experience are the result not simply of differences in place, but of deeply different points of view. As Dorothy Lee (4) has observed, there are fundamental differences in ways of thinking, which the languages of different societies provide for. Some societies are time oriented, with events having significance in relation to the past, the present, or the future. Their language provides for this time orientation. Other societies are much less time oriented and tend to value everything in terms of present existence. Events which we would think of as historical are viewed in such societies as a part of the existing state of affairs, or else they are not viewed as of any importance at all. When events are recounted, they are told without reference to chronological sequence, thus deemphasizing the element of time or history. Even "future" or anticipated events are a part of the existing reality, or else they are held to be unimportant. And the language of such a society provides for this kind of thinking. The language of a society carries the definition of human relationships, categorizing the moral and social and ethical and spiritual values of the group.

But of greatest importance for our present discussion is the fact that in every society there are ways of cataloguing experience that the child must learn if he is to become an acceptable, socialized member of that group. This learning is part of his experience from the cradle to the grave, and becomes a part of him and a vital force in shaping his personality. A statement made by the fact-finding committee of the Midcentury White House Conference on Children and Youth stresses the vital role played by culture in shaping the personality of the child:

> Culture is powerful and pervasive, changing the character of our biological drives, affecting our thinking, our emotions, and our perceptions. For example, there are distinct patterns of

> aggression, sibling rivalry, privacy, jealousy, loving, frustration, play, participation in the different cultures. What was there before culture entered the picture? Are human beings jealous by nature? There are some polygynous societies where co-wives exhibit so much jealousy that a man has to apportion himself with care and tact. There are other polygynous societies where an only wife will taunt and nag her husband until he brings her a co-wife, with whom she then lives amicably. Is jealousy an inborn trait, which some cultures suppress effectively? Or is it a potentiality, fostered by some, atrophied by other cultures? (8, p. 167).

Current thinking on the question raised by this quotation is that jealousy and related traits of personality are primarily the products of social living rather than innate human characteristics which can be transmitted through biological inheritance. To the extent that this is true, our task becomes one of understanding the cultural forces and pressures that result in the development of such traits under some circumstances, and that foster other traits under different conditions.

Our society appears to foster the development of competition and rivalry. Children are exposed to such learning at a very early age. In other societies this may be less true. Much of the remainder of this chapter is an attempt to illustrate the varying cultural pressures that come to bear on children who live and grow in contrasting cultures in different parts of the world. It will help us to remember that culture is an abstract concept, referring essentially to all the learned behavior of a people, including customs and values, art and technology, patterns of language and thought, and all the accepted ways of operating within a given society. Each of us, having grown up in and become a part of a particular society, tends to look at other groups in relative or comparative terms, using such expressions as "better than" or "worse than" or "more effective than" or "less desirable than" etc. In describing some of the cultural forces that influence children of other societies, it should be kept in mind that a practice good for children in one society may be quite undesirable for children in another society, inasmuch as the structure and objectives of the two societies are markedly different. In other words, we are not in a position to say that one society is "right" and another one "wrong" in their respective child-rearing practices. We are concerned with the fact that differences do exist and that they lead to markedly different personality attributes as the children experience their particular cultures.

SOME CENTRAL QUESTIONS ON THE EFFECTS OF CULTURE ON THE CHILD

Just how does culture influence the child's development? This general question can be answered, in part, if we can provide answers to certain more specific questions. Consider, for example, the question of *who is responsible for the care of the child.* If the answer seems obvious to us, it is probably because we take for granted the responsibility of the child's mother to provide for routine child care. We assume that the mother will therefore be the primary influence in the life of the baby and young child. There are societies, however, in which this is not the case. In some there are servants or nurses not biologically related to the child, retained for the special purpose of child care. In some the mother's primary responsibility is for food production or for work in the field, and the care of the baby and young child is in the hands of older women of the tribe, who may or may not be related biologically. The role of male relatives in child care is also variable from one group to another. The Trobriand Islanders assume that the child's maternal uncles will have a closer tie to the child, and more responsibility for his care and upbringing, than his biological father. Thus it is quite apparent that the question as to who cares for the child cannot be answered simply and easily for all children everywhere with the same answer.

Another question might have to do with the place or position a child holds in relation to his family, and to adults in the community. In some, for example, a child is not really viewed as a person, or even as being essentially human, until he reaches an age beyond the preschool years. This is in marked contrast, obviously, to our society, which places great emphasis on the individual needs of children and admonishes parents to regard their children with love, respect, and dignity. We not only regard the period of childhood with great importance as a foundation and forerunner of adult personality, but we cherish childhood and respect it for its own sake, as a period of life having validity of itself, apart from what it may portend for the future. Similarly, one society may value children as economic or cultural assets, while another may tend to view children as liabilities. And one group may place special significance on certain features of individual children—their sex, their position in the family (oldest, youngest, etc.)—at the expense of other features. We could certainly conclude that children are not viewed in the same way by adults in all societies.

Another central question about cultural effects on the child has to do with *what is allowed and what is forbidden.* Child behavior which is accepted and even encouraged in one group is sharply curtailed and perhaps severely punished by another group. Examples of this are too numerous to present in detail, but one illustration is the attitude of different social groups toward sexual curiosity and experimentation on the part of children in different societies. In our own—while enlightened parents are aware of the natural curiosity of their children toward sex—sex play and experimentation is severely controlled. In some societies, however, it is ignored; in others it is a matter of humor and joking on the part of adults.

Still another central question has to do with the nature of discipline, *the amount, kind, quality of disciplinary measures* used in the group. In our society (while there is a great deal of variation, of course) there is a great deal of hand-slapping, threatening, scolding, and deprivation of privileges. In some societies there are purposeful efforts to frighten children into being good; in others, while fear is not purposely used, there may be threats of great bodily harm, or of dire consequences in the form of magical or supernatural events, which are designed to keep the child in line.

Other questions would have to do with the *kinds of learning experiences provided for children in order to induct them properly into the adult society.* What are the experiences that teach the child what he must do, what he must not do, and what he must value, if he is to be an acceptable member of his group? Are these experiences ritualized and attended with great ceremony and attention? Or are they almost unnoticed incidents along the way—experiences that blend into a total pattern of living, which gradually provides the child with a definition of acceptable and unacceptable behavior? Are they formal, institutionalized training programs, as in the American schools and churches? Or are they retained exclusively as the province of a family, or of particular members of a family? These are part of the larger question of how a society organizes those of its experiences designed to socialize its children. These and perhaps many other fundamental questions underlie the concept of cultural effects on the child.

Scientists who study culture are extremely cautious about attributing the personality characteristics of a child or adult to any one particular child-rearing practice or cultural characteristic. There was a time in the study of cultures when anthropologists tended to see a special peculiarity of the adult members of a society as being the direct outcome of a special or peculiar child-rearing practice prevalent in that society. Current thinking, instead, emphasizes the total cultural context in which the child is living and growing and learning, and tends to view cultural effects as an unbroken network of experiences, with no single experience in the child's life especially meaningful apart from the total network. It is the cultural pattern then, not isolated practices or experiences, which seems to bring about personality qualities of the members of a society. Nevertheless, a keener insight into the nature of the child, and into the complex tasks of growing into a useful member of his society, with which he is confronted, may be achieved through study of the cultural practices of different groups. It is to this objective, the achievement of keener insight into the nature and tasks of the child engaged in the socialization process, that the next section of this chapter is devoted.

PARENTAL AUTHORITY VS. CHILD AUTONOMY

How much authority and control parents exercise over their children varies a great deal, of course, within a given society. It seems to vary with the social class, educational level, geographical area, and certainly with the personality characteristics of parents in America. Nevertheless, there are typical patterns of behavior which mark the relationships between parent and child in America, in contrast to those in Germany, or those in France, or in primitive groups in New Guinea or Samoa or Bali.

Orientals traditionally have been known for the respect shown by children toward their elders, in contrast with what appears to be disrespect on the part of American children. Historically, the German child was trained to respond obediently and unquestioningly to the authority of the father. But certain of the American Indian tribes have been observed to value a quite different kind of behavior on the part of a child. In some, aggressive and "unruly" behavior (by our standards) is encouraged and rewarded. Even if a child hits back at his parents, there are some societies in which it is viewed as a healthy sign that the child will become an appropriately aggressive adult.

A Hopi child is becoming a member of her society.
(Courtesy of Santa Fe Railway.)

Another significant difference lies in the kinds of properties and objects available to the child, and around which problems of discipline may arise. These vary greatly, of course, from one group to another, and the resulting differences in kind and degree of discipline are readily apparent. The following description of the childhood prohibitions and restrictions placed on the Hopi child, given by Dennis, is a vivid contrast to the middle-class American child's situation:

> The Hopi child is free from many of the frustrations which are continually imposed upon the modern city child. The primitive child, generally, lives in a much simpler material culture, where valuable objects are more rare and not so easily damaged as our own. He is surrounded by a minimum of breakable property, and in consequence there is no occasion to tell him not to spill things on the floor, not to pull books off the shelves, not to touch the telephone or the radio, not to climb on chairs or on stairs, not to put his hands on the windows, and not to pull the table cloth. He escapes a thousand and one other demands which are made upon the child in the American home. Among the Hopi, the property which the child might damage, such as ceremonial garments and masks, "best" clothing and jewelry, are kept either out of sight or out of reach. The child may touch everything which he sees. There is a striking absence in the Hopi home of the constant admonishment of the child not to handle or touch this and that (2, pp. 38–39).

FEEDING AND CLOTHING THE CHILD

It is commonly observed that people in different parts of the world dress differently and eat different kinds of food. Such variations in people are more than matters of mere curiosity or amusement for students of child development. We must understand not only that the child comes to learn the manner of dress and types of food of his people, but that he learns such things so well and so thoroughly and so consistently from a very early age that he accepts them as the reasonable ways of satisfying his food and clothing needs. There may even be significant emotional involvement if he is confronted with the need to revise his culturally learned habits. Thus, the kinds of conditioning the child experiences during the preschool period have a special bearing on his definition of appropriate food and clothing behavior during his whole lifetime. Some societies are typically flexible and adjustable when it comes to infant feeding. From the very beginning, the mother's breast is available to the infant and child whenever he cries. This pattern of marked "self-demand" feeding may be accompanied by a very relaxed, unhurried weaning, with no sharp break between the nursing period and the stage of eating solid foods.

In many cultures, there is relatively little emphasis on a matter that most of us in America take for granted: the teaching of a child to eat three meals a day. The fact that we succeed in conditioning our children to be "hungry" three times a day speaks less about the child's biological needs than it does about our cultural pressures. We could eat two meals, or four meals, or more, and serve our biological needs as well; but our children are taught, as early as possible, to adapt their eating patterns to the family's schedule. The description presented by Margaret Mead of the feeding behavior she observed in the village of Bajoeng Gede in Bali is of interest:

> Feeding babies falls definitely into two categories: (1) suckling, in which the infant, after it is a few weeks old, is held high above the mother's breast and nurses down, and (2) giving solid food to the infant, which is done in the bath. The mother prechews a mixture of rice and banana and builds a mound on the baby's face. When it opens its mouth to protest, she pushes some food in. When older children are given food, they display related behavior, pushing the food into their mouths with the flat of their hands, or turning their coconut shell plates straight over their faces. Feeding is something done *to* a baby, and later something that one does to oneself . . . (5, pp. 46–47).

Cultural variations in clothing the child are also observable from infancy onward. Some societies swaddle the infant tightly, restricting his body movements during the early months of life. American children not accustomed to such swaddling or restriction of movement typically protest loudly if their arms and legs are suddenly held firmly. Children in societies that practice swaddling have been observed to cry, when freed briefly of their restrictive clothing, until returned to the comfort and security of their close wrappings! Other societies not only fail to provide such closely wrapped support for their infants, but provide little or nothing in the way of clothing for a child until he is well past the preschool years. In some such cases, there is much close body contact between child and mother or other adult, which appears to be an important element of emotional security in early childhood. In our own society, we claim that the objective of clothing the preschool child is his own comfort and our own convenience. However, mothers and nursery-school teachers who struggle in wintertime with that strange daily "ritual of the snowsuit" might argue that our culture still leaves something to be desired in the way of convenient clothing for children.

Still another way in which variation in child training may be demonstrated is the conditioning some children receive, at a very early age, in body control. Balinese children, for example, are given rigorous training in the making of formal gestures, as reported by Mead:

> At its various anniversary ceremonies its hands are cupped to receive and hold water, its palms pressed together in prayer, its arms shaped to receive the essence of the offerings. Whenever anything is offered it, its mother pulls out its right hand from under her arm, and if a gift is given, she will cup one hand under the other, repeating on behalf of the child a formal thanks—literally, "I ask." Words are put into the child's mouth from its first days, elaborate phrases coupled with "I am just a little baby," "I have as yet no name," so that in verbal and postural terms the child is fitted passively into the etiquette long before it would be able to enact it without these initial cues. But at the 210th-day birthday, babies sit and repeat over and over the gestures through which they have just been put, the hands of the parents occasionally playfully reinforcing them.
>
> Dancing is taught by alternately pressing the child's hands into position and making the gesture oneself, inducing the child to imitate it as the adult hums a dance tune. Hand dancing is learned in arms, before the child can walk, and a child may be set down to go through a beginning dance routine before it can keep its balance. Walking, like dancing, is taught by holding the child from behind, or with the aid of a walker, a single bamboo rail set up in the middle of the yard (5, p. 47).

Mead goes on to point out that the Balinese child is not allowed to creep in the fashion of Western babies. When the child reaches the age at which it would engage in crawling behavior, if he shows evidences of crawling or creeping he is generally picked up quickly and held off the floor. To the Balinese, such creeping behavior is "animal-like" and is regarded as undesirable for human children. In view of these early trainings, it is interesting to note that the Balinese people are unusually graceful in their walking and body movements. Whether this adult gracefulness can be attributed entirely to early training is not clear, but there does seem to be some relationship.

TRAINING FOR CONTROL OF ELIMINATION

Considering the sameness of the biological needs, in view of the human condition, it is remarkable that so much variation can be found in the experiences of children as they acquire the acceptable patterns of toileting behavior of their societies. In part, this variation can be accounted for by the differences in emotional attitudes associated with elimination in various societies. American parents would certainly know the meaning of the question, if the researcher inquired of them as to the problems they experienced in toilet training their children. We even have commercial devices in our automated society designed to awaken a child if he should be so faulty as to urinate in his bed!

By contrast, when parents in some primitive societies were asked about their methods and problems associated with toilet training, they could not understand the question. There were no methods, and there were no problems. Mead also gives some insight into this difference in her description of the Balinese culture:

> Elimination is treated very lightly. No fuss at all is made over urination by an infant; children urinate playfully into their baths, little boys learn to make elaborate patterns in the dust. Adults simply turn aside from a group to urinate . . . A child's chief learning from the culturally imposed elimination habits is to watch where it is and to move away from inappropriate spots. It never has to go far, so that emphasis on foresight and self-control, which American children learn and generalize to other areas of life, is missing (5, pp. 47, 48).

TRAINING FOR SOCIAL DEVELOPMENT AND ADJUSTMENT

Americans are very much concerned with the social behavior of their young children. Our middle-class society tends to place a high value on getting along well in groups and being an effective group member. In recent generations, as our society's knowledge of the importance of the early preschool period has increased, we have accordingly emphasized the preschool period as a time when children should learn to play and mingle well and cooperatively with other children. We emphasize, for example, that the child learn to share, to wait his turn, to be considerate of the needs and feelings of others, and in general to be liked by others. There is a fundamental assumption underlying this cultural value, a child should be able to trust other people and that if he shows respect for and interest in other children, such feelings will be reciprocated by others in his behalf.

A remarkably keen insight into cultural differences in this area of social living is afforded by a recent study of French children and parents, carried out by Martha Wolfenstein (9) as a part of Columbia University's research project in Contemporary Cultures. Wolfenstein took advantage of the Parisian family custom of taking their children to the park, which provided an ideal setting in which to make detailed observations of the children in their play, and also of the nature of the interaction between the children and their parents. Some of her observations are reported here in order to illustrate the contrast between these French families and the American modes of parent-child and child-child interaction:

> The adults do not seem interested in friendly overtures between children of different families, showing little of the usual eagerness of American parents that their children should make friends and be a success with their age-mates. French adults seem to be much more on the alert for negative behavior of other children toward their charges.
>
> These tendencies are illustrated in the behavior of a grandmother and her two-and-a-half-year-old grandson, Marcel. The grandmother seats herself on a bench facing the sand pile, to which Marcel goes, waving back at her across a few feet as if it were a long distance. He keeps looking at her while he plays,

> and she praises his sand pies. When a little girl steps on one of them, the grandmother scolds her roundly. Repeatedly the grandmother enters the sandbox and takes the little boy away from the others, telling him to stay in his own little corner. She makes frequent negative comments about the other children, remarking to me, "Have you ever noticed in children how some of them have the spirit of evil (*l'esprit du mal*)? Marcel, however, never destroys other children's things; he is very well brought up (*très bien èlévè*)." The little boy, though on the whole he seems friendly toward other children, has the idea of demarcating his own little space and safeguarding it from intrusion. Thus, when another boy sits down on the cement edge of the sandbox where Marcel has a row of prized sand pies that grandmother has helped him make, he is anxious about the other boy getting too close and makes a barrier with his hand between the other boy and the sand pies; then, becoming increasingly uneasy about these fragile possessions, he starts gently pushing the other boy away . . . In such little daily experiences the child learns from the attitude of the adult to carry over into the world outside the home the feeling of separateness and the need to guard one's own against possibly dangerous intruders (9, p. 100).

It would be a mistake, of course, to assume that American children never show possessiveness or concern for protecting their sphere of action from the intrusion of other children. It would also be incorrect to assume that such possessiveness is never encouraged by American parents and grandparents. Nevertheless, Wolfenstein's observations so consistently supported this tendency as a cultural theme in the interaction of children and adults in the Paris parks that it would appear to be a valid cultural difference. She points out clearly, in other parts of her report, that even when French children are playing in a community park their lines of social interaction are much less with the other children than with their own parents. Play materials and toys are not used to encourage sharing, taking turns, or for the increase in social interaction among children. They are regarded as property, as belongings, and it is critical to keep the lines of ownership clear.

One contrast here is in the American movement of the twentieth century toward providing nursery-school experience for its preschool children. A significant part of the motivation to provide such experience seems to be the wish of parents to have their children learn to adjust easily and smoothly to living, playing, and working cooperatively with other children. As we shall see in Chapter Thirteen, there are other fundamental objectives of nursery schools, as expressed by the professional nursery-school teacher. Nevertheless, the motivation on the part of the parents involved would seem to be, at least in large part, this matter of social adjustment.

Wolfenstein cites a number of incidents from her observations that support her contention that sharing among French children is actively discouraged. Children are punished for making overtures to other children in the form of socialized play during the preschool years:

> A girl of about two has picked up a leather strap from a neighboring group. Her nurse reproves her, takes her by the hand, and returns the strap. A little later a boy of about the same age, belonging to this neighboring family, plays with the little girl, picks up her pail, and keeps it while the little girl is fed by the nurse. The boy's grandmother becomes aware that he has the pail, hits him on the buttocks, scolds, and taking him by the hand, returns the pail to the girl's nurse. In front of the nurse she repeatedly hits the boy about the head and ears (9, p. 101).

Contrasts may also of course be drawn between the American and other societies besides the French with respect to this matter of children's social development. Child socialization in the Israeli kibbutz affords such a contrast, since the kibbutz operates to achieve a totally different kind of parent-child relationship, and child-child relationship, than that to which we are accustomed. In the Israeli kibbutz, which is a communal settlement with little or no private property, living conditions are so markedly different for children and families than those elsewhere that the effects on children's social development are of special interest. The following description by Kenkel of living conditions and social interaction is revealing:

> A kibbutz is a cooperative society in the fullest sense of the term. There is almost no private property. The house in which a person lives belongs to the kibbutz. The food he eats

> at the communal dining hall is furnished by the kibbutz. Each member receives his clothes and personal effects from the community storeroom. Medical bills are paid by the group, and even a small vacation allowance is furnished each member. All the goods and services that an individual needs are supplied, without the necessity for payment, by his kibbutz.
>
> In [some types of kibbutz] the rearing of children is a community responsibility. Children live not with their parents but in special children's homes, where they are cared for and educated by special nurses and teachers. Like adults, children receive all of the necessities of life and all of the "luxuries" that the society can provide from the kibbutz. Parents have no direct responsibility for the economic needs of their children (3, p. 165).

Preliminary research investigations by Rabin (6, 7) indicate that the children reared in the kibbutz appear to be healthy and sound from the psychological standpoint, and that their social adjustment is very adequate. How well such children would adapt to living conditions outside the kibbutz is a somewhat different question, and needs to be investigated.

CULTURAL INCONSISTENCIES AND CONFLICTS

In discussions of the effects of culture on the development of individuals it would be easy, but erroneous, to conclude that a given society places consistent pressures on the growing child to become a particular kind of personality. While there are definite and powerful cultural forces which influence the life, behavior, and development of a child, some of which have been illustrated in this discussion, a given society is not always consistent in the kinds of forces that it directs toward a child. Particularly in a culture as complex as those of Western European and American civilizations, there are inevitably cultural forces that are inconsistent with each other and that result in cultural conflict for the child. A simple example of this would be a child in our own society who is sensitive to both of the following kinds of demands: (1) he should be modest and somewhat self-effacing, not too forward or presumptuous in his relations with adults or with his peers; and (2) he should be self-assertive and demonstrate his ability to take initiative and show other qualities of leadership. The first of these two cultural pressures represents a portion of our society's expectations of a child if he is to be easily accepted by others and liked by people. The second pressure relates to our society's emphasis on success, which is often defined in terms of personal achievement and aggressive interpersonal relationships.

This discussion is not intended to characterize such cultural forces as being "right" or "wrong," but merely to point up the developmental problems that confront a child by virtue of the fact that he lives in a cultural complex which is not entirely coherent or self-consistent. In the case of the example given here, the child's essential task is to achieve a reasonable balance between over modesty and self-effacement on the one hand, and over aggressiveness and self-seeking on the other. Cultural pressures such as these do not inevitably prevent the achievement of balanced self-development, but instead represent complicating factors that make this achievement a more difficult and complex task.

Another kind of cultural inconsistency should also be noted. In addition to the simultaneous operation of two conflicting forces, there is another, somewhat different sort of inconsistency which occurs in the form of discontinuities over significant periods of time. These are best illustrated by changes in expectations, demands, and privileges from one time to another. An example of this sort of cultural discontinuity during the preschool period is provided by the toileting situation. Our society places no heavy demands on a child with respect to toilet control while he is emerging from infancy into the toddler period during his second year. During the middle and later preschool period there are, however, very definite pressures on the child to conform to the socially approved routines for elimination of body wastes. These are age-graded expectations, and the society is merely asserting its right to expect different levels and types of behavior in keeping with different age levels and maturity levels of the child.

A more serious and significant kind of cultural discontinuity of this general type would be illustrated if the society actively demanded a pattern of behavior at one level that it later insisted be destroyed and replaced by a competing or conflicting pattern. Perhaps a form of such a discontinuity exists in rigidly taught "stork-type" stories of sex and reproduction, which must be destroyed and replaced by realistic understanding. And in overly rigid early instruction in religion that involves learnings that must be destroyed in order for the child to achieve further progress in religious education, a kind of discontinuity exists.

These are examples of "blind-alley" learning, which considers that a child can be allowed or even encouraged to build up a false structure of concepts and habits that may be satisfactory to him and his parents for a time, but that inevitably must be destroyed, often at considerable emotional expense to the child, at a later date. A distinction should be made between discontinuity, as illustrated here, and learnings and habit patterns geared to the level of the child but that have the added feature of being "open-ended"—providing a sound basis for further learnings and higher habit patterns.

It is undoubtedly true that some societies present more inconsistencies and cultural discontinuities to the child than others. Ruth Benedict (1) made a penetrating analysis of some of the discontinuities that seem to characterize our American society. Many of her comments about the inconsistencies prevalent in our culture focus on the problems of the older child and adolescent in attempting to achieve adult roles for which their childhood has not prepared them. Inconsistencies of major significance were not analyzed for the preschool period.

It should not be assumed that the simpler, nonliterate societies necessarily provide a smoother, easier transition between childhood and adulthood than our own. Less advanced societies are not always free from inconsistencies and discontinuities. However, each society's modes of socializing its children, including the possibly inconsistent and frustrating modes, are relevant only within the total context of that society's way of life.

THE SIGNIFICANCE OF SUBCULTURES

A somewhat different kind of inconsistency within our society is that brought about by its extremely complex makeup. It is hardly appropriate to speak of the American culture without at least qualifying the phrase by noting the presence of a large number of cultural components, or subcultures. These have been variously defined by different writers, and what constitutes a true subculture for one person may not be so classified by all persons. Nevertheless, there are special groups, some of them geographically determined, others determined by special common features of religion, or social class, or vocational or professional affiliation. To the extent that these culture groups foster their own special sets of values, philosophies, ways of life, etc., they have significance for understanding the child. The Midcentury White House Conference Committee on Children and Youth stressed this in its report:

> There is no such thing as *the* environment of *the* American child. We all know that, broadly speaking, a Southerner has a pattern of family relationships, an attitude toward a settled existence, toward the land, toward the stranger, toward efficiency that is different from the patterns of a person from the North or the Midwest. Again, the functioning farm provides a different background of experience from that of the suburb or the city street. Within the city, there is difference occasioned by the income bracket of the family; and within the income bracket, there is the pattern that is affected by the occupation of the father. Miners and sanitation workers and college instructors have approximately the same income but, as a rule, they provide different designs of living for their children (8, p. 165).

The significance of culture to child behavior, and to our reactions to children with different backgrounds, is brought out in this further quotation from the same report:

> We cannot treat children as if they all felt and evaluated and interpreted and reacted to experience in the same way. Neither can we treat great differences in reaction and attitude as if they were always due to individual peculiarity. When a Navajo boy calls a robin's egg "green," he is not color blind or ignorant; he is classifying colors as his culture classifies them. When a Mexican boy said he had an angel whispering in one ear and a devil in another, he was neither peculiar nor emotionally disturbed or even poetic; he was voicing his culture's expression of inner conflict (8, p. 166).

SUMMARY

Culture refers to the learned behavior of a people. It includes such diverse elements of one's social world as technology, finance, politics, religious values, art, ethics, music, and patterns of family living and child-rearing. Even the manner in which individual children are taught to categorize their experiences is a reflection of cultural conditioning.

The manner in which parents and children relate to each other is, at one and the same time, a reflection of their culture and a determiner of the culture of the future. That is, each society defines acceptable and reasonable limits to the manner in which children and parents interact. This interaction, in turn, has its impact on the child's personality, which will be reflected in the kind of relationship he will eventually seek to establish with his own children.

Markedly different techniques of child-rearing and of satisfying basic needs, such as those for food and clothing, may be discerned from one society to another. The exact meaning of these cultural differences with respect to personality formation is far from clear, since any society's child-rearing practices are meaningful only within the total context of that society's way of life. It is clear, however, that culture is a powerful and pervasive force that enters into the determination of the child's way of organizing and viewing his social and objective world.

REFERENCES

1. Benedict, Ruth, "Continuities and discontinuities in cultural conditioning," *Psychiatry*, 1938, 1:161–167.
2. Dennis, W., *The Hopi child*, New York: Appleton-Century-Crofts, 1940.
3. Kenkel, W., *The family in perspective*, New York: Appleton-Century-Crofts, 1960.
4. Lee, Dorothy, "Being and value in a primitive culture," in C. E. Moustakas (ed.), *The Self*, New York: Harper, 1956, pp. 120–139.
5. Mead, Margaret, and Macgregor, Frances C., *Growth and culture*, Putnam, New York, 1951.
6. Rabin, A. I., "Kibbutz children—research findings to date," *Child.*, 1958, 5(5):179–184.
7. Rabin, A. I., "Behavior research on collective settlements in Israel: Infants and children under conditions of 'intermittent' mothering in the kibbutz," *Amer. J. Orthopsychiat.*, 1958 (28):577–586.
8. Witmer, Helen L., and Kotinsky, Ruth (eds.), *Personality in the making*, New York: Harper, 1952.

9. Wolfenstein, Martha, "French parents take their children to the park," in Margaret Mead and Martha Wolfenstein (eds.), *Childhood in contemporary cultures,* Chicago: Univ. of Chicago Press, 1955, pp. 99–117.

CHAPTER TWELVE

What are the traditional functions of the family? ∽ *In what respects are these functions being modified?* ∽ *In what way does the family create needs among its members, as well as satisfy their needs?* ∽ *What evidence is there that specific patterns of parental behavior lead to specific personal qualities in children?* ∽ *What are the sources of rivalry between siblings?* ∽ *In what respect does a child participate actively in determining the kind of parents he has?*

THE CHILD AND HIS FAMILY

THE CHILD'S CULTURE is mediated for him first by his family. That is, it is within the family setting that the child normally experiences the first and most vital impacts of his cultural world. We have not yet examined in any detail the many complexities of the interaction processes between the child and his family members; nor have we noted any specific effects on the child's developing personality that result from the peculiar, unique relationship he sustains to each family member. The purpose of this chapter, then, is to examine such relationships and increase our understanding of the varieties and richness of the types of relationships within the family, as they bear on the development of the child. We shall look first at the basic nature and organization of the family, at the major family functions, and view the family as a setting for interaction among family members. Then we shall examine the parent-child relationship, attempting to understand the effects of each on the other. Finally, we will pay attention to the interaction between and among siblings within the family, in an effort to understand the role of brothers and sisters in development during early childhood.

THE NATURE OF THE FAMILY

Some definitions of the family give emphasis to family structure, membership, and organization. Others stress the functions of the family as a group. Still others emphasize the roles of family members and the relational qualities among members as the basis of definition. Burgess and Locke's widely accepted definition of the family includes some elements of all these different emphases:

> [The family is] a group of persons united by ties of marriage, blood, or adoption; constituting a single household; interacting and communicating with each other in their respective roles of husband and wife, mother and father, son and daughter, brother and sister; and creating and maintaining a common culture (3, p. 8).

This definition conveys well the general, abstract meaning of the concept "family," but there is also a private, personal meaning for this term, which is a unique experience for every individual; that is, the functional, operating definition of the family which each of us carries with us, based on our own special experiences and reactions to family life as we have participated in it. From this point of view, it may never be possible to provide one definition of the family acceptable to all persons, for, just as every individual is different from every other, every family, too, has its own unique qualities. As Burgess and Locke express it, each family develops and maintains a kind of culture of its own. This culture contributes, among other things, an operating definition of "family" for its members —especially for its children.

It is difficult for children to conceptualize the abstraction "family" apart from their own experiences as members of a family group. What it means to be a brother; what it means to be a father; what it means to be a husband or wife; these and other basic familial roles are defined for the child as he witnesses their performance in day-by-day interaction among family members. One obvious example, then, of the role of families in the lives of children is the functional definitions of family life they provide for their children. We shall examine a number of other contributions of families to the attitudes, values, and concepts of children at various points throughout this chapter.

FAMILY FUNCTIONS

The family of which we are speaking at this point should be further defined as the *nuclear group* comprising a single household in our society; that is, we do not ordinarily include cousins, uncles, aunts, nieces, nephews, and in-laws. While there are variations that may sometimes include a grandparent in this nuclear group, we are speaking now of the more typical household consisting of husband and wife and their children.[1] This is in contrast to the *extended* family, common to some other societies, which may include a larger kinship group within the single household.

Various students of family life have provided us with classifications of family functions. While there is not perfect agreement among these specialists, the list provided by Winch appears to cover the primary areas of basic family functioning rather well:

1. *The economic function:* concerned with the family's production and consumption of goods and services, provisions for domestic division of labor, and handling of economic dependency needs.
2. *The status-conferring function:* concerned with the family's role in determining the status of its individual members by establishing subcultural attributes which define family status and by providing a status orientation for its members.
3. *The reproductive function:* concerned with the family's right and responsibility to have children.
4. *The functions of socialization and security-giving:* concerned with the family's role in providing the child with a foundation of psychological security for becoming a productive member of the larger social group (14).

CHANGES IN FAMILY FUNCTIONS

Looking at the family from a historical perspective, we note that there have been important changes in the structure and function of families over the years. Families are smaller; they are more mobile; they do not produce as much in the way of goods and services in the home as was once true. From the economic standpoint they are primarily purchasing

[1] There are other obvious variations: adopted child, step-relationships, foster parent-child relationships, missing parent, etc.

consumer units. The status-conferring function of the family still exists, but perhaps with less influence than in earlier generations. For example, with increased social and geographic mobility there is less concern about who one's father is and relatively more concern about the attributes of the individual under consideration. The child stands relatively more on his own merits as he enters the world of social, educational, and economic action. The importance of status-conferring activities of the family rests, to a great extent, on the degree to which the family actively orients its members to aspire to a kind or degree of status in society.

The reproductive function remains exclusively the right and responsibility of the family, but there is striking evidence of change here also: decreases over several generations in size of family; increased acceptance by large segments of society of the notion of family planning, as well as the emphasis on the prevention of conception; some significant beginnings of the practice of artificial insemination in cases of couples not otherwise able to have children; and the large number of illegitimate births typical of current vital statistics reports.

If anything, the functions of security-giving and socialization take on increased significance in view of the changes occurring in the other major areas of family functions; that is, to a marked degree the stability of family life as we know it appears to be dependent on the ability of families to satisfy needs of their members in terms of these two vital functions.

THE FAMILY AS A UNIT OF INTERACTING PERSONALITIES

One approach to understanding the family is to view its members as individuals, each of whom has his own special needs, motives, resources, habits, behavior patterns, attitudes, and feelings. The family, then, becomes a kind of "arena" within which these members interact, making use of their own resources and those of the group in an effort to satisfy their needs in an ongoing, changing relational process with each other. This "needs" approach to family life is a very useful one. It helps us to understand the individual and the nature of his relationship to other family members. We can appreciate better, for example, the child reacting with hostility to his newly arrived baby brother, if we can truly appreciate the threat this interloper may represent. The threat may well be in the form of a new competitor for the mother's affection, which is a prime source of need gratification. We can appreciate more fully that the behavior of this older child may well be indirect, unspoken, and poorly understood by the child himself, as he seeks reassurance that his source of affection is still available, or as he attempts to deal with the reality of his overwhelming feelings of loss as it becomes evident to him that his source of affection is not as available as before.

In general, the behavior of each individual in relation to the other family members is a lawful, channeled effort to satisfy the needs and drives that arise both from the biological forces within the individual and from the social experiences with other individuals. But the family as a unit of interacting personalities does more than satisfy the needs of its members. In addition, in the process of meeting the needs of its members, it also plays a very powerful role, in the lives of its children especially, in the *creation of new needs.*

Needs arise in persons both from internal, biological sources, and from more or less external sources in the social and objective environment. For example, a child needs food if he is to survive and maintain normal growth and health. But, with certain possible exceptions, there aren't any *particular* foods he must have in order to survive and maintain normal health and growth. There are classes of foods which are essential to optimal development, to be sure. But to say, for example, that every child "needs" a certain minimum quantity of spinach in his daily or weekly diet would be absurd. Similarly, no biological food needs are involved in the manner in which food is conveyed from plate to mouth. Yet it is apparent, with respect both to the *kinds of foods* we learn to need and to the *manner of eating* we come to rely on, that the family can play a significant role in teaching the child to need certain things, including the need to behave in certain ways.

We are, of course, using the term *need* in two somewhat different senses here, to refer both to biological necessities and to learned behavior that becomes routinized and satisfying. From the psychological standpoint, both of these senses of the term are valid and meaningful, since both become bases for significant behavior. Truly, the family serves to direct and to channel the biological drives and needs of its members and to provide definitions of acceptable behavior that can be used to satisfy needs. Thus, the family is a unit of interacting personalities, and not only serves to satisfy the needs of its members, but serves to create and to channel its members' needs.

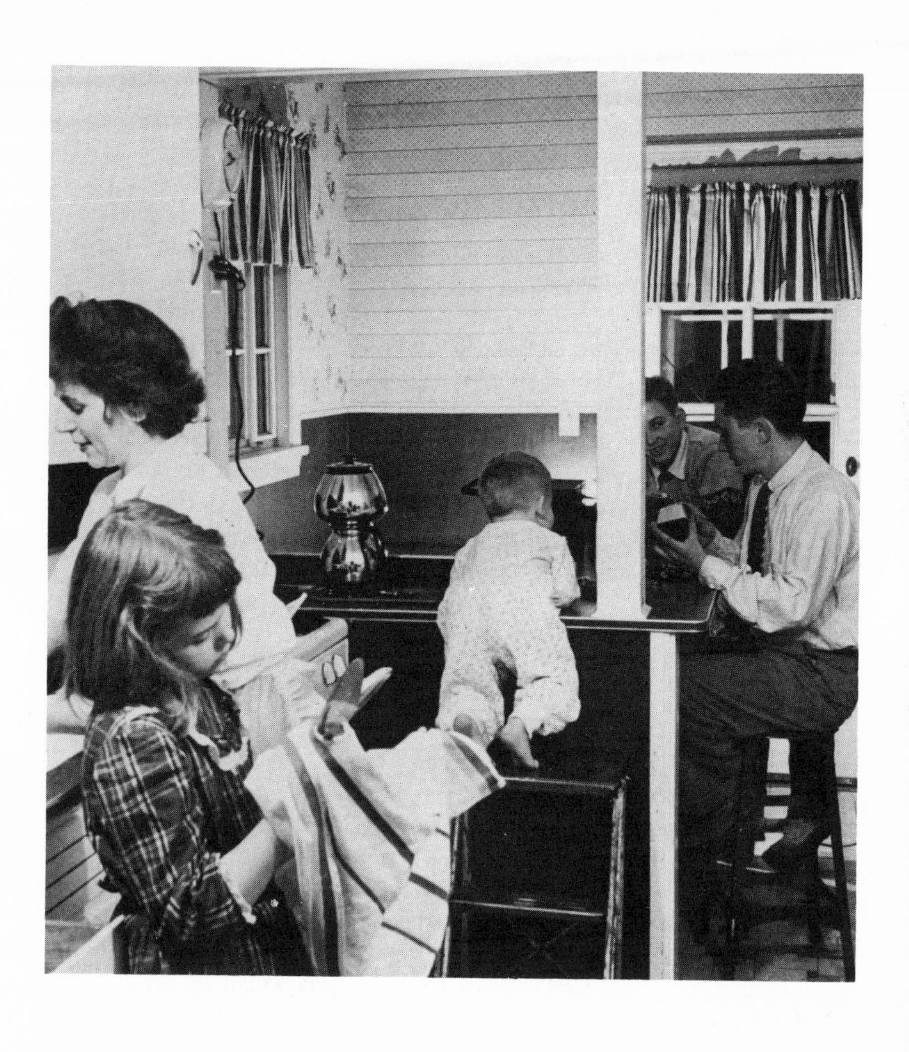

The family: a unit of interacting personalities.
(Courtesy of Gesell Institute of Child Development.)

The interaction process is not a simple one in which one individual merely manifests a need and another individual provides satisfaction for the need. There are degrees of need satisfaction and there may be a wide variety of techniques for bringing about satisfaction of a given need. The family will sometimes be more effective—sometimes less so—in providing satisfactions for its members. These normal variations in family operating efficiency are to be expected and do not necessarily reflect either weakness or instability. Another aspect of this interaction approach to the family is the reciprocal nature of the relationships among family members. Within the family we rarely encounter "one-way" relationships in which one individual influences another without also being influenced, in turn, by that other person. In the ongoing relationship between husband and wife, for example, what a man says to his wife may affect her behavior, and the change in her behavior may very well influence the man's next response. So also, the relationship between parent and child is not a one-way relationship, but a continuing, complex, reciprocating one in which the child influences the parent and vice versa.

SPECIAL FORCES AFFECTING FAMILIES, AND INTERACTION AMONG FAMILY MEMBERS

Cultural Forces In Chapter Eleven we noted that the child's culture is mediated for him and interpreted to him largely through the family, at least while he is young and highly dependent on his family. In turn, the family operates within a cultural setting that defines for it the appropriate forms of family life and family membership behavior. The culture, being the learned behavior of a people, defines the acceptable and legitimate marriage relationships and the foundation for family life. Cultural forces play vital roles in determining who shall be members of a family group and the manner in which they shall interact with other family members. An example would be those cultural taboos which regulate sexual behavior within the family. In our society the idea of sexual behavior between family members not related by marriage, e.g., brother and sister, or father and daughter, is abhorrent. While such incest taboos are also true in most other societies as well, the definition of incest and the manner of regulation of sexual behavior within the family is a cultural force of considerable significance. Other cultural forces come to bear also on the family and its members: the patterns of working, playing, and worshipping together, as well as defining patterns of authority and responsibility within the group, and working out methods of socializing children and bringing them to a point of independent control of their own behavior.

From this discussion, then, we may conclude that needs of individuals are not the only factors which determine the nature of interaction among family members. Cultural pressures and forces also play vital roles.

SOCIAL AND ECONOMIC STATUS FORCES

The socioeconomic status of families is also known to be a factor in determining the nature of family life and the kinds of interaction among family members. It is self-evident that families differ with respect to their abilities to provide tangible goods and services for the use of their members: automobiles; housing; homemaking conveniences; quality and amount of food and clothing; recreation facilities; books; education; special instruction in music, art, dancing, etc.; and the countless other things contingent on the family's economic resources. Even such things as medical care, surgery, orthodontic services, psychological services, nursery schools, and other specialized services are to a considerable extent available to some families much more readily than to others, depending on economic status. But beyond the mere ability to pay for such goods and services, it is apparent that there are very real differences from one family to another with respect to the degree of interest in and demand for such things. This is partly a matter of ability to pay and also partly a matter of tastes, values, beliefs, and interests. Socioeconomic status includes both of these considerations.

Even child-rearing methods appear to be related to socioeconomic status. Patterns of authority and parental control over children differ from one social class to another, and techniques of child guidance and discipline are related to social class. Bronfenbrenner (2) notes that middle-class parents tend to be more permissive than lower-class parents in the care of infants. It is the middle-class families in which parents make strenuous efforts to learn about children and to follow the recommendations of medical and psychological authorities. Their guidance of their children places a high value on education and on pushing their children toward achievement of those behavior patterns which represent status and respectability to the middle-class society. These parents are less likely to use physical punishment in dealing with young children than are parents of the working class. Sewell and Haller (12) argue that middle-class children also fare better than children of lower classes with respect to personal adjustment. Their explanation for this difference is that the middle-class child experiences less conflict between his family's and the larger society's expectations than is true for the lower-class child.

Sears, Maccoby, and Levin (11) studied the child-rearing practices of 379 mothers of 5-year-old children. The socioeconomic status of these mothers was classified by the investigators as either "middle class" or "working class." They found that the middle-class mothers imposed fewer restrictions on their children and made fewer demands upon them than did the working-class mothers. Middle-class mothers were more likely to overlook aggressive behavior of children toward parents, compared with lower-class mothers. In general, the middle-class mothers were less punitive and more permissive toward their children than were the lower-class mothers.

THE CHILD AND HIS PARENTS

Social and behavioral scientists have, for many generations, been concerned about the effects of child-rearing practices on the personalities of children. Philosophers and religious leaders have shared the concern of these scientists on this question, since it bears directly on the issues of character and moral development as well as on the achievement of competence, success, and on generally healthy adjustment and adaptation to social living. In spite of the historical interest in this question it is only within recent history that we have had any organized research efforts to discover precise effects of parent behavior on the development and adjustment of children. Because we are new at research of this kind, there are still many gaps in our knowledge; many important questions remain to be answered, and many of these questions await the development of more refined research procedures than the ones presently available. Nevertheless, there are some important facts and principles of which we can be fairly certain that can be noted. Among these, for example, is the fact of the fundamental importance of adequate mothering in the early development of infant and child, discussed in previous chapters.

The effects of specific parental practices on the personality development of children has been investigated with mixed results. The effects of early weaning, bottle feeding, early toilet training, etc., have at different times been described as having serious effects on personality of the growing child. Realistically, however, the research on such questions has been inconclusive. Orlansky (10), in a comprehensive summary of research on infant-care practices, is very critical of hasty and emotion-laden conclusions on the basis of limited evidence. He shows that there is little justification for the conclusion that any one specific practice, of those mentioned, has predictable effects on child personality.

Similarly, with preschool children, it would be unwise to assume that any single parental practice produces specific, predictable results in child development and behavior. The total personality of each child is, to a marked degree, the product of the relationship he sustains with his parents. The child's immediate behavior in a given situation, as well as the long-range characteristics that mark him as a consistently unique personality, are both dependent on the quality of the relationship he holds with his parents. In examining the parent-child relationship, however, it is important to distinguish two somewhat different aspects of the parent's total effect on the child. First, we may analyze particular child-care practices which may bear on the child's behavior and development. These would include such considerations as breast vs. bottle feeding in infancy, weaning practices, type of toilet training provided, disciplinary measures used, etc. Perhaps more basic, we should consider the fundamental qualities or characteristics of the parent as a personality. Some lines of evidence would indicate that this second consideration is a more vital influence in the child's life than any particular child-care practice that is followed. Furthermore, it has been argued that specific child-care practices have relatively little meaning apart from the feelings and attitudes of the persons who participate in them. Thus two different mothers may apply the same techniques but with quite different results, not only because the children are different in the first place, but also because the two mothers may hold different feelings toward the children as they apply the techniques, and may also hold markedly different feelings about the "rightness" or "naturalness" of the techniques. These are complicating considerations, which make it difficult to trace the precise effects of particular child-rearing practices.

In a careful, well planned study of the effects of home environment on the behavior of nursery-school children, Baldwin (1) paid particular attention to certain parental characteristics that he described as warmth, democracy, and indulgence. Fifty-six children between the ages of 36 months and 60 months were given nursery-school behavior ratings concerned with a large number of personal and social characteristics. Of the three parental variables—democracy, warmth, and indulgence—democracy was the most significant in relation to child characteristics. Children whose parents were highly democratic tended to be more active and socially outgoing than the others. The social behavior included both hostility and domineeringness as well as friendly and cooperative behavior. These children tended to have a high social status in their groups, being favored by the other children. In addition, they rated high in such qualities as intellectual curiosity, originality, and constructiveness. On the other hand, children whose parents were high in indulgence tended to be apprehensive and were lacking in skill in muscle activities.

The results are not as clear cut as this discussion might imply. For example, Baldwin's democratic parents were probably somewhat higher in native intelligence than his less democratic parents. Therefore, the intellectual curiosity and creativity of their children may have been due, in part, to superior native endowment. At the same time, the results were clearly indicative of a relationship between home atmosphere and child behavior. In this respect, the study was consistent with the experience of other research and clinical workers. Baldwin's study also brought out the fact that democracy in the home is a factor which operates *in relation to* the other qualities of warmth and indulgence; that is, it appears to be the interaction of such home qualities with each other, in their special combinations, which counts. Hence, it is not realistic to ascribe child behavior to one home condition in isolation from others.

The personality and adjustment of mothers, as a factor in the healthy development of infants and children, has received considerable attention in the research literature of child development. One example of such research studies was an investigation by Lakin (7) of the personality characteristics of mothers whose infants cried excessively. Lakin assumed that there may be many other factors involved in excessive crying of infants, including constitutional factors in the infants themselves and gross environmental factors. At the same time, there are also psychogenic factors related to the personality of the mothers, as revealed in this material taken from Lakin's summary:

> Intensity of competitiveness with own mothers appeared to be greater among mothers of colicky infants. Resentment

> at lack of support and greater emotional distance in relation to both parents were marked among these individuals. It is suggested that the quality of the primary relationships, in these cases, may have led to the expectation of denial and/or rejection in regard to ostensible sources of support in the environment, and to have affected personal and role self-concept adversely.
>
> Heightened ambivalence toward role and role function appears to be more characteristic of the experimental subjects. Awareness of a sense of inferior status and conflict with respect to frustrated vocational or other ambitions are frequently involved in this ambivalence. Some aspects of role function are more frequently identified by these individuals as submissive or as painful. Greater "conscientiousness" on the part of some of these women—the need to be viewed as "excellent wife and mother"—may be in the nature of reaction formation to the aforementioned ambivalent feelings.
>
> Poorer concept of self with respect to role function appears to be characteristic of the colicky infants. The ambivalence and contingent guilt feelings may play the chief part in the feelings of inadequacy experienced by these women. They may underlie the feelings of frustration, disappointment, and defeat in the mother-infant interaction and emphasize the felt difficulty in coping with the demands of motherhood.
>
> Mothers of colicky infants more frequently have less adequate marital adjustments. Some of these individuals felt that they have less support from husbands while others revealed conflict about accepting such support. Resentment, competitive elements, and self-assertive role-related strivings were more in evidence for the experimental subjects.
>
> Mothers of colicky infants seemed to experience greater tentativeness, insecurity, and lack of facility in the carrying out of mothering activities than did mothers of control infants. Their attitudes are more frequently those of uncertainty, wavering between possible courses of action, rather than those of prompt and efficacious mothering (7, p. 38).

If it is true, then, that a mother's feeling about her own mother, her personal ambitions, her self-concept, her marital adjustment, and her feelings of insecurity enter into the determination of the amount of crying her baby does, then it would appear safe to assume that such factors would also bear on the preschool child's struggle to achieve selfhood.

Levine (9) has noted that the development of normal reactions to stress among animals is dependent on the handling of the animals during their infancy. He discovered that rats that had received both painful shocks as well as gentle handling were more adaptive and constructive in their responses to stress at a later period in their development. Groups of rats that were not stimulated during infancy were inclined to be sluggish and to cower in a corner when placed in a strange situation. Their responses to stress were generally maladaptive in comparison with those that had received either positive or negative stimulation during infancy; in contrast, those that had been stimulated from infancy on tended to be far more active, adaptive, and constructive in their later responses to new and strange situations.

While animal research does not provide for direct translation into the theory of human behavior and development, there would seem to be important implications here, suggesting the importance of at least a minimum of handling if the infant is to become prepared to deal constructively with the many stresses he will encounter during the growing years. This sort of research provides us with keener insights into the kinds of questions that need to be asked about child development. In addition, the general conclusions of this study find support in clinical evidence of the faulty growth patterns of children who did not receive sufficient stimulation during infancy.

IDENTIFICATION AS A CENTRAL PROCESS IN PARENT-CHILD RELATIONSHIPS

There is a powerful striving on the part of a child to incorporate certain of the parental characteristics into his own personality. Mannerisms, posture, ways of moving, inflections in speech as well as kinds of words used, attitudes toward things, people, and institutions; all these and many more become parts of the child through the central process of identification. We could add to the list an almost infinite variety of types of things that can be accounted for through this process and provide countless examples of the way in which it operates. But first, our task is to understand the nature of the process itself. What is meant by identification, and how does it operate in the child's life?

We have all had the experience of watching a motion picture or a television program and of participating psychologically in one or more of the roles being portrayed. It is natural for a young girl, for example, to feel herself taking the role of the beautiful and sophisticated actress. The boy watching the exploits of a dashing, handsome, and powerful hero participates by feeling some of the strength, daring, and wisdom of the heroic figure. These commonplace examples of identification that we experience in everyday life should not lead us to believe that it is strictly a fantasy process, which relates solely to entertainment or to daydreaming. In the child, the process of identification goes far beyond "entertainment" and relates directly to the very heart of the matter of personality development.

EFFECTS OF CHILD CHARACTERISTICS AND BEHAVIOR ON PARENTS

Recently, some significant research was conducted concerning the effects of a severely mentally retarded child on family members and family behavior. Farber (4), commenting on the results of this research, notes that considerable evidence exists to the effect that the presence of a handicapped child in the home creates special problems and crises for the rest of the family. There is less material available, however, dealing directly with the effects of normal children on their parents. We know some of the obvious effects: when the first baby arrives the routine of the parents is markedly changed, and different parents, depending on their motives and their abilities to adapt to these changed routines, may vary greatly in their toleration of such demands.

One student of child development, after completing her course of training, was married and became the mother of a handsome baby boy. As she was paying a visit to friends and former teachers in the college community where she had attended school, she was asked the inevitable question: "Does it help any, having been a student in child development, when it comes to having children of your own?" The answer was somewhat mixed: "Oh, yes! It helps a lot and makes it more fun, knowing more about what to expect of him, and being more appreciative of his needs . . . but you know, you teachers never really told us what it's like being on call 24 hours a day!" Perhaps it is never quite possible to explain this to someone who has always taken sleep for granted.

But interruption of routines and changes in living habits, which undoubtedly occur with almost all families when the first baby arrives, still tell only a small fraction of the story; they explain only the general features of what it means to live with any baby or child. When we begin to explore the potentials of each child for being unique and for revealing different aspects of himself from one time to another, we see that each child brings out different aspects of the parent's total personality. Moreover, the same child at different times brings out quite different aspects of the parent's total capacity to respond. At one time a child is passive, loving, dependent, obedient, and submissive. The mother's response to this may be tender, affectionate, proud, and contented. The child calls forth from the mother a feeling of satisfaction and success in her role. But at another time the same child may be willful, disobedient, unruly, hostile and aggressive. This behavior calls forth quite different aspects of the mother's capacity to respond, including sharp words, commands, spanking, unhappiness, disappointment, guilty feelings, and feelings of failure in her role as mother.

The diagram below attempts to illustrate some of the features of parent-child interaction (Fig. 12.1). It depicts a small fragment of the continuing process of give and take between mother and child. In this case, a child's question, "Who is God?" arising out of curiosity and limited knowledge and experience, is directed toward the mother. The mother's answer, however, involves more aspects of her personality than mere "knowledge." Her response to the child reflects not only her knowledge of theological concepts, but her sense of values about God and man, her attitudes toward people and things, her sense of personal worth, and her conviction of her importance as an influence in the life of her child. All these and perhaps many other facets of the mother's total self are somehow involved in her response to the child's question. Moreover, her response will affect other aspects of the child's self than his mere knowledge; he, in turn, deals with his mother's response by incorporating it to a greater or lesser extent into the various significant regions of his personality: attitudes toward people and things, feelings about himself, skills, adequacies, and competence as a person.

The never ending cycle of parent-child interaction is appropriately viewed as a dynamic system; that is, it is constantly undergoing change; it is continually being revised in interaction with each of the personalities involved. One of the implications of this philosophy of parent-child relationships is that actions by one person lead to reactions by another—less on the basis of the intent of the first person than on the basis of the reaction capacity of the second. The action may call forth particular aspects of that

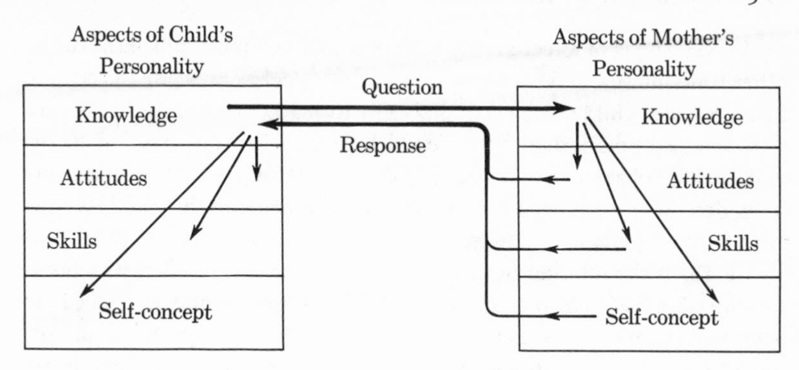

Fig. 12.1. A diagrammatic representation of a brief unit of interaction between child and parent.

capacity at different times, but it is never merely what one says or does that brings this reaction; it is the perception of what one says or does by the other person, and the other person's needs and capacities for response, which determine the reaction.

It follows then that a mother's response to her child is bound to vary with her mood, her degree of fatigue, her preoccupation with other matters, and many other considerations. This makes consistency of reaction a most difficult and perhaps even unnatural condition in parent-child relationships. Yet consistency of parent behavior is one of the goals prescribed by many authorities on parent-child relationships. Consistency, of course, may be overdone. At the same time, there are sound reasons for the belief that the child's sense of security, as well as his ability to get along with the people and things of his world, are heightened by consistent behavior by his parents. One solution to this problem lies at the very heart of the parent-child interaction system, and is based on the fact that parental reactions to child behavior can be more objective (and more consistent) if parents do not allow guilt feelings or defensive reactions to interfere with the basic relationship. Consider the child who shows hostile, aggressive behavior. Dealing with such behavior is never simple, and there is no easy prescription for the "right" way to handle it. But the problem becomes much more acute in the mother who must deal not only with the child's hostility but with her own feelings of inadequacy, guilt, frustration, and failure if she blames herself every time the child behaves that way. At one time she may feel very much at fault for her child's behavior, and perhaps she may indulge the child or be very accepting of the child's hostility. In this mood, she is in effect saying, "After all, it's my fault, not his." At another time, however, she may have very strong defenses against accepting blame for her child's behavior; she seeks to place the responsibility with someone else—his father, or the child himself. Then her reaction to the undesirable behavior may be entirely different. It would not be surprising if, under these circumstances, physical punishment of the child, who is after all the "guilty party," were the result.

Perhaps the solution to such difficulties lies in this mother, who needs to understand herself and the reasons she feels guilty, and who needs to overcome her feelings of inadequacy. She also needs to arrive at a philosophy of parent-child relationships that does not rely on finding the "guilty party" and punishing that person. If she can learn to see the behavior of herself and her child as natural and normal reactions to stresses and forces in their lives, and not to have guilt feelings about her role in it or to place blame on her child or husband for it, she is then in a better position to deal constructively with the undesirable behavior itself. But the behavior of neither the parent nor the child can be seen realistically without reference to the behavior of the other. To carry this one step further, the behavior of the child at one stage in his development is, in part, the outcome of the kind of relationship he sustained to his parents at previous stages. If, for example, the child's early language behavior was rewarded by fond motherly attention and consideration and his language became an important means to the achievement of need satisfaction, it is likely that he will rely heavily on the use of language to achieve need satisfaction in subsequent stages of development.

Language behavior should also be mentioned, not only as one of the outcomes of parent-child interaction, but as a significant mode or means by which interaction is carried on. In fact, the fundamental role of communication processes in parent-child interaction can hardly be overstated. Gardner (5) has presented an outline of some of the basic considerations in understanding communication processes as they affect parent-child relationships. He stresses the importance of parental willingness to listen actively and appreciatively to the child's efforts at communication.

SIBLING INTERACTION: THE CHILD AND HIS BROTHERS AND SISTERS

Interaction between the child and his brothers and sisters also forms one of the bases of the child's total socialization process—the process of learning to be a competent person in his world of people and things. His relationship with his brothers and sisters is a significant factor in determining what he thinks of himself, as well as being basic to his attitudes toward other people. In this section we shall consider some of the features of sibling relationships that bear directly on the child's achievement of a healthy pattern of personal growth.

With siblings, as with parent-child relationships, it is not possible to predict specific outcomes that may result from given conditions. For example, the idea that the youngest child in a family will inevitably be spoiled has stemmed, in popular thinking, from the observation that *some* youngest children are pampered, overprotected, and babied. There is no question but that this does occur in individual cases. But it is the pampering, overprotecting, babying type of relationship that leads to any peculiar qualities in the personality of the child—not the fact that he is the youngest. The role of the child's position in the family, then, is usually an indirect role, in that it may intensify certain tendencies on the part of parents, or older siblings, to react in certain ways. Being the youngest child does not *necessarily* or *inevitably* lead to "spoiling."

Similarly, being the oldest child in a family with several younger siblings does not necessarily lead to frustration and consequent abnormal development by being displaced in the affectional role with the parents. There is, in the situation of being the oldest child, the *possibility* that unhappiness, frustration, and bitterness will result as younger children replace him in the dependent relationship with loving parents. But the frustrating threat of being displaced in the relationship with loving parents is not unique to the oldest child; again, it is the feeling or perception of the possibilities in the situation of being the oldest child that appears to be of major significance, as opposed to the fact.

Effects of Ordinal Position There are a number of common beliefs about the effects of being the oldest child, or being the youngest, or of being an only child. These are examples of kinds of sibling situations that *may* have a bearing on the child's growth, but that may be modified considerably by the attitude of the parents toward whatever sibling condition exists as well as by the resources of the child himself. For example, some research indicates that oldest children and only children tend to talk more and to speak in a more adult manner, compared with other children. However, this situation, which may well be true of children *on the average*, will not necessarily obtain in the case of the family that makes special efforts to develop the language behavior of all its children, or in cases where the mental growth of a younger child may be more rapid than was true of the older child. Any sibling position we might mention—oldest child, youngest child, middle child, only boy in a family of girls, only girl in a family of boys, etc.—has its special possibilities both for need satisfaction and for need frustration. No one position appears to have a peculiar advantage over all the others, nor is any one sibling position necessarily more conducive to maladjustment or faulty development.

In spite of these general statements, there are some trends that suggest that particular combinations of sibling arrangements may have at least indirect affects on behavior and development. One example, a study of the effects of age, sex, and intelligence on sibling attitudes toward each other done by Smalley (13) revealed that jealousy is more likely to occur in girl-girl combinations than in boy-boy or boy-girl combinations. This study also pointed out that boy-girl combinations are more likely to lead to friendly and protective attitudes on the part of siblings, as compared with same sex combinations. It was also noted that the greater the age differences between siblings, the greater is the likelihood of friendly and protective attitudes, with less likelihood of jealousy.

An interesting and sometimes difficult situation which may arise in sibling relationships is the forming of a "coalition" by two or more children in relation to one or more other siblings. A typical coalition results when the oldest of three children adopts a protective attitude toward the youngest, particularly in defense of the youngest against the intrusions or attacks of the second, or middle, child. This can be understood, in part, as the result of the greater maturity and sense of responsibility of the oldest child, who may have progressed further in identifying with the parent role and hence becoming "parentlike" in his relationships with the youngest child, who is probably the most dependent of the three. It is also understandable if the middle child, having neither the sense of responsibility nor the privileges and status of the oldest or the dependence and protection accorded the youngest, may compensate for his situation through aggressive behavior directed toward the youngest. Such an adjustment undoubtedly aggravates and intensifies the situation, and serves as a force to unite the older and younger siblings even closer in their developing coalition. This is only one example of the several possible coalitions in sibling relationships, but it reveals the complexity of the forces in operation in the child's life as he learns to deal with brothers and sisters. Guidance on the part of parents who find these situations developing is based on an understanding of the forces that are operating in the lives of their children. For example, their awareness of the middle child's possible sources of frustration can enable them to take special measures to see that this child gets a reasonable share of attention and that he is not deprived of privileges and responsibilities that he is mature enough to handle just because he has an older sibling. Also, they can see to it that the youngest child does not get an undue amount of babying and special privilege by virtue of his being the youngest. In the long run it is no advantage, and may be detrimental, to the youngest child to be protected too much against the situations that normally arise in sibling relationships.

One critical issue in the handling of sibling relationships by parents is the question of fairness and equitability in their treatment of their children. It is only reasonable that if one child gets special privileges consistently that are denied the others, then *all* the children, including the privileged one, are at a disadvantage. Such unfairness heightens resentments and intensifies rivalries out of proportion to the normal competitiveness among brothers and sisters. As a result distorted attitudes of resentment and bitterness can carry over into one's adult relationships, not only with the brothers and sisters, but with friends and associates and within one's marital and parental experiences.

Intensive studies of the effects of certain sibling relationships on development of children have been made by Koch (6). Her subjects were 5- and 6-year-olds from two-child families, in which she compared first and second-born children with respect to a large number of personality characteristics. Koch found that the first-born children tended to be more given to anger, were rated as more intense emotionally, as reacting more violently to defeat in competitive activities, as reacting less favorably to sympathy and approval from adults, as more inclined to give alibis, and as exhibiting better articulation in speech. In general, the first-born children appeared to be more intense, anxious, defensive, and concerned about status. These findings, which are supported by the results of other research studies, are of particular interest in relation to a finding by Lasko (8) that mothers were more child centered and protective of their first-born children, but less warm than they were with their second-born children. Again, this leads us to conclude that there may be important differences associated with ordinal position and sibling relationships in the family, but that they are probably an indirect result of the sibling position, and more directly the result of differences in attitude and treatment afforded them by their parents. Evidently there are very complex reasons behind the fact that parents treat older children differently from younger ones. Perhaps one of the major factors in this differential treatment is the greater experience, the lower level of tension and anxiety, and the tendency to be more relaxed and to find more satisfaction in the child-rearing process, all factors that are likely to be true with second or younger children.

One of Koch's more interesting findings pertained to the sex of the children in the pairs of children. She observed that second-born males with an older sister were more sissyish, on the average, than were first-born males with either a younger sister or younger brother. Children with brothers were judged to be more competitive, ambitious, enthusiastic, and less wavering in decision than were children with sisters. Also, Koch noted that children from opposite-sex sibling pairs as compared with those of same-sex sibling pairs were judged to be more self-confident, inclined to recover more speedily from emotional upset, be more cheerful, kind, healthy, curious, tenacious, friendly to adults and children, and less wavering in decision. There were significant differences between boys with a younger sister and boys with an older sister. The latter tended to be less jealous, less exhibitionistic, and less inclined to take leadership.

SUMMARY

The family may be viewed as a unit of interacting personalities striving to use their varied resources to satisfy individual and group needs. The traditional functions of the family—economic, reproductive, status-conferring, socializing, and security-giving—are gradually being modified. There is relatively greater emphasis on the family as a unit that plays the major role in meeting the personality needs of all its members, but especially its dependent children. The family not only satisfies needs of children and, in so doing, provides a basis for healthy personality development; it also creates additional needs in children, which must be learned if the child is to become socialized.

It is not possible to relate a specific pattern of parent behavior to a particular kind of personality development in the child with any assurance of regular and predictable results. However, evidence has been obtained of the importance of the home atmosphere and of the degree of personal maturity of parents as factors in the adjustment of children. Much of the child's adjustment is learned from his parents through the vital process of identification.

We are beginning to view the family in terms of interaction processes, in which the impact of children on their parents is as vital a consideration as the effect of parents on children. Thus, a given child may play a basic role in determining the kind of mothering he receives, because of the special combination of qualities that he brings to this interactional relationship.

REFERENCES

1. Baldwin, A. L., "The effect of home environment on nursery school behavior," *Child Develpm.*, 1949, **20**:49–61.
2. Bronfenbrenner, U., "Socialization and social class through time and space," in E. Maccoby, T. M. Newcomb, and E. L. Hartley (eds.), *Readings in social psychology*, New York: Holt, 1958, pp. 400–425.
3. Burgess, E. W., and Locke, H. J., *The family*, 2nd ed., New York: American Book, 1953.
4. Farber, B., "Effects of a severely mentally retarded child on family integration," *Monogr. Soc. Res. Child Develpm.*, 1959, **24**:(2).
5. Gardner, D. B., "Parent-child interaction and the theory of communication," *J. Home Econ.*, 1957, **49**(10):777–781.
6. Koch, H. L., "Some personality correlates of sex, sibling position, and sex of sibling among five- and six-year-old children," *Genet. Psychol. Monogr.*, 1955, **52**:3–50.
7. Lakin, M., "Personality factors in mothers of excessively crying (colicky) infants," *Monogr. Soc. Res. Child Develpm.*, 1957, **22**(1).
8. Lasko, J., "Parent behavior toward first and second children," *Genet. Psychol. Monogr.*, 1954, **49**:97–137.
9. Levine, S., "Stimulation in infancy," *Sci. Amer.*, 1960, **202**:8086.
10. Orlansky, H., "Infant care and personality," *Psychol. Bull.*, 1949, **46**:1–48.
11. Sears, R. R., Maccoby, E. H., and Levin, H., *Patterns of child rearing*, White Plains, N.Y.: Row, Peterson, 1957.
12. Sewell, W. H., and Haller, A. O., "Factors in the relationship between social status and the personality adjustment of the child," *Amer. Sociol. Rev.*, 1959, **24**:511–520.

13. Smalley, R. E., "Two studies in sibling rivalry: II. The influence of differences in age, sex, and intelligence in determining the attitudes of siblings toward each other," *Smith College Stud. Soc. Wk.*, 1930, 1:23–40.
14. Winch, R. F., *The Modern Family*, New York: Holt, 1952.

CHAPTER THIRTEEN

Why do "preschool" children need a school experience? ⁓ What are the major kinds of programs available for children under 6 years of age? ⁓ What are the primary objectives of nursery education? ⁓ In what respects do nursery schools provide a unique research resource? ⁓ What are the physical qualities of a good nursery-school plant? ⁓ How is the nursery-school teacher specially qualified for work with young children?

THE CHILD AND THE NURSERY SCHOOL

IN ONE VERY IMPORTANT SENSE, the term "preschool," applied to 3-, 4-, and 5-year-old children, is erroneous and quite misleading. It seems to imply that these children are not ready to have school experiences. Such an implication is correct only if we hold to the traditional belief that a "school" is a place to learn such academic skills as reading and arithmetic. But education has a much broader meaning, based on the idea that the child's total relationship with his world of people and things can become more meaningful through organized learning experiences. In this light, a school is an institution designed to help the child increase his competence in being an effective person, in all respects, in relation to people and things.

THE NEED FOR A SCHOOL EXPERIENCE

If we do not provide more schools for 3- to 5-year-olds, it is not because these children have no need or interest in school experiences; it is merely because our society has as yet failed to recognize the significance of this period in the child's total educational development, and to find reasonable means of supporting financially what is admittedly an expensive program. The serious student of child development, however, is aware that the young child himself is not really "preschool" age. It would be more appropriate to qualify our school programs as "post-early childhood," since they are not geared to the needs of children of ages from 3 to 5. These children need group experiences that, for the most part, cannot be provided in private homes by ordinary families. This is no reflection on the homes or the families, but merely that homes and families, designed to accomplish their basic familial functions, are not capable of providing the range, richness, and variety of social, intellectual, and aesthetic experiences that characterize the program of a good nursery school.

Hymes has commented on the various arguments for and against nursery-school education. He notes that we are reluctant to pay the expenses of such programs and that we rationalize our reluctance by arguing that these children need their mothers—that nursery schools are a threat to family ties and solidarity:

> The reverse is more apt to be true. Good nursery schools and kindergartens strengthen families. They are primarily schools for children but they are schools for parents as well. Parents and teachers confer frequently in good schools. There are parent meetings that center around the common problems mothers and fathers of young children face. The skills of the parent do not grow rusty when a child under six goes to school. Family skills become keener, sharper. The home, as a center where children can find understanding, becomes more strong (2, pp. 141–142).

But the main argument for nursery schools is that the child himself is in need of an experience he cannot get in any other way. The central purpose of this chapter is to describe the kinds of schools that are intended to provide these experiences and to present their special features, including their objectives, programs, physical arrangements and facilities, and the qualifications of the professional people who operate them.

PROGRAMS FOR PRESCHOOL CHILDREN

There are many different sorts of programs available for children under 6 years of age. In quality they range from the very best of educational experiences in our entire society to the very poorest, and, unfortunately, it is often difficult for the nonprofessional to distinguish between the extremes. The schools that provide these programs also vary widely according to their types of administrative support and in the objectives of their programs. The major types of programs will be described briefly to illustrate the different ways of operating and the basically different objectives involved.

The Day-Care Program In many communities, particularly in large urban areas, there are extensive programs of day care for children of working mothers. Some of these provide for the care of preschool-age children during the entire working day, and usually include a noon meal as part of the program. While the objective of these services is primarily to serve families in which the mother is not able to care for her own child in the home, they have certain features in common with nursery schools. Sometimes these day-care services are regulated by state social-welfare agencies, which insure at least minimum standards for health, facilities, meals, and safety of children. However, it is difficult to enforce standards with respect to educational services in these programs; hence there are no guarantees that the child in a day care center will be treated in the light of his educational needs. The primary objective of these services is to protect the child and to meet his minimum needs in the absence of his mother.

Because of the nature of the service provided by day-care programs, it is not unusual for a child to participate for an extended period of time during the preschool years. Many of the children involved in such programs come from homes and communities that may be lacking in intellectual stimulation or may encourage distortions in personal and social adjustments. These facts, in combination with the full-day program typical of day-care services, point up the crucial role that can be played in the life of a child through such a service. The increased awareness of the significance and potentially positive influences of day-care services is reflected in rapidly expanding programs of this type, with emphasis on improved standards and attention to the educational and developmental needs of children as well as their routine care.

Some agencies are sponsored by community organizations and may receive some financial support from "red-feather" or community chest funds. Others operate on a private basis, with parent fees alone meeting the operating costs. Unfortunately, the personnel who staff such programs may not be well grounded in professional education in the field of child development. Moreover, because of the high costs of good programs of nursery education, it is an unusual day-care service that can provide quality facilities and equipment and that can offer the variety of experiences so necessary to the child.

University Nursery Schools Most state-supported institutions of higher learning—and many private universities and colleges as well—operate nursery schools as an integral part of their total educational program. The general objectives of such nursery schools are fourfold: (1) to provide for the total development of the young child, (2) to provide a laboratory and training facility for students, (3) to provide for parent education, and (4) to conduct research on various aspects of child development. Not all university nursery schools are equally concerned with all of these four objectives, of course. Furthermore, a few such programs may be designed to meet a somewhat different objective—to provide a service to families in the community who are in need of day care for a child. This, however, should clearly be understood as a separate objective and not the central purpose of the university nursery program.

Private Nursery Schools In some communities well qualified individuals have established private nursery-school facilities, operated primarily for the purposes of the educational development of the child. Again, primarily because of the cost of such programs, they are rarely found in any but the wealthiest communities, and their services are available only to those families who can afford to pay the high fees required to maintain such operations. It is particularly among private nursery schools that marked extremes in quality may be found. The parent seeking to enroll a child in a private nursery school would be well advised to observe the program and activities first, and to discuss the objectives and the methods of the nursery school with the director. The professional qualifications of the director and the teachers should be considered, also, along with the physical facilities, equipment, and program.

Cooperative Nursery Schools The movement toward the establishment of cooperative nursery programs in many communities has been gaining impetus partly because of their features of economy of operation, and partly because of increased parent participation, which many parents find challenging and stimulating. The unique feature of the parent-cooperative nursery school is that, while there is a professional staff employed to direct the over-all program, it is the parents themselves—mothers *and* fathers—who provide many of the routine services within the school. These include building maintenance and care of equipment, record keeping, and much of the actual teaching itself. Usually a schedule is worked out so that a mother whose child is enrolled in the cooperative participates by teaching perhaps one day a week. In the better operations of this type, there is active concern for parent education, and mothers and fathers attend the planning sessions for operating the school, which enables them to benefit from the group discussions and from the counsel of the professional in charge of the program.

Benefits to the child accrue in at least two ways: (1) he has the advantage of a nursery-school program that he might not otherwise have because of its prohibitive costs, and (2) he has the advantage of living with parents whose own development, life enrichment, and insights into child development have been greatly stimulated by their participation in the nursery-school experience.

While there are many things that operate to make the cooperative programs difficult, challenging, and sheer hard work, there is much to be said in favor of these ventures. Certainly, their success or failure is in large part the direct result of the degree of enthusiasm, vigor, energy, and creativity on the part of the professional person selected to organize and supervise the program. One outstanding community effort in the establishment of parent-cooperative nursery schools has been described recently by Katharine Whiteside Taylor (4), a leader in the cooperative movement. The parent-education function is particularly stressed by Mrs. Taylor, in addition to the direct benefits of the nursery schools for the children themselves. This parent-education function is carried out through parent observation of children in the groups, through special classes for the cooperating parents, and through actual participation as assistant teachers.

Nursery Schools for the Exceptional Child The establishment of nursery-school programs in hospitals—especially children's hospitals—and in special-service clinics for handicapped, disturbed, or otherwise exceptional children has become an increasingly common practice, and one that holds much promise for furthering the welfare of children and their families throughout the country. Such programs contribute a great deal by establishing a setting within which professional personnel from various specialized disciplines can work cooperatively for the benefit of a particular child. In addition, they provide a genuine therapeutic setting in which prescribed courses of action may be carried out in furthering the welfare of a child in need of special treatment programs: physical therapy, speech therapy, and psychological treatment of various kinds. Many large medical centers have long recognized the specialized needs of children who require surgery or long-term hospitalization and have incorporated special programs of play therapy that aid in the recovery and which stimulate healthy development of these unusual preschool children. In addition there are highly specialized programs, including nursery schools for children with cerebral palsy, orthopedic handicaps, sensory defects (blindness, deafness, etc.) and so on. The guiding philosophy of these programs is that children with special needs and handicaps are, first and foremost, children; their first and most fundamental need is to be treated with respect, dignity, and understanding in the same way as any other child. Beyond this, there are some special problems requiring the attention of skilled therapists and teachers, and in certain cases, requiring special equipment and facilities as well. The child-development student should be aware of the possibility of making a professional contribution by seeking a challenging career with this sort of agency; the possibilities for personal satisfaction in this work are unlimited.

OBJECTIVES OF THE NURSERY-SCHOOL PROGRAM

In the section describing the university nursery-school program, reference was made to four major objectives: (1) to provide for the total development of the young child, (2) to provide a laboratory and training facility for students, (3) to provide for parent education, and (4) to conduct research on various aspects of child development. In a comprehensive nursery-school program, all of these objectives are taken into consideration. No one of these objectives can be achieved *unless the nursery school provides a good environment and a good set of relationships that can work to the benefit of the child.* There is no such thing as a good research program in a poor nursery school; neither can there be effective parent

> other. They put the dishes away, then go into the bathroom. They come out of the bathroom and Christie runs up to the teacher and puts her arms around her. Laura and Christie then go over to a slide. . . .

This brief anecdote illustrates a number of things about the role of the nursery school in stimulating social behavior. First, it illustrates that much of the social behavior occurs in the spontaneous, free play that children initiate themselves, as opposed to organized activities prescribed by adults. Second, it illustrates the tenuous nature of social involvements among 3- and 4-year-old children. While there may be lasting friendships in the nursery-school group, children of this age are in need of stimulation from a wide variety of play companions, to learn how other people react and how to move freely from one social commitment to another without feeling deep loss or anxiety as one particular commitment terminates. Sometimes among 3-year-olds it terminates easily—as casually as it develops. Other times it terminates in a physical explosion of minor or major proportions. But in the well run nursery school there are so many opportunities for interaction in new social commitments that the effects of any one are tempered by the many others.

The anecdote also illustrates the important role played by good equipment in stimulating and furthering social play. In the midst of play, cooperative interaction among children takes on a delightful spontaneity that tends to produce keen satisfactions. It is good to be one with the others in a rich environment.

One of the prime advantages of the nursery school in aiding the child's social adjustment and development is that the child receives, from others in his same general age range, honest reactions to his own behavior. There is little in the way of pretense or social sophistication in the behavior of 3-year-olds toward each other. They show their feelings directly and openly, thus serving each other well in the general task of learning how one's behavior affects others. While the competent professional teacher is allowing and encouraging honest reactions from other children, she is also alert to the prevention of situations in which a child's social status is placed in serious jeopardy by his own actions or by those of other children. The good teacher is equally sensitive to the special social needs of children of all degrees of social competence, assurance, and skill. She is aware of the risks both of overprotecting the timid child from the active and sometimes boisterous social activities of her group, or of pushing such a child too vigorously in the direction of social participation. She knows that well grounded social adjustment must arise from within the child himself, as he gradually acquires the confidence and poise to feel good about his social ventures. This is in sharp contrast to a kind of social "technique" imposed upon him from the outside, or by an adult who is overly anxious to see children "play nicely" with others.

Social development takes time and practice; it takes a lot of good equipment, too, for it is around the hundreds of play situations that social development occurs. Equipment that leads naturally to social interchange is a part of the well planned nursery environment. It takes skill, experience, and foresight in a teacher to use materials and equipment competently in creating situations which lead to constructive social interaction. The well equipped nursery school can provide for an almost unlimited range and variety of socially stimulating experiences, in part because of the nature of the equipment itself. Van Alstyne (5) noted in 1932 that preschoolers spend 98 percent of their play time using equipment or materials. The range and quality of materials conducive to social development, as well as to sound contacts with other children and adults, gives the nursery school a real advantage in furthering healthy social growth.

Emotional development. The good nursery school does more than create an environment in which children can adapt to group living. Social development is important and is a reasonable objective for 3- and 4-year-old children. However, even social development itself is based to a significant degree on the personal emotional maturity of individual children. Individual emotional behavior and adjustment is, itself, a sphere of the child's life to which the nursery school can make significant contributions.

The range of emotional reactions experienced by a child in the normal course of events during a nursery-school day is potentially very broad, indeed. Emotions can range from keen excitement, delight, and joy to extremes of anger, resentment, despair, and jealousy. These emotions themselves are, of course, normal; the significant contribution of the school environment is the professional personnel who are equipped by training and temperament to deal constructively with these emotions, and who are able to use them as creative forces in the life of the child. The skilled teacher channels aggressive, hostile, and other "negative" emotions into harmless activities, but she also assists the child in coming to grips with his own emotions—the positive as well as the negative ones. Through her efforts—sometimes in verbalizing emotions for which the child has no words, sometimes in merely being an accepting person who has felt the same way and therefore can still respect the child who feels "that way"—she plays a significant role in helping the child to feel good about the person he is. This, of course, is the central thing about achieving emotional maturity—coming to accept oneself, including one's emotional self. It is in this sphere that the nursery school can make one of its most significant contributions to the child. The following simple anecdote offers an example:

> It is time to clear up the block-play area and prepare to go outdoors. Miss N instructs Brad: "You can start stacking the blocks on the shelves now, before we go outdoors." Brad looks at Miss N, scowling. He is kneeling, sitting on his feet, holding a long block in his right hand. As Miss N turns away to attend to something else, Brad hurls the block across the nursery school floor, narrowly missing the teacher's leg. She turns back to Brad, takes his hand and leads him to the block which he had thrown. Her actions make it obvious that he is to pick it up and return it to the block area. At the same time, her manner is neither unduly upset nor reproving as she remarks, almost casually, "You're angry at the teacher, Brad." She follows through, helping Brad get started in picking up other blocks and stacking them on the shelves.

In this incident, Brad was helped to have his anger verbalized by the teacher, who was mature enough emotionally to accept his immaturity without responding in kind. Experiences of this kind will gradually help him to understand that his angry feelings are natural enough; at the same time he will find it less necessary to resort to the physical manifestations of anger, first by letting words convey the feeling just as surely as the block conveyed it, then by finding more constructive channels of behavior that make it less necessary to feel the anger so keenly. One of the most significant elements of this little anecdote is that the teacher did not feel any personal threat in Brad's outburst of anger. She was able to recognize that Brad's anger was directed against her, at the moment, without feeling guilty, inadequate, or threatened. These latter feelings, had they been operating strongly in her at the moment, could have led to a "defensive" reaction on her part. This would have triggered a reprisal of some sort, perhaps in the form of punishment.

Other forms of emotional behavior also need acceptance and understanding in the nursery school. A child's emotional dependence on the teacher, for example, may indicate his need for continued reassurance of affection. This is understandable. But the wise teacher will see that a variety of emotional reactions in such a child, though they may appear on the surface to be unrelated to this emotional dependence, are really a part of the same general pattern. When a child shows strong resentments toward other children (who demand the teacher's time and attention) or grabs things away from other children (things which somehow symbolize the affection he is continually seeking), the skilled teacher can recognize the relatedness of these events and can gradually help the child to deal with the basic source of his emotional reactions. A competent teacher can work well on the relatedness of all elements in the child's total behavior, seeing the relevance of a single episode to the rest of the child's needs. While many mothers are aware of these problems and strive to see the relevancies, the opportunities for doing so and for working out feeling associated with these needs are an especially important contribution of a well run nursery school.

A major portion of the preschool child's energy and action is devoted to learning as much as possible about himself and about the world he lives in. This learning goes on at different levels of awareness: some things a child learns by acquiring a new word in his vocabulary and knowing how and when to use it; other things he learns by achieving a new and better way to relate to another child or an adult; and still others he learns by experiencing consistent boundaries of acceptable behavior. He also learns by expressing his innermost feelings and having them accepted, clarified, and reflected back to him by a respected teacher. Since the learning goes on in many different ways and at many levels of awareness in the child, a good nursery-school program makes provision for a richly varied set of experiences. These will include direct experiences with living things, both plant and animal life, and with a wide assortment of usable objects for creative action. The experiences will also include indirect resources for learning, particularly books and stories, which serve two major purposes in the life of the preschool child: they stimulate and provide for broadening of the child's world of understanding, along with pleasure and enjoyment, and they provide an excellent foundation for the child's further exploration of his world through books. The early discovery that books are a prime source of enjoyment and understanding becomes the basis for a sound approach to the world of literature. The nursery school is not only a place rich in its possibilities for learning about the world; it is also a place that can aid materially in developing long-range habits and values that serve the never ending process of personal exploration.

MOTOR AND PHYSICAL DEVELOPMENT. Young children need a healthfully balanced routine of rest and exercise to provide proper stimulation of physical growth. They also need a variety of kinds of play materials to encourage the development of body control and motor skills. These skills serve not only the health of the physical body, but also the social and emotional well-being of the child. Other things being equal, the child who is able to handle himself and to control the equipment of his environment with satisfaction and competence feels good about himself and his world, and is optimistic about the outcome of further encounters in that world.

Nursery-school play equipment is geared to the physical and motor capabilities of the young child. It is stimulating, attractive, and challenging, and, when put to use, it encourages the natural involvement of all of the child's muscle systems. Both gross motor activity—as in swinging, sliding, climbing on boxes and boards—and smaller, finer muscle coordination—as in painting, clay-working, cutting and pasting, working with puzzles—are thoroughly encouraged in the course of the regular nursery-school routine.

It is the policy of some nursery schools to engage the services of a nurse to give a brief but important physical inspection to each child on entrance to the nursery-school group each day. Communicable diseases spread rapidly among children this age, and such inspections are helpful in the control of disease. With proper inspections of this type, and with alertness on the part of the teacher for possible signs of excess fatigue, listlessness, fever, or unusual irritability, which often herald the beginning of illness, there is no reason to feel that the nursery-school child is being exposed to dangerous threats to his physical well-being in such groups. When evidence of a child's illness during the course of a nursery-school day is noted, the child may be removed from the group and isolated from the other children until his parents can take him home. Some well equipped nursery schools include a special isolation room where a child can be separated from the others in case of any such needs.

The threat of physical injury in a nursery school is also a consideration in view of the fact that there is typically a wide range of equipment for such climbing, swinging, and sliding activities as are appropriate for this age group. The number of adults present in the group to supervise activities and to keep the children within bounds is the most important safety precaution here, apart from the obvious advantage of reliable, sturdy, nontoxic, and safe equipment. In addition to the number of adults, however, the training of the nursery-school staff is of paramount importance. Part of this training consists of thorough understanding of the limits of children's abilities to look after themselves, to control their own bodies, and to get themselves out of predicaments. This should not be interpreted as a warning that children should be carefully guarded each moment in order to avoid an accident. There is every reason to assume that children can take considerable initiative and responsibility in the safety control of themselves and their environments. Knowing when to help and how to avoid situations in which excess help will be necessary are part of the professional knowledge of the qualified nursery-school teacher.

Nursery-school philosophy, in general, is to provide safe and appropriate equipment and materials, and then to allow children to explore the environment that is arranged for them. This philosophy capitalizes on the child's natural curiosity and enthusiasm as the prime motivating factor in his achievement of body control and control over the physical objects in his world.

Mental development. We have already noted that nursery school is not intended as a place for the achievement of traditional academic skills. There is no effort made to teach 3- and 4-year-olds to read and write or to engage in other studious work. Nevertheless, as Read (3) points out so effectively, there is a nursery-school "curriculum," and teachers make conscientious efforts to provide for a series of learning experiences that challenge and stimulate mental activity. The sources for mental development in the nursery school are almost without limit. A child who poured water into a bucket partially filled with sand and who observed for a few moments as the bubbles rose to the top of the water was engaged in a learning project. After thus observing with evident interest he commented briefly, and with some satisfaction, "There's air in that sand." Mental development, as was pointed out in Chapter Eight, is based, in part, on sensory experiences. In this respect the nursery school can make an unusual contribution. Through sensory exploration of his world the child may be assisted in the development of many concepts: concepts of size, shape, weight, distance, speed; of the physical properties of objects and materials; of growing things, both plant and animal, and many other concepts.

The well equipped and well planned nursery school takes into account the child's limited background of experiences, his level of insight and curiosity, and his need for tangible sensory experiences, and does not provide mere verbal abstractions in response to his questions. The teacher is prepared, in planning for the interests and activities of her program, for the varied and difficult questions that 3- and 4-year-olds are likely to ask. One young teacher had prepared carefully for an interesting project with baby chicks. She brought an incubator into the nursery school, with eggs nearly ready to hatch into chicks, for a period of several days. Each day, as a few more bedraggled new chicks struggled and pecked their way out of the shells, the children watched with all-consuming interest and fascination. One 4-year-old was finally able to organize the question that seemed to be troubling him as he pondered this mysterious event: "How did that chicken get inside the egg?" The ensuing discussion led to more questions, perhaps, than final answers, but the teacher saw this as an excellent opportunity to broaden her children's insights into some of the facts of life. By answering according to the child's level of experience and with respect for his question and his need to understand, she helped him achieve a rudimentary concept of reproduction that would not need to be destroyed later and replaced by any "hard realities." Perhaps the fundamental point here is that the so-called "hard realities" of the child's natural world, as well as of his social world, *can* be presented to him in such a way that they are meaningful and satisfying in his natural quest for understanding. The good nursery school is organized on the basis of this philosophy.

Aesthetic development. A child's awareness and appreciation of the aesthetic qualities in his world can begin very early and in very informal experiences. During the preschool period there should be ample opportunities for personal involvement with the central ingredients of a variety of aesthetic activities. Not yet ready for formal classes or lessons in music, a child profits mostly from rhythmic experiences which his body feels and to which he responds freely and naturally; not yet able to cope with lessons in painting or sculptoring, he needs materials with which he can experiment in color, texture, molding, and in feeling with his hands. Close observation of a group of preschoolers as they conduct the business of a clay table, a sand box, a table loaded with a variety of colorful paper materials, or a finger-painting table, will quickly convince the student that something important is going on. The child engrossed in his activity of the moment is experiencing with all the senses at his command the aesthetic qualities of the world around him. He is *seeing* the color, the form, the texture; he is *feeling* the warmth, the coolness, the hardness, the softness, the plasticity; he is *hearing* the sound of sand as it goes into a bucket, the sound of clay pounded on a firm table, or the sound of blocks as they are placed together or as they come tumbling down—but most of all he is *feeling with his whole body the personal participation* that makes him a part of the aesthetic world. In the long run, it is this kind of experience that makes the aesthetic world a part of him—and a very satisfying part.

Good nursery schools have lots of equipment and large supplies of materials, which encourage such participation. They are easily accessible to the children, and there is little emphasis on neatness or conformity to adult standards of design or control of aesthetic impulses in their relatively free use. There are limits, of course: finger painting is generally confined to a limited area of the nursery-school playroom, and the clay is not allowed to be thrown at other children. But such obvious "restrictions" are not such as to limit the child's imaginative use of creative materials. And there should be a noticeable absence of adult instruction in "how to make a turtle," or whatever needs to be made with the clay. For 3- and 4-year-olds it is not critical that one know how to make something which meets adult specifications of reality. What counts is having the materials available and providing the children with the freedom to express their inner needs and concerns through a variety of creative media.

Providing a Laboratory for Professional Education in Child Development Basic facts and principles of child development, published in scientific articles and textbooks and available to students in formal university courses, need to be incorporated into the "live" experience of the child-development student through work with flesh and blood children. The student who works with real, live children must learn to perceive each preschool youngster as a unique individual, and how to be responsive to the needs of each. No more appropriate setting for this training for the many professional careers in the broad field of child development has been devised than the laboratory-nursery school.

A training laboratory is organized carefully and designed to induct the student gradually into increasing responsibilities for individual children as well as for the over-all operation of the program. It is also designed to integrate with the student's gradually increasing theoretical knowledge and insight into psychological, biological, sociological, and educational principles. Thus the effective nursery-school training laboratory provides for some beginning laboratory experiences early in the students' college career, and gradually expands and intensifies these experiences as the student progresses toward graduation.

The laboratory is also a place for making observations and deriving further knowledge about children in general. This research function of the preschool laboratory is sometimes overlooked, but needs to be given some consideration here. Some of our most valuable insights about children —their growth characteristics and their psychological and social behavior —have been derived through careful observation of nursery-school groups. Many nursery-school laboratories have facilities for one-way-vision observation booths, which increase their potentials for research activities. In addition, many laboratory-nursery schools operated by universities and hospitals provide special examination rooms for the conducting of research studies with individual children. One such nursery-school laboratory is shown in Figure 13.1, which provides a view of the observation booth. This observation facility screens the observers from the children, giving the students and researchers an adequate and well ventilated space for writing and record-keeping.

The laboratory-nursery school also becomes a center for research into parent-child relationships. Not only is there a great deal of observable contact between parent and child in the daily routine of bringing children and picking them up; there is also considerable opportunity for teachers and researchers to conduct interviews and examinations with parents. Collection of considerable data about child-rearing methods of the home, patterns of family life and daily routine, etc., and the combining of such information with known data about individual children in the nursery school provides unique opportunities for the serious investigator to organize our knowledge of the effects of parent behavior on child development.

Still another contribution that the laboratory-nursery school provides

Fig. 13.1. Observing in a child-development laboratory. This view is from the interior of the observation booth from which there is one-way vision. (Monkmeyer Press Photos.)

is parent education. Most such nursery schools conduct some form of parent-education activities, through meetings and special classes, through individual counseling with parents, and through parent conferences, which may include discussion of the child's nursery-school behavior and also the results of special examinations which have been given, etc. There is also opportunity to evaluate the effects of such parent-education programs. These activities could not easily be conducted in other settings.

THE PHYSICAL PLANT

There is no one right way to construct the building which houses the nursery school. In different parts of the country the physical plant will be determined, to some degree, by weather and climate and by the natural surroundings that offer special features for outdoor play. The size and complexity of the building will be determined, in part, by considerations of economy and the number of children and staff to be involved. But the needs of the children are paramount. Safety needs are of special significance, inasmuch as preschool children are not sufficiently aware of the potential hazards of their world to assume full responsibility for automobile traffic, heating and electrical facilities, etc. It follows that the nursery-school building is designed to protect the child from ordinary hazards and to provide a safe environment in which exploration and freedom of movement can occur without serious threat. Outdoor playgrounds are separated, usually by sturdy fencing material, for the sake of providing freedom of movement within an area that can adequately be supervised. Movement in and out of the fenced areas should be under adult supervision; hence gates are usually equipped with latches beyond the reach of the children.

The outdoor play area should provide for a variety of quiet and active functions. Slides, swings, climbing apparatus, sandboxes, boards, barrels, and the like are standard equipment. But with imagination and sensitivity to the needs of children, excellent use can be made of natural features of the playground area. Trees, logs, rocks, small streams, pools, etc., have all been incorporated into excellent outdoor play areas without destroying the essential safety features.

The indoor playrooms are designed to take hard wear from active children day in and day out. A tough floor covering that can be kept clean without a hard wax finish is desirable. The room itself should be well lighted from both natural light and artificial fixtures. Ventilation is another consideration. Heating equipment should be of a type which cannot burn a child. The playroom is designed for flexibility of use. One large playroom which can be partitioned in a variety of ways with low, child-height screens is generally preferable to a series of small, fully partitioned rooms. Even toileting facilities for children need not be completely partitioned off into a separate room; there is no essential reason for making toileting behavior a secretive function in children of this age.

In evaluating the physical facilities and arrangements in a nursery school, consideration should be given to such questions as: Do they provide for smooth operation of the program? Do they encourage healthy contacts between children and adults and minimize the need for direct adult supervision? Do they provide for adequate storage, yet accessibility to equipment and materials? Do they eliminate or minimize safety hazards? Do they encourage social interaction and eliminate unnecessary frustration for both children and teachers? Do they provide for a reasonable balance of sensory stimulation, physical activity, and quiet contemplation? Are there possibilities for dramatic play, musical and artistic activities, etc., which do not require undue emphasis on "don't" from teachers? Are there ample provisions for books and records? Would it be possible to introduce a small animal, such as a guinea pig, into the nursery school without throwing everything into chaos?

QUALIFICATIONS OF THE NURSERY-SCHOOL EDUCATOR

The training program for the preparation of nursery-school teachers should include considerable emphasis on human growth, psychology, and sociology. It should also include work in biology and physiology. Ideally, it includes a sufficiently broad and stimulating background of academic experiences so that the teacher will know how to provide challenging experiences in the natural and biological sciences for her children. The competent nursery-school teacher is a specialized person in two main ways. First, she is especially educated in the fundamentals of child development and is thoroughly familiar with the characteristics of children of ages 2, 3, 4, and 5. Her background in child development—in addition to providing her with general knowledge of the stages and needs of the preschool child —makes her especially sensitive to the unique qualities of behavior in individual children. In nursery school, as at perhaps no other level in our whole educational system, it is paramount that children be viewed as individuals, and that the relationship between teacher and child be a one-to-one relationship so far as possible. Conversely, it is important to de-emphasize a primarily group oriented approach.

The second fundamental way in which the competent nursery-school teacher is specialized is with regard to her understanding of her own personal adjustment and temperament. It is axiomatic in nursery education that effective relationships between teacher and child are dependent on the degree to which the adult has insight into his or her own personal adjustment and needs. Preparation for nursery education, in fact, is largely a matter of achieving a high degree of insight into the dynamics of human behavior, which includes understanding the motives for one's own behavior. The sensitive teacher will have had many occasions to see her own temperament reflected in the behavior of her children, and will have profited from these insights. This should not imply in any sense that one must be "perfectly" well adjusted in order to qualify for work with young children. Aside from the fact that there is probably no such person as the "perfectly" well adjusted teacher, it is not especially compatible with the practical growth needs of young children that they be surrounded by perfect adults. But it is a reasonable goal to provide children with professional persons who are aware of their own anxieties, sources of frustration, insecurities, wishes, and values. It is reasonable, also, that these adults be motivated to grow and to improve their capacities for self-understanding as well as for the understanding of children. The two are really inseparable.

SUMMARY

Children between 3 and 6 need a school experience that contributes to all aspects of their total development. In effective programs for young children, whether they be called day care, laboratory-nursery schools, private or cooperative nurseries, there are provisions in the form of a physical plant, materials and equipment, program and, especially, qualified personnel, which contribute to that total development.

The nursery-school program is not intended merely as a preparatory experience for kindergarten and grade school. Nursery education is valid in and of itself in helping the child toward self-realization.

The qualified nursery-school teacher has an excellent education in child development, and has become particularly sensitive to the needs of

3-, 4-, and 5-year-old children. She has learned to view each child in terms of his special needs and his readiness to move toward new and higher levels of mental, physical, social, and emotional action. The teacher necessarily has insight into his or her own personal adjustment and needs, as well.

REFERENCES

1. Chittenden, G. E., "An experimental study in measuring and modifying assertive behavior in young children," *Monogr. Soc. Res. Child Develpm.*, 1942, 7(1).
2. Hymes, J. L., Jr., *The child under six*, Washington, D.C.: Educational Services, 1961.
3. Read, Katherine H., *The nursery school,* 3rd ed., Philadelphia: Saunders, 1960.
4. Taylor, Katharine W., "A community-wide program of parent education," *Children*, 1962, 9:9–14.
5. Van Alstyne, D., *Play behavior and choice of play material of preschool children,* Chicago: Univ. of Chicago Press, 1932.

CHAPTER FOURTEEN

Are society's responsibilities toward its children in conflict with its responsibilities toward itself? ∽ What relationships exist between a child's values and the image he has of himself? ∽ What is society's stake in the self-concept of its children? ∽ How does society determine the personal values of its children?

THE CHILD AND THE SOCIETY

WE NOTED in earlier chapters that the basic strivings in a child are directed ultimately toward self-realization; that is, the fundamental need that motivates the child to action and that directs his behavior is the need to become whatever he is ultimately capable of being. In the normal course of events many situations arise that obstruct progress toward optimum self-development. Some of these are merely temporary conditions, inhibiting the child's immediate satisfaction of his need for self-realization. Other events may have serious and long-lasting effects, which reduce the probability of his ever being able to achieve true self-realization. The loss is not merely a loss to that child but is, in a larger sense, a loss to society. Furthermore, our society has many resources for increasing the probability of self-realization among its children. The benefits do not merely accrue to the individual child; they accrue also to the larger society and to mankind.

CONCEPTS OF THE CHILD AND SOCIETY

One view of the relationship between the child and society holds that the child is inherently evil and that society's role is to curb and suppress his evil tendencies. Thus, society has been viewed as a great controlling agent that forces the individual to conform to its standards of goodness or risk the consequence, which is rejection by society. The long-term process of inducting the child into acceptable behavior and teaching him to conform has been viewed by some as the essential elements of the socialization process.

Another view (the one here held) is that the function of suppressing and curbing the natural tendencies of the child is, at best, only one aspect of the relationship between child and society. The other major aspect of the relationship is society's responsibility for bringing the child to the fruition of his own resources. The child is not only the product of his genetic inheritance; he is also the product of his social world—the society which he inherits. But, *the society is also the product of its children.* Society's investment in its children is an investment in its own future. Enlightened concern for the welfare of the child includes a great deal more than sentimentality in the care for dependent and helpless children. It includes a forward-looking awareness that tomorrow's society can be no better than the people who will comprise it. It realistically recognizes the fact that the complexities of social organization are meaningless if the people for whom those organizations are intended are not capable of achieving selfhood within the social structure. The manner in which any society views and treats its dependent persons is one important measure of the maturity and stability of that society. Treatment of the aged, the young, or the handicapped—regardless of their age—is an index of the concept a society has of itself—of the purposes of its existence and of the motivating forces behind its agencies and institutions.

PSYCHOLOGICAL ECONOMY

The key concept underlying this book is that the child's major task of development is essentially a task of self-definition and self-enhancement. In the process of sorting—selecting and rejecting ideas about the self—central to this task, the child naturally encounters many situations in which he must choose among alternatives. Though his choices may seem undirected and whimsical to his parents and other people—indeed, to the child himself—his behavior is directed primarily by the self-concept that he has already achieved, and that he wishes to achieve. If a given course of action is consistent with his notion of who he is, then, other things being equal, he will choose that course over courses that would force him to be less consistent with his self-image. We may refer to this as "psychological economy" in the sense that there are "credits" (experiences that lead to self-enhancement) and "debits" (experiences that lead to self-debasement). The net cumulative effect of both kinds of experiences is one's self-evaluation, and is, like the value of stock on the open market, subject to continual fluctuation. For the healthy child there is continual striving for improvement of this self-image through the choices and decisions involved in daily living.

The choices and decisions of the infant and the young child are extremely limited by the alternatives available to him. With maturation and experience, however, come an ever expanding range of possible alternatives of action. These require not only more decisions on his part, but increasingly fine discriminations among the kinds and qualities of alternatives open to him. The increasing scope of the child's world leads him into situations in which the mere discrimination of two clear-cut alternatives and selection of the one most consistent with the idealized self-image is no longer sufficient. Instead, he is forced to choose from among many degrees and qualities of alternatives, and his choices are the more complex in that he cannot be aware of all the possible subtle, long-range consequences of his decisions. Nevertheless, choices there must be, and an understanding of the basis for the child's choices can be fostered at this point, perhaps, by a brief discussion of the problem of values.

THE PROBLEM OF VALUES

Self-realization is a continuing process, then, and must be seen less as a directly achievable goal than as a life-long program of understanding, ever more precisely, the potentialities of one's self. A central aspect of this long-term process is the problem of personal values, which determine the course of one's action whenever there are alternatives. Thus, values coexist with the self-image. If one generally chooses a quiet evening at home in preference to an elaborate dinner and theater party, it is a reflection of his values. Similarly, if a child in the nursery school likes to dress up in adult clothing and engage in dramatic play, living in fantasy and identification with adult roles, in preference to outdoor play on jungle gym, swing, or slide, it is a reflection of his current value system.

But values run deeper into personality than the preference of one activity over another. Values include the more basic considerations of what is *right* to do, say, and feel, and what is *wrong*. Values represent a basic orientation to one's world of people and things. It is a selective orientation, such that what one perceives in his world, and how one reacts to his world, are directly dependent upon his value system. The things that arouse emotion—joy, sympathy, anger, humor, jealousy—are a reflection of values. Such complex states of feeling as love, affection, patriotism, and religious experience all are manifestations of value systems that serve to direct and to channel one's actions and to focus those actions on particular aspects of these complex states. The motivation to strive for achievement in any significant endeavor—art, education, science, literature—or to develop unusual competence in a skill—athletics, music, crafts—is a reflection of one's value system.

In general, then, we may conceive of values as a central feature of personality that serves to stimulate and to direct the activities of a person and that plays a vital role in one's selective orientation to his world of people and things. But what is the source of a child's personal value system? How can we account for the achievement of this fundamental determiner of a person's thoughts and actions?

A major portion of the child's value system is already established, and very powerfully so, at the time he enters the world. A child is not born into a value vacuum; he is born into a society that has had a long and complex history of evolution of values. The very first treatment he receives is a reflection of the value system of his society. Whether he is breast fed or bottle fed; how soon he is given nourishment of any kind; when he is started on solid foods; when and how he is weaned; what manner of discipline he receives and from whom; what educational activities he is exposed to and at what ages; how much freedom he experiences; the responses he receives to his angry and hostile acts, and to his fears; all these and many more are the aspects of the child's world which reflect the value system of his society. But note that all these value influences have their beginnings long before the child can question their "rightness" or "wrongness." To ask the infant whether he approves of his society's methods of discipline would be something like asking a blind child to compare his experiences with those of the sighted child. The blind child cannot do this, because he cannot perceive the world of the sighted child. Similarly, the ordinary child cannot perceive that his particular society's value system is only one of an infinite number of possible value systems. To him, the way people around him do things is not so much the "right" way or the "wrong" way as it is the *only* way, simply because he has no basis for understanding that there

Moving into the stream of society.
(R. Frank Sponholz.)

may be alternatives. Yet the basic patterns of interacting with people and things and of selecting aspects of one's world to which to relate are developed first by those early experiences within the structure of an already established value system. They become the standards against which all new experiences are evaluated, and the criteria for determining the rightness and goodness of new and potential relationships with the world.

To be sure, a significant component of one's value system has its roots in biology. That is, one's biological inheritance and resulting maturational processes are also reflected in values to a degree. This seems to operate in an indirect manner, as in the case of the development of a special talent. For example, it is unlikely that a person who is color-blind or who has no special artistic talent would ever develop an intense interest in the activity of oil painting. The relatively low place such an activity would probably have in his personal value system would be clearly associated with his biological inheritance. In a similar manner, the person with that special combination of qualities that are essential to the professional pianist—rhythm, muscular coordination, musical memory, etc.—is much more likely to develop musical values than one who does not have those qualities. A basic reason is that our society rewards excellence—with status, prestige, and money—and excellence is to a degree based on biological capacity. Society's rewards tend to enhance the value of the activity for which one is rewarded; lack of reward tends to lower the value.

Values, then, are the result of an interaction between unique individual qualities and a society that encourages some systems of thinking and acting while discouraging others. Our society, which places a high general value on education, provides tangible and intangible rewards to the individual who learns to place the same high personal values on education and, to a marked degree, fails to reward the individual who does not learn to value education, or who does not have the natural ability to make use of the educational processes that are provided. In one sense, any society is acting in its own self-interest by instilling in its children those values that will preserve and enhance that social organization. To do otherwise is to risk the eventual disintegration of that society, or an explosively abrupt evolution into a new form of society, the newness and unpredictability of which would be intolerable to many of its members. It follows that social change proceeds at a relatively slow pace. Nevertheless, social evolution inevitably occurs, and with it an attendant revision of value systems. Indeed, a major source of conflict between generations is the conflict of values between parent and child, which is an inevitable part of social evolution.

The major point, of course, is that society plays a primary role in determining the nature of the child's personality. Even the physical and biological qualities of the child are influenced in powerful and subtle ways by social processes. Some of the biological tendencies and qualities are rewarded while others may be actively punished and discouraged. Nothing in this discussion reduces or detracts from the importance of inherited characteristics; nevertheless, the vital role society plays in shaping the fundamental nature of the child cannot be ignored. But society is not merely a *cause* of the child's personality development. In the larger sense, society is also the *result* of the personal qualities and characteristics of its members. It is healthy or unhealthy, strong or weak, moral or immoral, dynamic or static, in direct proportion to the health, strength, morality, and dynamic nature of its constituent members. It should be clear from this that society's stake in the child is its own preservation and enhancement. Its communities, its educational and recreational services, its children's welfare agencies, its hospitals and health services, its churches and libraries—all these are part of society's investment in its children, and they are indeed a vital part, even if considered only from the standpoint of society's self-interest.

SOCIETY AS A RESTRICTIVE AGENT

One essential function of society is to place limits on individual activities and behavior, which might otherwise threaten to disrupt one or more aspects of social organization. It does this in part through legislation and law enforcement. Inevitably this means that certain otherwise accessible means and channels of self-realization are closed to the individual who wishes to operate within acceptable social limits. Society says, in effect, that the child must learn to conform or else he will not be granted status or other forms of need satisfaction. But the pressures to conform are far more subtle, and often more compelling, than those existing in the form of laws. Pressures to think, feel, and believe in certain ways come to bear upon the child before he is old enough or experienced enough to recognize any alternative ways of thinking, feeling, and believing. Pressures regarding body cleanliness, wearing apparel, manner of eating, modes of communication, ways of exchanging goods and services, and means of expressing deference to persons of higher status—all these are part of the complex of pressures brought to bear on the child. Their net effect is to reinforce his need to conform, at least within broad limits, or run the risk of being ostracized from the social group.

Society, and its means of communication, even define for the child the ways in which he may perceive his world. If, for example, his society's language has a rich and complex vocabulary pertaining to a given aspect of the world, the child may come to make very fine discriminations in his perception of that aspect of the world. If, on the other hand, his society's language provides only for crude, general distinctions among component parts of that aspect of the world, then the child will be more restricted in the ways he can refer to it, and he will be relatively more limited in his ability to perceive its finer details.

SOCIETY AS A MEANS TO SELF-REALIZATION

Any given society also serves to define for the child acceptable kinds of self-definitions. Further, it instructs the child in the techniques and methods he must use to achieve acceptable self-definition, and it helps him to develop essential skills. Society provides many channels by which the child may become more free, or more nearly that which represents his potential self. Its schools, its libraries, its museums, its churches and recreation programs—all participate in the process of self-fulfillment for the individual child. For many years in America we have engaged in a grand experiment called free public education, intended to bring about the greatest possible educational improvement for the largest number of children. Some critics of American education have questioned whether it is a part of the business of public education to concern itself with personal adjustment and development. Perhaps a more appropriate way to ask the question would be, "What are the particular aspects of personal self-development and self-realization that are uniquely or primarily the functions of public education?"

Historically there has been little need, until very recently, for people to concern themselves with *all* children in order to insure the self-preservation and well-being of their own society. What happened to children in far-away cities, or in Africa or Asia, was of little concern to parents of children growing up in a middle-class American home. There was so much space separating those children in far-away places from one's own children that the personal well-being and the personality development of these distant children seemed to have little or no bearing on one's own child or his happiness. But modern societies can no longer afford to dwell in such psychological and social isolation. We are too acutely aware that what happens to a child in a slum of some sprawling city, or in an isolated mountain cabin, or in an Israeli kibbutz, or in a Chinese communal settlement, will, in a sense, happen to the whole world. All children will live in the same world as our own—a shrinking world in which communication and transportation and political and economic needs bring people ever closer, and in which the possibility of remaining aloof and isolated from the conditions of the world's children becomes increasingly less.

Society, then, has both rights and responsibilities regarding its children. Its rights, in general, take the form of the expectation that its children will learn to abide by reasonable laws and codes of behavior, which protect its individuals and groups from exploitation. Its responsibilities, in general, take the form of providing increasingly efficient means toward the goal of self-realization for all its children. Thus, rights and the responsibilities are not necessarily in conflict with each other. The fufillment of responsibilities toward children does not represent merely a charitable ideal; it is a practical means—perhaps the *only* practical means—of insuring survival and enhancement of society itself.

SUMMARY

Society has a vital stake in its children, which goes beyond the responsibility to control them and limit their behavior to that which is acceptable and comfortable to live with. There is also the responsibility for providing a world of objects and a world of people that actively assist the child in his efforts toward self-realization. "Society" is an abstraction that does not exist apart from its constituent membership. It can only be as strong and productive as those members. Therefore society's stake in the child is its own self-preservation and self-enhancement.

INDEX